1580

Library

05/08/14

~~Athens MA~~

America MA

Theology

Sources and Contexts of
The Book of Concord

D0838861

Sources and Contexts of

The Book of Concord

Edited by
Robert Kolb and James A. Nestingen

Fortress Press   Minneapolis

SOURCES AND CONTEXTS OF THE BOOK OF CONCORD
Copyright © 2001 Augsburg Fortress. All rights reserved. Except for brief quotations in critical articles or reviews, no part of this book may be reproduced in any manner without prior written permission from the publisher. Write: Permissions, Augsburg Fortress, Box 1209, Minneapolis, MN 55440.

Cover design: Joseph Bonyata
Interior design: Peregrine Graphics Services

Library of Congress Cataloging-in-Publication Data

Sources and contexts of the book of concord / edited by Robert Kolb and James A. Nestingen.
    p. cm.
Includes bibliographical references and index.
ISBN 0-8006-3290-7 (alk. paper)
    1. Konkordienbuch. I. Kolb, Robert, 1941– II. Nestingen, James Arne.
BX8068 .S68 2001
238'.41'09031—dc21

2001023950

The paper used in this publication meets the minimum requirements of American National Standard for Information Sciences — Permanence of Paper for Printed Library Materials, ANSI Z329.48-1984.

Manufactured in the U.S.A.   AF1-3290
05   04   03   02   01   2   3   4   5   6   7   8   9   10

Contents

Preface

While the Reformation movement led by Martin Luther was conceived in Wittenberg, in the midst of the university's enterprise of teaching and learning, the Lutheran church that it produced was born at Augsburg, through a public act of confessing the faith. This confessing took lasting form in a document. The Lutheran princes, municipal representatives, and theologians assembled at Augsburg in June 1530 directed their testimony of the biblical message toward church and world in the Augsburg Confession. This act of confessing was preserved as a written statement of faith, the birth certificate and charter of the Lutheran church. This confessional document addressed specific issues of concern to the Christian community in a series of articles intended to define the teaching of Scripture for the situation of that day.

Again, in 1537, as they prepared for the council called by Pope Paul III, Lutheran theologians subscribed to a confession of faith composed by Luther, the Smalcald Articles. These articles also treated fundamental elements of biblical teaching under dispute within the specific context of the time. Forty years later, Lutheran churches confessed their faith in the Formula of Concord, again with reference to twelve topics being debated within their own historical context.

In each of these cases, sixteenth-century Lutherans defined their faith and their church by proclaiming and teaching the content of Scripture within the nexus of their own setting and circumstances. Implicit in this observation is the fact that, like all historical documents, the living confession and exposition of the Christian faith found in the Book of Concord can be better understood when the conditions and issues of the time are clearer. This clarity can in part be obtained by reading other documents from the period that shed light on the debates and concerns that moved the theologians of the time to address the questions posed for their church. Indeed, the documents in the Book of Concord are understandable as they were written also for those who live in the very different circumstances of the turn of the twenty-first century. But their contents may be digested more thoroughly with the aid of information and insight regarding the debates and discussions of their own time. Such insights and information may be gained from contemporary documents.

This volume is intended to support the study of the sixteenth-century Lutheran confessions. It presents fourteen texts that help illumine the situations in which the authors of these confessions perceived themselves. Some of these documents have previously appeared in English translation, but in almost every case they are out of print. In this collection, several documents are available that have not previously been at the disposal of readers of English. To aid instructors and students in their study of the confessions, we also make suggestions in this preface for the use of other available translations of documents that can shed light on the confessional texts.

The Documents in This Volume

Chronologically, Luther's catechisms were the first of what would later be called the Lutheran confessions to appear in print. Luther composed his catechisms on the basis of a great deal of preparatory work, by himself and by others. Some of his own attempts to reformulate the medieval catechetical tradition for evangelical use are available in English already.[1] At the same time that he was writing and preaching on the fundamentals of biblical learning during the 1520s, the reformer was urging other colleagues in Wittenberg and elsewhere to create a primer of the faith for families, teachers, and pastors to use in the instruction of young people. One of the early attempts, *A Booklet for Laity and Children,* appeared in 1525 (document #1); it demonstrates how one person among Luther's disciples, under his influence, perceived the catechetical task to which the reformer addressed his own efforts in 1528 and 1529. Luther himself finally took the writing of the children's catechism (the Small Catechism) and the accompanying teacher's guide (his Large Catechism) in hand. He did so in part because others in his circle had not found time to produce these works that he considered most urgent, in part because one of his students had indeed produced his own catechisms. Johann Agricola, among the brightest and best of Luther's earliest students, prepared instructional materials for the pupils in the schools of Eisleben, where he was rector. These works reflected his antinomian views, which had brought him into sharp disagreement with the Wittenberg theologians, led by Philip Melanchthon and Martin Luther, at just this time. His *One Hundred Thirty Common Questions* (document #2) also illustrates how those in the Wittenberg circle understood the task of catechizing the young; at the same time it reveals how Agricola's use of the law of God differs from that of Luther and Melanchthon. Luther's own catechism represents his attempt to counteract the influence of Agricola in the field of Christian education.

At the same time that Luther felt compelled to devote his energies to meet the pressing needs for the instruction of the young, imperial politics was driving Lutheran governmental officials and theologians to explain their program for the reform of the church in doctrine and life. Emperor Charles V called an imperial diet for late spring 1530 in the city of Augsburg. There, he demanded, the Evangelical princes and cities of his empire were to justify their alterations in ecclesiastical practice. When the delegation of Elector John of Saxony arrived in Augsburg, a new publication by the leading Roman Catholic theologian in Germany, John Eck, greeted them. His *Four Hundred Four Articles* gathered citations from writings of the Wittenberg reformers and other authors who

---

1. See, e.g., Luther's *Personal Prayer Book* (1522) (*LW* 43:3–45).

opposed the papal party into one malodorous potpourri of heresies, associating Luther, Melanchthon, and their colleagues with Anabaptist and sacramentarian ideas of various sorts (document #3). Some of the citations from the Wittenberg theologians themselves were taken out of context and given a heretical spin. The Lutherans, led by Melanchthon, recognized that they would have to make clear that the faith they confessed belonged solidly to the catholic tradition of the whole church.

Melanchthon therefore set to composing such an exposition of the faith, the Augsburg Confession. It treated two kinds of articles or topics: first, those that demonstrated the catholicity of the Lutherans and clarified their teaching on the fundamental issues of the public debate over reform, and second, those that offered the Lutheran view of how reform of essential practices in the life of the church should be accomplished. In his exposition of the catholic core of Wittenberg teaching, Melanchthon was able to use Luther's brief summary of his own theology, which concluded his *Confession on Christ's Supper* of 1528,[2] as well as the confession of faith prepared in anticipation of an Evangelical political alliance in summer 1529, the Schwabach Articles (document #4), and the articles of doctrine composed in the Marburg Colloquy of October 1529 (document #5). Since the eighteenth century, scholars have also spoken of the Torgau Articles, memoranda forged by theological advisors to the electoral Saxon court. Whether these memoranda were composed at Torgau or not remains unclear, and exactly what role the memoranda played in Melanchthon's actual drafting of the final articles of the Augsburg Confession is uncertain as well.[3] This volume contains the translation of one of the memoranda long viewed as significant in the process of formulating Articles XXI through XXVIII of the Confession (document #6) even though its actual place in their composition cannot be defined and similar sources that may have been used in the process cannot be identified.

The Augsburg Confession was presented to the Emperor on 25 June 1530. Charles immediately created a commission to refute the Lutheran statement of the faith. During the following five weeks, that commission fashioned a Confutation of the Augsburg Confession (document #7). Although the imperial officials refused to give a copy of this Confutation to the Evangelical princes, the stenographic notes taken by the officials' staff provided Melanchthon with a text to which he could reply. He did so in the *Apology of the Augsburg Confession*. How his mind was developing the doctrine of justification by faith alone at this time is also revealed in a series of theses in the genre of the academic disputation that he authored for use in Wittenberg in 1531 (document #8). The texts of

2. WA 26:499–509. *LW* 37:360–72.

3. The editors are grateful to Professor Dr. Gottfried Seebaß of the University of Heidelberg for his assistance in unraveling the tangled web of scholarship surrounding the preparations that resulted in the composition of the Augsburg Confession; he presented his analysis in an unpublished essay, "Die kursächsischen Vorbereitungen auf den Augsburger Reichstag von 1530—Torgauer Artikel?"

both the Confutation and this disputation shed light on the argument he set forth in the Apology.[4]

This volume contains no documents relating to the historical context of Luther's Smalcald Articles and Melanchthon's Treatise on the Power and Primacy of the Pope. However, the development of Wittenberg theology in the mid-1530s is partially elucidated by writings from Luther's and Melanchthon's hands published in the first half of the 1530s. Some of these texts are available in English translation.[5]

The Formula of Concord, the last of the Lutheran confessional documents of the sixteenth century, attempted to resolve a series of disputes that had plagued the Lutheran churches as a result of the political and theological crises generated by the so-called Smalcald War, waged by Emperor Charles V against the leading princes of the Evangelical Smalcald League in 1546–47. His military victory over Elector Johann Friedrich of Saxony and Landgrave Philip of Hesse in April 1547 encouraged the emperor to endeavor to impose religious uniformity on his German empire, albeit in a tentative form that would be superseded by the final decisions of the Council of Trent. His religious policy was issued in a document dubbed the Augsburg Interim by its foes (document #9).

In an attempt to ward off imperial pressure to conform to this policy, Charles's military ally, the new Evangelical elector of Saxony, Moritz, requested his counselors to provide a substitute policy that would appear similar enough to the Augsburg Interim to prevent imperial military action against him. Under considerable pressure from the electoral court, the Wittenberg theologians (under Moritz's jurisdiction because of the settlements made after the Smalcald War) worked together with court officials and local Roman Catholic representatives to formulate such an alternative policy. Although his estates refused to adopt the policy and although its provisions were introduced only piecemeal in various parts of his land by electoral decree, the document prepared for consideration in December 1548 at the electoral diet in Leipzig became a matter of controversy when foes of Moritz and his approach to church life published a draft of the proposed policy, calling it the Leipzig Interim (document #10). Its regulations and doctrinal formulations, as well as its spirit of compromise, fueled fires of controversy among the students and followers of Luther and Melanchthon for a generation.

One of the leading theologians of the period, who later played a primary role in the composition of the Formula of Concord, Martin Chemnitz, set down his

---

4. Melanchthon's theology of justification also appears in the 1540 version of his commentary on Romans, translated as *Philip Melanchthon: Commentary on Romans*, trans. Fred Kramer (St. Louis: Concordia, 1992).

5. E.g., see Luther's "Theses Concerning Faith and Law" (1535) (*LW* 34:105–32); "The Disputation Concerning Man" (1536) (*LW* 34:133–44); "The Disputation Concerning Justification" (1536) (*LW* 34:145–96); "Lectures on Galatians" (1535) (*LW* 26:1–461 and 27:1–149); see also the third edition of Melanchthon's *Loci* (2d ed., 1535), *Loci Communes 1543, Philip Melanchthon*, trans. J. A. O. Preus (St. Louis: Concordia, 1992).

thoughts on these controversies a decade after their outbreak, in 1561. Not published until seventeen years after the Formula was drafted, after the death of its author, the document nonetheless reveals the approach to the disputes plaguing the Lutheran churches that guided this influential theologian as he provided leadership in resolving the issues that divided Lutherans in his day (document #11). This volume offers three chapters from this discussion of the controversies. A number of Chemnitz's other writings in English translation are also available for student use.[6] Also, the first of the stages of formulation of the text of the Formula of Concord, Jakob Andreae's *Six Christian Sermons on the Divisions Which Have Continued to Surface among the Theologians of the Augsburg Confession . . .* may be obtained in English translation.[7]

One of the most critical issues at the time of the work on the Formula of Concord was the christological support for the Lutheran understanding of the real presence of Christ's body and blood in the Lord's Supper. Among the instruments used to criticize this part of Lutheran teaching was the argument based on selected citations of the ancient fathers of the church. Two of the authors of the Formula of Concord, Martin Chemnitz and Jakob Andreae, were commissioned to marshal patristic argument in behalf of the position of the Formula's eighth article, that on the doctrine of the person of Jesus Christ. Their Catalog of Testimonies on this topic was published with some printings of the Book of Concord when it appeared in 1580 and has often been printed as an appendix of the Book of Concord ever since (document #12). The two English translations of the Book of Concord of the second half of the twentieth century did not include it; therefore it is offered in this volume as an important exposition of the thought and method of the authors of the Formula of Concord.

The ninth article of the Formula of Concord, on Christ's descent into hell, was added to the Formula as a kind of appendix to Article VIII, on Christology. Certain Lutheran ministeria had discussed the proper interpretation of the descent into hell, but no burning controversy compelled inclusion of a treatment of this teaching. It was most likely discussed because of the desire to oppose Calvinist teaching on the topic. The text of the Formula refers readers to the published form of a sermon by Luther, attributed to Torgau in 1533 (though actually preached in Wittenberg a year earlier), and thus it has become

---

6. For background on Articles III and IV of the Formula of Concord, on justification and good works, see Chemnitz's *Examination of the Council of Trent, Part I,* trans. Fred Kramer (St. Louis: Concordia, 1971), 385–663; for Article VII of the Formula of Concord, on the Lord's Supper, see Chemnitz's *Repetitio sanae doctrinae de vera praesentiae corporis et sanguinis Domini in coena* (Leipzig, 1561), translated as *The Lord's Supper,* trans. J. A. O. Preus (St. Louis: Concordia, 1979); for Article VIII of the Formula, on Christology, see his *De duabus naturis in Christo* (1570; Leipzig, 1578); translated as *The Two Natures in Christ,* trans. J. A. O. Preus (St. Louis: Concordia, 1971); and on a number of subjects, but particularly the doctrine of election (Article XI), see his *Die fürnemsten heuptstück der christlichen Lehre . . .* (Wolfenbüttel: Conrad Horn, 1569); translated as *Ministry, Word, and Sacraments, an Enchiridion,* trans. Luther Poellot (St. Louis: Concordia, 1981).

7. See *Sechs Christlicher Predig von den Spaltungen . . . ,* translated in *Andreae and the Formula of Concord,* trans. Robert Kolb (St. Louis: Concordia, 1977).

a secondary part of the Formula's text (document #13). The sermon treats the subject only lightly in the midst of proclaiming the resurrection of Christ.

The Book of Concord was removed from its place of authority in the church of electoral Saxony as part of the religious policy of Elector Christian I, the son of Elector August, who had led and supported the efforts that resulted in the Formula of Concord. Christian's brief reign ended in 1591 and with it the "Crypto-Calvinism" promoted by his court. The reintroduction of the theology of the Book of Concord in Saxony was accomplished in part through the Saxon Visitation Articles composed in 1592 by the new Lutheran theological staff of the electoral government (document #14). These Visitation Articles became part of the regular publication of the Book of Concord in electoral Saxony. They reveal something of the thinking of contemporary adherents of the theology of the Formula of Concord.

With Thanks

A collection such as this is the product of many contributors. The editors express their deep appreciation to the translators of the individual documents; it has been a joy to work with each of them. One of these colleagues deserves special mention. Jacob A. O. Preus devoted his retirement to the careful study of the historical texts of the period preceding the Formula of Concord and also gave encouragement and support to fire the energies of a succeeding generation of confessional scholars before his death in 1995. His translation in this volume signals a much larger contribution to the study of Martin Chemnitz, and the editors also profited much from his encouragement as our work began.

In addition, our thanks are extended to Clinton J. Armstrong, Gerhard H. Bode Jr., and Erik Herrmann for their work on the most tedious aspects of editing. We also are grateful for the editorial support of those with whom we have worked at Fortress Press, above all Henry French and Michael West.

―――――――――

The study of the Lutheran confessional documents provides a reminder of what the first adherents of the Lutheran confession of the faith proclaimed as the heart of the biblical message and how they went about the process of confessing that message. Thereby it sets forth the definition of the doctrinal content of Scripture at the core of Lutheran theology. The study of these confessions also provides an understanding of the standpoint that Lutherans represent in the ecumenical conversation to this day. Finally, through this study we provide orientation for meeting the challenges of confessing Christian teaching in the twenty-first century, for the confessional documents furnish a hermeneutic for interpreting God's Word and formulating its message in our own time. This volume is designed to broaden and deepen historical knowledge of and insights into the Lutheran tradition. Therefore, we hope that it serves as a tool for continuing confession of the Christian faith.

Abbreviations

ANF	*The Ante-Nicene Fathers: Translations of the Writings of the Fathers down to 325 A.D.,* ed. Alexander Roberts and James Donaldson. Grand Rapids, Mich.: Eerdmans, 1980–87.
Ap	Apology of the Augsburg Confession
Br	*Briefe*
BSLK	*Die Bekenntnisschriften der evangelisch-lutherischen Kirche.* Göttingen: Vandenhoeck & Ruprecht, 1930, 1991.
CCL	*Corpus Christianorum, Series Latina.* Turnholt: Brepols, 1953–.
CIC	*Corpus Iuris Canonici,* ed. Emil Friedberg, 2 vols. Leipzig: Tauchnitz, 1879/1881.
Commentary	Zwingli, Ulrich. *Commentary on True and False Religion, 1525,* ed. Samuel Macauley Jackson and Clarence Nevi Heller. 1929; Durham, N.C.: Labyrinth, 1981.
CR	Melanchthon, Philip. *Corpus Reformatorum. Opera quae supersunt omnia,* ed. C. G. Bretschneider and H. E. Bindweil. Halle: Schwetschke, 1834–60.
CSEL	*Corpus scriptorum ecclesiasticorum latinorum.* Vienna: Gerold, 1866–.
DB	Deutsche Bibel
Denzinger	*Enchiridion symbolorum definitionum et declarationum de rebus fidei et morum . . . ,* ed. Heinrich Denzinger and Peter Hünnermann. Freiburg: Herder, 1991.
Ep	Epitome of the Formula of Concord
Fathers of the Church	*The Fathers of the Church: A New Translation.* Washington, D.C.: Catholic University of America Press, 1947–.
FC	Formula of Concord
LCC 24	Works by Ulrich Zwingli, in *Zwingli and Bullinger,* ed. G. W. Bromiley, *Library of Christian Classics,* 24. Philadelphia: Westminster, 1953.
Library of the Fathers	*Library of the Fathers of the Holy Catholic Church.* Oxford: Parker, 1838–85.
Loci	Melanchthon, Philip. *Loci Communes Theologici, 1521,* in *Melanchthon and Bucer,* ed. F. J. Taylor, *Library of Christian Classics* 19. Philadelphia: Westminster, 1969.
LW	Luther, Martin. *Luther's Works.* St. Louis: Concordia and Philadelphia: Fortress, 1958–86.

MPG	*Patrologiae cursus completus: Series Graece,* ed. Jacques-Paul Migne. 161 vols. Paris & Turnhout, 1857–66.
MPL	*Patrologiae cursus completus: Series Latina,* ed. Jacques-Paul Migne. 221 vols. Paris & Turnhout, 1859–1963.
NPNF	*A Select Library of the Christian Church. Nicene and Post-Nicene Fathers,* ed. Philip Schaff. Grand Rapids, Mich.: Eerdmans, 1986–89.
NRSV	New Revised Standard Version of the Bible
On Providence	Zwingli, Ulrich. *On Providence and Other Essays,* ed. Samuel Macauley Jackson and William John Hinke. 1922; Durham, N.C.: Labyrinth, 1983.
SCh	*Sources chrétiennes.* Paris: Cerf, 1942–.
SD	Solid Declaration of the Formula of Concord
WA	Luther, Martin. *Dr. Martin Luthers Werke.* Weimar: Böhlau, 1883–1993.
WADB	Luther, Martin. *Luthers Werke: Kritische Gesamtausgabe. Bibel.* 12 vols. Weimar: Böhlau, 1930–85.
ZSW	Zwingli, Ulrich. *Ulrich Zwingli (1484–1531): Selected Works,* ed. Samuel Macauley Jackson. Philadelphia: University of Pennsylvania Press, 1901.

Contributors

CHARLES P. ARAND is associate professor of systematic theology at Concordia Seminary, St. Louis, Missouri.

ROBERT KOLB is professor of systematic theology and director of the Institute for Mission Studies at Concordia Seminary, St. Louis, Missouri.

THOMAS MANTEUFEL is associate professor of systematic theology at Concordia Seminary, St. Louis, Missouri.

JAMES A. NESTINGEN is professor of church history at Luther Seminary, St. Paul, Minnesota.

OLIVER K. OLSON has taught church history at Saint Olaf College, Northfield, Minnesota; Lutheran Theological Seminary, Philadelphia, Pennsylvania; Marquette University, Milwaukee, Wisconsin; and Luther Seminary, St. Paul, Minnesota.

J. A. O. PREUS† was president of Concordia Theological Seminary, Springfield, Illinois, and president of the Lutheran Church–Missouri Synod.

ROBERT ROSIN is professor of historical theology at Concordia Seminary, St. Louis, Missouri.

WILLIAM R. RUSSELL is assistant professor of religion at Midland College, Fremont, Nebraska.

MARK D. TRANVIK is assistant professor of religion at Augsburg College, Minneapolis, Minnesota.

TIMOTHY J. WENGERT is professor of the history of Christianity at the Lutheran Theological Seminary, Philadelphia, Pennsylvania.

A Booklet for
Laity and Children

Translated by Timothy J. Wengert

Introduction

Near the end of 1524, Nicholas Hausmann, Evangelical preacher in Zwickau and correspondent of Luther, wrote to Luther in a now-lost letter asking that Wittenberg provide some guidance in the instruction of children. Luther responded on 2 February 1525 that Justus Jonas and John Agricola had been asked to produce some material for this purpose.[1] A month later, on 26 March, Luther reiterated that a catechism had been demanded from these authors.[2] A few months later, Hausmann turned to the court of electoral Saxony, again asking for a catechism.[3] He also suggested that the worship service be translated into German, a request Luther fulfilled that Christmas with the Deutsche Messe. In the preface to this work, Luther called for a simple catechism and described its parts.[4] He also referred readers to his *Personal Prayer Book*, first published in 1522 but revised in 1525, as a source for catechesis.[5]

Either with or without Luther's direct involvement, a small booklet for the instruction of children and laity appeared in 1525 and was immediately translated into Latin and Low German (Niederdeutsch). A second, revised edition, which included portions of Luther's comments on Confession and Absolution, appeared early in 1526. The only surviving copy of the first edition was discovered in 1991 in the Herzog August Bibliothek of Wolfenbüttel, Germany.[6] It consists of the texts of the chief parts, called a lay Bible, explanations of the Creed and the Lord's Prayer excerpted from Luther's writings (including from

---

1. WA *Br* 3:431.

2. WA *Br* 3:462. When Agricola left Wittenberg in the summer of 1525 to be rector of the Latin school in Eisleben, the project was never completed. For one of Agricola's own catechisms, see below, pp. 13–30.

3. Cited in Ferdinand Cohrs, *Die Evangelischen Katechismenversuche vor Luthers Enchiridion*, 4 vols. (Berlin: A. Hofmann, 1900–1902), 4:247.

4. WA 19:76, 1–78, 24; *LW* 53:64–67. The preface was probably written in January 1526.

5. WA 10, II:375–406; translated in *LW* 43:3–45.

6. See Timothy J. Wengert, "Wittenberg's Earliest Catechism," *Lutheran Quarterly*, n.s., 7 (1993): 247–60. This discovery disproves Cohrs's theory that the Niederdeutsch edition was the first and that it was produced by John Bugenhagen. It is more likely that this booklet was produced by Stephen Roth, then a catechist in Wittenberg and later the city clerk in Zwickau. He worked on several catechisms during this time as well as Luther's sermons for the texts of the church year. The call number is QuH 132.7 (5) and the title page reads: *Eyn buchlin fur | die leyen vnd | kinder. | Wittemberg. | MDXXV. |*, 8°, 24 unnumbered leaves.

1

the *Personal Prayer Book*), prayers for morning and evening, table grace and blessing, and a short section on Confession written by the compiler. In one form or another, this booklet was published at least twenty-six times between 1525 and 1530.[7]

This booklet is an important forerunner to Luther's Small Catechism because it contained for the first time texts of the five chief parts, brief explanations written by Luther, daily prayers, and an explanation of Confession. It also demonstrates how important Luther's *Personal Prayer Book* was for early Wittenberg catechesis. Finally, it sets off the changes and improvements of Luther's Small Catechism in sharp relief.

A Booklet for the laity and children.

WITTENBERG.
M D XXV.

[A Woodcut of Jacob's Ladder]
A a b c d e f g h i k l m n o p q r s t v u w x y z.
Vowels: a e i o u y
Consonants: b c d f g h k l m n p q r s t w x z

THE TEN COMMANDMENTS
The First
You shall have no other gods before me.
The Second
You shall not take the name of the Lord your God in vain.
The Third
You shall sanctify the holy day.
The Fourth
You shall honor your father and your mother.
The Fifth
You shall not kill.
The Sixth
You shall not commit adultery.
The Seventh
You shall not steal.
The Eighth
You shall not bear false witness against your neighbor.
The Ninth
You shall not covet your neighbor's house.

---

7. For a partial list of printings, see Cohrs, *Die Evangelischen Katechismenversuche,* 1:187–92. A later version, first published in Wittenberg in 1529, included a collection of Bible passages assembled by Philip Melanchthon. (It was later published in 1543 and 1548.)

The Tenth

You shall not covet your neighbor's wife, servant, maid, cattle, or whatever is his.

Christ gives a short summary in Matthew 7[:12], "Whatever you want people to do for you, do the same for them as well. That is the Law and the Prophets."

THE CREED

I believe in God the Father almighty, maker of heaven and the earth.

And in Jesus Christ his only Son our Lord, who was conceived by the Holy Spirit and born of the Virgin Mary, suffered under Pontius Pilate, crucified, died and was buried, descended into hell, on the third day he rose again from the dead, ascended into heaven, sitting at the right hand of God the almighty Father, from where he is coming to judge the living and the dead.

I believe in the Holy Spirit, one holy Christian church, one community of saints, forgiveness of sins, resurrection of the flesh and eternal life. Amen.

THE LORD'S PRAYER

Our Father, you who are in heaven, hallowed be your name, your kingdom come, your will be done also on earth as in heaven, give us today our daily bread, and forgive us our debts as we forgive our debtors, and do not lead us into temptation, but deliver us from evil. Amen.

ON BAPTISM

Whoever believes and is baptized will be saved. Whoever does not believe will be damned. Mark 16[:16].

ON THE SACRAMENT [OF THE ALTAR]

Christ took the bread and said:

"Take and eat, this is my body, given for you. Do this in remembrance of me."

Afterwards he took the cup also and said:

"Take and all drink from it. This is the cup of the New Testament in my blood, shed for you for the forgiveness of sins. Do this as often as you drink it in remembrance of me."

End of the Lay Bible.

AN INSTRUCTION[8]

For all people to be saved three things are necessary. First, they must know what to do and what to leave undone. This is what the Ten Commandments teach.

---

8. The following first appeared in Luther's *Personal Prayer Book* (1522) (*LW* 43:13). Additions to that text and corrections to the translation are noted by square brackets.

Second, when they realize that they cannot measure up to what they should do or leave undone with their own powers, they need to know where to go to find the strength they require. This the Creed shows them.

Third, they must know how to seek and obtain that strength, [namely through prayer. The Lord's Prayer teaches them this.]

ON THE CREED[9]

The Creed is divided into three main parts, each telling about one of the three persons of the holy and divine Trinity. The first [is dedicated to] the Father, the second [to] the Son, and the third [to] the Holy Spirit. [For this] is the most important article of the Creed; all the others are based on it.

The First Part.

The Second Part.

The Third Part.

The First Part of the Creed

I believe in God, the Father almighty, maker of heaven and the earth. This means: I renounce the evil spirit, all idolatry, all sorcery, and all false belief.

I put my trust in no person on earth, not in myself, my power, my skill, my possessions, my [righteousness], nor in anything else I may have.

I place my trust in no creature, whether in heaven or on earth.

I set my hope and confidence only in the one, invisible, inscrutable, and only God, who created heaven and earth and who alone is superior to all creation. Again, I am not terrified by all the wickedness of the devil and his cohorts because my God is superior to them all.

I would believe in God not a bit less if everyone were to forsake me and persecute me.

I would believe in God no less if I were poor, unintelligent, uneducated, despised, or lacking in everything.

I believe no less though I am a sinner. For this manner of faith will of necessity rise over all that does or does not exist, over sin and virtue and all else, thus depending purely and completely upon God as the First Commandment enjoins me to do.

I do not ask for any sign from God to put him to the test.

I trust in him steadfastly, no matter how long he may delay, prescribing neither a goal nor a time, nor a measure, nor a way [for God to respond to me], but leaving all to his divine will in a free and genuine faith.

If he is almighty, what could I lack that God could not give or do for me?

If he is the Creator of heaven and earth and Lord over everything, who, then, could deprive me of anything, or cause me harm? Yes, how can it be otherwise than that all things work for good for me [Rom. 8:28] if the God, whom all creation obeys and depends upon, is well intentioned toward me?

---

9. The following first appeared in Luther's *Personal Prayer Book* (1522) (*LW* 43:24–29).

Because he is God, he can and wishes to do what is best with me. Since he is Father, he will do all this and do it gladly.

And since I do not doubt this but place my trust in him, I am assuredly his child, servant, and eternal heir, and it will be with me as I believe.

The Second Part

And in Jesus Christ, his only Son, our Lord: who was conceived by the Holy Spirit, born of the Virgin Mary, suffered under Pontius Pilate, was crucified, [died,] and was buried; he descended into hell, the third day he rose from the dead, he ascended into heaven, and is seated on the right hand of God, the Father almighty, whence he shall come to judge the living and the dead.

That is:

I do not only believe that this means that Jesus Christ is the one true Son of God, begotten of him in eternity with one eternal divine nature and essence— but I also believe that the Father has made all things subject to him, that according to his human nature he has been made one Lord over me and all things, which he created together with the Father in his divinity.

I believe that no one can believe in the Father and that no one can come to him by any ability, deeds, understanding, or anything that may be named in heaven or on earth, except alone in and through Jesus Christ, his only Son, that is, through faith in his name and lordship.

I firmly believe that for my welfare Christ was conceived by the Holy Spirit, apart from any human or carnal act and without any physical father or seed of man, so that he makes me and all who believe in him spiritual, cleansing me of my sinful, carnal, impure, damnable conception—all this through his and the almighty Father's gracious will.

I believe that for my sake he was born of the immaculate Virgin Mary, without changing her physical and spiritual virginity, so that according to his fatherly mercy he might render my sinful and damnable birth blessed, innocent, and pure, as he does for all his believers.

I believe that for my sin and the sin of all believers Christ bore his suffering on the cross and thereby brings blessing through every suffering and cross and has thus made them not only harmless but also salutary and highly rewarding.

I believe that Christ died and was buried to put my sin to death and bury it and do the same for all believers and, moreover, that he slew human death, transforming it into something that does no harm and is beneficial and salutary.

I believe that for me and all his believers Christ descended into hell to subdue the devil and take him captive along with all his power, cunning, and malice so that the devil can no longer harm me, and that he redeemed me from the pains of hell, transforming them into something harmless and beneficial.

I believe that he was resurrected from the dead on the third day to give a new life to me and all believers, thus awakening us with him by his grace and spirit henceforth to sin no more but to serve him only with every grace and virtue, thus fulfilling God's commandments.

I believe that he ascended into heaven and received power and honor over all angels and creatures and now sits at God's right hand. This means that he is King and Lord over all that is God's in heaven, earth, and hell. Hence he can help me and all believers against all troubles and against every adversary and foe.

I believe that Christ will return from heaven on the Last Day to judge those who are alive at that time and those who have died before that day, that all humankind, angels, and devils will have to appear before his judgment throne to see him with their eyes. Then he will redeem me and all who believe in him from bodily death and every infirmity and will eternally punish his enemies and adversaries and deliver us from their power forever.

The Third Part

I believe in the Holy Spirit, one holy Christian church, one community of saints, forgiveness of sins, resurrection of the body, and eternal life. Amen.

That is:

I believe not only that the Holy Spirit is true God together with the Father and the Son, but also that except through the Holy Spirit's work no one can come in and to the Father through Christ and his life, his suffering and death, and all that is said of him [in the Creed], nor can anyone appropriate any of this to himself. Working through the Spirit, Father and Son stir up, awaken, call, and beget new life in me and in all who are his. Thus in and through Christ the Spirit quickens, sanctifies, and awakens the spirit in us and brings us to the Father, by whom the Spirit is active and life-giving everywhere.

I believe that throughout the whole wide world there is only one holy, universal, Christian church, which is nothing other than the gathering or congregation of saints—[righteous] believers on earth. This church is gathered, preserved, and governed by the same Holy Spirit and is given daily increase by means of the sacraments and the Word of God.

I believe that no one can be saved who is not in this gathering or community, harmoniously sharing the same faith with it, the same word, sacraments, hope, and love, and that no Jew, heretic, pagan, or sinner can be saved along with this community unless they become reconciled with it and unite with it in full agreement in all things.

I believe that in this community or Christendom all things are held in common; what each one possesses belongs also to others, and no one has complete ownership of anything. Hence, all the prayers and good deeds of all the Christian community benefit, aid, and strengthen me and every other believer at all times, both in life and in death, and that each one bears the other's burden, as St. Paul teaches [Gal. 6:2].

I believe that there is forgiveness of sin nowhere else than in this community and that beyond it nothing can help to gain it—no good deeds, no matter how many or how great they might be; and that within this community nothing can invalidate this forgiveness of sin—no matter how gravely and often one may sin; and that such forgiveness continues as long as this one community exists. To this community Christ gave the power of the keys, saying in Matthew 18[:18], "Whatever you bind on earth shall be bound in heaven." He said the same to Peter as an individual, representing and taking the place of the one and only one church, "whatever you bind on earth," and so forth, Matthew 16[:19].

I believe that there will be a resurrection from the dead in the future in which all flesh will be raised from the dead through the Holy Spirit, that is, all humankind, good and evil, will be raised bodily to return alive in the same flesh in which they died, were buried, and decayed or perished in various ways.

I believe in an eternal life for the saints after the resurrection and in an eternal dying for the sinners. And I haven't a doubt about all this that the Father through his Son Jesus Christ our Lord and with the Holy Spirit will let all this happen to me. [This means] Amen, that is, this is [actually and certainly true].[10]

A blessing for when one arises in the morning.
Under the care of God: the Father, Son, and Holy Spirit.

RECITE THE CREED.
I believe in God the Father almighty, creator, etc.

PRAY THE LORD'S PRAYER.
Our Father, you who are in heaven, hallowed be etc.

Afterwards read something from the Bible and Psalms that may be used to strengthen your faith against all errors, sins, and assaults.[11]

WHEN YOU GO TO WORK
Recite the Ten Commandments and pray an "Our Father etc."

THE [TABLE] BLESSING
Psalm 144 [=104:27-28]
All eyes wait upon you, O LORD, and you give them their food in their season. You open your hand and satisfy every living thing with pleasure. "Our Father etc."

Prayer
Lord God, heavenly Father, bless us and these your gifts that we receive from your bountiful goodness, through Christ our Lord. Amen.

---

10. Here ends the excerpt from Luther's *Personal Prayer Book.*
11. German: *Anfechtung.*

THE THANKSGIVING [AFTER MEALS]

Give thanks to the Lord, for he is kind, and his goodness endures eternally. He gives food to all flesh. He gives fodder to the cattle, to the young ravens who cry to him. He has no desire for strong horses nor pleasure in anyone's legs. The LORD takes pleasure in those who fear him, who wait for his goodness.

"Our Father."

Prayer

We thank you, LORD God Father, through Jesus Christ our Lord, for all your blessings, you who live and reign in eternity. AMEN.

An evening blessing when one goes to bed
Under the care of God: the Father, Son, and Holy Spirit. Amen.

Psalm 63[:6-7]

When I think of you upon my bed, so was my conversation about you during the [night] watch. For you are my Helper, and under the shadow of your wings I will rejoice.

"Our Father etc."

And here one must get accustomed to recalling whatever one heard or learned during the day from the Holy Scripture and fall asleep thinking about it.

A Short Meditation on the Lord's Prayer.
Also on Confession.
A Short Exposition of the Lord's Prayer.[12]

The Soul: O our Father, who art in heaven, we your children dwell here on earth in misery, far removed from you. Such a great gulf lies between you and us. How are we to find our way home to you in our fatherland?

God, in Malachi 1[:6]: A child honors its father, and a servant his master. If then I am your Father, where is my honor? If I am your Lord, where is the awe and the reverence due me? For my holy name is blasphemed and dishonored among you and by you, Isaiah 52[:5].

The First Petition

The Soul: My Father, unfortunately that is true. We acknowledge our guilt. Be a merciful Father and do not take us to task, but grant us your grace that your name may be hallowed in us. Let us not think, say, do, have, or undertake anything unless it redounds to your honor and glory. Grant that we may enhance your name and honor it above everything else and that we not seek our

12. The following is an excerpt from Martin Luther's *An Exposition of the Lord's Prayer* (WA 2:128, 3–130, 18; *LW* 42:78–81), which first appeared in an edition overseen by Luther in 1519. The Bible references have been slightly rearranged to reflect the way they appeared in the text.

own vainglory nor further our own name. Grant that we may love and fear and honor you as children do their father.

God, in Isaiah 52[:5] and Genesis 8[:21]: How can my name and honor be hallowed in you, while your heart and mind are inclined to evil and are captive to sin, and since no one can sing my praise in a foreign land, Psalm 127[:4]?

The Second Petition

The Soul: O Father, that is true. We realize that our members incline to sin and that the world, the flesh, and the devil want to reign in us and thus banish your name and honor from us. Therefore, we ask you to help us out of this misery and to let your kingdom come so that sin may be expelled and we become righteous and acceptable to you, so that you alone may hold sway in us and we may become your kingdom by placing all our powers, both inner and external, in your service.

God in Deuteronomy 32[:39]: Him whom I am to help I destroy. Him whom I want to quicken, save, enrich, and make [righteous], I mortify, reject, impoverish, and reduce to nothing. However, you refuse to accept such counsel and action from me, Psalm 78[:10-11]. How, then, am I to help you? And what more can I do? Isaiah 5[:4].

The Third Petition

The Soul: We deplore that we do not understand or accept your helping hand. O Father, grant us your grace and help us to allow your divine will to be done in us. Yes, even though it pains us, continue to punish and stab us, to beat and burn us. Do as you will with us, as long as your will, and not ours, is done. Dear Father, keep us from undertaking and completing anything that is in accord with our own choice, will, and opinion. [For] your will and ours conflict with each other. Yours alone is good, though it does not seem to be; ours is evil, though it glitters.

God in Psalm 78[:9]: Your lips often voiced your love for me, while your heart was far from me [Isa. 29:13]. And when I chastised you to improve you, you defected; in the midst of my work on you, you deserted me, as you can read in Psalm 78[:9], "They turned back on the day of battle." Those who made a good beginning and moved me to deal with them turned their backs on me and fell back into sin and into my disfavor.

The Fourth Petition

The Soul: O Father, this is very true; "for not by his might shall a man prevail," 1 Samuel 2[:9]. And who can abide under your hand if you yourself do not strengthen and comfort us? Therefore, dear Father, seize hold of us, fulfill your will in us so that we may become your kingdom, to your glory and honor. But, dear Father, fortify us in such trials with your holy Word; give us our daily bread. Fashion your dear Son, Jesus Christ, the true heavenly bread, in our hearts so that we, strengthened by him, may cheerfully bear and endure the destruction and death of our will and the perfecting of your will. Yes, grant grace also to all members of Christendom and send us learned priests and pastors who do not feed us the husk and chaff of vain fables, but who teach us your holy gospel and Jesus Christ.

God, in Jeremiah 5[:5-6] and other passages: It is not good to take what is holy and the children's bread and throw it to the dogs [Matt. 7:6; 15:26]. You sin daily, and when I have my Word preached to you day and night, you do not obey and listen, and my Word is despised [Jer. 5:5-6; Isa. 42:20].

The Fifth Petition

The Soul: O Father, have mercy on us and do not deny us our precious bread because of that. We are sorry that we do not do justice to your holy Word, and we implore you to have patience with us poor children. Take away our guilt and do not enter into judgment with us, for no one is just in your sight. Remember your promise to forgive those who sincerely forgive their debtors. It is not that we merit your forgiveness because we forgive others, but we know that you are truthful and will graciously forgive all who forgive their neighbors. We place our trust in your promise.

God in Psalm 78[:8]: I forgive and redeem you so often, and you do not remain steadfast and faithful. You are of weak faith [Matt. 8:26]. You cannot watch and tarry with me a little while, but quickly fall back into temptation. Matthew 26[:40-41].

The Sixth Petition

The Soul: O Father, we are faint and ill, and the trials in the flesh and in the world are severe and manifold. O dear Father, hold us and do not let us fall into temptation and sin again, but give us grace to remain steadfast and fight valiantly to the end. Without your grace and your help, we are not able to do anything.

God in Psalm 11[:7]: I am just, and my judgment is right. Therefore sin must not go unpunished. Thus you must endure adversity. The fact that trials ensue from this is the fault of your sin, which forces me to punish and curb it.

The Seventh Petition

The Soul: Since trials flow from these adversities and tempt us to sin, deliver us, dear Father, from these so that freed from all sin and adversity according to your divine will we may be your kingdom and laud and praise and hallow you forever. Amen. And since you taught and commanded us to pray thus and have promised fulfillment, we hope and are assured, O dearest Father, that in honor of your truth you will grant all this to us graciously and mercifully.

And finally someone may say, "What am I to do if I cannot believe that I am heard?" Answer: Then follow the example of the father of the child possessed with a dumb spirit in Mark 9[:23-24]. When Christ said to him, "Can you believe? All things are possible to him who believes," the father cried with tear-filled eyes, "O Lord, I believe; help my faith [when] it is too weak!"[13]

ON CONFESSION[14]

The Scripture describes for us a single confession that is necessary for us, that God demands and will have from us, without which we cannot be saved. It flows from faith: that we confess from the bottom of our hearts before God that we are eternally lost and that all our works, however good they may be, are pure and horrible sins to God, and that we confess that we are saved through the pure grace and mercy of God revealed in Christ alone. He speaks of confession in Psalm 32[:5]: "I said, I will confess my transgressions to the LORD etc." And Christ confirmed this and spoke an absolution upon such a confession in Luke 18[:9-14], where the Pharisee and the tax collector both went up to the Temple to pray. The Pharisee stood and prayed alone in this way: "I thank you, God, that I am not like other people—robbers, crooks, adulterers, or even like this tax collector etc." And the tax collector stood at a distance, would not even lift his eyes to heaven, but instead beat his breast and said, "God, be gracious to me, a sinner." "I tell you," Christ says, "this one went down to his house justified, not the first." Here Christ absolves the tax collector and damns the Pharisee. For this confession must come from the bottom of the heart without hypocrisy or self-deception. Otherwise it is all over for us, and [we] cannot even recognize the grace and mercy of God—much less attain it! Yes, where such confession is truly present, there is also the grace of God—no matter how much your sins may weigh you down! In the same way we confess in the Lord's Prayer, where we acknowledge our sin in all the petitions.

The other confession, which one makes to the neighbor, is not laid upon us from God as a necessity. For without this kind [of confession] we can and may be saved. It is nevertheless helpful, comforting, and salutary, if you make this kind of confession to someone who possesses God's Word. For such a person can hold before us the holy Gospel, that is, the certain forgiveness of sins through the Word of God, so that you may be comforted, certain, and at peace in your conscience. Moreover, you can defy the devil, who up to now has led you astray with all kinds of assaults[15] and sins. For you cannot plague the proud devil in a better way, so that he will leave you alone and will not harm you, than by confessing his shameful deeds, with which he assaults you, to another Christian or by using some other way of bringing his deeds to light. And you will thus thwart him through the powerful Word of God, which a Christian to whom you confess will doubtless proclaim to you through the Holy Spirit. For we Christians, who are brothers [and sisters] and coheirs of the Lord Christ one with

13. Here ends the excerpt from Luther's *An Exposition of the Lord's Prayer*.
14. There is no parallel for this material in Luther's extant works.
15. German: *Anfechtung.*

another, have the power to distribute to each other the inheritance, that is, the forgiveness of sins, in the name and in the stead of the Lord Christ. He gave us this power in Matthew 18[:18], "Whatever you bind on earth shall be bound in heaven, etc.," as we have heard enough about in the third part of the Creed.[16]

To all this may God give us grace through Jesus Christ our Lord. Amen.

16. This reference seems to indicate that this section was written by the compiler, not by Luther.

One Hundred Thirty Common Questions

Johann Agricola

Translated by Timothy J. Wengert

Introduction

Early in 1525, Martin Luther asked Justus Jonas and John Agricola to write a catechism for the instruction of children. Their work on such a project was interrupted when Agricola, who had been born in Eisleben, returned there in the summer of 1525 to become rector of the newly established Latin school. Agricola continued to demonstrate his concern for catechesis and in late 1526 produced a Latin catechism, *Elementa pietatis congesta*. This was immediately translated into German for the adjoining girls' school—in which his wife, Else, was probably a teacher—under the title *Eine Christliche Kinderzucht, ynn Gottes wort vnd lere, Aus der Schule zu Eisleben*. In one form or another, it was printed ten times in 1527 and 1528.[1] As Agricola himself admitted, even this translation was too difficult for the girls' school. Thus, a year later, he was writing a preface to a new catechism, translated here.[2] It enjoyed immediate, though short-lived, success, having been printed ten times in 1528–29 and thereafter only once.[3]

John Agricola (ca. 1494–1566) studied under Luther beginning in 1516 and accompanied him to the Leipzig Disputation in 1519. Agricola was also friends with Philip Melanchthon and even planned in 1520 to move into Melanchthon's living quarters shortly after the latter's marriage. After arriving in Eisleben in 1525, he was passed over for a professorship in Wittenberg that eventually went to Melanchthon. After his tour as rector in Eisleben, he returned to Wittenberg in 1537, where he became involved in the so-called antinomian controversy with Martin Luther. He fled to Berlin in 1541, where he remained for the rest of his life.

In Eisleben, the contours of his (antinomian) theology began to take shape, resulting immediately in a dispute with Philip Melanchthon over the Saxon

---

1. For this catechism, see Ferdinand Cohrs, *Die Evangelischen Katechismenversuche vor Luthers Enchiridion*, 4 vols. (Berlin: A. Hofmann, 1900–1902), 2:3–83.

2. *Hundert und Dreissig gemeyner Fragestücke für die iungen kinder ynn der Deudschen Meydlinschule zu Eyßleben*. We use the version published by Cohrs, *Die Evangelischen Katechismenversuche*, 2:261–311.

3. In 1541, in a Latin translation produced in Berlin after Agricola had fled Wittenberg following the antinomian controversy with Luther.

Visitation Articles of 1528.[4] In the early part of the controversy, Agricola objected to the division of repentance into the (medieval) categories of contrition, confession, and satisfaction. Later he insisted that Melanchthon's emphasis upon sorrow for sin out of fear of punishment contradicted Evangelical theology because true sorrow for sin arose not from the law but from the Gospel and thus from true love for God.[5] This theological controversy is directly reflected in Agricola's catechism, the preface of which was written only two weeks before Martin Luther effected a reconciliation between the disputants during a special meeting at the Torgau castle.[6]

There is some reason to believe that George Spalatin, a councilor to Elector John of Saxony, and Philip Melanchthon objected to Agricola's catechism, with its attack on the threefold division of repentance and its denigration of the law and reason,[7] and wished to replace it. Melanchthon began to write his own catechism at this time but broke it off at the third commandment, most likely because of Luther's own work on the Small and Large Catechisms.

Luther, too, was probably familiar with the *One Hundred Thirty Common Questions*. His own catechetical works stood in marked contrast to those of Agricola. The law is placed prominently at the beginning of both catechisms.[8] There is no sign of the medieval concept of a tinder of sin remaining after Baptism.[9] Complex questions and answers are replaced by the simple "What is this?" and most biblical proof texting disappears. Moreover, Luther's explanation to the commandments reflects the compromise proposed by Luther at the Torgau castle, in that both fear and love mark the relation to the commandments.[10]

Portions of Agricola's catechism also reflect the basics of Wittenberg's theology and Luther's catechisms, indicating either that in these texts Agricola depended upon Luther's earlier work or perhaps even that Luther borrowed some ideas and phrases from Agricola. In any event, this catechism was produced by the most widely published author of such books before Luther's

---

4. WA 26:195–240; LW 40:263–320. See Timothy J. Wengert, *Law and Gospel: Philip Melanchthon's Debate with Johann Agricola of Eisleben over Poenitentia* (Grand Rapids, Mich.: Baker and Paternoster, 1997).

5. He also accused Melanchthon of contradicting Luther's interpretation of Gal. 3:24 and insisted that Paul's exhortations were not law.

6. Luther insisted that Christians are repentant on the basis of both fear and love, the two responses to sin being indistinguishable to the conscience. He also argued that although there was a kind of general faith that preceded repentance, it was best to use the term "law" for that Word of God that terrified the conscience and preceded the Gospel.

7. See below, questions 71 and 8–9.

8. In contrast, see below, questions 13–16, 18, 47, 66, 75–82, 85–86, and 114–130. Note that Agricola consistently describes the Christian life as moving from the Gospel of God's Word to faith and finally repentance. Thus, he handles Baptism and the Lord's Supper first, then the Creed and the Lord's Prayer, and finally the Ten Commandments.

9. In contrast, see below, questions 29–33 and 43.

10. See Timothy J. Wengert, "Fear and Love in the Ten Commandments," *Concordia Journal* 21 (1995): 14–22.

catechisms of 1529 and provides unique insight into the state of Evangelical cat-echetics before Luther's work.

In this translation, we have tried to capture both Agricola's attempts at simplicity in language (see his preface) as well as certain awkward turns of phrases, so that the English reader may get a feel for the kind of pedagogy this booklet represented. Because Agricola often gave his own version of biblical texts, no attempt has been made to bring them into line with modern English translations.

Johann Agricola's One Hundred Thirty Common Questions for the Young Children in the German Girls' School in Eisleben: On God's Word, Faith, Prayer, the Holy Spirit, the Cross and Love, as well as Instruction on Baptism and Christ's Body and Blood

To the honorable Bartholomew Drachstet, my dear brother-in-law.[11] Peace from God!

A year ago I published my little children's booklet for our Latin school.[12] I have discovered, however, that it is too much to ask of the young girls in the German school that every evening in place of the Latin they bring home a small [translated] portion to their parents and repeat it for memory work or even recite the table blessing and grace.[13] For this reason, I have condensed things here and put them in question-and-answer form. For I confess that I am guilty of serving the young with foolish, childish questions and simplicity. And because you also take special pleasure in the same kind of childish speaking, I decided to dedicate these questions for the German school in your name. For both of us would like to see the young brought to faith and Christ. And I hope to God and am also certain that God will illumine many children in the two schools through his Spirit and after our death raise up the seed of Abraham [see Gal. 3:29] in them, Amen. Since writing and admonishing have no effect on the old, we want to see what God will do with the children. It's child's play and a fool's game that we present here. But ask an old fellow, and you'll soon see that he can't say boo about it.

Eisleben, Monday, 18 November, 1527.[14]

Jᴏʜɴ Aɢʀɪᴄᴏʟᴀ of Eisleben

1. Regarding the saints' knowledge of God and salvation, everything about who God is consists in what and in how many parts? That is, of what does god-liness consist?

---

11. Bartholomew Drachstet, son of a prominent councilor to the counts of Mansfeld, was mar-ried to the sister of Else Moshauer, John Agricola's wife.

12. *Elementa pietatis congesta* (1527). See above, in the introduction.

13. Agricola may be referring to the *Christliche Kinderzucht*.

14. The original has 1528 as a typographical error.

Answer: Of two parts.

2. What are they called?

Answer: Word and faith.

3. What does the Word do?

Answer: The Word promises and pledges something to me.

4. What does faith do?

Answer: Faith believes and trusts God, that God is true and will do it.

5. What is the promise like?

Answer: God's promise is just like God.

6. What is God like?

Answer: Human nature and reason cannot understand God. He is too great and high. Thus, it also cannot understand God's Word.

7. Since it cannot understand it, what does it do?

Answer: It must believe it.

8. Is faith different from reason?

Answer: Yes, of course. Faith and reason are like day and night, Christ and Belial [2 Cor. 6:14f.].

9. Where is that written?

Answer: St. Paul says [1 Cor. 2:14; 1:21], "The natural, rational person does not understand what God is" and "The wisdom of this world did not know God in his wisdom."

10. How is this announced to the world?

Answer: The world experiences it through the preaching of the Gospel.

11. How does this happen?

Answer: God sends and selects people, preachers with calls, in whose mouths he places his Word. God through his Spirit is with the Word. And, because it is the Word of God, it never goes forth in vain and does not return without fruit [see Isa. 55:11]. So, a person listens to the preachers and believes their words. The believers see and recognize God's goodness, which is proclaimed to them, see their errors and transgressions, and call to God for help.

12. Where is this written?

Answer: In Romans 10[:12b-15a], "The Lord is generous to all who call upon him. For whoever calls on the name of the Lord will be saved. But how shall they call on him, in whom they have not believed? How shall they believe in him, of whom they have not heard? How shall they hear without a preacher? But how shall they preach, where they have not been sent?" Jeremiah 1[:12b], "I will keep watch over my words, so that I do it." In 1 Samuel [3:11] God says to Samuel, "See, I will do a thing in Israel, so that the ears of everyone who hears it will tingle."

13. What are the sermons of these sent ones called, who were and still are the preachers?

Answer: There are two sermons: one is of the law and the other is of grace. There have been two preachers: Moses and Christ.

14. Show me in the Scripture?

Answer: John 1[:17], "The law is given through Moses; grace and truth have come through Jesus Christ." Matthew 11[:13], "The law and the prophets lasted up to John."

15. What do Moses and the law preach?

Answer: The law forces and compels people through punishment and torture that they should love God above all else or else they must die an eternal death.

16. Recite!

Answer: Deuteronomy 17[:19], "Cursed are all who do not keep everything written in this book of the law, so that they do it."

17. What do the Gospel and Christ preach?

Answer: The Gospel preaches grace and forgiveness of sins through Christ. Recite!

Galatians 3[:13-14], "Christ has redeemed us from the curse of the Law in that he was made a curse for us (for it is written [Deut. 21:23], 'Cursed is everyone who hangs on a tree'), so that the blessing of Abraham might come among the gentiles in Christ Jesus, and we also might receive the promised Spirit through faith."

John 3[:16], "God so loved the world that he gave his only Son, so that all who believe in him may not be lost but have eternal life."

John 15[:13], "No one has greater love than this: that he lays down his life for his friends."

Romans 5[:8], "In this God proves his love for us, that Christ died for us while we were still sinners and enemies."

18. Would you summarize this?

The law says, you must love God more than yourself or you must die.

[Answer:] The Gospel says, I announce to you that God loved you first from the beginning and wants to bestow this love on you that you may love yourself so much. He also wants to give you the Holy Spirit, so that because of his goodness you can hate and let go of yourself, your life, property, and honor.

19. Tell me, what kind of person is God?

Answer: God is a righteous person.[15]

20. How do you know God is an upright person?

Answer: I know it from his Word that tells me many dear and good things about him, how he is kind and merciful.

21. How do you experience this?

Answer: I experience it in this way, that I receive help from him for body and soul.

22. What does he do to help your body?

Answer: He nurtures me, preserves my life, gives me food, drink, shoes, and clothing, and whatever else I need.

23. What does he do to help your soul?

---

15. German: *fromer man*. Literally, "upright man."

Answer: As soon as I was born from my mother, God let me come to his Word of grace and made me holy and believing in Baptism.

On Baptism

24. What is Baptism?

Answer: Baptism is a bath of rebirth.

25. What happens in Baptism?

Answer: Someone calls out the three holy names, God the Father, God the Son, and God the Holy Spirit, over us children and immerses us in the water as a sign that for Christ's sake we must forsake this life.

26. Recite!

Romans 6[:3], "Do you not know that all of us who are baptized in Christ Jesus were baptized into his death."

27. How is Baptism a bath of rebirth?

Answer: We are born in sin, but through the Word and faith we are freed from the inherited guilt.[16]

28. Would you recite the Scripture?

John 3[:5], "You must be born anew through water and the Holy Spirit."

29. In Baptism is a person freed from all inclinations [to sin] or not?

Answer: Baptism puts the inherited defect[17] in check through the Holy Spirit but does not take it completely away.

30. Give me a rough example.

Answer: The housemaid, when she banks the fire with ashes, stops the fire from burning and puts it in check. Nevertheless, the next morning she starts the fire up again, which during the night had lain hidden in the ashes.

31. Does something still cling to me?[18]

Answer: You will discover, my child, the older you get in years, that your flesh and blood and the sparks of the inherited defect[19] will be stirred up and burst into flames in you.

32. How and by what means will they burst into flames?

Answer: The devil has a strong breath. When he blows into the flesh, the ashes blow away from the coals, and they begin to glow again. Then the devil rouses the world and fans in you desire for pride, unchastity, anger, impatience, unbelief, fame, more possessions, and so forth, until your life becomes full of this and other things.

33. How do I put the fire out?

---

16. German: *erbschuld* ("original sin").

17. German: *erbschaden* ("original sin").

18. With this question, Agricola has reversed roles so that the questioner plays the part of the child. He may here be reflecting the kinds of catechetical questions asked in the confessional.

19. Here, Agricola borrows the medieval concept of a *fomes peccati*, or tinder of sin, left after Baptism. See Heiko A. Oberman, *The Harvest of Medieval Theology*, 3rd ed. (Durham, N.C.: Labyrinth, 1983), 126–28.

Answer: My child, every time you feel this poisonous spark you should remember the three holy names, fall on your knees, and call on God. In this way:

Dear, loving God and Father, I, a poor child, am growing up and maturing, and the poisonous sparks of my inherited defect are being stirred up and are luring me into all kinds of sins and disgrace. (At this point you must admit to God whatever troubles you the most, whether it is impatience or another evil inclination.) But because you allowed me to receive the rich blessing of Baptism and have begun to work on me through your Spirit, I beseech you, my dear God and Father, that you would not take from me the same blessing and Spirit but instead would richly impart them, so that this inclination would not overtake me nor knock me to the ground. Amen.

34. What is this struggle called?

Answer:

Repentance

35. How long will it last?

Answer: As long as we live, it will not cease. For just as we sin every moment, so you should cry to God every moment and admit your need to him.

36. Will God listen to me every time I ask him?

Answer: Yes. He is more inclined to give than you are to ask and receive. For that matter, he has more to give than he ever has to forgive.

37. How do I know this?

Answer: Christ says [Luke 11:9], "Knock and it will be opened for you; seek and you will find; ask and it will be given to you."

38. Does God like to be asked?

Answer: Yes. You cannot do God a greater honor than that you expect many good things from him. You cannot do him a greater dishonor and disgrace than that you do not demand much from him.

39. Oh, who wouldn't want to love God? Is this really certain?

Answer: Yes. Christ himself says this about God in Luke [11:13], "If you who are evil can give a good gift to another person, how much more can your heavenly Father give the Holy Spirit to those who ask him."

40. Hasn't God provided us with some further comfort, so that we might improve our faith, which isn't very strong?

Answer: Yes, there is one more comfort.

41. What is it called?

Answer: It is called the flesh and blood of Christ.

The following is an instruction about how children should be brought to Confession and to the Sacrament of the Body and Blood of Christ

42. The Priest: What do you want, my child?

The Child: Dear sir and father, I want to pour out my need to God and to you in his place.

43. The Priest: Tell me, child, what is your need?

The Child: We children are growing up and maturing, both in years but also in the inclination toward evil thoughts, and so forth. (Here recount your shortcomings.) And I know that no counsel can be given me except through God's Word. Therefore, I ask you for God's sake that because of God you would give me good counsel and comfort and would ask God to help me.

44. The Priest: Because of God, who for this very reason allowed his Son to die, I promise to you grace and forgiveness of sins.

45. The Priest: Do you want something more?

The Child: I also desire an external medicine, which my dear God and Father left on this earth for this very kind of bad behavior in my flesh and blood.

46. The Priest: Tell me what this medicine is.

The Child: I desire to hear the Word of Christ concerning the forgiveness of sins, attached to the sign of his flesh and blood with which my righteous God wants to help my soul. For I confess to God and to you, that as truly as I see and chew the bread and smell and taste the wine, so truly God desires for the sake of his Son not to impute this spark of the inherited defect and weakness to me. Instead, God wants to strengthen my faith and give the Holy Spirit.

The Priest: Take and eat the body of our Lord Jesus Christ for eternal life. Take and drink the blood of Christ our Lord for eternal life. Amen. Dear Children, may the Word feed your souls; the body and blood of Christ feed your bodies, so that you may be certain that God wants to preserve your body and soul to eternal life.[20]

The Child: Praise be to God our Father, who has deemed us worthy to come to the riches of his grace and saving food. We ask you, Father, that you would let your Holy Spirit grow and increase in us. Amen.

The Articles of the Christian Faith[21]

. 47. What does God require of us so that we might repay him for these aforementioned blessings?

1. Answer: He demands nothing of us, except this alone: that we trust and believe his words.

48. How do you believe?

2. Answer: I believe and confess with heart and mouth that there is one God and three persons, God Father, Son, and Holy Spirit.

---

20. This indirect reference to the real presence, coming in the middle of Wittenberg's dispute with Zwingli over the Lord's Supper, led to accusations that Agricola supported a sacramentarian position—charges he denied.

21. In the following (questions 47–61), Agricola employs a combination of a threefold division of the Creed with a more traditional twelvefold division. He may have used portions of Luther's *Personal Prayer Book* (WA 10, II:392–94; *LW* 43:24–29) as a guide.

49. What do you confess about God, the Father?[22]

3. Answer: I confess that God the Father is almighty, the maker of heaven and earth.

50. How do you understand this?

4. Answer: I confess that the capabilities and strength of all creatures come from the almighty Father, for he made heaven and earth.

51. What do you believe about Jesus Christ?

5. Answer: I also believe in Jesus Christ, his only Son.

That is?

I confess that Jesus Christ is the only begotten Son of the Father from eternity.

52. What does "our Lord" mean?

6. I confess that Jesus Christ is our Lord, who guards and protects us in all troubles into which the devil, sin, and our own flesh try day and night to bring us, and that he will be our Lord until the last day.

53. "Who was conceived by the Holy Spirit, born of the Virgin Mary?"

7. I confess that the only begotten Son of the Father, himself God, became a human being, conceived by the Holy Spirit and born of a virgin named Mary; and he became our brother.

"Suffered under Pontius Pilate, crucified, died, and was buried, descended into hell?"

8. I confess that God let his dearest Son die on the cross, where he suffered the fear of death, felt eternal hell himself, and overcame it, so that we may be reconciled with God and be lord over all our enemies. I also confess that, apart from the death of the Son, Jesus Christ our Lord, no one can attain God's grace and salvation, whether with works or merits.

54. "On the third day rose again from the dead?"

9. I believe and confess that Christ Jesus, our flesh and blood, rose from the dead, that he took death and hell captive for our benefit, so that they could no longer harm us, that is, so that God would strengthen our weakness and spare us in the fear of death, as he spared his Son and only allowed him to go under for a short time.

55. "Ascended into heaven, sitting on the right hand of God the Father almighty?"

10. I confess that our brother Christ Jesus, who had just been battered on the cross so that he hardly looked human at all, at the same time rules and fills all things with God and has power over all things in heaven and on earth.

56. "Whence he shall come to judge the living and the dead?"

11. I confess that the crucified Christ will sit in judgment on the Last Day and will condemn those who did not believe in him and save those who expected life and blessings from him.

---

22. In the following section, Agricola divides the Creed into twelve sections in accord with the medieval tradition, which held that each of the twelve apostles wrote a single article.

57. "I believe in the Holy Spirit?"

12. I confess that Christ sent a Holy Spirit to earth, who strengthens the weak in faith, comforts the terrified conscience, extends a hand to those about to fall, stops them from falling, and directs them forward again and again, through and through. With very little effort, things improve. For the Holy Spirit helps us in our weakness and prays for us.

58. "One holy Christian church, where there is one communion of saints?"

13. I believe that the Holy Spirit has called a community out of Jews and gentiles to be the holy shrine of God. It has one Baptism, one faith, one Lord, one God, and one Spirit [see Eph. 4:4-6]. Thus Christians in India and Persia know and believe what we know and believe, from the [land of the] setting of the sun to [the land of the] midnight [sun].

59. "Forgiveness of sins?"

14. I believe that one person has to forgive the sins of another through the Gospel in God's place, not seven times, but seventy times seven [Matt. 18:21-22], without counting, without bounds, as often and as much as we need without stopping. We sin every moment. Every moment forgiveness of sins is available through the Word upon which the communion of saints is founded.

60. "A resurrection of the flesh?"[23]

15. I also believe that my body, which is to be devoured by the worms, will rise again as he [Christ] has already been raised.

61. "And eternal life?"

16. I believe that the same body and my flesh, eaten by worms, will live eternally with God. Therefore, I can bravely despise it, even if for the sake of the Christian community, God's Word, or the forgiveness of sins I must lose my life here in time.

62. By what means is the Christian church built?

Answer: Through the Word of the Gospel, Ephesians 1[:13].

63. In what does the Christian church consist?

Answer: In the Word of the Gospel or of the forgiveness of sins and in faith.

64. Who preserves and directs it?

Answer: The Holy Spirit directs it and makes both the Word and faith effective. For against this foundation, even the gates of hell cannot prevail [see Matt. 16:18].

65. Where does the Holy Spirit, who calls forth the Word and faith, come from?

Answer: Christ purchased the Holy Spirit through his blood and death. Ephesians 4[:8], "He ascended to the heights and has taken captivity captive, and has given gifts to human beings."

66. How does a human being become a believer?

Answer: When the Father draws an unbelieving heart and allows it to be sprinkled with the blood of his Son, Christ Jesus, it becomes believing, cries over

---

23. This term is the traditional one in the German version of the Creed.

its unbelief (that is, is repentant, remorseful, and laments), and diligently takes care so that it does not henceforth spurn the one who has forgiven so much.

67. How does this sprinkling occur?

Answer: God allows the death, blood, and resurrection of Christ to be preached throughout the unbelieving world in this way: this death happened for the world's good; through the blood it is reconciled to God. God draws all who are moved by the blood and pleased with this proclamation of Christ and shows to them how all who are in Christ Jesus are his.

68. With which words is this preached?

Answer: Romans 3[:24-26a], "We are justified without any merit, by his grace through the redemption that came to pass through Christ, whom God has put forward as a throne of grace, through faith in his blood, so that he could prove the righteousness that counts in his presence in that he forgives the sins which prior to this occurred under divine patience, sins that he bore, so that he at this time may prove the righteousness that counts in his presence."

Hebrews 12[:22a, 24], "You have come to the mediator of the new testament, Jesus, and to the blood of sprinkling that pleads there better than that of Abel."

Likewise [John 1:29], "Behold the Lamb of God, who takes away the sins of the world."

Romans 8[:32b], "Since God gave his only Son for us, how shall he not also give us all things with him?" [Isa. 53:5,] "Through his stripes we are healed, and for the sake of the sins of his people he smote him."

69. Did not Christ make an exchange with me and give me his property and honor for my disgrace?[24]

Answer: Yes.

70. How does this exchange occur?

Answer: St. Paul says in 1 Corinthians 1[:30], "Christ is made by God FOR US into wisdom, righteousness, salvation, and redemption," so that I can boast of his wisdom and holiness as my own. And whenever my unrighteousness and sin try to distress me, I ride on Christ's righteousness as on a carriage and silken pillow.

71. The Pope never taught us this, did he?

Answer: Absolutely not. For the Pope said that people have to consider their sins, confess, and through works do satisfaction for them, and that thereby they would be righteous before God and worthy of grace. But the Gospel preaches first the satisfaction of Christ—who made satisfaction for us and changed us from being enemies, since we did not know that we did such evil, into friends. Secondly, the Gospel also preaches that we should repent, as all the writings of the apostles show.[25]

---

24. Here, Agricola may be depending on Luther's *Freedom of a Christian* (WA 7:55, 6–36; LW 31:351f.), itself dependent on Augustine.

25. This movement from Christ's satisfaction to repentance is the opposite of that found in the Visitation Articles of 1528. This entire section contains an attack against the notion of repentance and law found there.

72. Tell me a Scripture passage.

Answer: St. Paul first preaches to the Romans in chapters 1 to 11 how the people become God's heirs. However, afterwards [chapters 12 to 14] he admonishes the believers so that they would want to continue on and not let go of [their inheritance] but instead offer their own bodies for this new life [see Rom. 12:1] and change their actions.

73. If a person preaches freedom in this manner, won't crass Christians result who will use this freedom for much evil?

Answer: St. Paul was not afraid of this but instead preached the Word of the resurrection and satisfaction of Christ among gentiles and Jews. For had he first oppressed and accused the people with laws, fear, and terror before God's judgment and an examination of their sins, they would never have said [Rom. 3:8], "We want to do evil, so that good may come."

74. With what should they comfort themselves when they see that many misuse freedom in this way?

Answer this way. St. Paul says, "God's sure foundation consists in this and has this seal: the Lord knows his own, and whoever calls on the name of Christ departs from unrighteousness," 2 Timothy 2[:19].

75. Explain to me this verse from Paul [1 Cor. 1:21]: "The world with its wisdom did not know God's wisdom. Therefore, through foolish preaching God wanted to save those who believe in it." What does "God's wisdom" mean?

Answer: God's wisdom was that he wrote into our hearts a living idea, by which we, as by an implanted law, would remember the good that we should do. And because the evil of humanity was greater than this idea, God wanted to help this idea and chose his very own people and gave to them a written legal code, so that they would know what God wanted to have from them.

76. How did God rule this people?

Answer: Through pure wisdom. God entrusted them [with the law], smote them, told them of the punishment if they did not have him as their God, and so forth. But it was all to no avail.

77. What is "the wisdom of the world"?

Answer: The world judges that if God were its friend, he would comport himself in a friendlier way and therefore not slay, murder, or threaten. And although it will not tolerate this from God, nevertheless it cannot change things. Therefore, they set up the sword, the wheel, and the gallows, which make people upright by using fear of punishment.

78. What is the "foolish preaching"?

Answer: God realized that the following was true, that the more he smote them, the more rotten they became. Therefore he thought, "I clearly see that I must first love the world and do good to it. I will behave foolishly and will win it with good deeds. I will give it my Son, who will open my heart to them."

79. Does God accomplish something with this foolishness?

Answer: Yes, he accomplishes everything.

80. How?

Answer: "When [God] struck Israel, he turned his back," Isaiah [57:17] says. However, when the world becomes aware of this goodness and love of God for us, it "enters the kingdom of heaven with force" [Luke 16:16], and no one can prevent it. And what no one could accomplish before with punishments or threats, they now risk body and soul with the desire and joy of their hearts—without necessity or force.

81. Does worldly wisdom understand this?

Answer: No, it does not. Instead, it considers this to be foolishness, that someone wants to make evil, crass people righteous by doing good. But this is God's highest wisdom: to make a virtue out of necessity.

82. Does God demand no good works?

Answer: God demands no good works for himself. For God does not need our goods or works. They are already his. However, he does want us to live in such a way on earth that other people may enjoy [what is] ours and praise God for it. God loved us first, therefore we should love our neighbor [see 1 John 4:11, 19].

83. How much must I love my neighbor?

Answer: As much as you love yourself.

84. How do I love myself?

Answer: I want very much that everyone honors me, gives me aid, and counsel in all my concerns. I feed, clothe, wash, and bathe my body. I take care of all its needs. I also have the responsibility to do this for my neighbor, and this pleases God very much.

85. How are law and Gospel divided?

Answer: The law says, "You are to love God above all things or else you must die." The Gospel says, "I [God] am too high for you, and I simply want everyone to know how much I love you, how favorable I am toward you. But if people want to do what pleases me, they love the brother [and sister], whom they can see, and take care of their needs."

86. Recite the Scripture.

Answer: Galatians 4[:9], "You have known God, or rather been known by him."

1 Corinthians 8[:3], "Whoever loves God is known by God."

1 Corinthians 13[:12], "Then I will know even as I am known."

87. Do I earn something through the service of love?

Answer: No. As little as I earn in taking care of my body and myself, so little do I earn when I serve my neighbor out of the responsibility and need of my life.

88. How does this happen?

Answer: Because of faith, I am now rich and a child of God. But because "I no longer live but Christ lives in me" [Gal. 2:20], so my life is only for the sake of others.

89. Where is faith active?

Answer: Only in God's sight.

90. Where is love active?

Answer: Only in relationship to my neighbor.

91. In what does the Christian life consist?

Answer: In faith and love. For God enters into us through faith, remains in us, enlightens us, and reaches the neighbor through us.

92. What are true good works?

Answer: Those done to serve the neighbor.

93. Who is served by the works of monks, priests, and nuns?[26]

Answer: They serve only themselves. Therefore such deeds do not belong to God, nor are they good works.

94. Recite the Scripture.

Answer: "They serve me with human commandments, that I have not bidden nor ordered" [see Matt. 15:9].

Concerning the Cross

95. Where does all human suffering come from?

Answer: From God.

96. Can't evil people hurt us?

Answer: No. God's will is always present.

97. Prove this.

Answer: In Job [41:1; Vulgate], God says, "I will not awaken the Behemoth in fury." St. Paul [1 Cor. 10:13]: "A true God, who will not let you be tempted above what you are able to bear." God does it, St. Paul says. Matthew 4[:1], "Jesus was led by the Holy Spirit into the wilderness, in order to be tempted by the Devil."

98. To whom does this happen for the good?

Answer: TO US. For St. Paul says, 1 Corinthians 10[:13], "Next to the temptation God creates a way out, so that you can bear it."

Job [40:14b], "The one who made them will attack them with his own sword."

99. Is all suffering—bodily and spiritual—from God?

Answer: Yes. Therefore, we should not get angry or murmur against him, but rather endure it.

100. Recite the Scripture.

Answer: Romans 12[:2b], "So that you might test what is the good, acceptable, and perfect will of God."

Psalm 27[:14], "Wait on the Lord. Be comforted and let your heart hold fast. And wait on the Lord."

---

26. Eisleben and its county, Mansfeld, were still divided at this time between the Evangelical and papal parties.

On Prayer

101. Who commanded us to pray?

Answer: Christ, when he said, Matthew 21[:22?; =John 16:24a and 23b], "Until now you have not prayed, but whatever you would ask the Father in my name, he will give it to you."

102. What does prayer mean?

Answer: To request something good from God in faith.

103. Why "in faith"?

Answer: Because God wants to give, so you must do him the honor and believe that he is truthful and can give it. Otherwise, you put the lie to God's words.

104. What should I ask from God?

Answer: You should ask God for everything that you need in body and soul.

105. Who will teach me what I need?

Answer: Christ has done you the service of comprehending all needs in the Lord's Prayer. For he says [Matt. 6:9], "When you want to pray, you should ask in this way, 'Our Father in heaven . . .'"

The Lord's Prayer[27]

106. What does "Our Father in heaven" mean?

Answer: You are always our Father, you who have begotten us as a father, have made all things, and do not despise us when we ask you for something but will also give us what we need.

107. What does "Hallowed be your name" mean?

Answer: Give so that we preach and teach your name rightly on earth, praise it when you show us grace and mercy, and call on it in suffering and death.

108. What does "Your kingdom come" mean?

Answer: Make us righteous and give us the Holy Spirit.

109. What does "Your will be done" mean?

Answer: Give grace, Father, so that we may endure your will with patience and not become angry if it should occur to us that things are turning out differently for us than we had wanted.

110. What does "Give us today our daily bread" mean?

Answer: Give us everything that we need here in this temporal life, understanding in the government, health to serve other people, smart and reasonable princes and lords, peace and unity, so that we with our wives and children may possess nourishment (crops and flour) in abundance and might get along honorably and well with other people.

111. What does "Forgive us our debts as we forgive our debtors" mean?

---

27. One possible source for the following section may be Luther's expositions of the Lord's Prayer in, among other places, his *Personal Prayer Book* (WA 20, II:393, 9–409, 22; *LW* 43:29–38).

Answer: Do not count old debts. Only be silent and cover our debt in heaven. On earth we would really like to pardon from our hearts all those who hurt us.

112. What does "Lead us not into temptation" mean?

Answer: Protect and hold us, dear Father, whenever we are attacked by our temporal and eternal enemies, and do not let us go under.

113. What does "Deliver us from evil" mean?

Answer: Free us from all misfortune of body and soul. Protect us from disgraceful poverty, from worldly disgrace, from syphilis, leprosy, pestilence, and all evil. Amen.

114. Should the Law of Moses also compel Christians?[28]

Answer: Christians do out of desire and love everything that God demands of them. For they are sealed by the spontaneous Spirit of Christ. Therefore, no law should compel them. For [1 Tim. 1:9] "to the righteous no law is given." In addition, as soon as the Gospel becomes a matter of compulsion and rules, then it is no longer the Gospel.

115. How then should we use it?

Answer: As Christians use all creatures over whom they are lords: without reservation of conscience, to God's glory and their use, when, where, and as often as they desire. As they might use Greek and Latin books and histories, so they use Moses and everything that he wrote, as long as he doesn't bother our conscience or compel us.

116. Why is Moses given to the Jews?

Answer: Moses is the Jewish common law.[29] And just as the Romans and we Germans follow imperial law, so the Jews had to follow Moses, as an external order that has nothing to do with the gentiles, Acts 15[:10].

The Ten Commandments

117. What does (1) "You shall have no other gods before me" mean?

Answer: I will be your God. If you lack something in body or soul, so you should take refuge in me, and I will give it to you.

118. What does (2) "You shall not take the name of God in vain" mean?

Answer: "There is only one name under heaven by which we shall be saved," which name, because it is useful, we should rightly use in suffering and death, in fortune and misfortune; we should praise this name, call upon it, and search and find comfort through it.

119. What does (3) "Keep the Sabbath holy" mean?

Answer: You should wait only upon that to which God calls you and not begin anything on your own.

---

28. These questions again reflect the struggle with Philip Melanchthon (and later with Luther) over the nature of the law.

29. Literally: *Sachsenspiegel*, the traditional law of the Saxons. See Luther's address to this question in *How Christians Should Regard Moses* (1525) (WA 16: 363–93; *LW* 35:161–74).

120. What does (4) "Honor your father and mother" mean?

Answer: You should do for your father and mother what they have done for you: feed them, take care of them in their old age, and know that they were given to you by God.

121. What does (5) "You shall not kill" mean?

Answer: You should be quiet and meek toward everyone, showing no anger or displeasure, not with thoughts, gestures, words, or deeds.

122. What does (6) "You shall not commit adultery" mean?

Answer: You shall not practice being unchaste in heart, thought, word, action, or gesture.

123. What does (7) "You shall not steal" mean?

Answer: You shall not take advantage of anyone in trade. God wants instead to support you richly and well without harming your neighbor.

124. What does (8) "You shall not bear false witness against your neighbor" mean?

Answer: You shall say the best and nicest things about all persons, cover up their disgrace, protect them from harm, and further their welfare.

125. What does (9) "You shall not covet your neighbor's house" mean?

Answer: You should not begrudge people what God has given them and therefore not be jealous that it is going better for others with respect to body, honor, favor, property, or fame than for you.

126. What does (10) "You shall not desire your neighbor's wife, child, manservant, maid, oxen, donkey, or anything else that belongs to him" mean?

Answer: You should wait on whatever God does with you, hold him to be your God, and not allow any creature to stand in your way.

127. Divide these commandments?

Answer: The first have to do with God; the last, with the neighbor.

128. How do the first three have to do with God?

Answer: The first concerns God's honor; the second, God's name; the third, God's work.

129. How do the last seven have to do with the neighbor?

Answer: The fifth concerns the neighbor's body and life; the sixth the neighbor's wife and child, the ones he cherishes the most next to himself; the seventh, his property and possessions; the eighth, his honor and good reputation.[30]

130. Summary of the entire thing: Why was the Holy Scripture given?

Answer: St. Paul says in 2 Timothy 3[:16f.], "All Scripture, given by God, is profitable for teaching, for correction, for improvement, for training in righteousness, so that God's people may be skilled in every good work." One must first teach and then correct those who do not want to follow the teaching.

The Gospel says to all flesh: You are free from all laws, even you Jews from the entire law of Moses, just do not use your freedom in a fleshly manner [see Gal. 5:13].

---

30. Other editions, not overseen by Agricola, include explanations of the fourth, ninth, and tenth commandments.

This is the infant formula and children's broth for sucklings. Whoever has the ability and time may set before the children and young people who have already cut teeth and can walk on their own, a good roast with gravy, and give them good wine to drink. That is, such a person may write articles to prove that Christ is God's Son, that there is a resurrection of the dead, and the like.

END OF THIS BOOKLET.

John Eck's Four Hundred Four Articles for the Imperial Diet at Augsburg

Translated by Robert Rosin

Introduction

In May 1530, the princes and municipal representatives of the German imperial diet began to assemble in the city of Augsburg, called together by Emperor Charles V to discuss a number of matters. The chief items on the emperor's agenda were the defense of his Austrian domains against the Turkish invasion and the rebellion of Luther's followers against the Roman church. Within two days of the arrival of Philip Melanchthon and the entourage of Elector John of Saxony in Augsburg, a new publication appeared on the streets of the city, accusing the Saxon theologians of a multitude of heresies. This collection of "four hundred four articles" was cast in the form of theses, or "articles," designed for academic debate. It therefore constituted a formal challenge regarding the entire spectrum of the church's doctrine to all opponents. Claiming to delineate the public teaching of the Wittenberg Reformation, it contained academic propositions composed by its own compiler against followers of Luther and other reform movements as well as citations from the works of a broad range of voices calling for the reform of the church. This publication imposed upon Melanchthon and the other representatives of Lutheran reform the necessity of going beyond the explanation of their measures of reform that they had originally planned to present to the emperor. It compelled them to confess their adherence to the core of catholic teaching, to the heart of the biblical message, in the presentation of their call for reform to Charles.

The compiler of this polemical piece was a professor of theology from the University of Ingolstadt in Bavaria, John Eck. Like all professors of his age, he was no stranger to academic disputation. In fact, he had used disputations as a weapon against reform movements throughout the previous decade. Eck's initial regard and respect for Luther had turned to criticism when the Wittenberger's Ninety-five Theses appeared in 1517 and Eck's opinion of them was requested by the Bishop of Eichstätt, Gabriel von Eyb. The two university professors confronted each other in the Leipzig Debate of June 1519. There, Eck had elicited Luther's admission that popes and councils could err. This disputation in Leipzig had provided Eck with a successful platform for building his own career, for the theological faculties of the Universities of Louvain and

Cologne found that Eck had defeated Luther and his Wittenberg colleagues in the debate. Thereafter, theological differences between Eck and Luther were framed with personal enmity. Eck led the prosecution of Luther as a heretic and was a leader among the German theologians seeking Luther's excommunication. In 1520, Eck journeyed to Rome to assist in drafting the bull excommunicating Luther and returned to Germany with Girolamo Aleander to promote the condemnation of the Wittenberg professor as a heretic.

Eck made his career as a foe of all forms of Protestant reform. In 1525, he published his *Enchiridion of Commonplaces against Luther and Other Enemies of the Church*.[1] In May and June 1526, he joined the Roman Catholic publicist Thomas Murner in a public disputation against Johannes Oecolampadius in the town of Baden in the Swiss Aargau. He participated in a similar disputation against the Swiss reforming party in Bern in January 1528. Thus, he had practiced a mode of attack upon reform movements that he used once again in Augsburg, in his *Four Hundred Four Articles*. In addition to reprinting some of his own critiques of various reformers, Eck assembled citations from the Wittenberg theologians, such Swiss reformers as Ulrich Zwingli and Johannes Oecolampadius (whose sacramental theology the Wittenberg reformers rejected), and other "radical" reformers, including several Anabaptist writers and preachers. Some citations accurately reflected the thought of their authors. Others, though accurate, were taken out of context or expressed only one part of the author's argument and thus ascribed a scandalous or absurd opinion to the author. In other cases, Eck actually cited his sources falsely or twisted their intent in order to demonstrate that the Lutheran reform movement embraced a wide range of departures from catholic teaching.

Especially in its first twenty-one articles, the Augsburg Confession met the accusation of heresy and deviation from catholic tradition lodged in Eck's work. Both in the Confession's positive presentation of Christian teaching and in its condemnations of historic heresies, the influence of the *Four Hundred and Four Articles* is revealed.

Eck continued to play a vital role in leading Roman Catholic opposition to the Reformation. He led the team appointed by Emperor Charles V to compose the Confutation of the Augsburg Confession later in 1530, and he also played a prominent part in negotiating with Melanchthon and other Evangelical theologians at Worms and Regensburg in 1540 and 1541.

This translation has been produced from an original printing of the work.[2] The edition of Wilhelm Gussmann, *D. Johann Ecks Vierhundertundvier Artikel zum Reichstag von Augsburg 1530*, has been consulted, particularly in the com-

---

1. Translated by Ford Lewis Battles (Grand Rapids, Mich.: Calvin Theological Seminary, 1978).

2. *SVB DOMINI IHESV ET MARIAE PATROCINIO. Articulos 404. partim ad disputationes Lipsicam, Baden. & Bernen. attinentes, partim vero ex scriptis pacem ecclesiae perturbantium extractos, Coram diuo Caesare Carolo V. Ro. Imp. semper Augu. ec. ac proceribus Imperii, Ioan. Eckius minimus ecclesiae minister, offert se disputaturum, vt in scheda latius explicatur Augustae Vindelicorum. Die & hora consensu Caesaris posterius publicandis.* Ingolstadt, 1530.

position of the notes.[3] Gussmann provides references from other editions of the volume, in which Eck more specifically identified where he had found many—but not all—of his citations. Therefore, Gussmann's notes should be consulted for further study. His notations of paraphrase or other alterations in the cited texts have been repeated here. English translations of Eck's sources have been indicated when they are available.

The Four Hundred Four Articles of John Eck

Under the patronage of the Lord Jesus and Mary. Four hundred and four articles, some dealing with the disputations at Leipzig, Baden, and Bern, some drawn from the writings of those disturbing the church. John Eck, the least of the church's ministers, offers to debate these articles before Emperor Charles V and the princes of the empire as explained in greater length in Augsburg, on the day and at an hour published hereafter with the consent of the emperor.[4]

For a number of years, many false apostles have been arising and are trying to tear the people away from the unity of the catholic faith and have been corrupting all Germany with errors, impieties, and blasphemies. Because of this, what was once held as most Christian has now become the dregs of all errors. For the sake of the faith and the church, I have quickly selected these few items from their infinite body of errors, even as the enemies of the faith launch their writings and offer to debate them in the shadows for the common people. According to the judgment and disposition of our most glorious prince and lord, Charles V, forever full of majesty, the Roman emperor of Spain, Germany, Sicily, and Catholic King and our most merciful lord and lord of all the princes of the Holy Roman Empire and particularly of our most serene prince and lord, Ferdinand,[5] King of Hungary and Bohemia, archduke of Austria, and so forth, and of our most illustrious princes of the celebrated house of Bavaria,[6] I offer to contend in broad daylight regarding these points noted below against any assailant of the catholic truth. I offer this in order to protect our doctrines and overthrow the false doctrines of the adversaries, to the praise of God, the increase of the faith, and the strengthening of the weak.

---

3. Kassel: Edmund Pillardy, 1930.

4. This title is in a typical form for the titles of theses offered for public disputation. Eck used this form, the form in which Luther's Ninety-five Theses on indulgences of October 1517 were cast, to challenge his Lutheran opponents to formal debate, hoping to repeat his success in Leipzig against his Lutheran opponents.

5. The younger brother of Emperor Charles.

6. The princes ruling in Bavaria, the land in which Eck was serving at the University of Ingolstadt.

To God alone be glory.

In order that Your Holy Majesty and the Christian world may see and judge the impieties of the adversaries, I have selected just a few items from their infinite body of errors. But I also have held these things in check from top to bottom with my assertions, and I offer to respond to all of them in behalf of the faith and the church.[7]

The Assertion of Eck

With total confidence in the Holy Spirit, I assert that the articles of Luther concerning this shameful affair condemned by Pope Leo X were legitimately condemned as heretical, erroneous, and scandalous. I anathematize and condemn them, and I freely declare that all those who agree with the bull[8] are Christian men. But those who oppose the bull are schismatics and are enemies of the faith who should be counted by Catholics as heathen and tax collectors. So we present all of these forty-one articles as follows, ready to take on the attacks of any opponent and to defend the positions of the church.

The Articles of Luther are as follows:

1. It is a heretical but commonly made statement that the sacraments of the New Testament give justifying grace to those who put no obstacle in the way.[9]

2. To deny that sin remains in the baptized child is to trample on both Paul and Christ.[10]

3. The tinder of sin, even if no actual sin is present, keeps a soul from entering heaven when it leaves the body.[11]

4. The imperfect love of the dying necessarily carries with it great fear that by itself is enough to produce the punishment of purgatory and prevent entrance into the kingdom.[12]

---

7. This statement is part of the form for public academic disputation.

8. Eck refers here to the papal bull, *Decet pontificem Romanum,* issued by Pope Leo X on 3 January 1521, condemning Luther as a heretic. Eck had played a major role in obtaining this condemnation.

9. *Resolutiones disputationum de indulgentiarum virtute* (1518) (conc. 7, WA 1:544; *LW* 31:106–7).

10. *Resolutiones Lutherianae super propositionibus suis Lipsiae disputatis* (1519) (conc. 2, WA 2:410; *LW* 31:317).

11. *Resolutiones disputationum de indulgentiarum virtute* (1518) (conc. 24, WA 1:572; *LW* 31:153–54).

12. A combination of words from *Resolutiones disputationum de indulgentiarum virtute* (1518) (conc. 14, 15, 24, WA 1:554, 555, 572; *LW* 31:123–26, 153–54).

5. There is no basis either in Holy Scripture or in the ancient Christian teachers [for the teaching] that there are three parts to penance:[13] contrition, confession, and satisfaction.[14]

6. A person is made a hypocrite—indeed, made a great sinner—by the contrition that results from self-examination and reflection and detesting sins, by which a person, filled with bitterness of the soul, surveys the years and ponders the gravity, multitude, and foulness of those sins, the loss of eternal blessedness, and the approach of eternal damnation.[15]

7. In regard to what is taught on this point about contrition, there is a different proverb that is most true and appropriate, namely, that not to do penance is the highest penitence, and a new life is the best penitence.[16]

8. Do not in any way presume to confess venial, or even mortal, sins because it is impossible to know all mortal sins. Thus in the early church only manifest mortal sins were confessed.[17]

9. In wanting to confess absolutely everything, we only show we are unwilling to leave anything for God's mercy to forgive.[18]

10. No sins are forgiven unless a person believes that when a priest forgives, they are forgiven. Indeed, sin would remain unless a person believes it *is* forgiven. The forgiveness of sin and giving grace are not sufficient. Instead a person must believe that sin is forgiven.[19]

11. Do not in any way trust that you are absolved on account of your contrition. Rather trust you are forgiven on account of Christ's word: "whatever you loose," and so forth [Matt. 18:18]. So trust that if you have obtained the absolution of a priest and firmly believe you are absolved, you truly will be absolved without anything having to do with contrition.[20]

12. If it were possible for people who are not contrite to confess, or for a priest who is not serious but only jesting to absolve, these people are truly absolved if they believe that they are absolved.[21]

13. In the Sacrament of Penance or remission of guilt, the Pope and bishop do no more than the lowest priest. In fact when there is no priest, any Christian—even a woman or a boy—can do just as well.[22]

---

13. The Latin term *poenitentia* may carry the meaning of (1) the Sacrament of Penance, (2) penitence, or (3) repentance. This translation endeavors to capture the most accurate focus of the use in specific cases, but twenty-first-century readers must remember that the three aspects of this single Latin term coalesced in the minds of sixteenth-century readers.

14. *Ein Sermon von Ablaß und Gnade* (1517) (WA 1:243), paraphrased.

15. *Sermo de poenitentia* (1518) WA 1:319, paraphrased.

16. *Sermo de poenitentia* (1518) WA 1:321, paraphrased.

17. *Sermo de poenitentia* (1518) WA 1:322.

18. *Sermo de poenitentia* (1518) WA 1:323.

19. *Resolutiones disputationum de indulgentiarum virtute* (1518) (conc. 7, WA 1:543; *LW* 31:104).

20. *Sermo de poenitentia* (1518) (WA 1:323), paraphrased.

21. *Sermo de poenitentia* (1518) (WA 1:323), paraphrased.

22. *Ein Sermon von dem Sakrament der Buße* (1519) (WA 2:716; *LW* 35:12).

14. No one ever ought to tell a priest he is contrite, and no priest should ever ask about contrition.[23]

15. Great is the error of those who come to the sacrament of the Eucharist depending on the idea that they have confessed, that they are not conscious of any mortal sin, and that they have said their prayers and are prepared. All these eat and drink to their judgment. On the other hand, if they believe and trust that they will receive grace there, this faith alone makes them pure and worthy.[24]

16. It would be good for the church to decide in a general council that the laity should commune in both kinds, and that those who are already communing under both kinds are not heretics but just schismatics.[25]

17. The church's treasures from which the Pope gives indulgences are not the merits of Christ and the saints.[26]

18. Indulgences which render good works unnecessary are pious frauds perpetrated on believers. Indulgences can be counted among those things that are lawful, but they are not counted among those things that are expedient.[27]

19. Indulgences given to those who sincerely pursue them do not result in forgiving the punishment that divine justice demands for actual sins.[28]

20. Those who believe that indulgences are salvific and produce spiritual fruit are deceived.[29]

21. Indulgences are necessary only for public offenses and are rightly given only to those who are hardened and show no patience.[30]

22. Indulgences are neither necessary nor useful for six categories of people: the dead or the dying, the sick, those with legitimate impediments, those who have not committed offenses, those who have committed offenses but not ones that are public, and those who have changed for the better.[31]

23. Excommunications are only external punishments and do not deprive a person of the church's common spiritual prayers.[32]

---

23. *Sermo de poenitentia* (1518) (WA 1:322).

24. *Sermo de digno praeparatione cordis* (1518) (WA 1:330), paraphrased from three distinct points.

25. *Ein Sermon vom Sakrament des Leichnams Christi* (1519) (WA 2:742; LW 35:50; see also WA 6:79). This statement refers to the Hussite movement in Bohemia and confirms Eck's accusation that Luther shared its heretical positions.

26. *Resolutiones disputationum de indulgentiarum virtute* (1518) (conc. 56 and 58, WA 1:605; LW 31:211–12).

27. *Resolutiones disputationum de indulgentiarum virtute* (1518) (conc. 58, 20, and 46, WA 1:610, 570, 600; LW 31:220, 150, 203).

28. *Resolutiones disputationum de indulgentiarum virtute* (1518) (conc. 5, WA 1:536–37; LW 31:93–94).

29. *Resolutiones disputationum de indulgentiarum virtute* (1518) (conc. 32, WA 1:587; LW 31:180).

30. *Resolutiones disputationum de indulgentiarum virtute* (1518) (conc. 13, WA 1:552; LW 31:120–21), paraphrased.

31. *Resolutiones disputationum de indulgentiarum virtute* (1518) (conc. 13, WA 1:552; LW 31:120).

32. *Sermo de virtute excommunicationis* (1518) (WA 1:639), paraphrased.

24. Christians ought to be taught that it is better to prize excommunication highly than to fear it.[33]

25. The Roman pontiff, Peter's successor, is not the vicar of Christ appointed by Christ himself in Saint Peter's place to be over all the churches in the whole world.[34]

26. Christ's word to Peter, "whatever you loose on earth," and so forth, extends only to those things bound by Peter himself.[35]

27. It is certain that neither the church nor the Pope is able to set up either articles of faith or laws about morals or good works.[36]

28. Even if the Pope, along with the greater part of the church, were to think this or that and even if they were not in error when thinking this, it is no sin or heresy to think the opposite. This is especially the case in something not necessary for salvation, until the time when a council rejects one opinion or approves another.[37]

29. The path has been cleared for us to talk about the authority of councils and to contradict freely what councils do, to judge their decrees, and to confess confidently whatever appears to be true regardless of whether it has been approved or rejected by any council.[38]

30. Some of the articles of John Hus[39] that were condemned in the council of Constance are most Christian, most true and evangelical, and cannot be condemned by the church universal.[40]

31. In every good work, a righteous person sins.[41]

32. A work done in the best possible way is a venial sin.[42]

33. It is against the will of the Spirit to burn heretics.[43]

34. To wage war against the Turk is to oppose God's visiting our iniquities on us through them.[44]

---

33. *Sermo de virtute excommunicationis* (1518) (WA 1:640), paraphrased.

34. *Resolutio . . . de potestate papae* (1519) (WA 2:180–82), paraphrased.

35. *Resolutiones disputationum de indulgentiarum virtute* (1518) (conc. 5, WA 1:536; *LW* 31:93).

36. It is uncertain what Eck is citing here, but it is likely that he was interpreting a passage in *Resolutiones Lutherianae* (1519) (conc. 10, WA 2:427).

37. *Resolutiones disputationum de indulgentiarum virtute* (1518) (conc. 26, WA 1:583; *LW* 31:172–73).

38. *Resolutiones Lutherianae* (1519) (conc. 1, WA 2:406, 404).

39. Eck had tried, with success, to associate Luther with the Czech reformer John Hus, burned at the stake during the Council of Constance in 1415 for heresy.

40. *Disputatio Lipsiae habita* (1519) (WA 2:279), paraphrased.

41. *Resolutiones Lutherianae* (1519) (conc. 1, WA 2:406).

42. *Resolutiones disputationum de indulgentiarum virtute* (1518) (conc. 58, WA 1:608; *LW* 31:216).

43. *Resolutiones disputationum de indulgentiarum virtute* (1518) (conc. 80, WA 1:624–25; *LW* 31:245), paraphrased.

44. *Resolutiones disputationum de indulgentiarum virtute* (1518) (conc. 5, WA 1:535; *LW* 31:92), paraphrased.

35. None are certain that they are not always involved in mortally sinning because the vice of pride is so deeply hidden [within the human being].[45]

36. Free will after sin is free in name only; in doing what is in oneself,[46] a person commits a mortal sin.[47]

37. Purgatory cannot be proven from the Sacred Scriptures in the canon.[48]

38. With respect to their salvation, souls in purgatory are not secure, at least not all of them. It also cannot be proven by means of reason or Scripture that they are beyond meriting or growing in love.[49]

39. Souls in purgatory sin constantly as long as they are still seeking rest and dreading punishments.[50]

40. Souls liberated from purgatory by the intercessions of the living are not as happy as when they make satisfaction themselves.[51]

41. Ecclesiastical prelates and secular princes would do nothing wrong if they were to put an end to all the mendicant orders.[52]

Eck

These articles are so atrocious that even their author, Luther, renounces some of them and is not willing to acknowledge them. Luther also lies when he says they have been misrepresented as his—for example, numbers 26, 29, and 41. But there is an old proverb—"one should be mindful of a lie"—because number 26 Luther wrote in *De resolutione indulgentiarum*, conclusion 5. Number 29 is in the resolution of the Leipzig Disputation right at the beginning, and number 41 is in a vernacular sermon on usury.

In addition, I take up the cause of positions I defended at Leipzig for nineteen days against Luther and Carlstadt without being vanquished.[53] If either they or their supporters will undertake to present anything new against these positions, I will more than give them satisfactory answers.

---

45. *Resolutiones disputationum de indulgentiarum virtute* (1518) (conc. 13, WA 1:553; *LW* 31:121).

46. The scholastic theologian Gabriel Biel (d. 1495), of the University of Tübingen, taught that if people "do what is in them," they can merit grace.

47. *Disputatio Heidelbergae habita* (1518) (conc. 13, WA 1:354; *LW* 31:40).

48. *Disputatio Lipsiae habita* (1518) (WA 2:324–26).

49. *Resolutiones disputationum de indulgentiarum virtute* (1518) (conc. 19 and 18, WA 1:564, 562; *LW* 31:140–41, 136).

50. *Resolutiones disputationum de indulgentiarum virtute* (1518) (conc. 18, WA 1:562; *LW* 31:136).

51. *Asterisci adversus obeliscos Eckii* (1518) (ob. 14, WA 1:298–99), paraphrased.

52. *Großer Sermon von dem Wucher* (1520) (WA 6:42).

53. In the Leipzig Disputation of June and July 1519.

The Conclusions of Eck at Leipzig[54]

42. Neither the declarations of Holy Scripture nor the holy fathers such as Augustine and others agree that when our Lord and master Jesus Christ said, "Repent," he meant the whole life of believers should be one of penitence, and for that reason this word "repent" could not be understood as sacramental penance.[55]

43. Even if people commit venial sins each day, we deny that the righteous person nevertheless sins in every good work, even in a blessed death. We also say it is wrong to hold that a righteous person can sin mortally while righteousness remains, or that after Baptism sin remains in the child from another will.

44. Moreover, we declare that a person should not be heard who says that repentance does not properly begin with hating sin by means of reflecting on sin's gravity and punishment, and that this actually makes a person an even greater sinner—a statement contrary to the Gospel and the holy fathers.

45. We judge it to be contrary to Holy Scripture and the practice of the church to say that God, in remitting guilt, also remits punishment and does not commute it into a punishment through temporal satisfactions imposed in part or in whole by the canons and injunction of the priest.

46. We do not accept that any priest (not to mention a prelate) can or should remit punishment and guilt to a person seeking such remission, or that the prelate sins in not fully absolving the person from punishment and guilt since this is contrary to the practice of holy mother church.

47. We consider it an error to hold that souls in purgatory make no satisfaction for the punishments of sins from the guilt of which they have been absolved but for which they have made no satisfaction. Likewise, it is not without error to say that God requires of one who is about to die no other punishment than death.

48. A person errs who, on the basis of the fact that an individual is given actively to evil but only passively to good, denies that the free will is master of human actions. So, too, that person is not without error who, contrary to the scholastic theologians, thinks that faith is corrupted by any sort of offense. Nor is that person without the greatest error who, with no thought of contrition, proclaims shamelessly that a person is absolved by faith alone.

49. Because it is contrary to truth and reason, we do not accept the idea that horror and a kind of despair arise out of the imperfection of love or faith in the souls of the dead, which makes an impact upon those in purgatory. And we do not accept that they experience this horror because of the fear of death and so, as it were, die reluctantly.

---

54. The following twelve theses were those penned by Eck for use in the Leipzig Disputation of 1519, first published as *In studio Lipsensi disputabit Eckius propositiones infra notatas contra D. Bodenstein Carlestadium* (1518). They are aimed against Luther's Ninety-five Theses on indulgences and other writings of that period.

55. Eck's attack on the first of Luther's Ninety-five Theses, WA 1:253; *LW* 31:25.

50. We deny as contrary to our faith and all reason that souls in purgatory merit greater grace, or that, if freed by the merits of others, their rewards are diminished. We also deny that souls in purgatory are not certain of salvation, or that they do not desire our petitions.

51. We deny the teaching that the merit of Christ's passion is not the treasury of the church out of which indulgences are given since this goes against the truth and against apostolic decrees, just as we think the keys are the most imperishable treasure of the church. Likewise, we piously believe that we are aided by the merits of the saints.

52. To say that indulgences do not bestow freedom is an error. Moreover, to say that indulgences are defective works and that a person is thus weaker because of them is the worst kind of error. So we believe that a person errs who says that one is bound to reject indulgences because the Lord says, "On account of myself I abolish iniquities" and does not say "on account of money" [Isa. 43:25].[56]

53. That the Pope is not able to remit the punishment for sin through indulgences is an error. Likewise, that he cannot absolve souls in purgatory from punishment is an error. Moreover, what we refuse to accept most of all is that those who are about to die or those who are weak, have legitimate impediments, or are without public offenses do not need indulgences.

54. We deny that the church of Rome was not superior to other churches before the time of Sylvester.[57] Instead, we have always acknowledged him who has the seat and the faith of the most blessed Peter as the successor of Peter and the general vicar of Christ.

Luther was subject to the judgment of the Paris faculty, to which he appealed before the legate of the apostolic throne. Convicted by the Parisians' opinion, Luther has exasperated them with his clamoring.[58]

At this point, I do not refuse to stand by the conclusions I undertook to defend against Zwingli and Oecolampadius and their followers before the twelve Swiss cantons,[59] even if Zwingli wants to flee into exile and make tracks to Rottenacker in Ulm or to Blaurer in Constance.[60]

---

56. In these theses, Eck was criticizing the positions of Luther expressed in earlier writings, e.g., in this thesis in *Resolutiones disputationum de indulgentiarum virtute* (1518) (conc. 18, WA 1:613; LW 31:224–25).

57. Pope Sylvester I held the papal office from 314 to 335.

58. When he appeared before the papal legate Thomas de Vio, Cardinal Cajetan, in Augsburg in October 1518, Luther appealed to the theological faculties of the universities of Basel, Freiburg, and Louvain, or, if they were not sufficient, Paris. Eck sought the judgment of several faculties upon the positions taken at the Leipzig Debate. The theologians of Cologne and Louvain condemned Luther fairly quickly upon the basis of Eck's report. The Parisian faculty rendered its decision in 1521, also condemning Luther on the basis of a wider range of his writings.

59. In the disputation or colloquy at Baden in the Aargau, at the end of May 1526.

60. Konrad Sam from Rottenacker was a leader of reform in the imperial city of Ulm; Ambrosius Blaurer, in the imperial city of Constance.

The Conclusions of Eck in Baden

55. Christ's true body and blood are present in the Sacrament of the Altar.

56. They truly are offered in the office of the Mass for the living and for the dead.

57. We ought to invoke Mary and the saints as intercessors.

58. Images of the crucifix and saints should not be done away with.

59. After this life, there is purgatorial fire.

60. Also, infants of Christians are born in original sin.

61. Christ's baptism, not John's, takes away original sin.

Added to these are all the other things Zwingli tries to attack in our true and indubitable faith.

Eck

I have noted on the negative side many godless things from Zwingli. Even this mad author himself was horrified when he thought about them. It was this sort of thing: frequently making the sign of the cross terrifies the soul just as the characters of the necromancers terrify the ignorant if they are given access to them. So he thinks they should abstain from making the sign of the cross in conducting the Mass. He writes to the Swiss that this was fabricated by me against him, but that I have spoken the truth is clear to anyone reading his *Epichiresis* on the canon of the Mass, folio 21, page 2.[61]

When he saw that his sect's stock had risen as a result of the disputation at Baden, Zwingli then subtly maneuvered to arrange for a disputation to take place at Bern.[62] I refuted the report on the disputation with substantial treatises, and no one offered a rejoinder. But because I now offer myself ready to defend counterconclusions on the side of the faith and the truth before the emperor and other princes of the empire, I propose the following.[63]

62. When our Lord Jesus Christ was ready to leave the world, he established prelates in the church through both himself and the Holy Spirit. They are his vicars, who have the power to govern and who both are said to be and are heads of the church. A person who foolishly rebels against them is abandoning Christ and the church.

63. The church of Christ and those who govern it fashion statutes and regulations to the honor of God and the betterment of the faithful. And even if these things are not specifically formulated in the sacred Scriptures, they are nevertheless obligatory in the forum of the conscience, so that a person who despises them scorns Christ.

61. Zwingli, *De canone missae epichiresis* (1523) (*CR* 89:597). A necromancer is a sorcerer who calls back the dead.

62. The disputation at Bern took place in January 1528. The city council issued its report as *Handlung oder acta gehaltner disputation zu Bern* (1528); Eck's critique was published as *Verlegung der disputation zu Bern* (1528).

63. The following theses were aimed against conclusions supported by the reforming party at the disputation at Bern.

64. Christ the Savior is our redeemer and righteousness. We should make ourselves participants in his passion and merit through the sacraments and good works. But if people in the church have the opinion, without a second thought, that we are saved in the church without good works and satisfaction, we are being presumptuous and sinning against the Holy Spirit.

Concerning the truth of [the presence of] Christ's body in the Eucharist, concerning the sacrifice of the Mass, concerning purgatory, and concerning the intercession of the saints, I assert once again against the people of Bern, and steadfastly affirm, my first five conclusions defended at Baden.

65. To say that marriage is commanded for every estate—also for the sacerdotal estate—in order to avoid fornication is the doctrine of Asmodeus.[64] It is clear that a person who thinks it is the chief virtue of a bishop to have a wife tramples on Christ even more grievously and opens up the Christian faith to ridicule throughout the whole world.

In addition to what has been mentioned above, we will bring up a few more of the innumerable errors and destructive and seditious publications of various people. We defend the opposite positions in behalf of the faith, in behalf of the church, and for the Christian empire.

New and Old Errors Now Given an Airing

On Christ

66. Christ experienced terrors of the soul even to the point of despair. Bugenhagen.[65]

67. In despair Christ cried out, "My God, why have you forsaken me." The Praemonstratensians at Magdeburg.[66]

68. The greatest cause of Christ's fear was his sense of being deserted and of divine wrath, in which he wavered between hell and life. In this fear, he experienced the loss of his gifts. So in this affliction and anguish, love was lost because when divinity withdrew itself, love ceased to burn. Melanchthon.[67]

69. After Christ's death, his soul had to suffer in hell and had to be attacked by demons in his suffering. Anton Zimmermann.[68]

70. Christ complained that he was forsaken by God, that is, that he was deserted by life, blessedness, and all good. Zimmermann.

---

64. Asmodeus is the evil spirit mentioned in Tobit 3:8 and 8:1-3. According to the Talmud, he was involved in Noah's drunken incest. That may be the reason why Eck used him here as one advocating fornication via marriage for clerics already married to the church.

65. Johannes Bugenhagen, pastor and professor in Wittenberg, *In librum psalmorum interpretatio* (1524), 34.

66. The work to which Eck refers here has not been identified.

67. Philip Melanchthon, Luther's colleague on the Wittenberg theological faculty, *In evangelium Matthaei annotationes* (1523) (*CR* 14:529), 45.

68. Anton Zimmermann, preacher in Weissenfels, *Ob auch die sele Christi . . . gelitten habe* (1525).

71. Christ is finite according to his humanity. So he truly grew in wisdom and grace. Zwingli.[69]

72. As a human being, Christ is the adopted son of God. Bugenhagen.[70]

73. Christ merited nothing for himself but everything for us. Luther.[71]

74. Christ did not rise from a closed sepulcher, nor did he enter into [the midst of] the disciples through closed doors. Bucer.[72]

75. Christ is not the head of the church according to his human nature. Haller.[73]

76. Christ no longer prays to God for us. Zwingli.[74]

77. Christ did not appear to St. Paul in person but only through angels. Zwingli.[75]

78. In Christ the two natures, human and divine, are comingled. Burgauer of Sankt Gallen.[76]

79. Christ did not have a rational soul, but in place of the soul he had divinity. The Lutheran Spelt in the book on the simple faith.[77]

80. According to his divine nature, Christ Jesus is, properly speaking, the essence of all things. Zwingli.[78]

81. Christ's humanity is not to be adored. Thus, it is not to be adored in the Eucharist. Zwingli.[79]

82. My soul hates the word "homoousios," that is, that the Father and the Son are the same essence. Luther.[80]

On the Holy Spirit

83. Since Christ's death, the Holy Spirit is his vicar. Bucer.[81]

84. Reason pretends to give honor to Christ by examining and meditating on his passion, but this is of no significance to Christ. Melanchthon.[82]

---

69. *Disputatio Bern.* (1528), 152, paraphrased.

70. *Annotationes in epistolas Pauli ad Galatas* (1525), 263, falsely cited.

71. *Contra malignum J. Eccii iudicium . . . defensio* (1519) (Article 14, WA 2:650).

72. Martin Bucer, reformer in Strassburg, participated in the disputation at Bern; *Disputatio Bern.* (1528), 160.

73. *Disputatio Bern.* (1528), 64, falsely cited.

74. *Disputatio Bern.* (1528), 206, falsely cited.

75. *Disputatio Bern.* (1528), 164.

76. Benedict Burgauer, pastor in Zurich, *Disputatio Bern.* (1528), 119, paraphrased. Some editions of Eck's work identify this as the ancient heresy of Eutyches.

77. Heinrich Spelt, *Der ainfeltig glaub* (1524), paraphrased. Eck identifies this as the ancient heresy of Apollinaris in some editions.

78. *Disputatio Bern.* (1528), 66. Eck identifies this as the heresy of Almaricus.

79. *Amica exegesis* (1527) (*CR* 92:693).

80. *Rationis Latominanae confutatio* (1521) (WA 8:117; *LW* 31:244). Eck identifies this as the ancient heresy of Arius in some editions.

81. *Disputatio Bern.* (1528), 8, paraphrased.

82. *In evangelium Ioannis annotationes* (1523) (*CR* 14:1210).

On Christ's Sepulcher

85. The sepulcher for Christ's body, which the Saracens control, is no more a concern to God than are oxen, according to what Paul teaches. Luther.[83]

On God

86. It is certain that all things, both good and evil, are done by God. Not only according to his permissive will but according to his proper will, he performs what is evil, as with David's adultery, and so forth. Thus the treachery of Judas is no less God's proper work than is the calling of Paul. Melanchthon.[84] That means that God wills sin.

87. God wanted himself to be recognized as foolish through folly, and a spiritual person sees God as foolish through folly. Melanchthon.[85]

On the Lord's Cross

88. It would be much better if the cross were lost rather than found, or if it were humbled rather than exalted. And it is an abuse for churches to be built or founded in honor of the wood on which God hung. Luther.[86]

89. It is a silly game and idolatrous error to encase a piece of the cross in gold and carry it around in the church, holding it out for people to kiss. Thus, if I were to have a piece of the cross, I would rather burn it to ashes. There are enough pieces of the cross in the world to build a house. I wish that no crown of thorns or no holy cross had ever seen the light of day. Luther.[87]

90. They have established a strange and horrifying festival at Trier on the basis of Christ's robe. Luther.[88]

On Mary

91. When Christ said to Mary, "What have I to do with you, woman?" [John 2:4] he meant to say, "Because you are my mother, you think I should do you some special favor because you deserve special status. But you should know that

---

83. *De abroganda missa privata* (1521) (WA 8:476; *LW* 36:228).

84. *In epistolas Pauli ad Rhomanos et Corinthios* (1522), H2, H4, paraphrased.

85. *In epistolas Pauli ad Rhomanos et Corinthios* (1522), M4, paraphrased.

86. A reference to relics from *Sermon von Kreuz und Leiden* (1522) (WA 10/3:369); and *Sermon von den Heiltumen* (1522) (WA 10/3: 33).

87. A reference to relics from *Sermon von Kreuz und Leiden* (1522) (WA 10/3: 369); and *Sermon von den Heiltumen* (1522) (WA 10/3:332).

88. A reference to the famous relic of the cathedral of Trier from *Sermon von Kreuz und Leiden* (1522) (WA 10/3: 369).

you have no more influence with me than the woman caught in adultery [John 8:3-11] or the Syrophoenician woman [Mark 7:24-30]." Melanchthon.[89]

92. Christ allowed Mary to err. And Joseph wanted to leave her because of the suspicion of adultery. Luther.[90]

93. When Christ preached, the centurion had faith greater than Mary because while Christ gave his mother great faith at the time of his conception and birth, her faith subsequently was not or was only rarely that great again. In the meantime, he let it waver. Luther.[91]

94. Contradicting the statement that the blessed virgin was conceived without original sin has not been condemned. Luther.[92]

95. We are certain that we are just as holy as Mary. Therefore, we do not want to have her as an advocate. Luther.[93]

96. It is deception and blasphemy when we use the epistle about the wisdom of God and the Gospel about the birth of Christ on the day of the nativity of Mary. Luther[94] and the Nurembergers.[95]

97. The "Salve regina" and the "Regina coeli"[96] do not effect anything but rather do injury to Christ since they ascribe to a creature what properly is God's. Luther.[97] Heiden in his booklet.[98] Freißleben at Weiden.[99]

98. Your prayer, Luther says to listeners, is just as precious to me as Mary's because you can help me just as much as she can. Luther.[100]

99. Christ was not willing to give in to the curiosity of Mary as she asked for a miracle when the wine was running out [John 2:4]. Zwingli.[101] Luther.[102]

100. The barrier of Mary's virginity was opened and torn in birth. Luther.[103]

101. There is no festival I hate more than the festival of the conception of Mary and the festival of Corpus Christi. Luther.[104]

---

89. *In evangelium Ioannis annotationes* (1522) (*CR* 14:1077).

90. *Sermon am 1. Sonntag nach Epiphaniae* (1523) (*WA* 12:413); and *Vom ehelichen Leben* (1522) (*WA* 10/2: 288; *LW* 45:31–32). The second sentence is falsely cited.

91. *Kirchenpostille*, gospel for the third Sunday after Epiphany, *Dr. Martin Luther's sämmtliche Werke* 11 (Frankfurt am Main: Hyder & Zimmer, 1868), 59.

92. *Grund und Ursach* (1521) (art. 28, *WA* 7:429; *LW* 32:79), paraphrased.

93. *Sermon von der Geburt Mariä* (1522) (*WA* 10/3: 316).

94. *Sermon von der Geburt Mariä* (1522) (*WA* 10/3: 315), paraphrased.

95. The reference has not been identified.

96. Two medieval hymns to Mary, literally: "Hail, Queen," and "Queen of Heaven."

97. *Sermon von der Geburt Mariä* (1522) (*WA* 10/3: 321, 322).

98. Sebald Heiden, cantor in Nuremberg, *Adversus hypocritas calumniatores . . . de inversa cantilena, quae Salve regina incipit, defensio* (1523).

99. Johann Freißleben, preacher in Weiden, *Das Salve regina nach dem richtscheydt . . . . ermessen und abgericht* (n.d).

100. *Sermon von der Geburt Mariä* (1522) (*WA* 10/3: 322).

101. *Disputatio Bern.* (1528), 209, paraphrased.

102. *Kirchenpostille*, gospel for the second Sunday after Epiphany (*WA* 17/2: 65–66).

103. *Kirchenpostille*, gospel for the first Sunday after Epiphany, identified in some editions as the source for this citation, does not have such a passage (*WA* 52:104–10).

104. *Sermon auf unsers Herrn Fronleichnamstag* (1523) (*WA* 12:581).

On the Apostles

102. The apostolic council [Acts 15] was wrong when it commanded that converted gentiles abstain from eating blood and from eating what was strangled. Therefore, they were corrected by Paul in Colossians [2:16]: "Let no one pass judgment on you," and so forth.[105]

103. The Gospel was not preached as clearly and purely in the age of the apostles as it is by me. Thus they call me Elijah, Daniel, and the Man of God. Luther.[106]

104. The apostles were not believers when they were baptized. That is why Christ wanted the apostles to baptize people first and then teach them what to do and what not to do [Matt. 28:19]. The preachers in Nuremberg.[107]

On St. Paul

105. Paul wished to be damned for his brethren [Rom. 9:3]. Melanchthon.[108] So Moses was willing to be led to the devil and to be condemned in body and soul for the people [Exod. 32:32]. Luther.[109]

106. Many have asserted that it is highly likely that the epistle is not from the apostle James and is not worthy of the apostolic spirit. Luther.[110]

On the Gospels

107. The evangelists wrote contradictions. This is clear in many places where they cannot be harmonized. But we believe all the apostles were able to err. Brunfels.[111]

108. The opinion that there are just four Gospels and just four evangelists ought to be done away with. Brunfels.[112]

109. We have to assert there is no Scripture that can be proved to be Scripture except the Old Testament. Brunfels.[113]

110. If the apostles had not commented on the Gospel with their epistles, the Gospels would be nothing but nonsense, deaf, and lifeless narration. And credit is due not to the evangelists but to Peter, Paul, James, and John that what we have about practices and rites is correct. Brunfels.[114]

---

105. Part of the polemic of Eck's Roman Catholic colleague, Caspar Schatzgeyer, in his *Wider herr Hansen von Schwartzenbergs . . . püechlin . . .* (1527), C4, paraphrased.

106. *An die Ratherrn aller Städte* (1524) (WA 15:39; LW 45:361), paraphrased.

107. The Nuremberg ministerium, *Ain gut unterricht und getrewer ratschlag . . .* (1525), H4, paraphrased.

108. *Annotationes in epistolas ad Rhomanos et Corinthios* (1522), H3, paraphrased.

109. *Predigt am 6. Sonntag nach Trinitatis* (1522) (WA 10/3: 253), paraphrased.

110. *De captivitate Babylonica* (1520) (WA 6:568; LW 36:118).

111. Otto Brunfels, lay theologian of Strassburg, *Problemata* (1524), a3.

112. *Problemata* (1524), a2, paraphrased.

113. *Problemata* (1524), b3.

114. *Problemata* (1524), b3.

111. The New Testament has lost its power as has the Old. Therefore, we are not to hold to any Scripture but only to the Spirit, according to the eternal Gospel. The spiritualists and certain people at Zwickau, according to what Emser says.[115]

On the Saints

112. Those who worship the saints for temporal benefit are little better than those who strike a deal with the devil for money. Luther.[116]

113. Prayers to saints for escaping any temporal evil are to be avoided since they cannot help us. Melanchthon.[117]

114. We have access to God only through Christ. Therefore, confidence in saints collapses. Luther.[118]

115. Christ alone has been given to us as an example for life; the saints have not. Zwingli.[119]

116. The worship of saints has reached the point where it would be better if there were no saints' festivals and their names were unknown. Luther.[120]

117. It is the work of the devil when people run here and there to the churches dedicated to saints. Luther.[121]

118. God cannot permit anyone to say, "St. Peter is my apostle." Luther.[122]

119. No one knows if it is St. James or a dead dog or a horse buried there in Compostella or in Toulouse. Luther.[123]

120. The first person depicted as Christopher was no saint—a ridiculous story that any learned person would laugh at. Billikan.[124]

121. When it comes to what the priests read today about Christopher in church, there is nothing that is not suspect. And this is true not just about Christopher but about two others, namely, Gregory and Margaret. Billikan.[125]

---

115. Eck may have had in mind two works of his Roman Catholic colleague from ducal Saxony, Jerome Emser: *Ein missive oder sendbrive* (1525) and his *Wyder den falschgenanten ecclesiasten und warhaftigen ertzketzer Martinum Luther* (n.d.).

116. *Decem praecepta* (1518) (WA 1:411), paraphrased.

117. *In obscuriora aliquot capita Geneseos annotationes* (1523) (CR 13:761).

118. *Predigt am Johannistage* (1522) (WA 10/3: 302–13).

119. *Handlung der versammlung in . . . Zürich* (1523) (CR 88:74).

120. *Decem praecepta* (1518) (WA 1:420), paraphrased.

121. *Decem praecepta* (1518) (WA 1:422), paraphrased.

122. *Predigt am Pfingstmontage* (1522) (WA 10/3: 164).

123. *Predigt am Jakobstage* (1522) (WA 10/3: 325). The thesis refers to important pilgrimage destinations.

124. Theobald Billikan, pastor in Nördlingen, *Perornata eademque verissima D. Christophori descriptio* (n.d.), a3, paraphrased.

125. *Perornata eademque verissima D. Christophori descriptio* (n.d.), a3.

On the Saints

122. Saints ought to be honored more on account of their teaching than on account of their lives. Luther.[126]

123. Since Christ's ascension, nobody has ascended into heaven, and nobody will do so until the last judgment. Luther.[127]

124. I have the same equal access to the Father as did Peter and Paul. Luther.[128]

125. Great idolatry has resulted from the invocation of saints. Luther.[129] Zileisen.[130] Glait.[131] and Stiefel.[132]

126. I would not give two cents for the merits of Saint Peter when it comes to helping an individual. People cannot help themselves. Any beggar would be of more use to me than Saint Peter. For what more can Peter have than you or I have? Luther.[133]

127. The names of saints should not be put into the canon of the Mass, but rather only names of devils since the saints are also devils. Luther. And Luther calls the Church of All Saints the Church of All Devils, and he calls Saint Benno[134] also the Devil of Meissen.[135]

On Relics

128. The relics of saints are nothing but the seduction of the people. Thus they ought to be buried in the ground right away. Luther.[136]

129. The blessed dead are not members of the body of Christ. Zwingli.[137]

---

126. *Predigt am Johannistage* (1522) (WA 10/3: 201).

127. *Sermon auf das Evangelium Luc. 16* (1523) (WA 12:596).

128. *Predgt am Johannistage* (1522) (WA 10/3: 202).

129. *Predigt auf den 2. Advent* (1520) (WA 7:71), paraphrased.

130. Ulrich Zeuleyß, *Daß die heyligen für Gott nicht anzurüfen . . . eyn kurtzer undterricht* (1524), A2–3, paraphrased.

131. This reference to the work of Oswald Glaib or Glait, a Moravian Anabaptist, has not been identified.

132. Michael Stiefel, Luther's colleague in the Augustinian order, *Das euangelium von dem verlornen sün* (1524), d4, paraphrased; also cited in some editions is Johannes Lonicer, *Bericht büchlin* (1523), d3–4.

133. *Sermon von dem unrechten Mammon* (1522) (WA 10/3: 28), paraphrased.

134. The canonization of Bishop Benno of Meissen (1010–1106) by Pope Adrian VI in 1523 had drawn Luther's harsh criticism. His grave had attracted pilgrims seeking indulgences in the late medieval period.

135. *Von dem Greuel der Stillmesse* (1525) (WA 18:3; LW 36:317), paraphrased; *Bericht . . . von beider Gestalt des Sakraments* (1528) (WA 26:568), paraphrased.

136. *Sermon von den Heiltumen* (1522) (WA 10/3: 334).

137. *Disputatio Bern.* (1528), 196, falsely cited.

On Miracles

130. Miracles do not prove that saints ought to be invoked. The devil has also unleashed his tricks. Oecolampadius.[138] Zwingli.[139]

131. Miracles have not been performed to confirm faith. Zwingli.[140]

On Jerome

132. The commentaries of Jerome and Origen are nothing more than nonsense and folly when compared to Melanchthon's commentaries, for they only deliver their own ideas rather than Pauline or Christian ones. Melanchthon is actually closer to Paul. Luther.[141]

133. Contrary to Jovinian,[142] Jerome superstitiously extols virginity. There are a lot of superstitious things like this in Jerome rather than godly things. Melanchthon.[143]

134. Jerome did not write adequately against Jovinian. Rather than use erudition against him, he twists the matter by flaunting authority, and he twists passages of Sacred Scripture, not to say he corrupts them. Who knows if Jerome was one of those of whom it is said in Ezekiel that when a prophet erred and spoke untruths, "It is I the Lord who has deceived that prophet" [14:9]. Luther.[144]

135. If there were a book from Vigilantius[145] about the relics of saints as there is from Jerome, I think it would have been written in a more Christian manner than Jerome's. Luther.[146] For Jerome is unparalleled as immodest, a vain jester. Zwingli.[147]

136. Books ought to be composed by Christians who have an understanding of Christ. And on account of this failing, many interpreting the Scriptures, including Jerome, have been wrong in many places. Sacred Scripture does not allow several meanings as they imagine with literal, allegorical, and so forth. Rather, there is a single, very simple sense of Scripture. Luther.[148]

---

138. Johannes Oecolampadius, reformer of Basel, *Disputatio Bad.* (1526), A2, paraphrased.

139. *Handlung der versammlung in . . . Zürich* (1523) (*CR* 88:539), paraphrased.

140. *Handlung der versammlung in . . . Zürich* (1523) (*CR* 88:539–40), paraphrased.

141. Preface to Melanchthon's *Annotationes in epistolas ad Rhomanos et Corinthios* (1522) (WA 20/2: 310).

142. Jovinian was a contemporary of Jerome, whom Jerome attacked because Jovinian taught that virginity was not a higher state than marriage.

143. *Annotationes in epistolas ad Rhomanos et Corinthios* (1522), O3.

144. *De votis monasticis iudicium* (1521) (WA 8:611; *LW* 44:306–7), paraphrased.

145. Vigilantius was a contemporary of Jerome, whom Jerome bitterly attacked for his alleged denial of the cult of saints, celibacy, and monasticism. Vigilantius's own works are not extant.

146. *Sermon von dem Heiltumen* (1522) (WA 10/3: 334).

147. *Uslegen und gründ der schlussreden oder artikel* (1523) (art. 20, *CR* 89:212), paraphrased.

148. Preface to the Old Testament, WADB 2:217–19; *Decem praecepta* (1518) (WA 1:507–8).

On Gregory [I, called the Great]

137. Jerome and Gregory erred when they took away from us the right to judge any and all doctrine. Luther.[149]

138. Jerome errs when he forbids circumcision. Melanchthon.[150] And he is off by a long shot from the view of St. Paul. Luther.[151]

On Augustine

139. Augustine thinks the human creature is the image of God because there is intelligence, memory, and will in the soul. But this fiction has been concocted not only without the authority of Scripture but even without reason. Melanchthon.[152]

On Thomas [Aquinas]

140. A dove is depicted in the ear of St. Thomas. I think it should have been a young devil, that he might be worshiped. Luther.[153]

On Saint Francis

141. Saint Francis foolishly erred and fell as he committed himself and his brothers to poverty. So he drew the Gospel as well into temporal poverty, contrary to Christ. Luther.[154]

On Bernard

142. Bernard, Francis, and Dominic remained in great errors along with the godless. They worshiped the Pope in ignorance, believing that everything from him was right and was from God, which is expressly contrary to the Gospel. Luther.[155]

143. In establishing his order, Francis erred as a human being. Could it be that all the fathers erred when taking vows? Luther. For they fell into pious error when they took vows, and yet God tolerated this folly in his elect. Luther.[156]

---

149. *Predigt am 8. Sonntage nach Trinitatis* (1522) (WA 10/3: 263), paraphrased.

150. *Loci communes rerum theologicarum* (1521) (111, CR 21:198), Loci, 125. •

151. *Acht Sermon* (1522) (WA 10/3: 20; *LW* 51:78).

152. *Annotationes in epistolas Pauli ad Rhomanos et Corinthios* (1522), P3.

153. *Sermon von dem Heiltumen* (1522) (WA 10/3:335).

154. *Predigt am Tage Allerheiligen* (1522) (WA 10/3: 404), paraphrased.

155. *De abroganda missa privata sententia* (1521) (WA 8:451; *LW* 36:190), paraphrased.

156. *De votis monasticis iudicium* (1521) (WA 8:580, 614; *LW* 44:256, 311); *Themata de votis* (1521) (WA 8:33).

On Benedict

144. Benedict boasts with impious hypocrisy and perverse jealousies. Luther.[157]

On the Nicene Council

145. Certain forms of penance were established by the Council of Nicea. I am not about to comment on the spirit in which the fathers made their decree. And as I see it, a good part of the Gospel—in fact, the heart of the Gospel—is obscured by this tradition. Melanchthon.[158]

146. In the holy Council of Nicea, faith and the Gospel were not to be found, and human traditions prevailed. Luther.[159]

On Noah

147. Although Noah was subject to judgment and was already judged as he heard the Word of God and the condemnation of its sentence, he was nevertheless snatched away by the mercy of God. Luther.[160]

148. Noah's flood was the same one the heathen write about, calling it Deucalion's.[161] Zwingli.[162]

On the Limbo of the Fathers

149. Christ descended to hell, not to a limbo of the fathers, which is a term unknown to the Sacred Scriptures. But Christ truly descended to hell so that he might see every place that was filled with desperation. Thus Christ praises God that he freed him from that utterly desperate hell, by whose chains he would have been lost if the hand of the Lord had not been there. Bugenhagen.[163]

150. That the Old Testament patriarchs descended into limbo is a fiction. Haller.[164]

151. The bosom of Abraham is nothing but the Word of God. Luther.[165]

---

157. *De votis monasticis iudicium* (1521) (WA 8:656; LW 44:380).

158. *Loci communes rerum theologicarum* (1521) (52, CR 21:137), Loci, 69.

159. *De votis monasticis iudicium* (1521) (WA 8:617; LW 44:316).

160. In fact, Melanchthon, *In obscuriora aliquot capita Geneseos annotationes* (1523) (CR 13:790).

161. Deucalion and Pyrrha, king and queen of Thessaly, were the only survivors of a great deluge sent by Zeus, according to ancient Greek mythology.

162. *Von klarheit und gewisse oder unbetrogliche des worts Gottes* (1522) (CR 88:354); *Clarity and Certainty*, 69.

163. *In librum psalmorum interpretatio* (1524), 485.

164. *Disputatio Bern.* (1528), 64, paraphrased.

165. *Sermon auf das Evangelium Luc. 16* (1523) (WA 12:595).

On the Old Testament

152. I want the Law of Moses to be seen as foolish gentile laws, that is, as civil law. Melanchthon.[166]

153. That part of the law that has the Decalog or moral precepts is made outmoded by the New Testament. Melanchthon.[167] Out of Moses' Decalog, Luther makes eight commandments and Zwingli makes eleven.

154. The Old Testament can either be followed today or it can be set aside. Thus Jerome erred in asserting that it has been abolished. Luther.[168]

155. Those who are circumcised are not sinning [by being circumcised], nor are those who neglect circumcision. Melanchthon.[169]

156. The reason the Mosaic law was abrogated is that it was impossible for it to be kept. Melanchthon.[170]

157. By his death, Christ confirmed the Old Testament. Weidensee.[171]

158. The Old Testament is no testament but a type of a testament. Melanchthon.[172]

On the New Testament

159. The New Testament is nothing other than the promise of all good apart from the law with no regard for our righteousness, for good is promised to us without condition while nothing is demanded from us in return. Melanchthon.[173]

160. Whatever is done under compulsion of the law is sin. In the New Testament, there are no precepts that coerce us but rather only exhortations and appeals. Luther.[174]

161. Christ did not come to make a [new chosen] people or to impose [a new] law. Melanchthon.[175]

On the Gospel

162. The Gospel in no way commands anything. Melanchthon.[176] It also prohibits nothing. Luther.[177]

---

166. *Loci communes rerum theologicarum* (1521) (*CR* 21:201), Loci, 129.
167. *Loci communes rerum theologicarum* (1521) (*CR* 21:193), Loci, 121.
168. *Von weltlicher oberkeit* (1523) (WA 11:256; *LW* 45:97), paraphrased.
169. *Loci communes rerum theologicarum* (1521) (52, *CR* 21:198), Loci, 125.
170. *Loci communes rerum theologicarum* (1521) (52, *CR* 21:198), Loci, 127, paraphrased.
171. Eberhard von Weidensee, pastor in Magdeburg, *Antwort auf die zwei elenden buchlein D. Johan Mensing . . .* (1526), D3.
172. *Loci communes rerum theologicarum* (1521) (52, *CR* 21:208), Loci, 133.
173. *Loci communes rerum theologicarum* (1521) (52, *CR* 21:193), Loci, 120.
174. *Ad librum Ambrosii Catharini responsio* (1521) (WA 7:760).
175. *In evangelium Ioannis annotationes* (1523) (*CR* 14:1060).
176. *Annotationes in epistolas ad Rhomanos et Corinthios* (1522), D3, paraphrased.
177. Preface to the New Testament (1522) (WADB 2:201–2), paraphrased.

163. Christ's testament is confirmed by faith, by which we believe his death. Weidensee.[178]

164. Christ removed all punishment in the New Testament, and he permits his Word alone to be active. Luther.[179]

165. [166][180] The Gospel is nothing but preaching about Christ's resurrection. Thus works are completely set aside. Luther.[181]

166. [167] Scripture does not distinguish between law and Gospel. Thus you might think that only what Matthew, Mark, Luke, and John wrote is Gospel and the books of Moses are nothing else but law. But the doctrine of the Gospel is interspersed through the books of the Old and New Testaments. Melanchthon.[182]

167. [168] Just as circumcision is nothing, so Baptism is nothing, and participation in the Lord's Supper is nothing. Melanchthon.[183]

On Angels

168. [169] The wicked do not have their own guardian angels. Having angels only extends to the elect. Bugenhagen.[184]

On the Church

169. [170] Only the predestined are in the church. The evil or wicked are not of the church. Bucer.[185]

170. [171] Whoever is in the church cannot be condemned. Zwingli.[186]

On Contingent Matters

171. [172] All things that happen happen according to divine predestination. Thus our will has no freedom. For according to his predestination, all things happen to all creatures by necessity. Melanchthon.[187]

172. [173] All things happen by absolute necessity. Luther.[188]

---

178. *Antwort auf die zwei elenden buchlein D. Johan Mensing . . .* (1526), D3–4.

179. *Sermon am Pfingsttage* (1522) (WA 10/3: 156).

180. The edition in use for this translation omits number 165 at this point. The number of the translation follows the Gussmann edition with the thesis numbers in the original in brackets.

181. *Sermon am Auffahrttage* (1522) (WA 10/3: 189).

182. *Loci communes rerum theologicarum* (1521) (52, CR 21:139), Loci, 71.

183. *Loci communes rerum theologicarum* (1521) (52, CR 21:209), Loci, 134, paraphrased.

184. *In librum psalmorum interpretatio* (1524), 519.

185. *Disputatio Bern.* (1528), 37, 42, paraphrased.

186. *Uslegen und gründ der schlussreden oder artikel* (1523) (art. 6, CR 89:56).

187. *Loci communes rerum theologicarum* (1521) (CR 21:87–88), Loci, 24. *Annotationes in epistolas ad Rhomanos et Corinthios* (1522), H1.

188. *Assertio omnium articulorum* (1520) (art. 36, WA 7:146).

173. [174] There is no difference between laws and Evangelical counsels.[189] Melanchthon.[190]

174. [175] There is only one Evangelical counsel, namely, virginity. Granted that it is not praised in the Scriptures. Luther.[191]

On the Commandments

175. [176] It is impossible for an Evangelical counsel to become a commandment. Luther.[192]

176. [177] God's commandments are impossible [to keep]. Melanchthon.[193] You are going about it wrong when you deny that our Savior commanded impossible things to do. Luther to Sylvester.[194]

On the Lord's Day

177. [178] "The Sabbath" does not indicate the religion of the Sabbath day. Since the law has been abrogated, all days are equal. Melanchthon.[195]

178. [179] There are some people who think the Sabbath still should be observed because we have Scripture to support this and not for the Lord's Day.[196]

179. [180] The Lord's Day was instituted only so that people could come together to hear the Word of God. Bucer.[197] It is not for resting. Os. Glait.[198] Carlstadt.[199]

---

189. In medieval theology, those works not commanded for all Christians but prescribed for those in monastic orders as works by which they strive toward Christian perfection. The Evangelical counsels included poverty, chastity, and obedience to religious superiors.

190. *In evangelium Matthaei annotationes* (1523), I3.

191. *Assertio omnium articulorum* (1520) (art. 30, WA 7:136).

192. *De votis monasticis iudicium* (1521) (WA 8:584; *LW* 44:262).

193. *Loci communes rerum theologicarum* (1521) (CR 21:107), Loci, 45.

194. *Ad dialogum Silvestri Prieratis de potestate papae responsio* (1518) (WA 1:649). Sylvester Prierias, a Dominican in the papal curia, was one of Luther's most strident opponents in the 1510s and 1520s.

195. *In obscuriora aliquot capita Geneseos annotationes* (1523), E5–6.

196. The citation has not been identified. Some editions label it as stemming from "Balthasar," probably the Anabaptist Balthasar Hubmaier, perhaps from his *Die uralten und gar neüen leerern urtail* (1526), D3.

197. Bucer in *Disputatio Bern.* (1528), 76, paraphrased. See also Zwingli, *Uslegen und gründ der schlussreden oder artikel* (1523) (art. 25, CR 89:247), paraphrased.

198. Oswald Glait in his *Handlung . . . in siben artickel beschlossen* (1526), a7, paraphrased.

199. Luther's former colleague Andreas Bodenstein von Carlstadt, *Von dem sabbat und geboten feyertagen* (1524), A2–4, falsely cited.

Sin

180. [181] The tinder [of concupiscence] truly is actual sin, actual absence of what ought to be there. It is a thing that is alive, and daily sin is a motivating force. Luther.[200] Rhegius.[201]

181. [182] Every sin is ignorance. Melanchthon.[202] And unconquerable ignorance does not excuse sin. Luther.[203]

182. [183] The distinction between venial and mortal sin is wrongly drawn today. Melanchthon.[204] For every sin is mortal according to its own nature, but it is venial for those who are in Christ. Luther.[205]

183. [184] Original sin is not sin but a natural defect like stuttering. Zwingli.[206]

184. [185] Original sin is really evil desire. Thus Scripture does not distinguish between actual or original sin. Melanchthon.[207]

185. [186] Original sin remains forever. Luther.[208]

Faith

186. [187] Faith alone justifies; works do not. For faith and works are exact opposites. Thus works cannot be taught without damaging faith. Luther.[209]

187. [188] An error in faith does not hurt so long as a person believes that Christ our Lord has saved us and redeemed us. Bucer.[210]

188. [189] There are no works so evil that they can accuse and damn those who believe in Christ. Luther. Where there is faith, no sin is injurious.[211]

189. [190] Those who once believed that Jesus Christ redeemed them have the seal of the Holy Spirit and are never able to commit a mortal sin. Bucer.[212]

190. [191] Christ established that there is no sin except for unbelief, and no righteousness except for faith. Luther.[213]

191. [192] It is fitting to elevate faith above all virtues. Luther. But it is taken away by every sin. Luther.[214]

---

200. *Assertio omnium articulorum* (1520) (art. 3, WA 7:110–11).

201. Urbanus Rhegius, reformer in Augsburg, *Novae doctrinae ad veterem collatio* (1526), xxi, paraphrased.

202. *Annotationes in epistolas ad Rhomanos et Corinthios* (1522), N1.

203. *In epistolam Pauli ad Galatas commentarius* (1519) (WA 2:538; *LW* 27:292).

204. *In evangelium Matthaei annotationes* (1523), 14.

205. In fact, in Heinrich Spelt, *Der ainfeltig glaub* (1524), F1, paraphrased.

206. *De peccato originali declaratio* (1526) (*CR* 92:371–72), paraphrased.

207. *Loci communes rerum theologicarum* (1521) (*CR* 21:97), Loci, 31.

208. *Resolutiones disputationum de indulgentiarum virtute* (1518) (conc. 4, WA 1:534; *LW* 31:89).

209. *De votis monasticis iudicium* (1521) (WA 8:600; *LW* 44:292).

210. *Disputatio Bern.* (1528), 35, paraphrased.

211. *De votis monasticis iudicium* (1521) (WA 8:608; *LW* 44:301); *Predigt am Pfingstmontage* (WA 10/3: 168).

212. *Disputatio Bern.* (1528), 43.

213. *Ad librum Ambrosii catharini responsio* (1521) (WA 7:764).

214. *Operationes in Psalmos* (1519) (WA 5:396 and 400, the latter paraphrased).

192. [193] We have no doubt at all that we are saved after we have been baptized because the promise made there cannot be changed by any sins. Thus someone who is baptized cannot lose salvation, even if that person wanted to, because there is no sin that can damn that person except for unbelief. All other sins are swallowed up by faith in an instant. Luther.[215]

193. [194] The only thing necessary is faith alone. All other things are entirely free, neither commanded nor prohibited. Luther.[216]

194. [195] Love does not justify but rather faith justifies; it is preferred to love. Melanchthon. Moreover, faith justifies without regard to works, good or bad. Melanchthon.[217]

195. [196] Only unbelievers are evil. For our works do not count in God's sight but only in the sight of other human beings. Zwingli.[218]

196. [197] Faith is not a matter of the past but of the future. Luther.[219]

197. [198] It is a pipe dream, unknown to Scripture, to say that "unformed faith"[220] is acquired. That is something that the prostitutes of the Pope teach. Luther.[221] "Unformed faith" is insanity. Melanchthon.[222]

Against Works

198. [199] No matter how laudable they seem to be, all the works people do are thoroughly offensive and are sins worthy of death. Melanchthon.[223]

199 [200] Evil deeds do not make a person evil. Luther.[224]

200. [201] The commandments are to be fulfilled prior to the performance of any work. Luther.[225]

201. [202] We are, have been, and always will be equals before God. Luther.[226]

202. [203] God does not care about our works. Luther. Or if they amount to anything before him, they are nevertheless all equal when it comes to merit.[227]

215. *De captivitate Babylonica* (1520) (WA 6:527; *LW* 36:59–60, 62).

216. *In epistolam Pauli ad Galatas commentarius* (1519) (WA 2:485; *LW* 27:213).

217. *Loci communes rerum theologicarum* (1521) (*CR* 21:135, 97), Loci, 147, paraphrased. *Annotationes in epistolas ad Rhomanos et Corinthios* (1522), C3, paraphrased.

218. *De canone missae epichiresis* (1523) (*CR* 89:572), paraphrased.

219. *Themata de votis* (1521) (WA 8:323).

220. "Fides informis" is "merely historical belief" or faith without accompanying deeds of love according to medieval theologians.

221. *Themata de votis* (1521) (WA 8:323).

222. *Annotationes in epistolas ad Rhomanos et Corinthios* (1522), Q1.

223. *Loci communes rerum theologicarum* (1521) (*CR* 21:106), Loci, 39.

224. *Tractatus de libertate christiana* (1520) (WA 7:61; *LW* 31:361).

225. *Tractatus de libertate christiana* (1520) (WA 7:56; *LW* 31:353).

226. *Operationes in Psalmos* (1519) (WA 5:169).

227. *De captivitate Babylonica* (WA 6:516, 514; *LW* 36:42, the latter paraphrased).

On Merits

203. [204] Paul bursts the pipe dreams of theologians who have invented "congruent merit" and "condign merit"[228] in order to obtain grace. Luther.[229] Rhegius.[230]

204. [205] Saying that our works are meritorious detracts from Christ's honor and merit. Haller.[231] For there is no merit at all in a person. Zwingli.[232]

205. [206] God's grace is not a quality within us. Melanchthon.[233] Someone who believes also loves. The priors of Nuremberg.[234]

Love

206. [207] The commandments are all to be followed in love. So those who do not kill still are sinning if they are not acting in love. Luther.[235]

207. [208] Love no longer exists in the eternal home. Zwingli.[236]

208. [209] A Christian always takes heed lest others be unsure of being in God's grace or unsure whether their works please God. For anyone who doubts this sins, and all that individual's works are lost. Luther.[237]

209. [210] This statement is absolutely certain, that we are absolutely certain of the remission of sins. The saints know they are in grace and their sins are forgiven. Melanchthon.[238]

210. [211] Acts of hope and faith are not differentiated in Scripture. Melanchthon.[239]

211. [212] I consider it a human fantasy that a disposition[240] is one thing while an action is something else. Therefore faith is nothing but a moving of the heart that is called to believe. Luther.[241]

---

228. Congruent merit was defined by medieval theologians as merit won by the performance of good works apart from grace and thus meritorious only because of the acceptance of God, whereas condign merit is won through the production of truly worthy works with the assistance of grace.

229. *In epistolam Pauli ad Galatas commentarius* (1519) (WA 2:509; LW 27:249).

230. *Materia cogitandi de toto missae negocio* (1528), lxxiii.

231. *Disputatio Bern.* (1528), 93.

232. *De canone missae epichiresis* (1523) (CR 89:578–80).

233. *Loci communes rerum theologicarum* (1521) (CR 21:158), Loci, 87.

234. *Grundt und ursach . . . wie und warumb . . . die mißpreüch bey der heyligen meß . . . geendert haben* (1524), D4.

235. *Resolutiones disputationum de indulgentiarum virtute* (1518) (WA 2:458; LW 31:132–33), paraphrased. *Operationes in psalmos* (1519) (WA 5:262).

236. *Disputatio Bern.* (1528), 197, falsely cited. *Uslegen und gründ der schlussreden oder artikel* (1523) (art. 25, CR 89:216–17), paraphrased.

237. *In epistolam Pauli ad Galatas commentarius* (1519) (WA 2:458; LW 27:173), paraphrased. *Operationes in psalmos* (1519) (WA 5:124), paraphrased. *Resolutiones disputationum de indulgentiarum virtute* (1518) (conc. 38, WA 1:594), paraphrased.

238. *Loci communes rerum theologicarum* (1521) (CR 21:189), Loci, 117.

239. *Loci communes rerum theologicarum* (1521) (CR 21:183), Loci, 111, paraphrased.

240. Latin: *habitus,* a component part of the human psyche, according to Aristotelian psychology.

241. *Operationes in psalmos* (1519) (WA 5:176).

212. [213] The freedom of the Gospel is this: all power of accusing and of condemning us has been crushed out of the law. That is, if you were to sin, you would not be condemned. Melanchthon.[242]

On the Sacraments

213. [214] The invention of sacraments is a recent thing. Luther. And there are only three sacraments: Baptism, Penance, and the Bread. Luther.[243] Other places he only posits two. Glait.[244]

214. [215] The sacraments of the New Law are no different from the sacraments of the Old Testament in terms of the efficacy of their signs. Luther.[245] Bucer.[246]

Baptism

215. [216] Baptism neither justifies nor profits anybody so much as does the faith in the word of promise that is added to Baptism. Luther.[247] Melanchthon.[248]

216. [217] Even in terms of the sign, Baptism is not a momentary thing but a permanent matter. Luther.[249]

217. [218] To baptize is incomparably greater than to consecrate bread and wine. Luther.[250]

218. [219] Thus Baptism cannot be performed except by a priest. Luther.[251]

219. [220] Baptism pertains no less to the second pardon than to the first. Melanchthon.[252]

220. [221] Repentance has no other sacramental sign than Baptism. Melanchthon.[253]

221. [222] It is pernicious to believe that the power of Baptism is set aside by sin in the case of a child of light. Luther.[254]

---

242. *Loci communes rerum theologicarum* (1521) (*CR* 21:194), Loci, 122.

243. *De captivitate Babylonica* (WA 6:562, 501, 572; *LW* 36:109, 18, 124, the last paraphrased).

244. *Handlung . . . in siben artickel beschlossen* (1526), a5–6, paraphrased.

245. *De captivitate Babylonica* (1520) (WA 6:532; *LW* 36:65).

246. *Enarrationum in evangelium Matthaei, Marci et Lucae libri duo* (1527) (1:150–52).

247. *De captivitate Babylonica* (1520) (WA 6:532; *LW* 36:66).

248. *Annotationes in epistolas ad Rhomanos et Corinthios* (1522), D1, paraphrased.

249. *De captivitate Babylonica* (1520) (WA 6:534; *LW* 36:69). *Ein Sermon von dem heiligen hochwürdigen Sakrakment baptismi* (1519) (WA 2:728), paraphrased.

250. *De instituendis ministris ecclesiae* (1523) (WA 12:181; *LW* 40:23).

251. *De instituendis ministris ecclesiae* (1523) (WA 12:181; *LW* 40:23), paraphrased.

252. *Loci communes rerum theologicarum* (1521) (*CR* 21:216), Loci, 141. *Annotationes in epistolas ad Rhomanos et Corinthios* (1522), P3–P4, paraphrased.

253. *Loci communes rerum theologicarum* (1521) (*CR* 21:215), Loci, 140. *Annotationes in epistolas ad Rhomanos et Corinthios* (1522), P4.

254. *De captivitate Babylonica* (1520) (WA 6:529; *LW* 36:61).

222. [223] Baptism is to be applied to the whole course of our life. Luther.[255]

223. [224] Christ's baptism is the same as John's. Zwingli. Thus John the Baptist preached the Gospel before Christ did. Zwingli.[256]

224. [225] The form of Baptism is not "in the name of the Father," but rather "I baptize you in the names of the Father and of the Son," etc. Zwingli.[257]

225. [226] Baptismal water is not to be blessed, and exorcism should not precede Baptism. But setting all ceremonies aside, we should use Baptism in the most simple way as Christ instituted it. Johannes Landsberger.[258]

226. [227] Infants should not be baptized. But when those baptized have come to the point of using reason, they should be rebaptized. Balthasar [Hubmaier].[259]

227. [228] Baptism does nothing for an infant unless it has its own faith. Luther.[260] Rhegius.[261] Weidensee.[262] Landsberger.[263] However, infused faith is a fiction. Oswaldus Glait.[264]

228. [229] It is not the working of Baptism but the blood of Christ that takes away original [sin]. Luther.[265]

Infants

229. [230] I believe that infants of Christians, even if they are not brought [to be baptized], are not condemned. Zwingli.[266]

230. [231] A child should not be hurried to Baptism because even God cannot give a baptized child faith when it is condemned. And he is able to give faith to an unbaptized child who is to be saved. Weidensee.[267]

---

255. *De captivitate Babylonica* (1520) (WA 6:572; *LW* 36:124), paraphrased.

256. *Vom touf* (1525) (*CR* 91:220–22; *LCC* 24:167), falsely cited.

257. *Vom touf* (1525) (*CR* 91:237, 336; *LCC* 24:144), falsely cited.

258. Johannes Landsberger, former Carthusian monk, *Ain gründtlicher bericht vom christlichen tauf* (1526), B1–B3, paraphrased.

259. *Vom dem christlichen tauf* (1525) is one of several of Hubmaier's tracts that may have supplied Eck with this summary of the Anabaptist preacher's position.

260. *Kirchenpostille* (WA 21:75–76), paraphrased.

261. *Wider den newen tauforden notwendige warnung* (1527), paraphrased.

262. *Eyn tractetleyn von dem glauben . . . der unmundigen und unvorstendtlichen kindelein* (1524), A2–A4, paraphrased.

263. *Ain gründtlicher bericht* (1526), C2–C3.

264. *Handlung . . . in siben artickel beschlossen* (1526), a5–6, paraphrased.

265. *Kirchenpostille* (WA 21:75–76), referred to in some editions, does not contain such a passage.

266. *Uslegen und gründ* (1523) (art. 67, *CR* 89:45), paraphrased.

267. *Eyn tractetleyn von dem glauben . . . der unmundigen und unvorstendtlichen kindelein* (1524), B6–B7.

231. [232] It is not certain, then, that a child dying after Baptism is saved. Weidensee.[268] A person does not know about a child dying without Baptism. Landsberger.[269]

232. [233] If someone were to bring up children and know that all of them are eternally condemned, that person should not be troubled on account of this or grieve. Weidensee.[270]

On [Sacramentally Bestowed] Character

233. [234] The character imposed in Baptism or Ordination is a fiction with no scriptural basis. Luther.[271] Melanchthon. Rhegius. Zwingli.[272]

On Confirmation

234. [235] Confirmation and Extreme Unction are not sacraments instituted by Christ. Luther.[273] Zwingli.[274]

On the Eucharist

235. [236] In the Eucharist, the substance of bread and wine remains because transubstantiation is a figment of sophists and Romanists. Pirckheimer.[275] Melanchthon.[276]

236. [237] I firmly believe not only that Christ's body is in the bread but also that the bread is Christ's body. Luther.[277]

237. [238] As Christ's body is in the bread where there is neither blood nor soul, so in the same way the blood is in the wine without body and soul. Luther.[278]

---

268. *Eyn tractetleyn von dem glauben . . . der unmundigen und unvorstendtlichen kindelein* (1524), A3–A4, paraphrased.

269. *Ain gründtlicher bericht* (1526), E2–E4, paraphrased.

270. *Eyn tractetleyn von dem glauben . . . der unmundigen und unvorstendtlichen kindelein* (1524), B6–B7.

271. *De captivitate Babylonica* (1520) (WA 6:567; LW 36:117), paraphrased.

272. Eck did not give references in any of his editions for the source of this statement in these three authors. In some editions, he added after Zwingli's name "and all the others."

273. *De captivitate Babylonica* (1520) (WA 6:549–50; LW 36:91, 118), paraphrased.

274. A precise reference to Zwingli's works was not given.

275. Willibald Pirckheimer, humanist in Nuremberg, who never officially supported the Reformation, *De vera Christi carne et vero eius sanguine* (1526).

276. Melanchthon had advanced this position in his theses for attaining the degree of Bachelor of Bible in September 1519 and conveyed his sentiments in a letter to Johann Heß (February 1520) (CR 1:137–39).

277. *De captivitate Babylonica* (1520) (WA 6:511; LW 36:34). Some editions add the name of the English reformer of the late fourteenth century, John Wycliffe, to this article, associating Luther with his "heresy."

278. *Bericht an einen guten Freund* (1528) (WA 26:603–5), paraphrased.

238. [239] The true body of Christ is not really in the Eucharist but only figuratively as in a sign. Zwingli.[279] Oecolampadius.[280] Capito.[281] Keller.[282] Rottenacker.[283]

239. [240] I do not know if it was a greater abomination to worship the golden calf in Dan [Exod. 32:1-6] or to worship that bread. Zwingli.[284]

240. [241] The Eucharist is the idol of Moazim, which, according to Daniel [11:38-39], we worshiped in the holy place and is true idolatry. Zwingli.[285]

241. [242] Christ's body cannot exist except in one place. Thus, if it was to be received by us, it would have to leave the right hand of the Father. Zwingli.[286]

242. [243] Miracles that are done in the Eucharist have Satan as their author. Oecolampadius. They proceed from the Father of Lies.[287]

243. [244] There is a great deal of danger in adoring the Eucharist. Therefore, it would be better not to adore it, following what the apostles did, nor is Christ there for the purpose of being adored. Luther.[288]

On Processions

244. [245] When the Eucharist is encased in gold and silver, paraded around in procession with pomp and external adoration, it is nothing more than a mockery of God. Luther.[289] Pirckheimer.[290] Lang.[291] Strauss.[292]

---

279. *Ad Matthaeum Alberum . . . de coena dominica epistola* (1524) (*CR* 90:322–24) *De vera et falsa religione* (1525) (*CR* 90:322–24), *Commentary*, 198–200.

280. Johannes Oecolampadius, reformer of Basel, *De genuina verborum Domini expositione* (1525), 5–7, paraphrased.

281. Wolfgang Capito, reformer in Strassburg, *Waß man halten und antwurten soll, von der spaltung zwischen Martin Luther und Andres Carolstadt* (1524), 2–4, paraphrased.

282. Michael Keller, reformer in Augsburg, *Etlich sermones von dem nachtmal Christi* (1525), C6–C8, paraphrased.

283. Konrad Sam refused responsibility for the tract published without his permission under the title *Ain schöner und wolgeteütschter grüntlicher bericht für den gemainen menschen, ober der leyb Jesu Christi im himel . . . zu suchen . . . sey* (1526), but Eck had attacked the ideas of this tract earlier and undoubtedly was referring to it here. In other editions, he also added Martin Bucer and Ambrosius Blaurer to the list of those who held this position.

284. *Ad Matthaeum Alberum . . . de coena dominica epistola* (1524) (*CR* 90:342).

285. *De vera et falsa religione* (1525) (*CR* 90:320), *Commentary,* 253, paraphrased.

286. *Eine Abschrift oder Kopie des Geleitbriefs an J. Eck* (1526) (*CR* 91:761), paraphrased.

287. *De genuina verborum Domini expositione* (1525), B1–B3, paraphrased.

288. *Vom Anbeten des Sakraments* (1523) (WA 11:449, 448; *LW* 36:295), paraphrased.

289. *Vom Anbeten des Sakraments* (1523) (WA 11:433, 445; *LW* 36:291, 278), paraphrased.

290. *De vera Christi carne* (1526), D1–D2, paraphrased.

291. Gussmann could identity no similar passage in the writings of the reformer of Erfurt, Johann Lange.

292. Jacob Strauß, reformer in Eisleben, *Ein kurtz christenlich unterricht des grossen jrrthumbs* (1523), A2–A4, paraphrased.

245. [246] Therefore it is an abuse of the Eucharist that it should be turned into a show or paraded around or reserved in an ark.[293] But that the Eucharist should be locked up like this is a sport of demons. Pirckheimer.[294] Glait.[295] Balthasar [Hubmaier].[296]

On Communion

246. [247] That no one should receive the Eucharist except with fasting is insanity more insane than any insanity. Thus it is ridiculous that a layperson does not take up the Eucharist in hand or handle the cup since laypeople could commune themselves. Luther.[297] Later, however, Luther prohibited this.

247. [248] Only those commune worthily who have consciences afflicted, disquieted, confused, in error, and weighed down by sin. Luther.[298]

248. [249] The greatest sins are committed at Easter due to the impious command of the Pope that people be compelled to go to Communion. And this is even worse than [the sins at] Carnival. Luther.[299]

249. [250] Trust my advice: a Christian in Lent and at Easter should neither confess nor come to this sacrament. And this is what the Christian should think: this is exactly why I will not do what this man, the Pope, commands; but I would do it if the Pope had not ordered it. Luther.[300]

Both Kinds[301]

250. [251] To deny both kinds to the laity is godless and tyrannical. And bishops sin who only give the one kind by itself. Luther.[302] Osiander.[303]

251. [252] The Greeks and others are not to be considered heretical or schismatics because they receive both kinds, but the Romans are. Luther.[304]

---

293. A reference to the reservation of sacramental elements and to the Corpus Christi procession.

294. *De vera Christi carne* (1526), B8, paraphrased.

295. Oswald Glait, *Handlung . . . in siben artickel beschlossen* (1526), a3, paraphrased.

296. *Ain ainfeltiger underricht auf die wort: Das ist der leib mein* (1526), D1–D2.

297. *Vom Mißbrauch der Messe* (1522) (WA 8:508; *LW* 36:165), paraphrased; *De captivitate Babylonica* (1520) (WA 6:566; *LW* 36:116); *Contra Henricium* (1522) (WA 10/2: 201–2).

298. *De captivitate Babylonica* (1520) (WA 6:526; *LW* 36:57), paraphrased.

299. *Acht Sermon* (1522) (WA 10/3: 50–51; *LW* 51:93), paraphrased.

300. *Von der Beicht* (1522) (WA 8:172).

301. This term refers to the elements of bread and wine that become the body and blood of Christ in the Lord's Supper.

302. *De captivitate Babylonica* (1520) (WA 6:506, 507; *LW* 36:27), paraphrased.

303. *Handlung eynes ersamen weysen rats zu Nürnberg* (1525), B3–B4, here ascribed to Andreas Osiander, a leading reformer in Nuremberg, paraphrased.

304. *De captivitate Babylonica* (1520) (WA 6:505; *LW* 36:24), paraphrased.

252. [253] It would be better to receive neither part than just one alone because it is a trap most harmful for souls to commune once a year under one kind. Luther.[305] Zwingli.[306]

253. [254] A layman lacking a desire for both kinds is ungodly and denies Christ. Luther.[307]

On Confession

254. [255] Confession, as it is now practiced, privately, cannot be supported by divine law. It was not practiced in this way originally, but instead at that time confession was made in public. Luther.[308] Zwingli.[309] Oecolampadius.[310]

255. [256] Whether secret sins fall under the jurisdiction of sacramental Confession cannot be proven in any way by reason or from the Scriptures. I suspect this was invented either by the greedy or by the curious. Luther.[311] Of the tyrants of the soul.[312] Oecolampadius.[313] Rhegius.[314] Strauss.[315]

256. [257] A priest ought to absolve the penitent from punishment and guilt, or the priest sins. Likewise, a superior sins in reserving cases for himself. Luther.[316]

257. [258] Circumstances are to be completely disregarded. The observance of places, times, persons does not matter. And if it is said that it matters, then it is another superstitious supposition. Luther.[317] Carlstadt.[318]

Penance[319]

258. [259] [The sacrament] of Penance lacks any [external] sign that is divinely instituted. Therefore it is not properly a sacrament but a path and a return to Baptism. Luther.[320] Melanchthon.[321]

---

305. *Ad librum Ambrosii Catharini responsio* (1521) (WA 7:767).

306. *Uslegen und gründ* (1523) (*CR* 90:2:124–25), paraphrased.

307. *Assertio omnium articulorum* (1520) (art. 16, WA 7:124), paraphrased.

308. *Contra malignum J. Eccii iudicium* (1519) (art. 7, WA 2:645).

309. *Uslegen und gründ* (1523) (art. 52, *CR* 89:393–95), paraphrased.

310. *In epistolam Joannis apostoli catholicam primam . . . demegoriae* (1524), 19, paraphrased.

311. *Confitendi ratio* (1520) (WA 6:161), paraphrased.

312. It is not clear to what Eck is referring with this expression.

313. *In epistolam Joannis apostoli catholicam primam . . . demegoriae* (1524), 19, paraphrased.

314. *Vom hochwürdigen sacrament des altars underricht* (1523), 3–5.

315. *Eyn verstendig, trostlich leer uber das wort Sanct Paulus* (1522), A2–A4, paraphrased.

316. *Resolutiones Lutherianae* (1519) (conc. 5, WA 2:423); *De captivitate Babylonica* (1520) (WA 6:546; *LW* 36:86), paraphrased.

317. *De captivitate Babylonica* (1520) (WA 6:548; *LW* 36:89), paraphrased.

318. *Subscriptas conclusiones Andreas Carolstadius adversus dominum Joannem Eccum defendet Lipsiae* (1519) art. 17, paraphrased.

319. See note 13 above.

320. *De captivitate Babylonica* (1520) (WA 6:572; *LW* 36:124), paraphrased.

321. *Loci communes rerum theologicarum* (1521) (*CR* 21:215), Loci, 140, paraphrased.

259. [260] Even if St. John has taught that fear is the beginning of penitence, it nevertheless does not follow that penitence begins from fear. Luther.[322]

260. [261] It is false and dangerous to think that penitence is the second plank after shipwreck. Luther.[323] Carlstadt.[324] Melanchthon.[325]

On the Keys

261. [262] The keys are not given except to the righteous and holy in spirit. Luther.[326] Oecolampadius.[327] Bucer.[328]

262. [263] To bind and to loose is nothing other than to preach the Gospel. Luther.[329] Zwingli.[330]

263. [264] Those laws about satisfactions by which we are taught to wipe out sins through our works are ungodly. Observe that the contrary has been condemned here by Christ, namely, everything about canon law and the rule of the Pope. Luther.[331]

Satisfaction

264. [265] No other satisfaction is required for sin but the death of Christ. Melanchthon.[332] Rhegius.[333] Zwingli.[334] Luther.[335]

265. [266] The Sacrament of Penance has been abolished by the prelates in the church. Luther.[336]

266. [267] Anybody can absolve anybody. So unlimited authority for hearing confessions is given to all brothers and sisters. Luther.[337]

---

322. *Disputatio Lipsiae habita* (1519) (WA 2:370).

323. *De captivitate Babylonica* (1520) (WA 6:529; *LW* 36:61), paraphrased, in opposition to a famous phrase from St. Jerome.

324. *Defensio adversus eximii D. Joannis Eckii . . . monomachiam* (1528) art. 2, paraphrased.

325. *Adversus Thomam Placentinum pro Martino Luthero theologi oratio* (n.d., *CR* 1:350–52), paraphrased.

326. *Resolutiones Lutherianae* (1519) (WA 2:93).

327. *In epistolam Joannis apostoli catholicam primam . . . demegoriae* (1524), 89, paraphrased.

328. *Enarrationes in evangelium Matthaei* (1523) (2:180–82), paraphrased.

329. *De instituendis ministris* (1523) (WA 12:184; *LW* 40:27–28).

330. *Disputatio Bern.* (1528), in fact a citation of Berchtold Haller.

331. *De votis monasticis iudicium* (1521) (WA 8:607; *LW* 44:299–300).

332. *Loci communes rerum theologicarum* (1521) (*CR* 21:215), Loci, 145, paraphrased.

333. Other editions substitute Bucer's name for that of Rhegius, a reference to Bucer's position, *Disputatio Bern.* (1528), 95–97, paraphrased.

334. *Uslegen und gründ* (1523) (art. 18, *CR* 89:111–13).

335. *Acht Sermon* (1522) (WA 10/3: 49; *LW* 51:92), paraphrased.

336. *Resolutiones disputationum de indulgentiarum virtute* (1517) (conc. 27ff., WA 1:584–86; *LW* 31:175–77), paraphrased.

337. *De captivitate Babylonica* (1520) (WA 6:547; *LW* 36:88), paraphrased.

Ordination

267. [268] The church of Christ does not know the Sacrament of Ordination. Luther.[338] But it is a figment invented by human beings. Zwingli.[339] Rhegius.[340] Amsterdo.[341]

268. [269] All Christians, as many as are baptized, are equally priests. And any layperson can consecrate churches, confirm children, and so forth. Luther.[342]

Mass

269. [270] The Gospel does not permit the Mass to be a sacrifice because to maintain the practice of masses under the name "sacrifice" is to deny Christ. Luther.[343] Rhegius.[344]

270. [271] A person can celebrate the Mass anytime and as often as one wants. Luther.[345] Yet a person cannot offer [the Mass] for another any more than one person can drink for anyone else. Zwingli.[346]

271. [272] They lie who say that the Mass of an evil priest is beneficial ex opere operato.[347] Luther.[348] It is clear that the name of "Mass" is improperly transferred to such a mass. Zwingli.[349]

272. [273] The office of the Mass is not effective when offered for the dead, for the troubled, or when applied to another person. Luther.[350] ·

273. [274] The Mass has been turned into Satan's sacrifice, and that happens by a common error. And also this is the worst idolatry and infidelity and is worse than pagan. Luther.[351] Rhegius.[352]

274. [275] We condemn and despise the Mass by the authority of the Gospel. Luther.[353] For it is deceitful and has nothing substantial in it. Zwingli.[354] Preachers of Nuremberg.[355]

338. *De captivitate Babylonica* (1520) (WA 6:560; LW 36:206).

339. *De vera et falsa religione* (1525) (*CR* 90:824), *Commentary*, 31, 257.

340. *Materia cogitandi* (1528), paraphrased.

341. It has not been identified to whom Eck is referring with this designation.

342. *De captivitate Babylonica* (1520) (WA 6:564, 566; LW 36:113, 115), paraphrased.

343. *De captivitate Babylonica* (1520) (WA 6:523, 524; LW 36:51–52), paraphrased.

344. *Materia cogitandi* (1528), paraphrased.

345. *De captivitate Babylonica* (1520) (WA 6:518; LW 36:44).

346. *De canone missae epichiresis* (1523) (*CR* 89:570–72), paraphrased.

347. "By the performance of the rite," that is, automatically.

348. *De captivitate Babylonica* (1520) (WA 6:520; LW 36:47), paraphrased.

349. *De canone missae epichiresis* (1523) (*CR* 89:567–69), paraphrased.

350. *De captivitate Babylonica* (1520) (WA 6:521; LW 36:48), paraphrased.

351. *De abroganda missa* (1521) (WA 8:457; LW 36:198), paraphrased.

352. *Ain summa christlicher leer* (n.d.).

353. *De abroganda missa* (1521) (WA 8:409; LW 36:185), paraphrased.

354. *De canone missae epichiresis* (1523) (*CR* 89:552–54), *Commentary*, 359–61, paraphrased.

355. Also identified as Philip Melhofer, *Offenbarung der allerheimlichisten heymlicheit der ytzigen baalspriester* (1525).

275. [276] Those celebrating the Mass today are idolaters. And they commit idolatry as often as they sacrifice. Luther.[356] Oecolampadius.[357]

276. [277] Private masses are to be abrogated. But on every Lord's Day and on those days alone, the simple Eucharist, just as it is, is to be consecrated. Luther.[358]

277. [278] Indeed, all masses are to be abrogated, whether public or private. Zwingli.[359] Bucer.[360] Capito.[361] Haller.[362] Blaurer.[363] Rottenacker.[364]

278. [279] Water should not be put into the cup at the Mass because it is an evil and unfortunate sign. Zwingli.[365] Luther.[366] Carlstadt.[367]

Canonical Hours

279. [280] I believe that those who read the [canonical] hours [of monastic devotion], empty as they are, sin more than those who skip them, for the former are hypocrites. There is hardly a greater sin than this mechanical worship of God, which is performed by bellowing through those canonical hours. Luther.[368] Thus the priors of Nuremberg have done away with matins and compline.

Marriage

280. [281] Marriage is not a divinely instituted sacrament, but it was invented by people in the church. Luther.[369]

281. [282] The conjugal duty is a sin and is plainly offensive according to Psalm 51. Indeed, not a single person practices it without sinning. Luther.[370]

282. [283] Priests ought to confirm all marriages that have impediments from papal law but not from divine law. Luther.[371] Every priest, indeed any

356. *De abroganda missa* (1521) (WA 8:442; *LW* 36:176).
357. *De genuina verborum Domini expositione* (1525), B3–B5, paraphrased.
358. *De abroganda missa* (1521) (WA 8:457; *LW* 36:198).
359. *Ad Matthaeum Alberum . . . de coena dominica epistola* (1524) (*CR* 90:336), paraphrased.
360. *Grund und ursach* (1524), C1–C3, paraphrased.
361. *Antwurt . . . auf bruder Conradts . . . vermanung* (1524).
362. The reference has not been identified.
363. The reference has not been identified.
364. The reference to the works of Konrad Sam is uncertain.
365. *Acta und geschicht* (1523) (*CR* 89:790–91), paraphrased.
366. *Contra Henricum* (1522) (WA 10/2: 201), paraphrased.
367. The reference has not been identified.
368. *De abroganda missa* (1521) (WA 8:454; *LW* 36:194).
369. *De captivitate Babylonica* (1520) (WA 6:553; *LW* 36:95–96).
370. *De votis monasticis, iudicium* (1521) (WA 8:654; *LW* 44:376); *Vom ehelichen Leben* (1522) (WA 10/2: 304; *LW* 45:49).
371. *De captivitate Babylonica* (1520) (WA 6:554–55; *LW* 36:98), paraphrased.

brother or anyone, can give himself a dispensation when it comes to the impediments decreed by the church. Zwingli.[372]

283. [284] It is lawful to marry the daughter of one's sister or to marry a niece. In the same way, children of two brothers or sisters may marry. Or a man may marry his wife's sister or someone connected by marriage. Indeed, no spiritual relationship impedes marriage. Luther.[373] Zwingli.[374]

284. [285] Marriages contractually arranged by parents against the will of the children are invalid. So the chapter[375] "On Clandestine Engagements" is from Satan. Luther.[376]

285. [286] If those entering into marriage have not reached age nineteen, the marriage is invalid. The Consistory of Zurich.[377]

286. [287] If anyone violates a virgin, he is not obligated to give her any more than a pair of shoes. A new law in Zurich that has fallen from heaven.[378]

Divorce

287. [288] When a man is impotent, the wife may seek a divorce. But if he is unwilling, then with the husband's consent, she may have intercourse with someone else or with her brother-in-law by a secret marriage. And let the offspring be considered those of the first man [who is to be] taken as the father. And the woman is saved, in a state of salvation. Luther.[379]

288. [289] For I prefer bigamy to divorce. Luther.[380] The Lutheran monks have demonstrated this in their lifestyle.

289. [290] If a wife does not obey her husband when he asks for her conjugal duty, let him call in a servant girl. In addition, he can seek a divorce on this account. Luther.[381]

290. [291] Divorce happens not only on account of adultery but also for more serious reasons. Think of a husband under a death sentence, insane, quarrelsome, withdrawing from his wife without her consent, and long absent in conjugal terms. The Zurich policy on marriage.[382] Luther.[383]

372. *Über die gevatterschaft* (1525) (*CR* 90:478–79).

373. *Vom ehelichen Leben* (1522) (*WA* 10/2: 280–81; *LW* 45:23–24), paraphrased.

374. *Über die gevatterschaft* (1525) (*CR* 90:470–72), paraphrased.

375. "Titulus" refers to a section in canon law, in this case *Corpus juris canonicis.* Decretal. Gregor. IX, lib. 4, tit. 3, *De clandestina dispensatione.*

376. *Vom ehelichen Leben* (1522) (*WA* 10/2: 286; *LW* 45:29).

377. *Ordnung und ansehen, wie hynfür in Zürich . . . eeliche sachen gericht sol werden* (1525) (*CR* 91:176–78).

378. *Zürich giengend uß etlich satzungen wider den eebruch* (1526) (*CR* 91:179), paraphrased.

379. *De captivitate Babylonica* (1520) (*WA* 6:558; *LW* 36:103), paraphrased; *Vom ehelichen Leben* (1522) (*WA* 10/2: 278; *LW* 45:19–20), paraphrased.

380. *Vom ehelichen Leben* (1522) (*WA* 10/2: 290–91; *LW* 45:33), paraphrased.

381. *Vom ehelichen Leben* (1522) (*WA* 10/2:291–92; *LW* 45:33), paraphrased.

382. *Ordnung und ansehen, wie hynfür in Zürich . . . eeliche sachen gericht sol werden* (1525) (*CR* 91:187), paraphrased.

383. *Vom ehelichen Leben* (1522) (*WA* 10/2:291–92; *LW* 45:33–34), paraphrased.

291. [292] When a divorce has been declared, the other innocent party is allowed to marry as long as the guilty party suffers no loss [in terms of the rights of inheritance]. Luther.[384] Melanchthon.[385]

292. [293] It is an error to nullify a marriage if one of the couple enters a monastery before the consummation. Luther.[386]

293. [294] Previous betrothals are not broken when a person later has coupled with a second mate. Luther.[387]

Celibacy

294. [295] Ordination does not prevent marriage or nullify a contract, but celibacy has been introduced by the devil. Luther.[388]

295. [296] Paul's words [1 Cor. 7:9] "I absolve" release all priests from celibacy. For there is a true and inseparable marriage between a priest and a woman [with whom he has been living], and such a marriage is approved by God's commands. The godless prohibition of such marriages is pure tyranny. Luther.[389] Zwingli.[390] Zell.[391] Blaurer.[392] Störer.[393]

296. [297] The Nicene Council permits the marriage of priests. Spengler in Nuremberg.[394] Zwingli.[395] Rhegius.[396]

297. [298] In Augustine's time nobody opposed the marriage of priests. Zwingli.[397]

298. [299] A priest or a bishop is allowed to marry—and even for a second, third, or fourth time, and so forth—regardless of whether the woman is a virgin or has been defiled. Luther.[398]

384. *De captivitate Babylonica* (1520) (WA 6:559; *LW* 36:104), paraphrased.

385. *Annotationes in epistolas ad Rhomanos et Corinthios* (1522), O4, paraphrased.

386. *De captivitate Babylonica* (1520) (WA 6:541; *LW* 36:79).

387. *De captivitate Babylonica* (1520) (WA 6:556; *LW* 36:100), paraphrased.

388. *De captivitate Babylonica* (1520) (WA 6:559; *LW* 36:104), paraphrased; *De votis monasticis iudicium* (1521) (WA 8:585; *LW* 44:261–62), paraphrased. Other editions refer as well to Johannes Bugenhagen, *De coniugio episcoporum* (1526), D8–E2, paraphrased.

389. *De captivitate Babylonica* (1520) (WA 6:557; *LW* 36:101–2), paraphrased.

390. *Uslegen und gründ* (1523) (CR 89:263–65).

391. The reference is uncertain.

392. *Antwurt uf Georgen Nüwdorfers fünft jm fürgehalten fragstuck* (1526), a2–a3, paraphrased.

393. Stephen Störer, Swiss reformer, *Von der priester ee disputation* (1523), A3, paraphrased.

394. Lazarus Spengler, lay leader of the Reformation in Nuremberg and Reformation publicist, *Eyn kurtzer außzug auß dem bebstlichen rechten . . .* (1530), B3, paraphrased.

395. *Handlung der versammlung in . . . Zürich* (1523) (CR 88:512).

396. *Ain sermon vom eelichen stand* (1525), b2, paraphrased.

397. *Handlung der versammlung in . . . Zürich* (1523) (CR 88:522), paraphrased.

398. *De digamia episcoporum propositiones* (1528) (WA 26:519–21), paraphrased.

Vows

299. [300] I wish I could persuade everyone either to renounce all vows or to avoid them. Luther.[399] Lambert.[400]

300. [301] If a vow is dispensable, then any brother can make that dispensation for his neighbor, or he could do it for himself. And if a neighbor cannot make that dispensation, then there is no law by which the Pope can do it. Luther.[401] Jonas.[402] Carlstadt.[403] Eberlin.[404]

301. [302] There is no example in the Scriptures of a lifestyle based upon a vow. Luther.[405] Blaurer.[406] Kettenbach.[407] Lambert.[408]

302. [303] Parents have the right to take their children who entered the monastery without the parents' consent out of those monasteries. If the Pope says otherwise, he lies. Luther.[409]

303. [304] Religious vows directly contradict the Gospel of Christ and Baptism, and they battle against faith and the Word of God. Luther.[410] Lambert.[411]

304. [305] To become a monk is to apostasize from the faith, to deny Christ, and to become a Jew. Thus their vows are condemned. Luther.[412]

305. [306] It is impossible for human beings to be continent. But just as it is necessary for a human being to eat and drink, to sleep, and so forth, so it is also necessary to have intercourse. So no man can be without a woman, and no woman can be without a man. Luther.[413]

---

399. *De captivitate Babylonica* (1520) (WA 6:538; *LW* 36:74).

400. Franz Lambert, reformer in Hesse, *Evangelici in minoritarum regulam commentarij* (1523), 5/5–5/7, paraphrased.

401. *De captivitate Babylonica* (1520) (WA 6:541; *LW* 36:79).

402. Justus Jonas, Luther's colleague at the University of Wittenberg, *Adversus Joannem Gabrum . . . Defensio* (1523), F2, paraphrased.

403. *Außlegung des XXX. capitel Numeri* (1522), d4–d6, paraphrased.

404. This reference to the work of Johann Eberlin von Günzburg, a reformer active in southwestern Germany, has not been identified.

405. *De votis monasticis iudicium* (1521) (WA 8:540; *LW* 44:262), paraphrased; *De captivitate Babylonica* (1520) (WA 6:540; *LW* 36:76).

406. *Warhaft verantwortung an aynen ersamen, weysen rat zu Constentz* (1523), 4–6, paraphrased.

407. This reference to the work of Heinrich von Kettenbach, reformer in Ulm, has not been identified.

408. *Evangelici in minoritarum regulam commentarij* (1523), a6–a7, paraphrased.

409. *De abroganda missa* (1521) (WA 8:446; *LW* 36:213); *De votis monasticis iudicium* (1521) (WA 8:627; *LW* 44:333).

410. *Themata de votis* (1521) (WA 8:331); *De votis monasticis iudicium* (1521) (WA 8:578, 591; *LW* 44:253, 273).

411. This reference has not been identified.

412. *De votis monasticis iudicium* (1521) (WA 8:600, 597; *LW* 44:288, 282).

413. *Vom ehelichen Leben* (1522) (WA 10/2: 276; *LW* 45:18); *De votis monasticis iudicium* (1521) (WA 8:632; *LW* 44:337), paraphrased.

306. [307] The state of virginity is lower than the state of marriage. There is no better state on earth. Luther.[414] Had St. Jerome known that marriage would be one of the church's seven sacraments, he would have set virginity aside and would have spoken more reverently about marriage. Certain people.[415]

307. [308] All vows are temporary and changeable. Luther.[416] Lambert.[417]

308. [309] A monk or priest cannot be a Christian. Luther.[418] Zwingli.[419]

309. [310] Rigid disciplines voluntarily assumed by people, like voluntary fasting, are condemned by Paul. Bucer.[420]

310. [311] We rightly think that all monasteries and cathedral churches and similar abominations ought to be completely abolished. Luther to the Duke of Savoy.[421]

311. [312] I advise everyone against entering religious orders unless a person realizes that the works of the members of the orders, no matter how difficult or holy, are in God's eyes no better than the works of farmers working in the fields. Luther.[422]

312. [313] Whatever is promised to people in secular matters is to be done. But in matters of conscience, whatever is promised to God is not to be done. Zwingli.[423]

313. [314] None of the saints became a saint through monasticism. Luther.[424]

Poverty

314. [315] Evangelical poverty is demanded of people by divine right, so vows [to live by this standard] should not be taken. Melanchthon.[425]

315. [316] Establishing a life of begging likewise clashes with the Gospel. Melanchthon.[426] Luther.[427]

---

414. *Vom ehelichen Leben* (1522) (WA 10/2:297–98; *LW* 45:47), paraphrased; *Das siebente Kapitel S. pauli zu den Corinthern* (1523) (WA 12:115–17; *LW* 28:11).

415. Gussmann identifies this as a citation from Desiderius Erasmus of Rotterdam, *Supputatio errorum in censuris Beddae,* 1527, *Desiderii Erasmi Roterodami Opera omnia* (Louvain, 1706), 9:589.

416. *De votis monasticis iudicium* (1521) (WA 8:649; *LW* 44:369).

417. This reference has not been identified.

418. *Sermon von der Tröstung des heiligen Geistes in der Verfolgung* (1522) (WA 10/3: 152).

419. This reference has not been identified.

420. *Disputatio Bern.* (1528), 88, paraphrased.

421. *Ein christlicher Sendbrief an Herzog Karl von Savoyen* (1523) (WA *Br* 3:151).

422. *De captivitate Babylonica* (1520) (WA 6:541; *LW* 36:78).

423. *Disputatio Bern.* (1528), 230, paraphrased.

424. *De votis monasticis iudicium* (1521) (WA 8:602; *LW* 44:291), paraphrased.

425. *Loci communes rerum theologicarum* (1521) (*CR* 21:127), Loci, 151, paraphrased.

426. *Annotationes in epistolas ad Rhomanos et Corinthios* (1522), V3.

427. *Großer Sermon von dem Wucher* (1520) (WA 6:41–42), paraphrased.

316. [317] Monasticism is of the devil. Zwingli.[428]

317. [318] Oh, that all monks and nuns would flee from the monasteries, and that monasteries, wherever they are in the world, would shut down. Luther.[429]

318. [319] All Carthusians, all monks and nuns, stray from that which has been ordained and from the freedom God grants when they suppose they are polluted by eating meat. Luther.[430] Lambert.[431]

319. [320] Take a look at the endless crowd of priests and monks with their masses, sacrifices, laws, doctrines, and all their works, and you will see nothing but a theater of Satan—godless people of perdition, reserved for the wrath of God in eternity. Luther.[432]

320. [321] Ecclesiastical ceremonies always obscure the freedom and the power of the Gospel, so it is proper to transgress them. Melanchthon.[433] The preachers of Nuremberg.[434]

321. [322] They are all human inventions—unctions, tonsures, ceremonial vestments, and the blessings of water, salt, palms, candles, herbs, consecrations of churches, altars, vases, and people, and so forth. Zwingli.[435] Lambert.[436] Bucer.[437] The preachers of Nuremberg.[438]

On Purgatory

322. [323] There is no purgatory after this life. Zwingli.[439] Osiander.[440] Oecolampadius.[441] Capito.[442] Bucer.[443] Lambert.[444] Rhegius.[445] Rottenacker.[446]

---

428. *Acta oder geschicht* (1523) (*CR* 89:739), paraphrased. Some editions refer also to Franz Lambert, *Evangelici in minoritarum regulam commentarij* (1523), b7, paraphrased.

429. *Acht Sermon* (1522) (WA 10/3: 23; *LW* 51:80).

430. *Acht Sermon* (1522) (WA 10/3: 25, 26; *LW* 51:81).

431. *Evangelici in minoritarum regulam commentarij* (1523), c2–c4, b6–b8, paraphrased.

432. *De abroganda missa* (1521) (WA 8:425; *LW* 36:153–54).

433. *In epistolas Pauli ad Rhomanos et Corinthios* (1522), L3.

434. *Handlung eynes ersamen weysen rats zu Nürnberg* (1525), C1–C2, paraphrased.

435. *Uslegen und gründ* (1523) (art. 26, *CR* 89:249–51), paraphrased. Other editions also mention Luther, *De captivitate Babylonica* (1520) (WA 6:561; *LW* 36:108), paraphrased; Melanchthon, *Loci communes rerum theologicarum* (1521) (*CR* 21:129), paraphrased; Loci, 61, and others.

436. This reference has not been identified.

437. This reference has not been identified.

438. This reference has not been identified.

439. *Uslegen und gründ* (1523) (art. 57, *CR* 89:414–16), paraphrased; *De vera et falsa religione* (1525) (*CR* 90:855–57), *Commentary*, 283–85.

440. *Wider Caspar Schatzgeyer . . . unchristlichs schreyben* (1525), F3, paraphrased.

441. *In epistolam Joannis apostoli catholicam primam . . . demegoriae* (1524), 94.

442. *Antwurt . . . auf bruder Conradts . . . vermanung* (1524), H3–H5, paraphrased.

443. This reference has not been identified.

444. This reference has not been identified.

445. *Materia cogitandi* (1528), paraphrased.

446. This reference to the work of Konrad Sam has not been identified.

323. [324] It would be safer to deny purgatory completely than to believe Gregory in the *Dialogs*.[447] Luther.[448]

324. [325] This is the downfall of anniversaries, vigils for the dead, depositions, the seventh, the thirtieth, fraternities, oblations, and other human fictions. Zwingli.[449] Chanting, organs, candles, ornaments, vestments, and chrism are falling into disuse. Luther.[450] Lambert.[451] Balthasar.[452]

325. [326] We have no command to pray for the dead. Therefore, you may pray once or twice for someone who has died, but after that you should stop lest you tempt God or fail to put your trust in him. Luther.[453]

326. [327] In addition, it is a matter of death and the devil that perpetual masses are founded on this, and repeated again every single year as if God had not heard them previously. God is mocked by this unbelief, and this sort of prayer is pure unbelief. Luther.[454]

327. [328] The office for the dead does as much for dead Christians as it does for dead cattle. The wretched priors of Nuremberg.[455]

328. [329] No Christians get themselves involved in masses and prayers for the dead unless they want to deny Christ, reject Baptism, and go against the entire Bible. The priors of Nuremberg.[456]

329. [330] If in your house you have a spirit who, when conjured up, seeks help through masses and prayers, then what you have most certainly comes from the devil. For since the beginning of the world, no [dead] soul has appeared [to the living]. God does not permit that. Luther.[457]

[Against Images][458]

330. [331] No images should be kept in church, but instead they should be destroyed and burned. Indeed, they should not be kept either in public or in private. They should not be painted or sculpted, for they are relics of the old idolatry and are against the second commandment of the Decalog [You shall

---

447. Pope Gregory I (ca. 540–604), a reference to his *Dialogi*, IV, 40, MPL 87:396–97. This passage served as important support for the medieval doctrine of purgatory.

448. *De abroganda missa* (1521) (WA 8:452).

449. *Uslegen und gründ* (1523) (art. 19, *CR* 89:157), paraphrased; *De vera et falsa religione* (1525) (*CR* 90:584), *Commentary*, 283–85, paraphrased.

450. *Ad librum Ambrosii Catharini responsio* (1521) (WA 7:734).

451. This reference has not been identified.

452. This reference has not been identified. It may refer to Balthasar Hubmaier.

453. *Sermon auf das Evangelium Luc. 16* (1523) (WA 12:596).

454. *Sermon auf das Evangelium Luc. 16* (1523) (WA 12:596).

455. *Grundt und ursach . . . wie und warumb . . . die mißpreüch bey der heyligen meß . . . geendert haben* (1524), J1, falsely cited.

456. *Grundt und ursach . . . wie und warumb . . . die mißpreüch bey der heyligen meß . . . geendert haben* (1524), K2.

457. *Sermon auf das Evangelium Luc. 16* (1523) (WA 12:597), paraphrased.

458. This topic title is not found in the edition used here but is present in other editions.

not make yourself a graven image, Exod. 20:4]. Zwingli.[459] Bucer.[460] Haller.[461] Carlstadt.[462]

[On Free Choice][463]

331. [332] This term "free will" came from Satan's teaching for seducing people away from God's way. In fact, this is a mere fantasy because the will contributes nothing toward its willing, and it is wrong [to say] that it is active in good works. Luther.[464] Carlstadt.[465] Rhegius.[466]

[Against Obedience and Princes][467]

332. [333] The designation "brother" does not permit a person to be superior to someone else, or to have any more legal or hereditary standing than anyone else, especially in spiritual matters. Luther.[468]

333. [334] We Christians are free, exempt from all the laws of all people, set free through Baptism. Luther.[469]

334. [335] No laws can be imposed on Christians by any legal right—whether by other human beings or by angels—unless the Christians desire them. Luther.[470]

335. [336] Subjects neither can nor will nor ought to bear your tyranny any longer. Luther to the princes.[471]

336. [337] The emperor and princes are involved in manifest lies, and they promulgate contradictory commands. Luther.[472]

337. [338] It is either the chief or the greatest sign of the Antichrist and most fallacious to say that the Pope has transferred the empire from the Greeks to the Germans. Luther.[473]

---

459. *Uslegen und gründ* (1523) (art. 21, *CR* 89:222–24), paraphrased.

460. *Grund und ursach* (1524), O2–O4.

461. *Die schlussreden, über welche Franciscus Kolb und Bertold Haller uf dem synodo zuo Bern Anno 1528 antwort und bericht geben*, (n.d.), A2, paraphrased.

462. *Von abthuhung der bilder* (1522), A2–A4.

463. This topic title is not found in the edition used here but is present in other editions.

464. *Assertio omnium articulorum* (1520) (art. 36, *WA* 7:145).

465. *Epistola adversus ineptam et ridiculam inventionem Eckij* (1519), A3–A4.

466. *Nova doctrinae collatio* (1526), paraphrased.

467. This topic title is not found in the edition used here but is present in other editions.

468. *De instituendis ministris* (1523) (*WA* 12:189; *LW* 40:33).

469. *De captivitate Babylonica* (1520) (*WA* 6:536; *LW* 36:72), paraphrased.

470. *De captivitate Babylonica* (1520) (*WA* 6:537; *LW* 36:72).

471. *Ermahnung zum Frieden auf die zwölf Artikel der Bauerschaft* (1525) (*WA* 18:294; *LW* 46:19–21).

472. *Zwei kaiserliche uneinige und widerwärtige Gebote* (1524) (*WA* 15:254).

473. *Ad librum Ambrosii Catharini responsio* (1521) (*WA* 7:748).

338. [339] I am sorry that I submitted to the emperor at Worms when he gave my teaching a hearing, since nothing really helps with tyrants. Luther.[474]

339. [340] There is no more noble secular law than that of the Turk, who has no canon or civil law. Luther.[475]

340. [341] The secular princes are foolish, and following their foolish brains they want to send the Holy Spirit to school and give him orders. And if the emperor were to command something, they want to look as though they were conscientiously carrying out what he had ordered. Luther.[476]

341. [342] The madness of the foolish is aimed at extinguishing faith because they want to force people to believe. Luther.[477]

[Seditious Expressions][478]

342. [343] God has handed princes over to the depravity of their minds, and he wants to put an end to them just as he wants to finish off the monasteries. Luther.[479]

343. [344] Secular rule lies at just as low a level as that of ecclesiastical tyrants, so the one will not perish without the other. Luther.[480]

344. [345] When princes ban Luther's [translation of the] New Testament, they act like Christ's murderers, such as Herod. They are acting like tyrants when they do that, as is the manner of the princes of this world. That is necessary so that they can live up to their titles. Luther.[481]

345. [346] Since the beginning of the world, a wise prince is the rarest of birds. For in general, they are either the biggest fools or the sorriest wretches. In fact, they are God's special agents and torturers. Luther.[482]

346. [347] The common folk have now become wise and prudent. And a powerful shock from the people and the common folk is close at hand for the, princes. I am afraid it cannot be stopped. Luther.[483]

347. [348] The Turk is ten times more wise and just than our princes. So how then could such fools succeed against the Turk? Luther.[484]

---

474. *Antwort deutsch auf König Heinrichs Buch* (1522) (10/2: 233), paraphrased.

475. *An den christlichen Adel* (1520) (point 25, WA 6:459; *LW* 44:203); Luther's citation of a common proverbial expression.

476. *Von weltlicher Oberkeit* (1523) (WA 11:246; *LW* 45:83-84), paraphrased. In some editions, Eck gives this work the title "Against Secular Authority" instead of its title "On Secular Authority."

477. *Von weltlicher Oberkeit* (1523) (WA 11:247; *LW* 45:84), paraphrased.

478. This topic title is not found in the edition used here but is present in other editions.

479. *Von weltlicher Oberkeit* (1523) (WA 11:265; *LW* 45:109), paraphrased.

480. *Von weltlicher Oberkeit* (1523) (WA 11:265; *LW* 45:109).

481. *Von weltlicher Oberkeit* (1523) (WA 11:267; *LW* 45:112), paraphrased.

482. *Von weltlicher Oberkeit* (1523) (WA 11:267, 268; *LW* 45:113), paraphrased.

483. *Von weltlicher Oberkeit* (1523) (WA 11:270; *LW* 45:116).

484. *Zwei kaiserliche uneinige und widerwärtige Gebote* (1524) (WA 15:277–78).

348. [349] In the halls of princes, the devil resides in the highest spot, and he has his throne there. Luther.[485]

[On the King of France][486]

349. [350] The kingdom of France is impiously called "most Christian" because of its ungodly service—the shedding of blood—to the Antichrist. Luther.[487] He has also treated the most noble king of England with the greatest insults, injuries, and reproaches.

[On Nobles][488]

350. [351] Highway robbery, this sin, is now an honor and an emblem of the nobility. Luther.[489]

351. [352] If the peasants prevail, then the devil is abbot. If the princes win out, his teacher[490] is an abbess. Luther.[491]

[On the Pope][492]

352. [353] The reign of the Pope is pure tyranny, the reign of the Antichrist with his guises. Luther.[493] Indeed, the Pope is the Antichrist himself, the son of perdition. Lambert.[494]

353. [354] The title "Pope" is recent. It was heard neither in the time of Nicholas nor in the time of Augustine. Zwingli.[495]

[Against the Clergy][496]

354. [355] Bishops ought to be serious men—married, laymen, advanced in years. Luther[497] and all the others.

355. [356] A bishop is not allowed to do anything else but to teach the Word of God. To preach the Gospel thus properly belongs to a bishop, so that it is not

---

485. *Auf des Königs zu England Lästerschrift* (1522) (WA 23:31–32).
486. This topic title is not found in the edition used here but is present in other editions.
487. *Ein christlicher Sendbrief an Herzog Karl von Savoyen* (1523) (WA *Br* 3:153).
488. This topic title is not found in the edition used here but is present in other editions.
489. *Decem praecepta* (1518) (WA 1:501).
490. Other editions read "mother."
491. *Ein Sendbrief von dem harten Büchlein wider die Bauern* (1525) (WA 18:401; LW 46:84).
492. This topic title is not found in the edition used here but is present in other editions.
493. *De captivitate Babylonica* (1520) (WA 6:537; LW 36:72).
494. This reference has not been identified.
495. *De canone missae epichiresis* (1523) (*CR* 89:573), paraphrased.
496. This topic title is not found in the edition used here but is present in other editions.
497. Eck attributes the passage to *De captivitate Babylonica,* but no similar passage can be found in that work; perhaps he was thinking of WA 6:557; LW 36:101–2. Luther did write something

permitted to substitute another man in the bishop's place to teach for him. So if he does not teach, he is not a bishop. Melanchthon.[498]

356. [357] There is to be no ecclesiastical [exercise of secular] authority over people. Bucer.[499] Therefore, bishops have wrongly usurped for themselves the jurisdiction that should be due secular princes. Luther.[500] Rhegius.[501] Zwingli.[502] Blaurer.[503]

357. [358] Ecclesiastical power is not from God. Luther.[504]

358. [359] Christ subjected himself and the church to secular authority. Haller.[505] This ruined the immunity of churches and the freedom of the clergy. Luther.[506]

359. [360] The civil power, not the ecclesiastical, has the right to make laws and statutes. Melanchthon.[507]

360. [361] To impose law on Christians is to tempt God. Zwingli.[508]

Statutes

361. [362] Therefore the statutes of the church do not obligate the conscience, nor do the ordinances of the apostles. Bucer.[509]

362. [363] Therefore we are not obligated to celebrate the feast days of saints, to fast in Lent, and to abstain from meat on six feast days, or to hold to other human precepts. Luther.[510] Osiander.[511] Rhegius.[512] Zwingli.[513]

363. [364] No prelate is able to excommunicate anyone, but rather, only the church can. Zwingli.[514] Haller.[515]

---

similar in *Wider den falsch genannten geistlichen Stand des Papstes und der Bischöfe* (1522) (WA 10/2: 112–14).

498. *Loci communes rerum theologicarum* (1521) (*CR* 21:224), Loci, 65, paraphrased.

499. *Disputatio Bern.* (1528), 12, paraphrased.

500. *Wider den falsch genannten geistlichen Stand des Papstes und der Bischöfe* (1522) (WA 10/2:110–12).

501. *Symon Hessus zeygt an Doctori Martino Luther ursach, warumb die Lutherischen bücher . . . verbrent worden sein* (1521), c1–c3, paraphrased.

502. *Uslegen und gründ* (1523) (art. 34–35, *CR* 89:404–5), paraphrased.

503. *Ermanung an eyn ersamen rath der stat Cönstantz* (1524), A2–A4, paraphrased.

504. *Wider den falsch genannten geistlichen Stand des Papstes und der Bischöfe* (1522) (WA 10/2: 110), paraphrased.

505. *Disputatio Bern.* (1528), 14.

506. *Ad librum Ambrosii Catharini responsio* (1521) (WA 7:752), paraphrased.

507. *In epistolas Pauli ad Rhomanos et Corinthios* (1522), L2.

508. *Uslegen und gründ* (1523) (art. 16, *CR* 89:93–94), paraphrased.

509. *Disputatio Bern.* (1528), 79.

510. *An den christlichen Adel* (1520) (points 18–19, WA 6:445–47; *LW* 44:182–83), paraphrased.

511. *Ain gut unterricht und getrewer ratschlag . . .* (1525), H3–H4, paraphrased.

512. *Materia cogitandi* (1528), paraphrased.

513. *Uslegen und gründ* (1523) (*CR* 89:247–48), paraphrased.

514. *Disputatio Bern.* (1528), 24, paraphrased.

515. *Disputatio Bern.* (1528), 21, paraphrased.

364. [365] We allow that the world has been miserably seduced by popes, by councils, by decrees of the fathers, by these traditions, or, more rightly put, by these snares of the devil. Luther.[516]

365. [366] No pope, no bishop, and no other person has the right to set a single syllable over any other human being. Luther.[517]

On Councils

366. [367] No human laws or constitutions bind an individual after that person has been justified. Melanchthon.[518]

367. [368] It was wrongly decided in council that essence does not generate nor is it generated. Likewise [it was wrongly decided] that the intellectual soul is the substantial form of a human being. Luther.[519]

368. [369] Statute C on the destruction of the heretics is clearly heretical. Melanchthon.[520]

369. [370] I declare that all the articles of Hus at Constance were thoroughly Christian, and they were condemned by the Antichrist and his disciples in the synagogue of Satan, gathered by the most wicked sophists. Luther.[521]

Listen to this, Holy Emperor: the perverter of the most holy and free Council of Constance now is appealing to a future council.[522]

370. [371] Hus and Jerome [of Prague] were burned contrary to the public promise [of safe conduct] given to them because it was decided in the council that a safe conduct is not there for protecting heretics. This is how our Germans have learned from the Romans to breech faith and break promises. Capito.[523]

371. [372] In the past, the princes of Germany were held in highest regard for their fidelity. However, in homage to the idol of Rome, they have learned to despise nothing more than fidelity, to the perpetual shame of the nation. Luther.[524]

372. [373] When called to Worms, I went even though I knew that the public assurance [of safe conduct] had been violated by the emperor. Luther.[525]

373. [374] In those things that are tied to faith, any Christian is pope and church to himself. Luther.[526]

516. *Ein christlicher Sendbrief an Herzog Karl von Savoyen* (1523) (WA Br 3:151).

517. *De captivitate Babylonica* (1520) (WA 6:536; LW 36:70).

518. *In epistolas Pauli ad Rhomanos et Corinthios* (1522), L2, paraphrased.

519. *De captivitate Babylonica* (1520) (WA 6:509; LW 36:31).

520. *Loci communes rerum theologicarum* (1521) (CR 21:133), Loci, 65. This refers to the statute of the Council of Verona, 1184, aimed at the elimination of the Waldensian movement.

521. *Assertio omnium articulorum* (1520) (art. 30, WA 7:135).

522. This is not a separate thesis but Eck's address to Emperor Charles V, inserted as a separate remark after the last item.

523. *Antwurt ... auf bruder Conradts ... vermanung* (1524), C4–C6, paraphrased.

524. *Contra Henricum* (1522) (WA 10/2: 180).

525. *Contra Henricum* (1522) (WA 10/2: 201), paraphrased.

526. *Operationes in psalmos* (1519) (WA 5:407).

374. [375] Every Christian is allowed to judge all doctrine because we are not bound to believe councils and the Pope. Luther.[527] Blaurer.[528]

[Seditious Expressions][529]

375. [376] It would really be laughable if sedition were to arise against bishops and their rule. For those who risk their resources and themselves for this cause are children of God, true Christians. And in a short time it is hoped things will develop so there may be no bishop, no prince under the sun, no cathedral, no monastery, and so forth. Luther.[530]

376. [377] Nothing is to be accepted unless it is expressed in the Holy Scriptures. Zwingli.[531] Bucer.[532] Blaurer.[533]

377. [378] I will not let you say that Sacred Scripture has more than one literal level of meaning. Zwingli.[534] Luther.[535] For Scripture will not allow multiple levels of meanings: literal, allegorical, and so forth.

378. [379] The literal understanding of the creation of the world in Genesis 1 is hypocrisy and carnal opinion regarding the way things are. Melanchthon.[536]

379. [380] The Book of Revelation was not from the evangelist John. The books of Baruch, Maccabees, and so forth are not to be accepted either. Luther.[537] Zwingli.[538]

[Against Laws][539]

380. [381] It is impossible for the Gospel to share authority with canon law. Luther.[540]

381. [382] I know that there is no government that may be profitably administered by laws. Luther.[541]

---

527. *Predigt am 8. Sonntage nach Trinitatis* (1522) (WA 10/3: 258–59), paraphrased.

528. This reference has not been identified.

529. This topic title is not found in the edition used here but is present in other editions.

530. *Wider den falsch genannten geistlichen Stand des Papstes und der Bischöfe* (1522) (WA 10/2: 111 and 140), paraphrased.

531. *Uslegen und gründ* (1523) (art. 5, CR 89:32–34), paraphrased; *Von klarheit und gewüsse* (1522) (CR 88:339–41), LCC 24, 60.

532. This reference has not been identified.

533. *Ermanung an eyn ersamen rath der stat Cönstantz* (1524), A1, paraphrased.

534. *Uslegen und gründ* (1523) (CR 89:398–99), paraphrased.

535. *Ad librum Ambrosii Catharini responsio* (1521) (WA 7:710), paraphrased.

536. *In obscuriora aliquot capita Geneseos annotationes* (1523), A7.

537. *De captivitate Babylonica* (1520) (WA 6:500; *LW* 36:16); preface to Revelation (1522) (WADB 2:202–4), paraphrased.

538. *Disputatio Bern.* (1528), 204, 203, paraphrased.

539. This topic title is not found in the edition used here but is present in other editions.

540. *De abroganda missa* (1521) (WA 8:459; *LW* 36:202).

541. *De captivitate Babylonica* (1520) (WA 6:554; *LW* 36:98).

382. [383] It is impossible to hold to both the Gospel and human laws at the same time. So it is impossible to keep the peace while upholding the laws at the same time. Luther.[542]

383. [384] There is no hope of a remedy unless we wipe out all human laws once and for all and then judge and rule everything according to the Gospel. Luther.[543]

[Whether to Take an Oath][544]

384. [385] There should be no taking of oaths in regard to temporal matters. For the person who demands an oath from another or who finds it necessary to take an oath must be a malicious spirit or frivolous, having no reverence for the truth. Melanchthon.[545]

385. [386] Christians are not allowed to swear an oath for any reason. Anabaptists.[546] For it is both wrong and contrary to Sacred Scripture to make demands on another person's good faith. Luther.[547]

386. [387] All those who contend in court for goods or for reputation are heathen. Luther.[548]

[Making War][549]

387. [388] If something is wrested from us, we ought not seek its return through judicial proceedings or war. Luther.[550]

388.[551] It is a diabolical doctrine that Christians may wage war. For all who go to war are the accursed children of Cain. Oecolampadius.[552]

---

542. *In epistolam Pauli ad Galatas commentarius* (1519) (WA 2:594; *LW* 27:375–76).

543. *De captivitate Babylonica* (1520) (WA 6:588; *LW* 36:107).

544. This topic title is not found in the edition used here but is present in other editions.

545. *In evangelium Matthaei annotationes* (1523), 17, paraphrased.

546. The Anabaptist doctrinal articles of Schleitheim, *Brüderlich vereynigung etzlicher Kinder Gottes, sieben Artikel betreffend*, composed 1527, published 1533, contained this teaching; see the translation of John C. Wenger, "The Schleitheim Confession of Faith of 1527," *Mennonite Quarterly Review* 19 (1945): 243–53, 251–52, on oaths.

547. *Von Kaufshandlung und Wucher* (1524) (WA 15:298–300).

548. *Von weltlicher Oberkeit* (1523) (WA 11:260; *LW* 45:102), paraphrased.

549. This topic title is not found in the edition used here but is present in other editions.

550. *Von weltlicher Oberkeit* (1523) (WA 11:249–50; *LW* 45:89), paraphrased; *Predigt am 4. Sonntag nach Trinitatis* (1522) (WA 10/3: 227).

551. The original is unnumbered.

552. *In epistolam Joannis apostoli catholicam primam . . . demegoriae* (1524), 57, paraphrased.

[Buying][553]

389. To buy and sell is a purely pagan thing. Luther.[554]

390. Even for such godly things as churches, benefices, and so forth, contractual agreements for buying or selling are usurious. Strauss.[555] Or they are at least unjust. Luther.[556]

[Holding Things in Common][557]

391. Holding all things in common is commanded in the New Testament. Melanchthon.[558]

392. Altars are to be done away with in the New Testament because that is precisely the place where Christ is crucified, dissected, buried, and eaten with the teeth. But instead a table is good enough for the Lord's Supper. Balthasar [Hubmaier].[559] Glait.[560]

393. No one should be concerned about being buried in a cemetery or consecrated place because it is certain that every place that is blessed by a human being is cursed by God. Glait.[561]

394. Evil spirits along with the damned will have a second chance to be saved. Johannes Denck.[562]

395. Those blaspheme who say that Turks and heretics should not be attacked with the Word of God, of which they know nothing. Rather, those who attack them with war and worldly violence or with a blast of censures are insane. Luther.[563]

396. Christ's word says that many false prophets would arise and seduce many people. I surely think this applies to the universities of this society. Melanchthon.[564]

397. The teachings of all schools, whether speculative or practical, are condemned. Luther.[565]

---

553. This topic title is not found in the edition used here but is present in other editions.

554. *Predigt am 4. Sonntag nach Trinitatis* (1522) (WA 10/3: 227).

555. *Haubstuck und artickel christenlicher leer* (1523), B2–B3, paraphrased.

556. This reference has not been identified.

557. This topic title is not found in the edition used here but is present in other editions.

558. *In epistolas Pauli ad Rhomanos et Corinthios* (1522), V4, paraphrased.

559. *Ein ainfeltiger underricht* (1526), C2–C4.

560. *Handlung . . . in siben artickel beschlossen* (1526), a4, paraphrased.

561. *Entschuldigung . . . Etlicher artickel verklerung* (1527), D2, paraphrased; *Handlung . . . in siben artickel beschlossen* (1526), a6, paraphrased.

562. The south German Anabaptist preacher, Hans Denk, *Wer die warhait warlich lieb hat, mag sich hierinn brüfen im erkandtnuß seynes glaubens,* n.d., A4–A6, paraphrased.

563. *Resolutiones disputationum de indulgentiarum virtute* (1517) (conc. 80, WA 1:624–25; *LW* 31:91–92), paraphrased.

564. *In evangelium Matthaei annotationes* (1523), 42.

565. *De votis monasticis iudicium* (1521) (WA 8:608; *LW* 44:300).

398. All moral virtues and speculative knowledge are not true virtues and knowledge but are sins and errors. Luther.[566]

399. I doubt whether the Creed was produced in writing by the apostles, although I do not doubt it was done by apostolic men. And yet I am enough in doubt that I wish it could be proved. Unless I am mistaken, Augustine did not believe this either. Rather, this was a mistaken formulation from the common people, not from impious opinion. Previously [this author commented that] that good man Augustine erred and was exceedingly gullible in his Christian simplicity. Another author.[567]

400. Pilate was not free to release Christ since he was compelled to use his power to serve the fury of the Jews. In the same way, it is a trivial matter to say, as Bede alleges about the humility of Mary, that Mary thereby deserved to become the mother of God. Another author.[568]

401. It is not clear to me whether it was clearly revealed to the Virgin Mary at the time of Christ's infancy that he was God and man. If Mary and Joseph had known that the boy Jesus was God and man and would not suffer anything except what was necessary, then why were they fearful and filled with anxiety [Luke 2:48], and so forth? Another author.[569]

402. Jesus did not want his death to be mournful but glorious, not deplored but adored. For he was to be applauded for the victory. Another author.[570]

403. It is proper and in keeping with God's Word that rebellion and tumult be stirred up. Hence I have no better proof that my teaching is from God than that it arouses discord, dissent, and tumult. Luther.[571] So it is that many of them have often said publicly to the common folk, "The gospel demands blood." Zwingli[572] and others.

404. There ought to be no ranking one person higher than another among Christians, no courts, nothing walled off or closed up, nothing mine, nothing yours, no cliques and no excommunication. And they want this frequently to be [the case]. Anabaptists.[573]

566. *Decem praecepta* (1518) (WA 1:427).

567. Other editions identify Erasmus, here cited from his opponent, Noel Beda, *Annotationes* (1526), 236–37, a paraphrase of Erasmus's *Suppputatio errorum* (1527), *Opera omnia*, 9:554–56.

568. Other editions identify Erasmus, here cited from his opponent, Noel Beda, *Annotationes* (1526), 264–65, reproducing Erasmus's *Paraphrasis in Joannis evangelium*, *Opera omnia*, 7:637.

569. Other editions identify Erasmus, *Suppputatio errorum* (1527), *Opera omnia*, 9:607.

570. Other editions identify Erasmus, here cited from his opponent, Noel Beda, *Annotationes* (1526), 254–55, reproducing Erasmus's *Paraphrasis in evangelium Lucae*, *Opera omnia*, 7:461.

571. *Auf des Bocks zu Leipzig Antwort* (1521) (WA 7:280, 281), paraphrased.

572. *Uslegen und gründ* (1523) (CR 89:321–22), paraphrased.

573. This reference has not been identified.

Who, however, is this Luther [that] I may understand him? For he longs to be heard. [He has said:]

"I was the first one whom God put in this field." "I certainly have never done anything evil." "If I had wanted to proceed impetuously, I would have brought about tremendous bloodshed." "Moreover, I could well have started the game at Worms in such a way that the Emperor himself would not have been safe." "I was also the one to whom God first revealed this so that I might proclaim these words to you." "Yet you have no idea how much work it is to fight with the devil. I know him well and he knows me well. For I indeed have eaten a pinch or two of salt with him,[574] and I would have died because of him already long ago if there had not been confession."[575]

We reject and anathematize all these articles noted above, both those from Luther himself as a man clearly familiar with the devil and those from people who, being infatuated with his errors, have grown progressively deaf. We reject and anathematize them because they are heretical, scandalous, false—either offensive to godly ears and misleading to the simple folk or plainly seditious and disruptive to the public peace. In regard to this I am prepared to give an account in public disputation at the pleasure of the most holy emperor, with God's help and the intercession of the noble Virgin Mary and all the saints.

To God alone be glory.
Eck will publish the day and hour of the disputation
in accord with the choice of the holy emperor.
Printed in Ingolstadt.
1530.

---

574. This expression in German means "to get into a fight with someone."

575. An amalgam of quotations from *Acht Sermon* (1522) (WA 10/3: 8–9, 18–19, 61–62; *LW* 51:72–73, 77, 98).

The Schwabach Articles

Translated by William R. Russell

Introduction

At the imperial diet in Speyer in April 1529, Emperor Charles V insisted that the princely and municipal adherents of Luther's reformation return to papal obedience in compliance with the Edict of Worms of 1521, which had prohibited Lutheran teaching and reform in the Holy Roman Empire. At Speyer, the princes who were following Luther's plans for reform drew up a testimony of their faith, in Latin *protestatio*, which earned them the name *Protestant*.

Soon after the close of the diet, Landgrave Philip of Hesse, in consort with the government of electoral Saxony and several South German cities (above all Ulm, Strassburg, and Nuremberg), began to organize a defensive alliance against the stated intentions of Emperor Charles to suppress their faith. Luther and Melanchthon opposed any princely federation organized to defend their faith if its members could not agree on a common confession of that faith. Elector John of Saxony supported this position, as did the court of Margrave George of Brandenburg-Ansbach. At meetings in Schwabach, in the county of Brandenburg-Ansbach, in October 1529, a set of seventeen articles of faith, which the Wittenberg theologians had drafted in late summer, were presented to representatives of the governments seeking a defensive confederation. Although the issue of confessional unity frustrated efforts at forming such an alliance, the articles did provide a bond between the Brandenburg, Hessian, and Saxon officials, and the articles formed a basis for discussion between Saxon theologians and Swiss theologians at Marburg in early October. As Elector John sought an understanding with Emperor Charles in the spring of 1530, these articles served his emissaries as a description of the doctrinal position of the electoral Saxon church. Melanchthon took them in hand as he prepared the text of the Augsburg Confession a few months later.

This translation is based on the text as found in WA 30/3:81–91. The text is also found in *BSLK*.

The Schwabach Articles

The First Article.

It is firmly and unanimously maintained and taught that there is only one true God, maker of heaven and earth. In the one, true, divine essence, there are three inseparable persons: God the Father, God the Son, God the Holy Spirit. It is maintained and taught that the Son, begotten of the Father from eternity to eternity, is true God, by nature, with the Father. The Holy Spirit, who is from both the Father and the Son, is also from eternity to eternity true God, by nature, with the Father and the Son. All of this may be clearly and authoritatively proved by the Holy Scripture: John 1[:1-4], "In the beginning was the Word, and the Word was with God, and the Word was God . . . all things came into being through him"; Matthew 28[:19], "Go, therefore, and make disciples of all nations, baptizing them in the name of the Father and of the Son and of the Holy Spirit"; and similar passages, especially in the Gospel of St. John.

The Second [Article].

Only the Son of God became a real human being, born of the pure Virgin Mary with complete body and soul.[1] Neither the Father nor the Holy Spirit became human, as the heretics called the Patripassionists, have taught.[2] Also, the Son did not take on the body alone, without the soul, as the Photinians have taught,[3] because he himself quite often speaks about his soul in the Gospel: "My soul is troubled unto death" [Matt. 26:38]. John 1[:14] clearly states that the Son of God became a human being: "And the Word became flesh." In Galatians 3[=4:4], it is written, "But when the fullness of time had come, God sent his Son, born of a woman, born under the law."

The Third [Article].

This same Son of God, true God and human being, Jesus Christ, is a single indivisible person. He suffered for us, was crucified, died, was buried, and on the third day rose from the dead, ascended into heaven, sits at the right hand of God, and is Lord over all creatures, and so forth. Therefore, it should not be believed or taught that only the human Jesus Christ or his humanity suffered for us, because here God and human being are not two persons but one indivisible person. It should be maintained and taught that God and the human being (or the Son of God) has truly suffered for us, as Paul says in Romans 8[:32], "He did not withhold his own Son, but gave him up for all of us." 1 Corinthians 2[:8], "None understood this; for if they had, they would not have crucified the Lord." And there are many similar passages.

---

1. This confession is directed against the heresy of Apollinaris, who taught that Jesus Christ was not a complete human being, but that the divine Logos had been joined to a human body and spirit, replacing the human soul.

2. The modalistic monarchians of the third century taught that God is not three persons but rather plays three external roles as Father, Son, and Holy Spirit. Their opponents labeled them "Patripassionists" because the opponents concluded that they must then teach that the Father was crucified.

3. Photinus (d. 376) was rejected by the ancient church above all because he taught that there is no distinction between the persons of the Father and the Son. This view was also ascribed to his followers.

The Fourth [Article].

Original sin is a real, genuine sin, not just a mistake or a weakness. Rather, this kind of sin condemns all people who stem from Adam and separates them from God eternally—if Jesus Christ had not intervened on our behalf and taken this sin and all sins that result from it upon himself. Through his suffering, he made satisfaction for this original sin and in himself completely removed and destroyed it (as Psalm 50[=51:7] and Romans 5[:6-11] so clearly write about such sin).

The Fifth [Article].

Therefore, because all people are sinners and are subject to sin, death, and the devil, it is impossible by one's own power or good works for a person to do enough to become once again righteous and upright. Certainly one cannot prepare oneself for, or bring about, righteousness. On the contrary, the more a person tries to work it out alone, the worse it becomes for that person. There is, however, only one path to righteousness and redemption from sin and death: that a person, apart from any merit or work, believes in the Son of God, who suffered for us, and so forth, as said above. This faith is our righteousness. God intends to impute righteousness to and regard this faith as our righteousness, uprightness, and holiness. All who have such faith in the Son of God are given the forgiveness of all sins and eternal life. For the sake of the Son of God, they shall be accepted into divine grace and are children in the kingdom of God, and so forth, as St. Paul and St. John in his Gospel teach so richly: Romans 10[:10], "For one believes with the heart and so is justified"; Romans 4[:22], "his faith was reckoned to him as righteousness." John 3[:16b] says, "everyone who believes in him should not perish, but have eternal life."

The Sixth [Article].

Such faith is not a human work nor possible by our power. Rather, it is God's work and gift, which the Holy Spirit gives through Christ and effects in us. This faith is not mere illusion or a presumption of the heart, as the false believers maintain. Rather, faith is a powerful, new, vital essence. It bears much fruit; it always does good toward God (by praising, thanking, praying, preaching, and teaching) and toward the neighbor (by loving, serving, helping, offering counsel, giving, and suffering all kinds of evil until death).

The Seventh [Article].

To obtain such faith or to give it to us human beings, God has instituted the preaching office or spoken Word (that is, the Gospel), through which he has this faith proclaimed, along with its power, benefits, and fruits. God also bestows faith through this Word, as through an instrument, with his Holy Spirit, when and where he wills. Apart from it, there is no other instrument or way, passage or path, to obtain faith. Speculations [about what happens] apart from or previous to the spoken Word, as holy and good as they appear, are nevertheless useless lies and errors.

The Eighth [Article].

With and alongside of this spoken Word, God has also instituted external signs: Baptism and the Eucharist. Through these, alongside the Word, God offers and gives faith and his Spirit and strengthens all who desire him.

The Ninth [Article].

Baptism, the first sign or sacrament, consists of two parts: of the water and the Word of God. When one baptizes with water and speaks God's Word, it is not just mere water or pouring (as the blasphemers of Baptism teach). Rather, because God's Word is with it, and it is founded on this Word, it is a holy, vital, powerful thing. As Paul says in Titus 3[:5] and Ephesians 5[:26]: "the water of rebirth and renewal by the Holy Spirit, etc." In addition, such baptism is extended and conveyed to small children. God's words, on which it rests, are as follows: "Go and baptize in the name of the Father, Son, and Holy Spirit" (Matthew 28[:19]) and "the one who believes and is baptized, will be saved" [Mark 16:16]. This must be believed.

The Tenth [Article].

The Eucharist, or Sacrament of the Altar, also consists of two parts: the true body and blood of Christ are truly present in the bread and the wine, according to the word of Christ: "this is my body, this is my blood" [Matt. 26:26], as even the other side admits. These words foster and produce faith and exercise faith in all who desire this sacrament and do not act contrary to it in that faith, just as Baptism produces and bestows faith when one desires it.

The Eleventh [Article].

Private confession should not be compelled by laws, any more than Baptism, the sacrament, or the Gospel should be compelled. They should be free. Still, we know how very comforting and salutary, beneficial and good it is for afflicted or erring consciences. This is because in it absolution—that is, God's Word and judgment—is spoken. Through this absolution, the conscience is freed from its anxiety and set at peace. Also, it is not necessary to enumerate all sins; one may, however, recount those that sting and disturb the heart.

The Twelfth [Article].

There is no doubt that there remains and is on earth one holy Christian church, until the end of the world. As Christ says in Matthew 28[:20]: "And remember, I am with you always, to the end of the age." This church is nothing other than believers in Christ, those who hold to the articles and parts [of Christian teaching] mentioned above and who believe and teach them and who are persecuted and martyred in the world because of this. For where the Gospel is preached and the sacrament rightly used, there is the holy Christian church. It is not bound by laws and external practices to places and times, to specific persons and observances.

The Thirteenth [Article].

On the last day, our Lord Jesus Christ will come to judge the living and the dead. He will redeem those who believe in him from all evil and bring them into everlasting life. He will rebuke those who do not believe and the godless, and he will condemn them, together with the devil, to eternity in hell.

The Fourteenth [Article].

In the meantime, until the Lord comes in judgment and all political power and lordship are abolished, we should maintain and be obedient to secular author-ity and lordship as a walk of life ordained by God to protect the upright and to curb the evil. A Christian, if properly called to such a walk of life, may well serve or even exercise leadership in it without damage or danger to faith and salva-tion. Romans 13[:1-7] and 1 Peter 2[:13-16].

The Fifteenth [Article].

It follows from all of this that the doctrines prohibiting marriage and ordinary meat and food for priests and clergy, together with all monastic life and vows, are simply condemned doctrines of the devil because they seek and intend [to obtain] grace and salvation through them, and they are not left free, as St. Paul says in 1 Timothy 4[:3]. Of course, Christ alone is the only way to grace and salvation.

The Sixteenth [Article].

Above all, the Mass is to be abolished as an abomination, for it previously was held to be a sacrifice or work by which one person might acquire grace for another. Instead of such a mass, a godly order of service is observed: the holy sacrament of the body and blood of Christ is distributed in both kinds to each person, according to each person's faith and need.

The Seventeenth [Article].

We also abolish the ceremonies of the church which oppose God's Word. We allow the others to be free to be used or not, in accord with love, so that we might not carelessly offend without reason or disturb the general peace unnecessarily.

The Marburg Articles

Translated by William R. Russell

Introduction

Among the most formidable problems facing the German princes engaged in reformation was the public dispute over the Lord's Supper between the Swiss reformers, led by Ulrich Zwingli of Zurich and Johannes Oecolampadius of Basel, on the one hand, and the followers of Martin Luther, on the other. Luther taught that the bread and wine in the Lord's Supper are the body and blood of Jesus Christ, while Zwingli and Oecolampadius held that Christ's body and blood are represented by the bread and wine.

In the weeks following the emergence of the new imperial threat to the Reformation at the Diet of Speyer in April 1529, Landgrave Philip of Hesse took the lead in trying to bring together representatives of the two sides, in hopes that doctrinal agreement might lead to a political alliance between the German "Protestants" and the Swiss Reformed cantons. Therefore he invited representatives of both sides to his castle in Marburg at the beginning of October 1529. There, in the first four days of the month, Zwingli and his colleagues from Zurich, Oecolampadius and one fellow pastor from Basel, and three representatives of the church of Strassburg met with Luther, Melanchthon, and others from Wittenberg along with Andreas Osiander from Nuremberg, Johannes Brenz from Schwäbisch-Hall, and Stephan Agricola from Augsburg. Luther was paired with Oecolampadius, and Melanchthon with Zwingli, in private conversations before the entire group came together. The participating theologians agreed on fourteen articles of faith composed by Luther himself, but an agreement eluded them on the Lord's Supper. Melanchthon used these articles as one of the bases of the Augsburg Confession.

This translation is based on the two manuscripts that were written and signed by both the Evangelical (that is, "German") and Reformed (that is, "Swiss") parties at the conclusion of the colloquy at Marburg in early October 1529. These respective manuscripts were taken by each party and published independently (WA 30/3:160–71). The text is also found in *BSLK*.

The Marburg Articles

The following articles were written at Marburg and subscribed on 3 October 1529.[1]

1. We on both sides believe and maintain[2] unanimously that there is only one true God, who is by nature God and is the maker of all creatures. This same God, who is one in essence and nature, is triune in persons: Father, Son, and Holy Spirit, etc. This is precisely what the Council of Nicea concluded and this is what is sung and recited by the entire Christian church throughout the world in the Nicene Creed.[3]

2. We believe that neither the Father nor the Holy Spirit, but rather the Son of God the Father (who is truly and by nature God), became a human being. He was born of the pure Virgin Mary, through the action of the Holy Spirit (without the seed of a man). He was bodily complete, with body and soul like any other person,[4] without any sin, and so forth.

3. [We believe] that this same Son of God and Son of Mary, the undivided person Jesus Christ, was crucified, died, and was buried for us, rose from the dead, ascended into heaven, is sitting at the right hand of God, is Lord over all creatures, and will return to judge the living and the dead, and so forth.

4. We believe that original sin is born in us and inherited from Adam. It is this sin that brings condemnation upon all people. Indeed, if Jesus Christ had not come to help us through his death and life, we would have had to die eternally on account of it and would not be able to enter into the kingdom of God and be saved.

5. We believe that we are redeemed from this sin and all other sins, along with eternal death, if we believe in this Son of God, Jesus Christ, who died for us, and so forth. Apart from this faith, no works, social standing, or [monastic] order, and so on, would be able to free us from a single sin, etc.

6. [We believe] that this faith is a gift of God which we are unable to earn with any preceding deeds or merit.[5] Nor are we able to manufacture it by our own power. Rather, the Holy Spirit gives and creates this faith in our hearts wherever he wills, when we hear the Gospel or the Word of Christ.

---

1. Luther actually wrote these articles on 4 October 1529, as a summary of the negotiations that had concluded a day earlier.

2. The phrase "we believe and maintain" covers the first fourteen articles, in which the two sides agreed, and is repeated in Article XV, where both agreement and disagreement are noted.

3. In a marginal note on the Swiss manuscript, Zwingli commented that "the Germans sing, we recite [the Creed]," WA 30/3:160.

4. This confession is directed against the heresy of Apollinaris, who taught that Jesus Christ was not a complete human being but that the divine Logos had been joined to a human body and spirit, replacing the human soul.

5. A reference to the scholastic concept of "meritum de congruo," which, for example, in the theological system of Gabriel Biel, sprang from deeds done apart from grace, on the basis of "purely natural powers," which could not merit eternal rewards but that did earn the gift of grace, which in turn enabled the performance of works worthy of salvation.

7. [We believe] that faith such as this is our righteousness before God, for the sake of which God justifies us, imputes us, and regards us as godly and holy apart from all works and merit. Through this faith, God rescues us from sin, death, and hell. By grace, God receives and saves us for the sake of his Son, in whom we believe. Through the righteousness of the Son of God, we enjoy and participate in life and all good things. [Therefore, the entire monastic way of life and vows, when regarded as contributing to righteousness, are completely condemned.][6]

On the External Word[7]

8. [We believe] that the Holy Spirit, properly speaking, gives this faith or his gift to no one apart from preceding[8] preaching, or the spoken Word, or the Gospel of Christ. Rather, the Holy Spirit works and creates faith through and with this spoken Word where and in whom he wills. Romans 10[:14-17].

On Baptism

9. [We believe] that Holy Baptism is a sacrament established by God to create this faith. Moreover, because God's command, "Go baptize" [Matt. 28:19], and God's promise, "the one who believes" [Mark 16:16], are in it, it is not merely an empty symbol or sign among Christians, but a sign and act of God by which our faith is fostered. Through it, we are born again to life.

On Good Works

10. [We believe] that this faith is bestowed through the work of the Holy Spirit, and through it we are regarded as—and become—righteous and holy. This faith effects good works through us: love of neighbor, prayer to God, and endurance in all kinds of persecution.

On Confession

11. [We believe] that Confession or seeking counsel from one's pastor or neighbor is to be done freely and without coercion. It is indeed beneficial to those whose consciences are distressed, afflicted, or burdened with sins, or have fallen into error, above all because of the absolution or comfort of the Gospel, which is what true absolution is.

---

6. The sentence in brackets is an addendum by the Reformed theologians participating in the colloquy. See the translator's note below.

7. Article VIII is the first to be given a title.

8. A play upon the medieval scholastic concept of "preceding" works or merit. Only the Word of God comes before or paves the way for faith.

On Government

12. [We believe] that all government, secular laws, courts, and ordinances, wherever they are, exist as a true, good walk of life. They are not forbidden, as some papists and Anabaptists teach and maintain.[9] [We believe] that a Christian who is called or born into this walk of life can quite well be saved through faith in Christ, etc., just as in the walk of life of a father and mother, husband and wife, and so forth.

13. [We believe] that if what we call tradition (a human ordinance in spiritual or churchly matters) is not contrary to the clear Word of God, then we may freely keep it or lay it aside, so long as, among the people with whom we associate, unnecessary offense is avoided and the weak and the common peace and so forth are served through love. [{We believe} also that the doctrine forbidding the marriage of priests is a doctrine of the devil.][10]

14. [We believe] that it is proper to baptize children. Through Baptism they are brought to God's grace and into Christendom.

On the Sacrament of Christ's Body and Blood

15. Regarding the Supper of our beloved Lord Jesus Christ, we all believe and maintain that we should make use of both kinds, according to the institution of Christ [and that the Mass is not a good work with which a person attains grace for another, whether alive or dead].[11] Also, the Sacrament of the Altar is a sacrament of the true body and blood of Jesus Christ, and the spiritual reception of this body and blood is particularly necessary for every Christian. Similarly, the use of the sacrament, like the Word, is given and ordained by God Almighty so that weak consciences might be moved to faith through the Holy Spirit. Although we have not at this time agreed whether the true body and blood of Christ are bodily in the bread and wine, each side is able to display Christian love to the other (as far as conscience allows). Both sides are praying diligently to Almighty God, that he would confirm us in the right understanding through his Spirit. Amen.

[Translator's note: The following three addenda are contained only at the conclusion of the manuscript copy that was taken to Zurich by the Reformed theologians. The Lutherans signed this manuscript, as well as their own copy of the articles, which did not contain these changes. WA 30/3:170–71.]

---

9. This sentence originally read, "They are not forbidden as the Pope and his party maintain." The change to the present text was made before both sides signed the articles at the conclusion of the colloquy, WA 30/3:167.

10. The sentence in brackets is an addendum by the Reformed theologians participating in the colloquy. See the translator's note below.

11. The sentence in brackets is an addendum by the Reformed theologians participating in the colloquy. See the translator's note below.

Before the title "On the External Word," the following should be inserted: Therefore, the entire monastic way of life and vows, when regarding as contributing to righteousness, are completely condemned.

In the fifteenth article, after the words "we should make use of both kinds, according to the institution of Christ," the following should be inserted: that the Mass is not a good work with which a person attains grace for another, whether alive or dead.

After the thirteenth article, by way of conclusion, the following should be inserted: [We believe] also that the doctrine forbidding the marriage of priests is a doctrine of the devil.

MARTIN LUTHER
JUSTUS JONAS
PHILIP MELANCHTHON
ANDREAS OSIANDER
STEPHAN AGRICOLA
JOHANNES BRENZ
JOHANNES OECOLAMPADIUS
HULDRICH ZWINGLI
MARTIN BUCER
CASPAR HEDIO[12]

JOHANNES OECALAMPADIUS
HULDRICH ZWINGLI
MARTIN BUCER
CASPAR HEDIO
MARTIN LUTHER
JUSTUS JONAS
PHILIP MELANCHTHON
ANDREAS OSIANDER
STEPHAN AGRICOLA
JOHANNES BRENZ[13]

12. The Evangelical manuscript lists the signatures in this order.
13. The Reformed manuscript lists the signatures in this order.

The Torgau Articles

Translated by William R. Russell

Introduction

When Emperor Charles V issued his invitation to the imperial estates to gather in Augsburg in late spring 1530, he demanded from the princely followers of Luther an explanation of why they were instituting changes in their churches. As supporters of the reform movement condemned by the Edict of Worms of 1521, Elector John of Saxony and other Evangelical princes recognized the seriousness of their situation within the empire. Therefore, the elector commissioned his theologians to prepare such a statement soon after he received the call to the imperial diet on 11 March 1530. The Wittenberg professors Martin Luther, Philip Melanchthon, Johann Bugenhagen, and Justus Jonas began working on drafts of their position and their understanding of reform almost immediately.

Since the eighteenth century, scholars have spoken of the "Torgau Articles" in connection with these drafts, but they disagreed on precisely which text or texts should be so designated since the term was not used in the sixteenth century.[1] In his *Urkundenbuch zu der Geschichte des Reichstages zu Augsburg im Jahre 1530,* I (Halle, 1833), Karl Eduard Förstemann presented a fresh interpretation of the documentary evidence surrounding the electoral Saxon deliberations in preparation for the diet at Augsburg, provoking a century and a half of debate over the nature of the documents he presented there and other similar policy drafts. Translated here is his document A (I:68–84, with consideration of that text as edited by Theodor Kolde, *Die Augsburgische Konfession, lateinisch und deutsch* [Gotha, 1896], 128–39), largely coincident with the document designated in the analysis of *BSLK* as the "Torgau Articles." The relationship of this text to that of the later articles of the Augsburg Confession and ways in which it might have been directly used by Melanchthon remain unclear. It does not read like a formal or finished treatise; rather, it reads more like a set of preparatory or preliminary notes. This explains why, at various points, the document includes editorial comments and strategic notes that indicate where and what additional information or argumentation could possibly be added. It is possible that Melanchthon had a more refined draft at hand in Augsburg.

---

1. The editors were guided in their orientation to the "Torgau Articles" and the historiography on the documents that have been given this title by Professor Dr. Gottfried Seebaß of the Evangelical Theological Faculty of the University of Heidelberg. He generously shared his unpublished essay "Die kursächsischen Vorbereitungen auf den Augsburger Reichstag von 1530—Torgauer Artikel?" with us.

The Torgau Articles

[Preface]

Because some people charge My Most Gracious Lord—to be sure unfairly—that his Electoral Grace is abolishing all worship and promotes pagan, unbridled living and disobedience (from which would follow the dissolution of all Christendom), it is necessary that My Most Gracious Lord first make it clear that his Electoral Grace is zealously instituting and promoting proper, true worship, and that he desires whatever is God-pleasing. In addition, for the sake of God's praise and honor, he is enduring danger, expense, and trouble, which he would not do if he did not think he was serving God. For everyone knows how his Electoral Grace conducts his life: that, God be praised, you continually seek peace and until now, in these matters, have often helped to maintain and make peace, etc.

(In this section, it would be good to prepare a long and rhetorical preface.)[2]

Second, this is also obvious and as plain as day: My Most Gracious Lord is very zealously arranging for the holy gospel to be diligently preached and the ceremonies associated with it to be observed in the lands of his Electoral Grace. It must be conceded, even by our opponents, that the doctrine taught, written, and practiced in the lands of his Electoral Grace is Christian and consoling and contains no error, even though this renewal has been undertaken without the permission of a general council. Because our opponents themselves now admit that the doctrine in itself is correct, they should not accuse My Most Gracious Lord of abolishing worship and tolerating unchristian doctrine or practices, and so forth. Rather, his Electoral Grace knows and does not doubt that this is proper, true worship that your Electoral Grace allows in your lands and that this doctrine is Christian, comforting, and salutary for all God-fearing people.

Now the disagreement is primarily about certain abuses, which have been introduced through human doctrines and opinions. We intend to report and demonstrate in an orderly manner for what reasons My Most Gracious Lord has allowed some abuses to be set aside.

[1.] On Human Doctrine and Human Ordinances[3]

First, although worship does not consist of human doctrines, My Gracious Lord has had the customary ecclesiastical ordinances maintained in his electoral lands, as long as they are not contrary to the Gospel. He has also had the peo-

---

2. This editorial note, inserted in Latin, is an indication that the text here translated was regarded as a preliminary draft.

3. This title is written in German, as are the titles to Articles III, V, VII, and X. The titles of Articles II, IV, and IX are written in Latin. The titles of Articles VI and VIII are given in both German and Latin.

ple informed through preaching that such ordinances are to be maintained for the sake of peace. This is public knowledge, and it can be seen that divine services are conducted with greater devotion and earnestness in his Electoral Grace's lands than among his adversaries.

Second, there are many human ordinances which cannot be observed without sin. Accordingly, My Most Gracious Lord wants no one to be compelled by force to observe such practices contrary to God's command, for this reason: the Scriptures say in Acts 4[=5:29]: "We must obey God rather than human authority." The same is also commanded in the *Canons*, Distinction 8: that every custom, however old it might be or however long it has been preserved, should yield to the Scriptures and the truth, etc.[4]

Some people, however, let themselves be told that no change is to be permitted without approval of the church or the Pope and that the sins which arise from the doctrines of human invention are much more tolerable and less hurtful than the schism which has now begun through such changes. Furthermore, these same people say that we, as schismatics, are severed members of the church, that the sacrament is invalid among us, and so forth, as such people like to bellow, and so on.

On account of these accusations, it is necessary to answer: they may applaud obedience as much as they can, but this saying remains sure: "We must obey God rather than human authority" [Acts 5:29]. Furthermore, Galatians [1:8]: "But even if an angel from heaven should proclaim to you a gospel contrary to what I proclaimed to you, let that one be accursed!" From that it clearly follows that those people are not condemned who give up false doctrine and ordinances, but rather those people are condemned openly by St. Paul who hold on to false doctrine and ordinances, etc.

Moreover, the unity of the Christian church does not consist of external human ordinances. Therefore, even if we practice different ordinances than each other, we are not members who are cut off from the church because of this, and the Holy Sacraments are not invalid [among us] because of this.

Differences in external human ordinances are not contrary to the unity of the Christian churches, as this article, which we confess in the creed, clearly proves: "I believe in the Holy Catholic Church." If we are commanded to believe that the church is catholic, then the church is in the whole world and is not bound to a single place. Rather, everywhere, wherever God's Word and ordinances are, there the church is. Since external human ordinances are not the same everywhere, it follows that such variance is not contrary to the unity of the church. Also, Christ says, "My sheep hear my voice. They do not hear another's voice, nor follow it" [John 10:27]. And, "The kingdom of God is not coming with things that can be observed; nor will they say, 'Look, here it is! or There it is!'" [Luke 17:20-21]. And Paul says, "The kingdom of God is not food and drink" [Rom. 14:17].

---

4. *Decretum Gratianum*, pt. 1, dist. 8, chs. 4–6.

As Augustine wrote so clearly to Januarius, the unity of the church does not exist in external human ordinances.[5] And he also said that such human ordinances should be free and may be maintained or not observed.

Also, if it were to be a schism when external ordinances are altered, then it would be fairer to consider as schismatics those who first, contrary to all the ordinances of Christendom and the councils, prohibited marriage, as indeed the Council of Constantinople decreed that the marriage of priests should not be forbidden. Furthermore, they have introduced new ways of worshiping, which are contrary to God's Word. Contrary to the usage and practice of the ancient church, they have sold masses even though the ancient church knew nothing of such selling of masses.

In addition, all the citations from the fathers about schismatics—that the sacraments are not valid among them, and similar things—did not use the term "schismatics" for those who practice different external human ordinances, but rather for those who have strayed from God's Word in some article of faith. As Augustine clearly wrote to Cresconius and Jerome: "They are not schismatic unless they invent some heresy."[6]

We would like to enumerate, however, those human ordinances which may not be observed without sin, because it is necessary to discern the ordinances which are to be regarded as adiaphora. Much that is false has been preached and taught in the past within the church on this subject, for example, that fasting, distinctions in foods and clothing, special festivals, songs, pilgrimages, and similar practices are works through which one can win grace and the forgiveness of sins.

Now that is obviously such a dangerous and damnable error that even many among our adversaries have also had to concede this. They, too, have received comfort through our doctrine, which teaches the opposite: that the forgiveness of sin and grace are truly and certainly given to us through Christ, by grace, and that we receive these things only through faith in Christ, that for Christ's sake and through Christ's merit our sins are forgiven us apart from our merit. Therefore, if it is taught that people receive grace and the forgiveness of sins through the human ordinances mentioned above, then that is certainly an obvious blasphemy and completely contrary to the holy gospel. Paul clearly teaches that if we want to become righteous and win grace through our own work, then Christ has died in vain, Galatians 2[:21] and Romans 3[:28]: "For we hold that a person is justified by faith apart from works prescribed by the law." Also, Ephesians 2[:8, 9] says, "For by grace you have been saved through faith, and this is not your own doing; it is the gift of God—not the result of works." Therefore, those who teach that we receive grace through works of our own choosing (such as prescribed fasts or festivals or similar things) have done a great dishonor to Christ. They have ascribed the praise which belongs to Christ to works of their own choosing. In so doing, they have not given the proper recognition to Christ

---

5. Epistle 54 to Januarius, 2:2 (*MPL* 33:200; *NPNF*, ser. 1., 1:300–3).

6. A paraphrase of Augustine in *Contra Cresconium*, II:6ff.; *MPL* 42:470.

and his grace, but God prefers no higher honor than that we recognize and listen to Christ, as it is written, "This is my son, the beloved; with him I am well-pleased; listen to him!" [Matt. 17:5]. Furthermore, Christ says, "In vain do they worship me, teaching human precepts as doctrines" [Matt. 15:9]. Here it is certainly made clear that God does not regard observing human ecclesiastical ordinances as something that merits the forgiveness of sin.

Furthermore, Christ has forbidden that sin and righteousness be defined with reference to the distinction between foods. He intends that such things be left free. As St. Paul says, "Let no one condemn you because of food and drink" [Col. 2:16]. But now they look upon those who do not maintain distinctions between foods as heretics, even though Paul calls such a distinction the devil's doctrine [1 Tim. 4:1-3].

Therefore, if the correct Christian teaching concerning those ordinances which are regarded as adiaphora is granted, they may certainly be observed. As ordinances were initially made in the church regarding festivals or fasts, they were not intended to obtain grace, but rather that the people could know and learn when they should gather together or might otherwise observe outward practices, so that they might more willingly hear and learn through God's Word. But where such ordinances are required, as if they were necessary for receiving grace, or as if apart from such works no one could be a Christian, then we should oppose such an error both in our teaching and in our example, just as Paul did not want Titus circumcised in order to prove that such a work was not necessary or required to attain grace [Gal. 2:3].

Therefore, My Most Gracious Lord has forced no one to maintain the distinction between foods or prescribed fasts, but rather he has allowed such traditions to be set aside because it is obvious that people regarded them as works performed to receive the forgiveness of sin. So that this error not be reinforced, people ought not be forced to observe these ordinances.

In addition, our adversaries pronounce those who do not observe the distinction of foods heretics, thus making this practice a work without which no one might be a Christian. However, Christ says, "food does not make the person impure" [Matt. 15:11].

Also, the ancient canons demonstrate what is to be held regarding such human ordinances:

Distinction 4: It is forbidden to reinstate fasts which have fallen into disuse. Now, if such ordinances were abandoned through common practice, then it follows that they are not necessary for the Christian life. In this way, the penitential canons have fallen into disuse through common practice, and no one maintains that they sin if they do not observe them.[7] Thus many other ordinances have fallen into disuse as have many ancient canons, which are found in the decretals, for example, to fast on Wednesdays and Fridays. Furthermore, no one has observed all the fasts as they were commanded.

---

7. The reference is to *Decretum Gratianum,* pt. 1, dist. 4, ch. 6.

Also, distinction 12.5 speaks to this: "The Roman church knows that other ordinances of other times and places are not harmful for the salvation of one's soul."[8] Furthermore, Jerome and Augustine also write that one ought not to make a necessity out of such things.

From all of this, it is clear that what is commonly taught about human ordinances in his Majesty's, our Gracious Lord's lands, is without doubt sufficiently grounded in the Scriptures and the fathers.

[2.] On The Marriage of Priests

(These are the ordinances which may not be observed without sin.)

First, to forbid priests to marry is contrary to God. For Paul says, "It is better to marry than to be aflame with passion" [1 Cor. 7:9]. This is God's command, and it may be abolished by no human being. We also know that the church held for a long time, and the councils likewise commanded, that marriage not be forbidden for priests. Furthermore, they have used force to submit the priesthood in Germany to this prohibition—with difficulty. There was even a bishop of Mainz who was almost beaten to death when he proclaimed the papal prohibition.[9] Whatever good comes from it can readily be seen, and it is a matter of concern for those who want to protect marriage, for it will only get worse because the longer the world lasts, the weaker it becomes.

[3.] On Both Kinds [of the Sacrament]

Also the custom of receiving only one kind in the sacrament cannot be observed without sin. Christ commanded, "Drink from it, all of you" [Matt. 26:27]. Thus it is known that for a long time the church had administered both kinds to the laity, as we find in Cyprian and in the canons. Thus they also cannot explain how this practice originated or who prohibited the administration of both kinds.

[4.] On the Mass

Up to now, they have taught that the Mass is a work, through which the one who observes it obtains grace, not only for oneself but also for others—indeed that it acquires grace for others, even though the priest is not upright. On this basis, they have established many masses for the dead and living to obtain all kinds of things: that merchants might succeed in their dealings, that hunters might have success on the hunt, and so forth. Therefore masses are endowed,

---

8. *Decretum Gratianum*, pt. 1, dist. 12, ch. 10.

9. This story is recorded in the Annals of Lambert of Hersefeld, which Melanchthon had had edited in 1525: at a synod at Erfurt in 1075, as he introduced new reform laws from Pope Gregory VII, Archbishop Siegfried of Mainz encountered such strong opposition.

bought and sold, and observed only for the sake of the belly. As a result, many pious people of our time have complained about this.

Some people now want to gloss over their position by saying that the Mass should be observed as a memorial, not to obtain grace for the dead or the living. They may color the matter as they will, but their books and writings are clear; in them we find how they have taught: that the Mass is a sacrifice which merits grace and takes away the sin of the dead and the living.

That this is an error, however, is demonstrable through Paul, who teaches us everywhere that we receive grace and have comfort only through faith in Christ. We believe that God is gracious to us and wants to accept and help us for Christ's sake. Thus the forgiveness of sins must be received through faith. It cannot be merited through the work of a priest on behalf of another. It is a great error that the people are directed away from faith to an external work. Therefore, this faith is to be so emphasized because it is the chief article and essence of the Christian life: that we have true assurance before God for the sake of Christ, and that he shows grace and wants to assist in every need.

Those people who sell masses do not talk about this faith. They boast only in their works. They want to save others with their works, even though Christ has done this once and for all. As Paul writes: "With one sacrifice he has perfected the saints" [Heb. 10:14]. Furthermore, the words in the holy sacrament also teach us its right use: "This is the cup of a New Testament" [Luke 22:10]. Now that which is called the New Testament is not our work; rather, it is the work of God, who offers and bestows something upon us, as one is accustomed to do in the making of a testament. Thus grace and the forgiveness of sin are offered and bestowed. If now this is promised, says Paul, we must receive it by faith [Rom. 4:13-16]. Therefore the Mass is not a work that merits something for another person. Rather, to the person who uses it, grace and the forgiveness of sins are offered. These things people receive as they believe that through Christ they receive such things. The Mass is instituted for the exercise and awakening of faith in those who use it.

It is an obvious abuse, however, that those who conduct the Mass for the sake of their bellies and money do so with no interest in God, for the most part, indeed with contempt for God. Therefore, if there were no other reason than this great, overwhelming abuse, that alone would warrant changing the current practice wherever the Mass is endowed. For Paul says that whoever does not use the sacrament worthily is guilty of the body and blood of Christ [1 Cor. 11:27].

On account of this, My Most Gracious Lord has mass celebrated for the congregation so that other people [in addition to the priest who conducts the mass] who are prepared to use the sacrament may receive it. This is its proper use, for Christ instituted it so that it should be celebrated in the church with others who are prepared to receive it. Paul also teaches the Corinthians that it should be observed in the presence of others and used with others [1 Cor. 11:17-34]. Thus they find in their hearts that they do not dishonor the body and the blood of the Lord. And, in order that the sacrament is not shown any disrespect, the people are often instructed as to why one ought to use it, and they are admonished to use it in this way.

Also, the Zwinglian doctrine has been refuted to the fullest extent possible, as the writings about it which have been published in My Most Gracious Lord's lands demonstrate. The people are diligently taught that in the Lord's Supper the body and blood of Christ are present and that they are given there, that faith is strengthened through it, so that we may receive the comfort that Christ desires to be ours and to help us, etc.

And do not doubt, My Most Gracious Lord, that such a mass is true and Christian worship, especially because there was only this kind of mass up to the time of Jerome and Augustine. It is not known from where the selling of masses comes or when private masses began.

[5.] On Confession

Confession has not been abolished but rather is maintained with such utter seriousness that pastors are commanded not to administer the holy sacrament to anyone who has not previously been examined and has not desired absolution. For absolution is most necessary, and it is comforting because we know that Christ commanded [us] to forgive sins—and that he desires that the word of the priest, through which sin is forgiven, be received as if it were Christ's voice and a pronouncement from heaven.

And the people are most diligently taught about the power of the absolution and the faith which belongs to it, so that they know what a great, comforting thing Confession and Absolution is. Yet, previously, the monks said nothing about the faith and absolution. They only tortured poor consciences with the enumeration of sins, which is something impossible for everyone on earth. Because of this, we do not compel people to enumerate their sins, because we do not find the enumeration of sins commanded in the Scripture. Indeed, it is impossible. As the psalm says: "Who can detect their errors?" [Ps. 19:12].

Furthermore, the command with respect to Confession [in electoral Saxony] is formulated like this: the priests are ordered to administer the sacrament to no one who has not received absolution from them. Otherwise there are no specifications for the people as to when or how often they should confess. Such a command would lead to a great abuse of the sacrament, as happened previously, when the people did not come to the sacrament willingly in order to be relieved of their sins, and thus the sacrament was greatly dishonored. Because absolution is a comfort for terrified consciences, it makes a mockery of this comfort to demand that someone who does not desire it be comforted. If we add to that specifications regarding times and frequency for making use of the sacrament, the result would be contrary to the rule of St. Paul because many who would be required to come to it would receive the body and blood of Christ unworthily [1 Cor. 11:29]. Those who would force such people to come to the sacrament would be guilty of dishonoring the sacrament.

The people [of electoral Saxony], however, are admonished to come to it earnestly through God's Word, and they are told that whoever wants to be a Christian is obligated to use the sacrament. Those who do not use it demonstrate that they do not want to be Christian, as the canon made at the Council of Toledo, Canon *Si qui intrant*, dist. 2, de consec., also says.[10]

[6.] On Jurisdiction

(On the Jurisdiction and Secular Authority of the Bishops)

My Most Gracious Lord has taken from the bishops no jurisdiction or secular authority. Rather, once the people no longer wanted to pursue justice in clerical courts, and because the clergy in many places abused their judicial power and the practice of excommunication, My Gracious Lord, based on his authority as elector, had to accept and hear cases as they reached his Electoral Grace. In any case, clerical judicial power to deal with such matters reverts to the sovereign if the clergy abuse their jurisdiction.

Second, the primary aspect of clerical jurisdiction is to punish false doctrine, which is commanded of the bishops in Scripture and canon law. Up to now, they have never used this jurisdiction. Instead, they have allowed all kinds of errors to be preached. At the present, if they want to suppress true doctrine under the pretense of their jurisdictional rights, then we cannot submit to their jurisdiction regarding such things. If the bishops would have promptly taken up these concerns from which the dispute has arisen, in an orderly and Christian manner, then much ill will might have been avoided.

Third, My Most Gracious Lord was not obliged to help the bishops attack the priests who had gotten married in order to make them remain obedient to the bishops, for My Most Gracious Lord could not, in good conscience, have given them aid for this purpose. However, it is much more the duty of every patron, according to clerical ordinances concerning the law of patrimony, to protect the servants of his churches from the illegal power of clerical prelates—especially if the patron is not under the same prelate—for the patron even has the power to place a capable priest in a parish against the will of the prelate who had placed an incompetent priest in it (canon *Decernimus* 16, q. 7).

Fourth, because evil is wrought in clerical courts regarding many marriage cases, it is necessary to seek another court. For example: [1] secret marriage promises, by which an honorable man has his child thievishly stolen, are upheld; [2] joining a spiritual "fellowship of grace" is permitted, tearing marriage vows in shreds; [3] the innocent party after divorce is not free to marry again, which is contrary to God's Word; [4] it is not necessary to recount what other abuses have happened to marriage up to now.

On account of this, we cannot assent to their authority and jurisdiction over such things. It must be considered whether it is even possible to set up such

---

10. *Decretum Gratianum*, pt. 3. De consecr. dist. 2, ch. 21, from the Council of Toledo in 400.

authority against everyone's desire, because they cannot force the people to seek such a judgment by burdening their consciences.

[7.] On Ordination

Similarly, as long as the bishops oppress the priests with this oath, namely, not to preach this doctrine and not to be married (which cannot be done without sin), then we cannot seek ordination with them because such an oath is against God. We must be more obedient to God than to human beings [Acts 5:29], and the canons permit forsaking bishops who compel people to act against God.

There are many disputed points which are not necessary to consider: whether priests must be ordained by bishops, whether the priestly estate is instituted to teach or to make a sacrifice by which grace is attained for others.

Furthermore, concerning the ceremony of ordination, we would be inclined to yield somewhat if there would be agreement on the chief article of faith [the doctrine of justification] and if the bishops submit themselves [to it].

For if they were willing to make peace, then we should at the least give up everything that we can yield with a good conscience, for the sake of peace—which is to be regarded as higher and better than all the external freedoms which can be thought of. Also, if this matter concerned only ourselves and not the government, land, and people, then we ourselves would act as a sheriff against the enemy, at our own risk.

But this is not just an academic exercise. All kinds of recklessness have been committed by the mob in this schism, and they have caused the government to be brought into the matter. One can easily see the ruinous, horrible scandal that comes from such divisions. In addition to this, consider what might happen in the future. It is an item of concern that not many Dr. Martins will come along after this, who will take charge of these great issues with such grace so as to guard against false teaching and conflict. If disunity remains and more wicked and impassioned people show up in the future—oh God, what will they incite! May God give grace, so that the princes on both sides will assess their responsibilities and take into consideration their most beloved children, to whom they can leave nothing better than the proclamation of the true religion and a good government. Up to now, some of the nonessential ordinances have been allowed to fall into disuse because they counteracted doctrine. If only we were permitted to teach the doctrine and they would accept it, we, for their sake, would maintain certain customs—as long as the doctrine was not harmed.

[8.] On the Vow

(On the Cloistered Life)

This matter of cloistered living does not affect My Most Gracious Lord because his Electoral Grace has not told the monks either to forsake the monastery or to enter the monastery. Instead, they should be asked why they are doing what they are doing. "It is a private matter and does not pertain to the church at large."

However, the reasons must still be indicated why, on the one hand, My Gracious Lord has not reinstituted monasteries and, on the other hand, why his Electoral Grace has tolerated those who have left [the monasteries].

There are three primary reasons why monastic life, as it has been observed up to now, is wrong and contrary to God. The first [reason] is that such living is undertaken with the idea that by it satisfaction is made for sins and grace is merited, as Thomas maintained with clear words: monastic life is comparable to Baptism. He said that becoming a monk takes away sin, as Baptism does. What is this other than giving human works and self-selected worship the honor which belongs to Christ? Christ has earned grace, which we receive through faith without our merit (Ephesians 2[:9]). Therefore, it is a great blasphemy to want to merit grace and pay for sin with the monastic life. Baptism has God's Word and institution, and it is God's work. Therefore, it takes away sin. However, the monastic life does not have God's Word. Thus, it stands among the vain human commands of which Christ speaks: "In vain do they worship me, teaching human precepts as doctrines" [Matt. 15:9]. On account of this, it is certain that the monastic life cannot take away sin since a human commandment is a vain service and monastic life is nothing more than such a command. Now so long as the vow of the cloister is an ungodly vow, which is viewed as a work through which grace is earned, then it is invalid and worth nothing.

The second reason [why monastic life is wrong]: it is also contrary to God's command for those who suffer the flames of passion to make a vow not to become married. Paul says, "It is better to marry than be aflame with passion" [1 Cor. 7:9]. And if such a vow is against the created order and nature of humankind, then it is also impossible. Now because it is against God's command and is impossible, it follows that such a vow is not [a real vow] and those who need the married life should and must leave the monasteries. For this reason, even the ancient canons allow young persons to leave the monastery.[11] Augustine writes as well that, even if those who leave the monastery and marry thereby commit a sin, it is still a true marriage and should not be dissolved.[12]

The third reason [why monastic life is wrong] is that some who up until now were in the monastery, even though they wanted and were able to live in marriage, were forced to participate in the abuse of the Mass for the dead, etc., and other unrighteous observances such as the invocation of the saints, etc. Therefore, they have a just reason to flee from such an unchristian existence, in which God's name is used to serve the belly, in order to avoid this sin against the Second Commandment.

11. *Decretum Gratianum*, pt. 2, ch. 20, q. 1, c. 10.
12. In Augustine's *De bono viduitatis*, c. 9 (*MPL* 40:437–38; *NPNF*, ser. 1, 3:444).

[9.] On the Invocation of Saints

It is taught regarding the saints that their examples of faith are beneficial for strengthening our faith, also that their good works serve as reminders to us to do likewise, each according to one's own calling.

However, to ask something of the saints or to expect something through their merits is an honor that belongs to God and to our Lord Christ alone. Therefore, we should not also call upon the saints as intercessors. Christ had commanded us to hold to him as the one intercessor and mediator. As Paul says: "There is also one mediator between God and humankind" [1 Tim. 2:5]. And Christ says: "Come to me, all who are carrying heavy burdens" [Matt. 11:28]. And the example of the usefulness of having a good advocate at court is easily refuted: it would be damaging to have such an advocate if the prince had ordered that a person should come directly to him.

[10.] On Singing in German

In general, what we maintain about adiaphora in ceremonies has been said above: if they do not promote doctrine but are viewed as works through which sin is taken away, then such worship is unrighteous and contrary to the Gospel.

Since ceremonies are supposed to support doctrine, we have adapted some German singing so that through such exercises the people should learn something. As Paul teaches in 1 Corinthians 14[:5, 19], in the church we ought not speak or sing anything that is unclear. Nevertheless, we do not make a law of this and also continue to sing Latin, as practice for the youth. These matters mentioned so far concern external ordinances and customs.

[Conclusion]

Now, if they desire to know what else My Most Gracious Lord allows to be preached, we would like to present articles in which the whole Christian doctrine is brought together in good order, so that they may see that My Most Gracious Lord has not permitted any heretical doctrine but rather has had the holy gospel of our Lord Christ preached in utmost purity. Also, many of our adversaries have to confess this: they have been better instructed about lofty and important issues through this doctrine, as it is preached in My Most Gracious Lord's lands, than they were previously taught by the "sentences-commentators" and "summa-writers." For example, among the summa-writers, we can find no finality to [discussions] about how to attain the forgiveness of sins through faith, about how to use the sacraments, about the distinction between political authority and the bishop's office, and [about] how far human ecclesiastical ordinances are to be observed.

The Confutation of the
Augsburg Confession

Translated by Mark D. Tranvik

Introduction

After the Protestant princes had presented the Augsburg Confession to Emperor Charles V and the assembled imperial diet on 25 June 1530, the imperial court began to plan a response. It enlisted the aid of some two dozen theologians faithful to Rome for the drafting of a critique and confutation of the Augsburg Confession. The group included the Ingolstadt professor John Eck, Bishop Johannes Fabri of Vienna, and the theologians Johannes Cochlaeus, Konrad Wimpina, Johann Dietenberger, and Julius Pflug. The papally appointed legate from Rome, Cardinal Lorenzo Campeggio, assisted the committee. These theologians brought their own thoughts and writings into their deliberations. Important among these were Eck's *Four Hundred Four Articles*.

After considering a broad attack on all the heresies that had appeared in recent years, along the lines of these *Four Hundred Four Articles*, the committee decided to focus simply on the text of the Augsburg Confession since imperial advisors and leading Roman Catholic princes found this broader approach, embracing all disputes that had arisen over the past decade, too polemical. By mid-July, the committee was working on a second draft of the imperial response. During the last two weeks of July, under the guidance of the imperial court, a document moderate in tone with argumentation based on Scripture was produced. The imperial secretary, Alexander Schweiss, read the German version of the Confutation to the imperial diet on 3 August. The committee had also prepared a Latin version, which was placed in the emperor's hands.

The imperial counselors insisted that the actual text of the Confutation should not be shared with Melanchthon and his colleagues unless they agreed to submit to it before they had heard it and had promised not to make any public response. The Evangelical theologians and governments rejected these conditions. Staff members took stenographic notes, and Melanchthon was able to use these notes to shape the Apology of the Augsburg Confession against specific points made in the Confutation in the final stages of preparing the text. These notes proved to be quite accurate when the text of the Confutation finally appeared in print. It was first published in 1559.

The argumentation of the Confutation shows marks of the thinking of traditional scholastic theologians, such as Eck and Cochlaeus, as well as those under the influence of Erasmian humanist reform ideas, such as Julius Pflug.

This English translation is based on the "Responsio Pontifica seu Confutatio Augustanae Confessionis," *CR* 27:82–184; and Herbert Immenkötter, ed., *Die Confutatio der Confessio Augustana vom 3. August 1530* (Münster: Aschendorff, 1979) (see also his *Der Reichstag zu Augsburg und die Confutatio* [Münster: Aschendorff, 1979]). Use was also made of an earlier English translation by Henry E. Jacobs as found in *The Book of Concord or the Symbolical Books of the Evangelical Lutheran Church* (Philadelphia: G. W. Frederick, 1883), 2:348–83.

The Confutation of the Augsburg Confession

Part I

Prologue

His Holy, Imperial, and Catholic Majesty, our most merciful lord, recently received a confession of faith subscribed to by the Elector of Saxony, several other princes, and two cities. His Holy Majesty, who seeks the glory of the most glorious God, the salvation of souls, the furtherance of Christian harmony, and the promotion of peace and unity in the German nation, not only read the Confession himself but also determined that a matter of such great importance needed the thorough and thoughtful consideration of others. Thus the Confession was given to several learned, mature, and honorable men of various nations for their consideration and inspection. These men were directed to praise and approve those items in the Confession that were Christian and correct. They were also to determine what was not in accord with the universal Christian church and indicate why this was the case. This task has been completed. The learned men mentioned above examined the Confession with great care and presented a reply to his Holy Imperial Majesty. As one might expect from a Christian emperor, this reply was read most carefully by his Imperial Majesty. It was then given to the other electors, princes, and estates of the Roman Empire for their examination. These parties also judged the document as orthodox and consistent with the Gospel and Holy Scriptures.

After meeting with the electors, princes, and estates, his Imperial Majesty, concerned to settle the disputes involving our holy orthodox faith and religion, ordered that this declaration be made.

Regarding the confession about matters involving the Christian and orthodox faith, which was presented to his Imperial Majesty by the Elector of Saxony and a few princes and cities of the Holy Roman Empire, the following Christian reply is given:

Article One

God. In the first article, they confess the unity of the divine essence in three persons in accordance with the Council of Nicea. This is to be accepted because it agrees with the rule of faith and the Roman church. The Council of Nicea, convened by Emperor Constantine, has always been held in the highest regard. At this council, 318 bishops, renowned for their holiness of life, martyrdom, and learning, defined and formulated this article on the essential unity of the three persons after careful investigation of the Holy Scriptures.

Likewise, their condemnation of heresies that are contrary to this article are also to be accepted, namely, the Manichaeans,[1] Arians,[2] Eunomians,[3] Valentinians,[4] and Samosatanes.[5] The catholic church has long condemned all of these false teachings.

Article Two

Original Sin. In this second article of their confession, we approve what is in agreement with the catholic church: that it maintains that inherited sin[6] is truly sin, condemning and bringing to eternal death those who are not reborn through Baptism and the Holy Spirit. They rightly condemn the Pelagians,[7] new and old, a group declared to be heretical by the church long ago.

However, this article's declaration that original sin means that humanity is born without fear and trust in God is to be completely rejected. As every Christian acknowledges, adults fail to fear and trust God, but this is not a fault found in infants, who lack the use of reason. So God said to Moses: "Your children had no knowledge between good and evil," Deuteronomy 1[:39].

Also rejected is their teaching that inherited or original sin is concupiscence, if they mean that concupiscence is a sin that remains a sin in children after their Baptism. The apostolic see has already condemned two articles by Martin Luther[8] where he taught that sin remains in infants after Baptism and the "fomes"[9] of sin hinders the soul's entrance into heaven. But if they are speaking

---

1. A religious group named after its founder Mani (d. 276). The Manichaeans advocated a stark dualism between powers of light and darkness. The Augsburg Confession, Article I, condemned the Manichaeans and other groups mentioned here.

2. Named after Arius (260–336), who denied that the Father and Son were of the same substance.

3. Named after Eunomius (d. 394), who believed similar to the Arians that the Son was not fully divine.

4. A gnostic sect from the second century.

5. Paul of Samosata taught in the third century that Jesus was a man who had received special gifts from the Holy Spirit.

6. *vitium originis,* often referred to as original sin.

7. Pelagius (ca. 400) stressed the ability of the human will to freely choose between good and evil.

8. The papal bull of Leo X, *Exsurge domine,* art. 2 and 3.

9. This refers to the "tinder" of sin. It means infants have an inborn disposition to sin that will eventually reveal itself.

in the manner of St. Augustine's teaching and call the inherited sin concupiscence in the sense that it ceases to be sin in Baptism, then this teaching can be accepted, for it is in accord with St. Paul, who said, "We are all born children of wrath" [Eph. 2:3], and that "in Adam we have all sinned," Romans 5[:12].

Article Three

The Son of God. There is nothing in the third article which is contrary to [the] Apostles' Creed and the correct rule of faith. These state that the Son of God became incarnate, assumed human nature into the unity of his person, was born of the Virgin Mary, truly suffered, was crucified, died, descended to hell, was resurrected on the third day, and ascended into heaven, where he sits at the right hand of the Father.

Article Four

Justification. In the fourth article, the Pelagians are condemned. They judged that human beings could merit eternal life by their own powers and without the grace of God. This condemnation is in accord with the catholic faith and is consistent with the early councils. It is also clearly in agreement with Holy Scripture. John the Baptist says: "No one is able to receive anything except what has been given from heaven," John 3[:27]. We also read that "every good gift and every perfect gift is from above, coming down from the Father of lights," James 1[:17]. Thus "our competence is from God," 2 Corinthians 3[:5]. Christ says, "No one can come to me unless drawn by the Father who sent me," John 6[:44]. And St. Paul asks: "What do you have that you did not receive?" 1 Corinthians 4[:7].

However, to reject human merit, which is acquired through the assistance of divine grace, is to agree with the Manichaeans and not the catholic church. St. Paul says: "I have fought the good fight, I have finished the race, I have kept the faith. From now on there is reserved for me the crown of righteousness, which the Lord, the righteous judge, will give me on that day," 2 Timothy 4[:7-8]. Paul wrote to the church at Corinth: "For all of us must appear before the judgment seat of Christ, so that each may receive recompense for what has been done in the body, whether good or evil," 2 Corinthians 5[:10]. God said to Abraham: "Do not be afraid, Abram, I am your shield; your reward shall be very great," Genesis 15[:1]. And Isaiah says: "See . . . his reward is with him and his recompense before him," Isaiah 40[:10]. In Isaiah 58[:7-8], it says: "Share your bread with the hungry . . . and your righteousness shall go before you, the glory of the Lord shall be your rear guard." Also the Lord said to Cain: "If you do well, will you not be accepted?" Genesis 4[:7]. The parable in the Gospel declares that we have been hired to work in the Lord's vineyard: "Call the laborers and give them their pay," Matthew 20[:8]. St. Paul, who had access to the mysteries of God, says: "Each will receive wages according to the labor of each," 1 Corinthians 3[:8].

All Catholics admit that our works of themselves have no merit but God's grace makes them worthy to earn eternal life. As St. John says: "They will walk with me, dressed in white, for they are worthy," Revelation 3[:4]. And St. Paul says to the Colossians: "Give thanks to the Father, who has enabled you to share in the inheritance of the saints in the light," Colossians 1[:12].

Article Five

The Office of the Ministry. Article Five, which says that the Holy Spirit is given by Word and sacrament, as through instruments, is approved. For it is written in Acts: "While Peter was still speaking, the Holy Spirit fell upon all who heard the word," Acts 10[:44]. And in John it says: "He on whom you see the Spirit descend and remain is the one who baptizes with the Holy Spirit," John 1[:33].

However, when they speak of faith, this is to be admitted insofar as they are speaking not of faith alone (which some unfortunately teach) but that faith which is to be understood as working through love (as Paul correctly teaches in Galatians 3[:5]). For in Baptism, it is not faith alone but also hope and love which are simultaneously infused, as Pope Alexander declares in the canon "Majores. Concerning Baptism and Its Effects."[10] John the Baptist taught this long before, saying of Christ: "He will baptize you with the Holy Spirit and fire," Luke 3[:16].

Article Six

The New Obedience. The sixth article, in which they confess that faith ought to bear fruit in good works, is valid and acceptable since "faith without works is dead," James 2[:17], and all of Scripture invites us to do works. The wise person says: "Whatever your hand finds to do, do with your might," Ecclesiastes 9[:10]. Also we read: "And the Lord had regard for Abel and his offering," Genesis 4[:4]. The Lord saw that Abraham would "charge his children and his household after him to keep the way of the Lord by doing righteousness and justice," Genesis 18[:19]. Similarly, we also find: "By myself I have sworn, says the Lord: Because you have done this . . . I will indeed bless you and multiply your offspring," Genesis 22[:16-17]. Thus the Lord regarded the fast of the Ninevites, Jonah 3, and the weeping and tears of King Hezekiah, 2 Kings 20[:5]. For this reason, the faithful ought to follow the counsel of St. Paul: "So, then, whenever we have an opportunity, let us work for the good of all, and especially for those of the family of faith," Galatians 6[:10]. Also, Christ says: "The night is coming when no one can work," John 9[:4] since "their deeds will follow them," Revelation 14[:13].

However, in the same article they attribute to justification by faith alone that which is wholly opposed to evangelical truth. The Gospel does not exclude good

---

10. According to Gratian, this was Pope Innocent III, X.3.42.3 (*CIC* II:644–46).

works, for "glory and honor and peace for everyone who does good," Romans 2[:10]. Why is this the case? Because David, Psalm 62[:12]; Christ, Matthew 16[:27]; and Paul, Romans 2[:6] testify that God will reward everyone according to their works. Moreover, Christ says: "Not everyone who says to me, 'Lord, Lord,' will enter the kingdom of heaven, but only the one who does the will of my Father in heaven," Matthew 7[:21].

Thus no matter how much a person believes, if that person does not do good works, then he or she is not a friend of God. "You are my friends," says Christ, "if you do what I command you," John 15[:14]. Consequently, it is not enough to say we are justified only by faith because justification pertains to faith and love. For St. Paul says: "If I have all faith, so as to remove mountains, but do not have love, I am nothing," 1 Corinthians 13[:2]. Here Paul witnesses to the princes and the entire church that faith alone does not justify. Rather, he teaches that love is the superior virtue: "Above all, clothe yourselves with love, which binds everything together in perfect harmony," Colossians 3[:14].

Nor is their teaching on justification approved by Christ: "When you have done all that you were ordered to do, say, 'We are worthless slaves,'" Luke 17[:10]. For if it is right to call the doers worthless slaves, how much more appropriate to say to those who only believe: "When you have believed all that you were ordered to believe, say, 'We are worthless slaves.'" This saying of Christ does not extol faith without works but teaches that our works bring us no credit from God, are not a cause for boasting, and that when compared with the divine reward are null and void. Thus St. Paul says: "I consider that the sufferings of this present time are not worth comparing with the glory about to be revealed to us," Romans 8[:18]. For faith and good works are gifts of God, to which eternal life is given through God's mercy. Their citation of Ambrose is not pertinent, for this church father is speaking specifically of works of the law. He says "apart from the law," but he actually means "apart from the law of the Sabbath and circumcision and revenge." This he says even more clearly when he cites St. James on Romans 4 concerning the justification of Abraham without the works of the law before circumcision. For how could it happen that Ambrose in his commentary would say something different than what St. Paul says in Romans: "For no human being will be justified in his sight by deeds prescribed by the law," Romans 3[:20]. In the end, he does not simply exclude works but says: "We hold that a person is justified apart from works prescribed by the law" [Rom. 3:28].

Article Seven

The Church. The seventh article of their confession, which affirms that the church is an assembly of saints, cannot pass without close examination, if by this they mean that wicked persons and sinners are to be separated from the church. For the Council of Constance condemned this and other teachings of

John Hus;[11] it plainly contradicts the Gospel. We read that John the Baptist compared the church to a threshing floor, which Christ will clear with his winnowing fork and will gather the wheat into his granary but burn the chaff with unquenchable fire, Matthew 3[:12]. Does the chaff not signify the wicked, and the wheat the good? Christ also compares the church with a net in which there are both good and bad fish, Matthew 13[:47-48]. And he compares the church with ten virgins, among whom there are five wise and five foolish ones, Matthew 25[:1-2]. For these reasons, this article cannot be accepted.

However, they deserve praise when they confess that the church is eternal. The church is the place of the promise of Christ, who promises that the Spirit will remain with it forever, John 14[:16]. Moreover, Christ himself promises to be with the church always, even to the end of the age, Matthew 28[:20].

They are also to be praised when they say that differences in church rites do not threaten the unity of faith. This refers only to particular (local) rites, as Jerome says: "Every province abounds in its own sense (of propriety)."[12] However, if their confession is extended to cover the practices of the universal church, then this article cannot be accepted. Along with St. Paul, we would oppose them and say: "We have no such custom" [1 Cor. 11:16]. All believers must observe the universal rites, as Augustine, whose testimony they often cite, so splendidly taught.[13] We presume that these practices originated with the apostles themselves.

Article Eight

What Is the Church? In the eighth article, in regard to evil or hypocritical ministers of the church, they confess that the wickedness of these ministers does not do damage to the sacraments and the Word. This is in agreement with the Roman church and the princes. Condemned for their false teaching are the Donatists[14] and Origenists,[15] who denied it was lawful to use the ministry of the wicked in the church. This same heresy was adopted by the Waldensians[16] and

---

11. John Hus (1372–1415) was condemned by the Council of Constance in 1415.

12. Jerome, Ep. 71, 6 (*CSEL* 55/7: 6–7; *NPNF*, ser. 2, 6:154).

13. Augustine, Ep. 54, *ad inquisitiones Ianuarii*, 1, 1, 1 (*CSEL* 34/1:159, 15–18; *NPNF*, ser. 1., 1:300).

14. The Donatists were a group in the early church (fourth and fifth centuries) who taught that a sacrament's validity was dependent upon the holiness of the one administering it.

15. A group from the sixth century with Donatist tendencies who had no connection with Origen of Alexandria (185–254).

16. The Waldensians were a rigorist group from the twelfth century. They originated with the reform preaching of Peter Waldo of Lyons.

the Poor of Lyons[17] and later by John Wycliffe[18] in England and John Hus[19] in Bohemia.

Article Nine

Baptism. In the ninth article, they confess that Baptism is necessary for salvation and that infants are to be baptized. This is approved and accepted. They correctly condemn the Anabaptists,[20] a group of people so seditious that they ought to be banished beyond the boundaries of the empire so that Germany might not suffer again the bloody and destructive tumult of five years ago when thousands were killed.[21]

Article Ten

The Holy Supper of Our Lord. The words of the tenth article contain nothing that would give cause for offense. They confess that the body and blood of Christ are truly and substantially present in the sacrament after the words of consecration. This should also mean they believe that under each form the entire Christ is present—the blood of Christ is no less present under the form of the bread through concomitance[22] than it is under the form of the wine and the reverse. Otherwise, in the Eucharist the body of Christ is dead and without blood, which would be contrary to the words of St. Paul: "We know that Christ, being raised from the dead, will never die again," Romans 6[:9].

In order to complete this article, it is necessary to add that the church, contrary to what some falsely teach, is able by the almighty Word of God in the consecration of the Eucharist to change the substance of the bread into the body of Christ. This has been definitively established by a general council in canon *Firmiter. De summa trinitate et fide catholica.*[23] They are to be praised for condemning the Capernaites,[24] who deny the true presence of the body and blood of our Lord Jesus Christ in the Eucharist.

17. Another name for the Waldensian movement.

18. John Wycliffe (1325?–84), theologian and church reformer from Oxford, was condemned at the Council of Constance for holding that a priest must be in a state of grace in order to worthily administer the sacrament.

19. John Hus (1372–1415) was a critic of the church from Prague who was also condemned at Constance, accused of holding a position similar to Wycliffe (see n. 18) on the worthiness of a minister who administers the sacrament.

20. A term that covers a wide variety of sixteenth-century groups who held a common belief that Baptism is valid only if it is preceded by a personal confession of faith, thus rendering infant baptism improper.

21. The Peasants' Revolt of 1524–26.

22. A teaching that holds the whole body and blood of Christ are present in either consecrated element.

23. The teaching of the Fourth Lateran Council (1215), cap. 1.

24. A designation for those who seemed to contend that physical flesh was consumed in the sacrament, based on a reference to John 6:52, where the people of Capernaum thought Jesus was referring to an actual eating or chewing of physical flesh.

Article Eleven

Confession. In the eleventh article, they assert that private absolution is to be maintained in the church along with confession. This is to be accepted as catholic teaching and consistent with our faith, for absolution is based firmly on the word of Christ: "If you forgive the sins of any, they are forgiven" [John 20:23].

However, two things are required concerning this article. First, their subjects should be compelled to make an annual confession as is required by canon law in *Omnis utriusque sexus. De poenitentiis et remissionibus.*[25] This has been the custom of the entire Christian community.

Second, their subjects should be admonished regularly by their preachers to examine their consciences diligently and, even though it is not possible to confess every sin, to confess all the sins of which they are aware. With regard to those that have been forgotten, let them confess in general and say with the psalmist: "Clear me, Lord, from hidden faults," Psalm 19[:12].

Article Twelve

Repentance. In the twelfth article, they confess that those who have sinned are able to have their sins remitted whenever they repent,[26] and that the church ought to bestow absolution on those who have come back to its fold. This is to be commended, for here they most justly condemn the Novatians,[27] who denied that repentance can be repeated. This is contrary to the prophet's promise of grace to sinners whenever they cry out in anguish, Ezekiel 18[:21]. It is also contrary to the merciful attitude of Christ our Savior, who responded to St. Peter by saying that in one day he should not forgive his brother only seven times but seventy times seven, Matthew 18[:22].

However, the second part of this article must be rejected. In maintaining there are only two parts to penance, they put themselves in opposition to the universal church, which from the time of the apostles has held and believed that penance consists of three parts: contrition, confession, and satisfaction. The ancient doctors Origen, Cyprian, Chrysostom, Gregory, and Augustine taught this in accordance with the Sacred Scriptures, particularly 2 Kings 12[:16] concerning David, 2 Chronicles 33[:16] concerning Manasseh, as well as Psalms 32, 38, and 102. For this reason, Pope Leo X of blessed memory condemned this in the teaching of Luther, who said: "That there are three parts to penance, namely, contrition, confession, and satisfaction, is found neither in the Holy Scriptures nor in the writings of the holy Christian doctors."[28] Hence, this part of the article cannot be admitted under any circumstances.

25. The Fourth Lateran Council (1215), cap. 21.

26. The word used here, *conversio,* was used in sixteenth-century theological Latin not only for "conversion" but also for "repentance."

27. Followers of Novatian who in the third century insisted that those who had fallen away could not be received back into the church.

28. The papal bull *Exsurge domine* of 15 June 1520, art. 5.

Also to be rejected is the teaching that faith is the second part of penance. It is well known that faith comes before repentance, for unless a person believes, that person will not repent.

Nor can we agree with that section which scorns the satisfactions belonging to penance. Such teaching is contrary to the Gospel, the fathers, the councils, and the universal catholic church. John the Baptist cries: "Bear fruit worthy of repentance," Matthew 3[:8]. St. Paul teaches: "For just as you once presented your members as slaves to impurity and to greater and greater iniquity, so now present your members as slaves to righteousness for sanctification," Romans 6[:19]. In a similar way he preached to the gentiles, saying "they should repent and turn to God and do deeds consistent with repentance," Acts 26[:20]. And Christ himself preached and taught: "Repent for the kingdom of heaven has come near," Matthew 4[:17]. Christ had commanded his apostles to preach and teach in this way, Luke 24[:47], and in his first sermon St. Peter faithfully follows these instructions [Acts 2:38]. So Augustine exhorts "that every person should judge himself with severity and in so judging himself he might not be judged by God."[29] This corresponds to what St. Paul says to the Corinthians, 1 Corinthians 11[:31].

Also, Pope Leo the Great[30] said: "The mediator between God and humanity, the man Jesus Christ, gave to church authorities the power to assign a work of penance to those who have made a confession and to admit to the sacramental communion those who have passed through the door of reconciliation by a healing act of satisfaction." And Ambrose[31] says: "Let the extent to which the conscience is troubled dictate the severity of the penance."

Accordingly, a variety of penitential canons were designated by the most holy Council of Nicea in order to account for the diversity of satisfactions. The heretic Jovinian[32] taught that all sin was equal, and therefore he did not admit to a variety of satisfactions. But we assert that the acts of satisfaction in penance should not be abolished by the church, for that would be contrary to the explicit words of the Gospel and the decrees of the councils and fathers. Those who have confessed and received absolution by a priest ought to carry out the work of satisfaction they were commanded to do. This is consistent with St. Paul: "He [Christ] gave himself for us that he might redeem us from all iniquity and purify for himself a people of his own who are zealous for good deeds," Titus 2[:14]. Christ made satisfaction for us that we might be zealous in good works and so fulfill the penitence commanded of us.

29. From a sermon attributed to Augustine. See Pseudo-Augustine, "Sermo 351," 4, 7 (*MPL* 39: 1542).

30. Leo the Great, Ep. 108, 2 (*MPL* 54:1011B–12A; *NPNF*, ser. 2, 12:80).

31. Wrongly attributed to Ambrose. See Pseudo-Ambrose, *De lapsu virginis consecratae*, 8, 34 (*MPL* 16:393A).

32. Jovinian taught near the end of the fourth century in Rome.

Article Thirteen

The Use of the Sacraments. The thirteenth article gives no offense and is to be accepted. Here they say the sacraments were instituted not only as signs which identify Christian people but much more as signs and testimonies of God's will toward us. However, we also ask that what they say about the sacraments in general should also be applied specifically to the seven sacraments of the church and that care should be taken so that they are observed by their subjects.

Article Fourteen

Ecclesiastical Order. When they confess in Article Fourteen that no one ought to preach the Word of God or administer the sacraments unless they have been rightly called, it should be understood that "those rightly called" refers to those called according to the laws and ecclesiastical ordinances that have been observed throughout Christendom. It does not refer to the call of Jeroboam[33] [1 Kings 12:31] or a circumstance where a mob of people forces its will upon the rest. This was not how Aaron was called [Exod. 28:1; Heb. 5:4]. This is the sense in which this article is to be received. Let them be admonished so that they might continue to follow proper procedures and allow no one to be admitted to their jurisdictions as a pastor or priest who has not been rightly called.

Article Fifteen

Ecclesiastical Rites. In Article Fifteen, they confess that those ecclesiastical rites that can be kept without sin ought to be observed since they promote peace and good order in the church. This we accept. Yet they are admonished that the rites of the church, whether of the church universal or of individual provinces, ought to be kept with Christian devotion. This has been the church's practice up to the present day, and it should continue to observe these rites in the future. And if in a few places these rites have been interrupted, the princes and city governments should take care that they are restored in their domains and that their subjects be exhorted to do things according to the ancient Christian form.

However, the appendix of this article is completely rejected. For it is false that human ordinances instituted to placate God and make satisfaction for sin are against the Gospel. This will be made clear when we examine the articles concerning vows, the choice of foods, etc. in more detail.

Article Sixteen

Temporal Government. The sixteenth article concerning civil magistrates is received with pleasure. For it agrees not only with civil law but also with

---

33. Jeroboam defied proper order and appointed priests who were not from the Levites.

canonical law, the Gospel, the Holy Scriptures, and the universal norm of faith. The apostle Paul admonished the church: "Let every person be subject to the governing authorities. For there is no authority except from God, and those that exist have been instituted by God. Therefore, whoever resists authority resists what God has appointed, and those who resist will incur judgment," Romans 13[:1-2].

The princes are to be praised for condemning the Anabaptists, who destroy all civil ordinances and prohibit Christians from using the magistracy and other civil offices, without which it is impossible to successfully administer the state.

Article Seventeen

The Return of Christ to Judgment. The confession of the seventeenth article is accepted. The entire catholic church knows from the Apostles' Creed and the Holy Scriptures that Christ will come on the last day to judge the living and the dead. They rightly condemn the Anabaptists, who teach there will be an end to the punishment of condemned persons and the devil and who imagine, like the Jews, the establishment of a righteous kingdom in this world, where all wickedness is suppressed, before the resurrection of the dead.

Article Eighteen

The Free Will. In the eighteenth article, they confess that the free will has the power to effect civil righteousness but that it lacks the power, apart from the Holy Spirit, to produce the righteousness of God. This confession is received and approved.

On this issue Catholics pursue a middle way, siding neither with the Pelagians,[34] who ascribe too much to free will, nor with the godless Manichaeans,[35] who take away all liberty. Both of these groups are in error. As Augustine says: "We firmly teach and preach that there is a free will in human beings."[36] For it would be an inhuman error to deny that people possess free will since it is in accord with human experience and often asserted by the Holy Scriptures, as the passages quoted below indicate.

Thus St. Paul says: "But if someone stands firm in his resolve, being under no necessity but having his own desire under control," 1 Corinthians 7[:37]. Also, the Wise One speaks of a righteous person: "Who has had the power to transgress and did not transgress, and to do evil, and did not do it?" Ecclesiasticus 31[:10]. And God says to Cain: "If you do well, will you not be accepted? And if you do not do well, sin is lurking at the door; its desire is for you, but you must master it," Genesis 4[:7]. God speaks through the prophet Isaiah: "If you are

---

34. See n. 7.
35. See n. 1.
36. *Hypomnesticon* 3, 3, 3 (*MPL* 45:1623), a writing classified as the work of Pseudo-Augustine.

willing and obedient, you shall eat the good of the land; but if you refuse and rebel, you shall be devoured by the sword" [Isa. 1:19-20]. More briefly, Jeremiah says: "This is how you have spoken, but you have done all the evil that you could," Jeremiah 3[:5]. In addition, Ezekiel says: "Cast away from you all the transgressions which you have committed against me, and get yourselves a new heart and a new spirit! Why will you die, O house of Israel? For I have no pleasure in the death of any one, says the Lord God; turn, then, and live," Ezekiel 18[:31-32]. And Paul says: "The spirits of prophets are subject to the prophets," 1 Corinthians 14[:32]. Similarly, he says: "Each of you must give as you have made up your mind, not reluctantly or under compulsion," 2 Corinthians 9[:7]. Finally, Christ refuted all the Manichaeans with one word when he said: "For you always have the poor with you and can show kindness to them whenever you wish," Mark 14[:7]. And he said to Jerusalem: "How often have I desired to gather your children together as a hen gathers her brood under her wings, and you were not willing," Matthew 23[:37].

Article Nineteen

The Cause of Sin. The nineteenth article is also approved and accepted. The source of evil is not God, the highest good, but the cause of sin is the rational will of humanity in its frailty. Humanity should not blame its misdeeds or wickedness on God but should rather look to itself, just as Jeremiah says: "Your wickedness will punish you and your apostasies will reprove you," Jeremiah 2[:19]. And Hosea says: "O Israel, thou hast destroyed thyself; but in me is thy help," Hosea 13[:9].[37] David also recognized in the Spirit that "God does not delight in wickedness," Psalm 5[:4].

Article Twenty

Faith and Good Works. Article Twenty does not so much contain the confession of the princes and the cities as the justification of the preachers' teaching. Only one thing concerns the princes and cities, namely, that good works do not merit the forgiveness of sins. This teaching has been rejected and disapproved above, and we will now show again that it is false. The passage from Daniel is well known: "Atone for your sins with righteousness, and your iniquities with mercy to the oppressed," Daniel 4[:27]. Also, Tobit says to his son: "Indeed, almsgiving, for all who practice it, is an excellent offering in the presence of the Most High," Tobit 4[:11]. Christ says: "So give for alms those things that are within; and see, everything will be clean for you" [Luke 11:41]. And if works are not meritorious, why does Wisdom say: "She gave to holy people the reward of their labors," Wisdom of Solomon 10[:17]? Why would St. Peter be so adamant about the

---

37. The NRSV reading, "I will destroy you, O Israel; who can help you?" follows Greek and Syriac translations; the Confutation translation follows the Hebrew.

importance of good works, saying: "Therefore, brothers and sisters, be all the more eager to confirm your call and election," 2 Peter 1[:10]? And Paul says: "For God is not unjust; he will not overlook your work and the love that you showed for his sake," Hebrews 6[:10].

We are not disparaging the merits of Christ, for we know that our works merit nothing in and of themselves unless they proceed from the merits of Christ's passion. For we know that Christ is "the way, the truth and the life," John 14[:6]. However, Christ, as the Good Shepherd, began to act and teach, Acts 1[:1], and gave to us an example in order that what he has done we might also do, John 13[:15]. He went through the desert, through the way of good works, with the intention that all Christians should follow him and bear the cross according to his will, Matthew 10[:38], 16[:24]. And whoever does not bear the cross is not a disciple of Christ. For John rightly says: "Whoever says, 'I abide in him,' ought to walk just as he walked," 1 John 2[:6].

Finally, let it be noted that their opinion regarding good works was condemned and rejected more than a thousand years ago at the time of Augustine.

Article Twenty-One

The Cult of the Saints. In the last and twenty-first article, they admit that we should remember the saints in order to imitate their faith and good works, but that the saints are not to be called upon for help. It is remarkable that the princes and the cities have allowed this opinion to be perpetuated in their domains since it has been condemned often by the Christian church. Eleven hundred years ago Jerome[38] triumphed over the heretic Vigilantius[39] on this issue. Long after him came the Albigensians,[40] the Poor of Lyons,[41] the Waldensians,[42] and the old and new Cathari,[43] all of whom were legitimately condemned by the church. This article of their confession, which contains errors rejected so many times before, must be condemned because it contradicts the teaching of the universal church.

Concerning the invocation of the saints, we have not only the authority of the entire church but also the agreement of the holy church fathers, such as Augustine, Bernard, Jerome, Cyprian, Chrysostom, Basil, and the other doctors of the church.

---

38. Jerome, *Contra Vigilantium,* especially c. 6 (*MPL* 23:359; *NPNF,* ser. 2, 6:417–23, esp. 419–20).

39. An opponent of Jerome, who was linked with the teachings of Jovinian (see n. 32).

40. A heretical group of the twelfth and thirteenth century from southern France with links to the Cathari (see n. 43).

41. See n. 17.

42. See n. 16.

43. The Cathari were a heretical group from the twelfth and thirteenth centuries that posited a radical dualism between the spiritual and material worlds. They denied the efficacy of the sacraments and condemned the institutional church.

Furthermore, the Holy Scriptures, consistent with this assertion of the catholic church, demonstrate that the saints should be honored, as Christ taught: "Whoever serves me, the Father will honor," John 12[:26]. If God sees fit to honor the saints, then why should we relatively insignificant human beings not do the same? Was not the Lord brought to repentance by Job when he prayed for his friends, Job 42[:10]? If the most compassionate God assented to Job, why would he not do the same for the blessed Virgin Mary when she intercedes? We read in Baruch: "O Lord Almighty, God of Israel, hear now the prayer of the dead of Israel," Baruch 3[:4]. This shows that the dead pray for us. In the Old Testament, Onias and Jeremiah did the same thing. Judas Maccabeus saw Onias, the high priest, with his hands outstretched and praying for the entire people of Judea. When a man of great age, majesty, and beauty appeared, Onias said: "This is a man who loves the family of Israel and prays much for the people and the holy city—Jeremiah, the prophet of God," 2 Maccabees 15[:14]. The Holy Scriptures also show that the angels pray for us. Why deny that this is the case with the saints? We read in the prophet Zechariah: "Then the angel of the Lord said 'O Lord of hosts, how long will you withhold mercy from Jerusalem and the cities of Judah, with which you have been angry these seventy years?' Then the Lord replied with gracious and comforting words to the angel who talked with me," Zechariah 1[:12-13]. Likewise Job testifies: "Then, if there should be for one of them an angel, a mediator, one of a thousand, one who declares a person upright, and he is gracious to that person, and says, 'Deliver him from going down into the Pit,'" Job 33[:23-24]. This is clearly stated in the words of that holy person, St. John the Evangelist: "When he had taken the scroll, the four living creatures and the twenty-four elders fell before the Lamb, each holding a harp and golden bowls full of incense, which are the prayers of the saints," Revelation 5[:8]. And later he says: "Another angel with a golden censer came and stood at the altar; he was given a great quantity of incense to offer with the prayers of all the saints on the golden altar that is before the throne. And the smoke of the incense, with the prayers of the saints, rose before God from the hand of the angel" [Rev. 8:3-4].

Finally, St. Cyprian, bishop and martyr at Carthage 1,250 years ago, wrote Pope Cornelius and asked: "Let the one who dies first never cease to pray for his brothers and sisters."[44] This holy man would not have written in this manner if he had not believed that after this life the saints pray for the living. He would have been admonishing Cornelius to do something in vain.

It should be noted that their argument is not strengthened when they say "there is one mediator between God and humankind," 1 Timothy 2[:5]; 1 John 2[:1]. His Imperial Majesty and the entire church confess that there is one mediator of redemption, namely, Jesus Christ. Nevertheless, there are many mediators of intercession. For example, Moses was a mediator and advocate between

---

44. Cyprian, Ep. 60, 5 (*CSEL* 3/2:694–95; *ANF* 5:352).

God and humankind, Deuteronomy 5[:5]. In the role of mediator, he prayed for the children of Israel, Exodus 17[:4]; 32[:11-13]. And St. Paul prayed for those with whom he was sailing, Acts 27[:23ff.], and asked for the prayers of the Romans, Romans 15[:30], the Corinthians, 2 Corinthians 1[:11], and the Colossians, Colossians 4[:3]. Moreover, when Peter was in prison, the church prayed to God for him without ceasing, Acts 12[:5].

Christ is our first and chief advocate. But it is also true that the saints are "members of Christ," 1 Corinthians 12[:12, 27]; Ephesians 5[:30]. They desire to conform their wills with the will of Christ. When they see that the head, Jesus Christ, prays for us, who can doubt that the saints should do the same thing?

Having considered all of these matters carefully, we request of the princes and the cities that they reject this part of their confession. We ask that they come into agreement with the holy universal and orthodox church and believe and confess what the entire Christian world believes and confesses regarding the veneration and intercession of the saints. For this teaching has been in all churches since the time of Augustine, who said: "The Christian people celebrates the memory of the martyrs with great devotion and follows their example in order that the community may partake in their merits and be helped by their prayers."[45]

Response to the Second Part of the Confession

Article Twenty-Two

Communion in Both Kinds. The practice of communing the laity under one kind is listed in the confession of the princes and the cities as an abuse. Also, in their jurisdictions the laity receive the sacrament under both kinds. Thus we will show that according to the custom of the holy church, it is wrong to say this is an abuse. In fact, the reverse is true. To give the laity the sacrament under both forms is an abuse and an act of disobedience according to the statutes and sanctions of the church.

In the early church, the saints received the sacrament only under the form of the bread. St. Luke says: "They devoted themselves to the apostles' teaching and fellowship, to the breaking of bread and the prayers," Acts 2[:42]. Here Luke mentions only the bread. Similarly, in Acts 20[:7] it says, "on the first day of the week, when we met to break bread." Also Christ, who instituted this most holy sacrament, after rising from the dead and meeting his disciples on the way to Emmaus, administered the Eucharist under one form, as it is written: "When he was at the table with them, he took bread, blessed and broke it, and gave it to them. Then their eyes were opened, and they recognized him," Luke 24[:30-31]. In their commentaries on this passage, Augustine, Chrysostom, Theophylact, and Bede—some of whom lived not long after the time of the apostles—affirm that the Eucharist is being spoken of here. It should be

---

45. Augustine, *Contra Faustum,* 20, 21 (*CSEL* 25/1:562; *NPNF,* ser. 1, 4:262).

noted that in John 6[:32-35] Christ mentions only the bread. St. Ignatius,[46] a disciple of St. John the Evangelist, mentions the bread alone in his letter to the Ephesians. Similarly, Ambrose,[47] in his books on the sacraments, speaks of "the communion of the laity."

At the Council at Reims,[48] it was determined that the priests, and not the laity, should take the sacrament of the body to the sick. There is no mention of the form of the wine. Hence it may be surmised that the viaticum was given to the sick only under one form.

The penitential canons agree with this. The Council of Agde[49] determined that a priest guilty of a criminal offense should be sent to a monastery and permitted only lay communion. At the Council of Sardica,[50] Bishop Hosius prohibits those guilty of sexual misconduct from receiving lay communion unless they repent. There has always been a distinction in the church between lay communion under one form and priestly communion under two forms. This was beautifully prophesied in the Old Testament concerning the descendants of Eli: "Everyone who is left in your family shall come to implore him for a piece of silver or a loaf of bread, and shall say, 'Please put me in one of the priest's places, that I may eat a morsel of bread,'" 1 Samuel 2[:36]. This Scripture clearly shows that the descendants of Eli, after they have been removed from the priesthood, will desire the part for priests, namely, the bread. Therefore, our laity ought to be content to receive the one part for a priest or under one form. For it is true that the popes in Rome, along with cardinals, bishops, and all priests, are satisfied with one form when they are not reading the Mass themselves or on their deathbeds. They receive the sacrament, which the Council of Nicea named the viaticum, only under the form of the bread. They would not do this if they thought it necessary for salvation to receive the sacrament in both forms.

It is true that in the early days of the church both forms were given to the laity (for they were free to commune under one or both forms). However, because of many dangers, this custom has been discontinued. When one considers the great number of people, among whom are the old, young, tremulous, weak, and mentally impaired, great care must be taken so that the sacrament is not violated by the spilling of the wine. The large number of people also makes it difficult to administer both forms because the wine, when kept for a long period, would go sour and cause nausea or vomiting in those receiving it. It could also not be taken to the sick without danger of spilling. For these and other reasons, the churches (whose custom had been to commune in both kinds) were led—undoubtedly by the Holy Spirit—to give only the bread. This was based on the reasoning that the whole Christ is under each kind and is no

---

46. Ignatius of Antioch, *Epistola ad Ephesios*, 1, 20 (*MPG* 5:661–62; *ANF* 1:57). Ignatius wrote in the first half of the second century.

47. Ambrose, *De sacramentis* 4, 4, 14–19 (*CSEL* 73:51–54; *Fathers of the Church* 44:302–4).

48. The Council of Reims met in 1049.

49. A mistaken reference. Actually, it was the Synod of Epaul that met in 517.

50. The Council of Sardica met from 342 to 343.

less received under one kind than under two. This was decreed by the highly respected Council of Constance[51] and by the Synod of Basel.[52]

In former times, it was a matter of freedom whether to receive the sacrament under one or both forms. However, the appearance of this heresy, which taught that it was necessary for salvation to receive both forms,[53] led the church, directed by the Holy Spirit, to forbid the laity from receiving both the bread and the wine. Sometimes the church must combat heresy by means of an opposite teaching. For example, there arose a few in the church who said that unleavened bread must be used in the Eucharist. The church responded for a time by saying that only leavened bread was to be used. Or, to cite another case, when Nestorius[54] wanted to teach that the Virgin Mary was the mother of Christ and not of God, the church for a time prohibited her from being called Christotokos, that is, the mother of Christ.

Therefore, we ask the princes and the cities not to allow this schism to enter Germany or the Holy Roman Empire nor to allow themselves to become separated from the practice of universal church.

The arguments that our opponents put forth are not convincing. For while Christ did institute both forms of the sacrament, nowhere in the Gospels does it say that he commanded the laity to receive both forms. The words in Matthew 26[:27] "Drink of it all of you" were directed to the twelve apostles, who were priests. Mark makes this clear when he says "And all of them drank from it," Mark 14[:23]. This has never been seen to apply to the laity. The custom of giving both forms to the laity has never existed in the entire church. At most, it is possible to say that this practice occurred among the Corinthians, the Carthaginians, and in a few other churches.

Concerning their reference to Pope Gelasius,[55] chapter *Comperimus,* de consecratione, dist. 2, if they examine this document they will see that it speaks of priests and not the laity. Hence their opinion that the administration of the sacrament under one form is contrary to divine law must be rejected. Above all, the conclusion to this article, which says that the eucharistic procession must be abandoned or disregarded because it separates [the elements of] the sacrament, is expressly rejected. On the basis of the Christian faith, they know, or ought to know, that Christ is not divided, but that the entire Christ is under each of the forms. Nowhere does the Gospel forbid the division of sacramental forms. This happens on Good Friday throughout the universal catholic church, although the consecration is made by the priest in both forms, who also should receive both.

---

51. The Council of Constance met in 1415.

52. The Council of Basel met in 1439.

53. A teaching associated with the Hussite movement.

54. Nestorius (381–451) was charged by his opponents with so strictly separating the human and divine natures of Christ that he was unable to refer to Mary as the mother of God.

55. For an explanation of the issue here, see Immenkötter, *Der Reichstag zu Augsburg und die Confutatio,* p. 71, n. 12.

The princes and cities are admonished to give all reverence and honor that is due to Christ, Son of the living God, our redeemer and glorifier, Lord of heaven and earth, since they believe and acknowledge that he is truly present in the Eucharist. They know that this has been piously believed and held by other Christian princes who were their predecessors in the faith.

Article Twenty-Three

The Marriage of Priests. In the second place, it is astonishing that they refer to the celibacy of priests as an abuse. They allow their priests to marry and call on others to do the same. This practice is the real abuse—the violation of priestly celibacy and the entrance into an unsanctioned marriage. That priests are forbidden to marry is testified to by Aurelius in the second Council of Carthage: "Since this [priestly celibacy] is the example taught by the apostles and is also the practice of the early church, let us maintain it."[56] And shortly before this, a canon says: "Let the bishops, priests and deacons, or those who administer the sacraments, as custodians of chastity, refrain from marriage."[57] As these words indicate, this is a tradition that has been received from the time of the apostles and is not a recent invention of the church.

St. Augustine, in his "Questions Concerning the Old and New Testaments," asks: "If it is held that it is lawful and good to marry, then why are priests not allowed to have wives?"[58] Also Pope Calixtus,[59] holy man and martyr, established 1,300 years ago that priests should not marry. The holy councils of Caesarea, Neo-Caesarea, Carthage, Agde, Gironne, Melfi, and Orleans have decided similarly. Since the time of the apostles, it has not been appropriate for priests to marry.

It is true that in the early church, because of a shortage of priests, married men were admitted to the priesthood. This is documented in the apostolic canons and in the reply of Paphnutius at the Council of Nicea. However, those who wished to marry were mandated to do so before obtaining the subdiaconate. This practice of the early church has been retained by the Greek church to the present day, as found in ch. *Si quis eorum*, dist. 32.[60]

However, by the grace of God the church grew, and there was no longer a shortage of priests. Thus, 1,140 years ago, Pope Siricius,[61] without doubt not apart from the guidance of the Holy Spirit, declared that priests should remain celibate, ch. *Plurimos*, dist. 82.[62] This position was also held by Popes Innocent

---

56. The second Council of Carthage (390), canon 2.

57. The second Council of Carthage (390), canon 2.

58. A work wrongly attributed to Augustine. See Immenkötter, *Der Reichstag zu Augsburg und die Confutatio*, p. 72, n. 15.

59. Actually dates back to Calixtus II, who was pope from 1119 to 1124.

60. D32, c. 7; *CIC* I:119–20.

61. Pope from 385 to 399.

62. D82, c. 3; *CIC*, I:115.

I, Leo the Great, and Gregory the Great. It is maintained in our day by the entire Latin church. Thus it is clear that the celibacy of clergy is not an abuse. For this practice has stood since the time of the apostles and church fathers and was received by the entire Latin church.

It should also be noted that the priests of the old law were separated from their wives at the time of their duty in the temple, as can be seen in the case of Zacharias, Luke 1[:5-25]. Since the priests of the new law must always be engaged in ministry, it follows that they should be celibate. Paul also taught that married people should not refrain from conjugal relationships except for a time when they give themselves to prayer, 1 Corinthians 7[:5]. Since a priest ought to always pray, he should always be celibate. These arguments have been cited previously in the writings of Jerome, Ambrose, and Augustine.

Furthermore, St. Paul says: "I want you to be free from anxieties. The unmarried man is anxious about the affairs of the Lord, how to please the Lord; but the married man is anxious about the affairs of the world, how to please his wife, and his interests are divided," 1 Corinthians 7[:32-34]. Therefore let a priest who wishes to continually please God flee from the cares of marriage and not look back, as was the case with Lot's wife, Genesis 19[:26].

Priestly celibacy was foreshadowed in the Old Testament. For example, Moses commanded those who were to receive the law not to approach their wives until the third day, Exodus 19[:15]. How much more then should priests, who receive Christ as legislator, Lord, and Savior, refrain from taking wives. The priests of the Old Testament were commanded to wear cloths over their thighs so as not to disclose their shameful flesh, Exodus 28[:42]. Bede noted that this was a symbol that priests in the future would be celibate. Also Ahimelech, when he was about to give the blessed bread to the servants of David, first asked whether they had kept away from women. David answered that they had for three days, 1 Samuel 21[:4-6]. Therefore, those who receive "the living bread that came down from heaven," John 6[:51], should also remain pure. Those who ate the Passover lamb had their loins girded, Exodus 12[:11]. How much more should those who eat our Passover lamb, Jesus Christ, gird their lives with celibacy just as the Lord commanded: "Purify yourselves, you who carry the vessels of the Lord," Isaiah 52[:11]. The Lord also said: "You shall be holy, for I the Lord your God am holy," Leviticus 19[:2]. Therefore let the priests serve God in holiness and righteousness all their days, Luke 1[:74].

The holy martyr St. Cyprian testified to receiving a revelation from God with the strict injunction that fervently warned the clergy not to live in a house with women.[63] Clerical celibacy has been commanded by councils and popes and has been revealed by God. Priests themselves have promised God to be celibate. Hence it cannot be rejected. The dignity of the Mass requires it, as well as the frequency of prayer and the liberty and purity of spirit so that God may be pleased, according to the teaching of St. Paul.

---

63. Pseudo-Cyprian, *De singularitate clericorum* 1 (*CSEL* 3:3/173).

It is clear that their teaching on clerical celibacy is the reappearance of the ancient heresy of Jovinian,[64] which was condemned by the Roman church and in the writings of Jerome.[65] St. Augustine noted that this heresy was soon extinguished and thereby unable to corrupt the priests.[66] Accordingly, the princes ought not to tolerate this teaching, for it brings shame and disrepute to the Roman Empire. Rather, they should conform to the universal church and not be moved by the arguments of those suggesting otherwise.

The writing of St. Paul, who says, "But because of cases of sexual immorality, each man should have his own wife and each woman her own husband," 1 Corinthians 7[:2], needs further clarification. According to Jerome, Paul is speaking here of one who has not made a vow.[67] St. Paul also says in this chapter: "If a virgin marries, she does not sin" [1 Cor. 7:28], which is not interpreted by Athanasius or Vulgarius[68] as referring to a virgin who has been consecrated to God. As to the verse "It is better to marry than to be aflame with passion" [1 Cor. 7:9], reference should be made to the sharp reply of Jerome against Jovinian and his use of another passage of Paul: "It is well for a man not to touch a woman" [1 Cor. 7:1].[69] For a priest is in a middle position where he neither burns nor marries. By the grace of God, he obtains divine assistance to restrain himself, using such means as prayer, vigils, fasting, and other ways of subduing the flesh.

When they teach that Christ said not all are fit for celibacy [Matt. 19:11], this must be admitted as true, and it should also be noted that not all are suited for the priesthood. However, let the priest pray so that he may be strengthened by the word of Christ regarding continence, as St. Paul says: "I can do all things through him who strengthens me," Philippians 4[:13]. For celibacy is a gift of God, Wisdom 8[:21]. When they base their argument in behalf of the marriage of priests on the command and ordinance of God as found in Genesis 1[:28], it is helpful to listen to what Jerome said about these words a thousand years ago: "It was first necessary to plant the forest in order that it might grow so that afterward it could be cut down."[70] This command was given so that humanity might multiply and fill the earth. Now that the earth is populated—even to the extent that the nations press upon one another—this commandment no longer applies to those able to be celibate. Empty, too, is their attempt to base this teaching on the commandment of God. Let them show where God has dictated that priests ought to marry. Besides, there are many places in the divine law where it

64. See n. 32.

65. Jerome, *Adversus Jovinianum* (*MPL* 23:221–352; *NPNF*, ser. 2, 6:346–416).

66. Augustine, *De haeresibus* 82 (*MPL* 42:46).

67. Jerome, *Adversus Jovinianum* 1, 7 (*MPL* 23:230; *NPNF*, ser. 2, 6:350–51).

68. Actually Theophylacticus (d. 1108). See Immenkötter, *Der Reichstag zu Augsburg und die Confutatio*, p. 75, n. 26.

69. Jerome, *Adversus Jovinianum* 1, 9 (*MPL* 23:232–34; *NPNF*, ser. 2, 6:352).

70. Jerome, *Adversus Jovinianum* 116 (*MPL* 23:246; *NPNF*, ser. 2, 6:359–60).

says that vows once offered must be kept, Psalm 50[:14]; Psalm 76[:12]; Ecclesiastes 5[:4-5]. Why do they not observe the divine law?

They also twist the teaching of St. Paul, as if the apostle by saying "Now a bishop must be the husband of one wife" [1 Tim. 3:2] were mandating that bishops be married. By that line of reasoning, Martin, Nicholas, Titus, John the Evangelist, and even Christ himself would not have been bishops. However, Jerome clarifies this command of St. Paul by saying it means a bishop cannot be a bigamist.[71] The truth of this interpretation is based not only on the authority of Jerome, which ought to be honored by all Catholics, but also on St. Paul, who writes concerning the selection of widows: "Let a widow be put on this list if she is not less than sixty years old and has been married only once," 1 Timothy 5[:9].

Finally, the event recalled from German history does not provide any evidence to the contrary.[72] As historians have shown, the reign of Emperor Henry IV was a time of great unrest in the empire. There was much tension and strife between the papal office and Henry IV's son, together with princes and nobles of the empire, between the secular and spiritual realms. As a result, the laity improperly administered the sacraments, used sacred unction for sordid activities, baptized, and did many other things that are contrary to the Christian religion. The clergy also exceeded their boundaries, a precedent which cannot be cited as law. It was not considered unjust to dissolve these sacrilegious marriages, which had no validity and were entered into against vows and the teachings of the fathers and the councils. In our time, the so-called marriage of priests is also not valid.

Therefore, they lament in vain that the world is growing old, and that this dictates that the strictures against priestly celibacy should be relaxed. For those consecrated to God have been given other means to remedy weakness. For example, let them avoid the company of women, abandon idleness, subdue the flesh by fasting and vigils, and be careful that the senses, especially the eyes and ears, are not exposed to things forbidden. Further, let them dash their little ones (their carnal desires) upon a rock (which is Christ). That is, as David taught [Ps. 137:9], let them regard Christ as their rock who helps them in their struggle against their weaknesses. Let them subdue their passions and submit frequently and devoutly to God in prayer. Without doubt, these are the most useful and effective means for keeping clergy of God pure in their service to God.

St. Paul correctly said that those who prohibit marriage promote a doctrine of demons [1 Tim. 4:3]. This was the teaching of Tatian and Marcion, about whom Augustine and Jerome have written. However, the church does not forbid marriage; indeed, it is numbered among the seven sacraments. It is thus consistent to expect of the ministers, who occupy a lofty and distinctive office, a superior purity.

71. Jerome, *Adversus Jovinianum* 1, 34ff. (*MPL* 23:268, and 270; *NPNF,* ser. 2, 6:371–72).

72. In Article XXIII of the Augsburg Confession, Melanchthon cites an incident from the eleventh century, when Archbishop Siegfried of Mainz encountered fierce opposition from the clergy when priests were compelled to take vows of celibacy.

They are incorrect when they say it is the command of God to be married. If that were true, then John the Evangelist, St. James, Lawrence, Titus, Martin, Catherine, Barbara, etc. would have sinned. Cyprian,[73] whom they cite, spoke not of a virgin who had retracted a solemn vow but of one who had resolved to live a celibate life, as the beginning of epistle eleven, book one, indicates. St. Augustine was very clear on this issue when he wrote: "It is damnable for virgins who have made a vow not only to marry, but even to wish to marry."[74] Given all these reasons, it follows that the abuse of marriage and the breaking of vows among the clergy are not to be tolerated.

Article Twenty-Four

Concerning the Mass. The items in this article concerning the Most Holy Mass are to be accepted insofar as they agree with the teaching of the Holy Roman and Apostolic Church. However, those things that are added which are contrary to the practices of the universal Christian church are to be rejected because they offend God, threaten Christian unity, and cause dissension, strife, and insurrection in the Holy Roman Empire.

Now we turn to the issues in this article. First, contrary to the practice of the entire Roman church, they celebrate the Mass in German and not in Latin. Moreover, they pretend to call upon the authority of St. Paul, who taught that in the church a language should be used that is understood by the people, 1 Corinthians 14[:9]. But this is a misunderstanding of the words of Paul. According to this view, the entire Mass would have to be read in German, something they themselves do not do. For the priest not only represents the local community but acts on behalf of the entire church. Thus it is not improper for a representative of the Latin church to celebrate the Mass in Latin.

It is also beneficial for the listener to hear the Mass in the faith of the church. Experience teaches us that devotion is greater at Mass among Germans who do not understand Latin than among those who hear the Mass in German. The words of St. Paul should also be understood to say that for all those lacking understanding an "Amen" is sufficient [1 Cor. 14:16]. It is not necessary that all words in the Mass be heard and understood. Rather, it is much more profitable if the meaning of the Mass, namely, the Eucharist offered in memory of Christ's passion, be pondered and contemplated. Support for this view can be found in the early church. According to the opinions of the fathers, the apostles and their successors up until the time of the Emperor Hadrian[75] celebrated the Mass only in Hebrew, a language unknown to Christians, especially the gentile converts.

---

73. Cyprian, Ep. 4, 2 (*CSEL* 3/2:474; *ANF* 5:357); the Confutators used the numbering of the letters according to the edition by Erasmus, Basel, 1521.

74. Augustine, *De bono viduitatis* 9, 12 (*CSEL* 41:318; *NPNF*, ser. 1, 3:444–46).

75. Hadrian was Roman emperor from 117 to 138.

But even if the first Christians celebrated the Mass in the language of the people, such a practice would not be necessary today. At that time, many were converted who did not know the mysteries and ceremonies of the faith, and thus it was important for them to understand the words. However, Christians today know from infancy the practices and customs of the church and thus understand how to conduct themselves at Mass.

With regard to their complaints concerning the abuses of the Mass, all sensible people agree that these things should be corrected. But it should not be called an abuse when those serving at the altar receive their living from that altar. This is not an abuse but rather something commanded by divine and human law. St. Paul asks: "Who at any time pays the expenses for doing military service?" 1 Corinthians 9[:7]. He also says: "Do you not know that those who are employed in the temple service get their food from the temple, and those who serve at the altar share in what is sacrificed on the altar?" 1 Corinthians 9[:13]. Even Christ himself says "the laborer deserves to be paid," Luke 10[:7].

Most reprehensible is the abolition, in certain places, of private masses. They reason that foundations with a fixed income are sought only for personal gain. However, the abrogation of these masses diminishes the worship of God, dishonors the saints, invalidates the ultimate will of the founder, robs the souls of the dead of their rights, and it steals and chills the devotion of the living. The abolition of private masses should not be tolerated. Nor is it the case, as they assume we teach, that Christ's suffering and death was on behalf of original sin and thus the masses were instituted for the sake of actual sin. Catholics have never subscribed to this teaching, and today, if asked, would deny being taught such a thing. The truth is that the Mass does not abolish sins—repentance is the remedy designed specifically for this malady. Rather, the Mass abolishes the punishment owed on account of sin, supplies the satisfactions, increases grace, provides holy protection for the living, and, finally, brings the hope of divine consolation and aid in time of need.

Also, their insinuation that Christ is not offered in the Mass must be rejected by all, just as the faithful have always condemned this view. Augustine condemned this error in the Arians, who denied that the Mass was a sacrifice for the living and the dead.[76] This teaching is contrary to the Holy Scriptures and the entire church. Through the prophet Malachi, the Lord predicted the rejection of the Jews, the call of the gentiles, and the idea of sacrifice according to evangelical law for which we are contending: "I have no pleasure in you, says the Lord of hosts, and I will not accept an offering from your hands. For from the rising of the sun to its setting my name is great among the nations, and in every place incense is offered to my name, and a pure offering," Malachi 1[:10-11]. This passage can refer to nothing other than the pure sacrifice of the altar, the Holy Eucharist. These words of Malachi have been cited by Augustine and other

---

76. Augustine, *De haeresibus* 53 (*MPL* 42:40).

Christians on behalf of the Mass against the Jews.[77] Among catholic princes, these words ought to prove more persuasive than all the other objections of their adversaries.

Malachi, speaking of the coming of the Messiah, also says: "He will purify the descendants of Levi and refine them like gold and silver, until they present offerings to the Lord in righteousness. Then the offering of Judah and Jerusalem will be pleasing to the Lord as in the days of old and as in former years," Malachi 3[:3-4]. In the Spirit, the prophet foresees that the sons of Levi, who according to Jerome are the evangelical priests,[78] offer sacrifices not with the blood of goats but in righteousness, just as in days of old. And the same spirit which inspired the writing of the prophet also inspires the church when it repeats these words in the canon of the Mass.

Similarly, the angel spoke to the prophet Daniel: "Many shall be purified, cleansed, and refined, but the wicked shall continue to act wickedly. None of the wicked shall understand, but those who are wise shall understand. From the time that the regular burnt offering is taken away and the abomination that desolates is set up, there shall be one thousand, two hundred ninety days," Daniel 12[:10-11]. Christ testifies that this prophecy, which is not yet fulfilled, must be fulfilled, Matthew 24[:15]. Therefore, the daily sacrifice of Christ will universally cease upon the arrival of the abomination—the Antichrist—just as it has already ceased or been abandoned in certain churches. In the place of desolation, churches are destroyed, deserted, and abandoned. The result is that the canonical hours are not sung, the Mass is not celebrated, the sacraments are not distributed, and there are no altars, images of saints, candles, or furniture. Therefore, all princes and faithful subjects of the Roman Empire ought to be warned never to allow or neglect anything which encourages those who are preparing the way of the Antichrist. As it is written: "The woman (that is, the church) fled into the wilderness, where she has a place prepared by God, so that there she can be nourished for one thousand two hundred sixty days," Revelation 12[:6]. And finally, St. Paul says to the Hebrews: "Every high priest chosen from among mortals is put in charge of things pertaining to God on their behalf, to offer gifts and sacrifices for sins," Hebrews 5[:1].

The external priesthood has not ceased in the new covenant but has been transformed into a better office. Therefore, even today, the high priest and the entire priesthood offer in the church an external sacrifice, which is nothing other than the Eucharist. In connection with this, it is helpful to recall that episode in the history of the apostles where, according to the new translation, Barnabas, Simeon, Lucius of Cyrene, Manaen, and Saul made a sacrifice, Acts 13[:1]. This should not be construed as a sacrifice made to idols, but rather as a reference to the Mass since it is called by the Greeks "*liturgia.*"

77. Augustine, *Adversus Iudaeos* 9, 12 (*MPL* 42:60–61).
78. Jerome, *Commentary on Malachi* (*CCL* 76A:931f.).

That already in the early church the Mass was known as a sacrifice is testified to by a number of holy fathers. Ignatius, a follower of the apostle John, states: "It is not permissible without a bishop to offer a sacrifice or celebrate the Mass."[79] Also, Irenaeus, a student of the disciples of John, says: "Christ taught a new sacrifice of the New Testament, which the church, receiving from the apostles, offers to God throughout the entire world."[80] This teaching, coming shortly after the time of the apostles, demonstrates that the new evangelical sacrifice was offered throughout the whole world. Origen, Cyprian, Jerome, Chrysostom, Augustine, Basil, Hilary, and others teach and testify that this was so, but we omit their words for the sake of brevity. Therefore, since the entire catholic church has taught, held, and observed this doctrine from the time of the apostles, it ought to teach and hold the same today. Indeed, it ought to be held and observed with that objective.

It should be noted that this does not contradict St. Paul, who says that by one sacrifice we are justified through Christ, Hebrews 10[:10]. For Paul is speaking here of the bloody sacrifice of the lamb upon the cross. This naturally only happens once, and from it all the sacraments, especially the sacrifice of the Mass, receive their power and effectiveness. Christ was sacrificed once on the cross, shedding his blood. Today, however, he is sacrificed in the Mass without violence and in a sacramental way that is veiled in mystery and in which he does not suffer, just as he was sacrificed figuratively in the Old Testament.

The sense of the word "mass" itself shows that the reference is to sacrifice since "mass" means "sacrifice" and received its name from the Hebrew word *misbeach* ("altar," or in Greek, *thysiastirion*) on account of the sacrifice received there.

It has already been shown that, strictly speaking, we are justified not by faith but by love. And when the Scriptures say we are justified by faith, this is to be understood as a "living faith" which works through love, Galatians 5[:6]. Justification occurs not only through faith, since faith is "the assurance of things hoped for," Hebrews 11[:1].

It is also not being denied that the Mass is a memorial of Christ's passion and the benefits of God. This has been prefigured by the paschal lamb, who was at the same time a victim and a memorial, Exodus 12[:1-14]. The passion is represented not only in word and sacrament but also in the sacred ceremonial actions and vestments of the church. In memory of the victim on the cross, the church offers the Eucharist anew in the mysteries to God, the almighty Father. Therefore the princes and cities are not to be blamed for keeping the one common mass in the church, as long as they observe the sacred canons upheld by all in the catholic church. However, the abolition of all other forms of the Mass[81] goes beyond what the faith allows.

---

79. The reference is not clear. See Immenkötter, *Der Reichstag zu Augsburg und die Confutatio*, p. 81, n. 39.

80. Irenaeus, *Contra haereses* 4, 17, 5 (*MPG* 7/1:1023; *ANF* 1:484).

81. Above all, private masses are meant here.

No one disputes that in times past all present were communed. Indeed, it is to be desired today that all were so disposed to receive the sacrament worthily! But if they regard one mass as beneficial, why would not a number of masses be even more advantageous? Rather, they have unjustly disapproved of the latter.

When all these arguments are correctly considered, we must ask the princes and others to repudiate this new form of the Mass, which has already been frequently changed, and restore the old form according to the rite and custom of all Christendom and the churches of Germany. Further, private masses should be resumed in accord with the wills of those who founded them. If such policies were followed, they would gain benefit and honor for themselves and bring peace and tranquillity to all of Germany.

Article Twenty-Five

Concerning Confession. Our views regarding Confession have been given above in Article Eleven. Their claim that Chrysostom supports their position is wrong because they falsely apply his words about public confession to sacramental and priestly confession. This he makes clear at the beginning of the passage: "You should not confess publicly or accuse yourself before others."[82] This is consistent with what Peter Lombard[83] and Gratian[84] said three hundred years ago and is also confirmed by other passages in Chrysostom. According to the latter's twenty-ninth sermon regarding Confession (speaking of the penitent): "In his heart there is contrition, in his mouth confession and in his work complete humility. This is perfect and fruitful repentance."[85] Here the three parts of repentance are clearly set forth. In his tenth homily on Matthew, Chrysostom prescribes a fixed time for Confession and describes how the open wounds of sin are healed through repentance.[86] But how can these sins be healed if they are not disclosed to the priest through Confession? Chrysostom refutes this view in several passages, an opinion corroborated by Jerome, who says: "Let us say someone has been bitten secretly by the devil and been infected with the poison of sin. If this same person who has been bit remains silent and does not repent, that is, does not confess his sin to his brother and teacher, then how can the teacher, who has the words of healing, be of use to him? For if a sick person is ashamed to reveal his illness to the physician, how can the latter heal that of which he is ignorant?" Therefore, let the princes and civil authorities believe the writings of these holy fathers rather than one single gloss in a decretal of Gratian which has been rejected by those knowledgeable in the divine law.

82. Chrysostom, *Ep. ad Hebrews 12:4,* homily 31, 3 (*MPG* 63:216; *NPNF,* ser. 1, 14:506–7).

83. Peter Lombard, *Sententiarum* 4, 17, 3 (*MPL* 192:881).

84. Gratian (twelfth century) organized the collection of canon law known as the *Decretum.*

85. Actually not a writing of Chrysostom. See Immenkötter, *Der Reichstag zu Augsburg und die Confutatio,* p. 85, n. 46.

86. Chrysostom, *Matthew 3:1,* homily 10, 2 (*MPG* 57:186; *NPNF,* ser. 1, 10:63–64).

Since a pure and sincere confession is not only necessary for salvation but also a vital part of Christian life and obedience, the princes and civil authorities should be admonished to conform their practices to the teachings of the orthodox church. For this teaching of our opponents, as Jerome makes clear, is nothing other than the old heresy of the Montanists,[87] which was condemned 1,200 years ago. The Montanists were ashamed to confess their sins. It surely is not proper to follow this teaching. It is much better to observe the rite of the ancient fathers and the holy Christian church so that confession be practiced according to the standard of the one orthodox faith in all domains, so that this great treasure of the church may be held in high esteem and practiced in conformity to historic church practice.

Article Twenty-Six

The Distinction of Foods. What they say regarding the distinction of foods and other traditions—things for which they have little regard—must be rejected. For we know from St. Paul [Rom. 13:1] that all authority is given by God and that ecclesiastical authority in particular has been given by God for the purpose of edification. For this reason, it is important that the laws of the holy catholic church be accepted with reverence and piety and be regarded as legitimate. If this is done, then people will be strengthened in their resolve to follow the divine commands, which themselves have their foundation in the Holy Scriptures. The person who despises or resists these laws gravely offends God, as we hear in the words of Christ: "Whoever listens to you listens to me, and whoever rejects you rejects me, and whoever rejects me rejects the one who sent me," Luke 10[:16]. A prelate is despised when his statutes are despised. As St. Paul says: "Therefore whoever rejects this rejects not human authority but God, who also gives his Holy Spirit to you," 1 Thessalonians 4[:8]. In a similar manner, St. Paul speaks to the bishops, saying: "Keep watch over yourselves and over all the flock, of which the Holy Spirit has made you overseers, to shepherd the church of God," Acts 20[:28]. If the prelates have the power to rule, then they have the power to make statutes for the well-being of the church and the growth of its members. St. Paul tells the church at Corinth to do all things in good order, 1 Corinthians 14[:40], which is not possible unless there are laws. He also says to the Hebrews: "Obey your leaders and submit to them, for they are keeping watch over your souls and will give an account," Hebrews 13[:17]. Here, St. Paul not only asks for obedience but also gives the reasons for that obedience.

We see that St. Paul made use of his authority not only in matters concerning the Gospel but also to establish many rules and ordinances. He prescribed laws for the election of a bishop [1 Tim. 3:1-7] and for widows [1 Tim. 5:3-9]. Concerning women, he said they should cover their heads [1 Cor. 11:5] and that they should be silent in church [1 Cor. 14:34]. He even provided guidelines for dealing with secular matters, 1 Thessalonians 4[:11], such as the civil courts,

---

87. A sect of the second century that advocated a high degree of discipline and ethical rigor.

1 Corinthians 6[:1-6]. To the Corinthians, he says very clearly: "To the rest I say—I and not the Lord," 1 Corinthians 7[:12]. Finally, he also says: "So then, brothers and sisters, stand firm and hold fast to the traditions that you were taught by us, either by word of mouth or by our letter," 2 Thessalonians[2:15].

Therefore, the princes and the cities are to be admonished to obey the statutes and laws of the church. For if they refuse to obey God, they may find that their own subjects will withdraw their obedience as was the case in the recent revolt involving the peasants. The princes must take care lest they be led astray by false doctrines. It is completely without foundation when they say the righteousness of faith is obscured by these ordinances. A person would have to be demented and insane to practice them without faith. For these laws were given to Christians and not to the Turks or Ishmaelites. As St. Paul says: "For what have I to do with judging those outside?" 1 Corinthians 5[:12].

When they extol faith above all, they oppose St. Paul and actually do violence to the meaning of his words. They confuse what he is saying regarding evangelical works with legal works. These errors we have refuted and condemned above.

Also false is their view that these church ordinances obscure the law of God. Indeed, these statutes help a person to keep the law. For example, fasting helps to suppress the desires of the flesh, so that a person does not fall into the sin of lust.[88]

It is also false to hold, as they do, that it is impossible to keep these ordinances. However, the church is not a cruel mother who makes no exceptions in the celebration of festivals and in rules concerning fasting, etc.

Furthermore, they falsely cite Augustine who, in his reply to Januarius, says the opposite of what they claim. For here Augustine very clearly says that what has been universally binding on the church should be universally observed.[89] However, in matters indifferent, or those things in which a person is free to keep or not to keep, St. Augustine says, by the authority of St. Ambrose, that the customs of each church should be observed. For instance, he notes: "When I come to Rome, I fast on the sabbath, but when I am here I do not."[90]

Persisting in their errors, they twist the meaning of Scripture. For Christ does not completely overthrow human law but only those ordinances opposed to the law of God. As he says in Matthew: "And why do you break the commandment of God for the sake of your tradition?" Matthew 15[:3]. In Mark he says: "You abandon the commandment of God and hold to human tradition," Mark 7[:8]. Also, St. Paul teaches in Colossians that no one is to be condemned for not following Jewish customs concerning food, drink, and the Sabbath, Colossians 2[:16]. When the church forbids meat, it does not do it on the grounds that the Jews did, namely, that it was unclean. Hence their citation of

---

88. One of the seven deadly sins, the sin of *luxuria* in Latin.
89. See the reference to Augustine in the Augsburg Confession, Article XXVI.
90. Augustine, *Ep. 54 ad inquisitiones Ianuarii* 2, 3 (*CSEL* 34/2: 161; *NPNF*, ser. 1, 1:300–301).

the words of Christ concerning that which goes into the mouth [Matt. 15:11] fails to appreciate the context in which this saying was uttered. Christ's intention was to correct the error of the Jews, who believed that food prepared with unwashed hands was unclean and that those who ate this food also became unclean. However, it is not the intention of the church to reintroduce these burdensome Jewish observances.

They also completely misunderstand Paul's words in his first letter to Timothy in which he says those who forbid meats partake in a "teaching of demons," 1 Timothy 4[:1-3]. Heretical groups such as the Tatianites,[91] Marcionites,[92] and Manichaeans[93] thought that meat was unclean. However, this contradicts St. Paul, who says "everything created by God is good," 1 Timothy 4[:4]. The church does not forbid meat because it is evil or impure but rather as an aid to keeping the commandments of God. When the laws are viewed in this way, all arguments against them fail.

If they would preach the cross, bodily training, and the value of fasting with an eye toward bringing the body under discipline, then their teaching could be approved. However, their desire to leave these things free must be rejected and condemned because such a view is contrary to the faith and discipline of the church. It is not right for them to support their position by noting the variety of church practices and citing Jerome, who said that individual provinces could accommodate their own tastes and customs.[94] This must be understood as applying to special rites in a specific area or region. However, the universal rights of the church ought to be universally observed.

Their arguments about Easter are also not convincing. The Roman popes convinced Christians in Asia to celebrate Easter on the same day as the whole church. This is the way Irenaeus must be understood.[95] Similarly, without causing offense to faith, the vigils of some apostles were observed with fasting in Germany but not in France.

Let the princes and cities be admonished to follow the teaching of Pope Gregory, who held that the customs of individual regions might be observed as long as they do not contradict the catholic faith, ch. *Quoniam consuetudinem*, dist. 12.[96] We are not ignorant of the fact that various and different rites are observed within the unity of faith without injury to the entire catholic church.

---

91. Affiliation with the sect called the "Encratites," an ascetic group that rejected, among other practices, the eating of meat, was falsely ascribed to the second-century theologian Tatian in the Middle Ages and Reformation period.

92. Marcion (85–160) repudiated the Old Testament and advocated a strict separation between the spiritual and natural worlds.

93. See n. 1.

94. Jerome, Ep. 71, 6 (*CSEL* 55:7; *NPNF*, ser. 2, 6:154).

95. For a fuller examination, see Immenkötter, *Der Reichstag zu Augsburg und die Confutatio*, p. 89, n. 61.

96. The reference here is unclear; Immenkötter suggests the possibility that it refers to Gregory the Great, Ep. 1, 75 (*MPL* 77:529–30; *NPNF*, ser. 2, 12:98–99).

However, let churches everywhere observe this common and universal faith, which has been delivered and received from antiquity.

Article Twenty-Seven

Monastic Vows. This article examines a variety of matters. When all the issues are given thoughtful consideration, it must be maintained that monastic vows have a firm foundation in the Old and New Testaments. It can hardly be ignored that thousands and thousands of holy men, having been the recipients of miracles and other wonders of God, have lived their lives in religious orders. Since this way of living has been approved for hundreds of years and been accepted throughout the Christian church, it is not to be tolerated that vows are carelessly broken without any fear of God.

In the Old Testament, God approved the vows of the Nazarites, Numbers 6[:1-4], and the vows of the Rechabites, who neither drank wine nor ate grapes, Jeremiah 35[:6-8]. God also demands that anyone who makes a vow must fulfill it, Deuteronomy 23[:21]. And anyone who retracts a vow comes to ruin, Proverbs 20[:25]. However, the vows of the righteous are pleasing to God, Proverbs 15[:8]. Also, God teaches us through the prophet Isaiah that monastic vows find favor with him: "For thus says the Lord: To the eunuchs who keep my sabbaths, who choose the things that please me and hold fast my covenant, I will give, in my house and within my walls, a monument and a name better than sons and daughters; I will give them an everlasting name that shall not be cut off," Isaiah 56[:4-5]. The ones being promised these things are none other than the ones Christ himself praises, namely, those who "have made themselves eunuchs for the sake of the kingdom of heaven," Matthew 19[:12], and those who deny themselves, take up their cross, and follow Christ, Luke 9[:23].

These are no longer governed by their own will but rather the will of the one whom they serve. An even better witness, St. Paul, testifies that those virgins who spurn the world and its enticements and maintain their virginity in the cloisters do better than those who get married. As he says to the Corinthians: "He who marries a virgin does well; and he who refrains from marriage will do better," 1 Corinthians 7[:38]. Paul says concerning a widow: "But in my judgment she is more blessed if she remains as she is" [1 Cor. 7:40].

Well known to all are the holy lives led by Paul the Hermit, Basil, Anthony, Benedict, Bernard, Dominic, Francis, William, Augustine, Clara, Bridget, and other similar hermits who forsook the splendor and riches of the world out of love for the Lord Jesus Christ. Condemned of old was the heresy of the Lampetians,[97] which the heretic Jovinian[98] attempted to revive in Rome, although without success.

---

97. A fifth-century sect that rejected the means of grace and all outward aspects of religious life in favor of an inner "freedom of the soul."

98. See n. 32.

Therefore, all the things said in this article against monasticism must be rejected. For example, when it is said that in the time of Augustine monastic life was voluntary and that vows were added afterward, it should be noted that the opposite is true: vows came before the monasteries.

Even though the nunneries are inhabited by the weaker sex, the holy nuns have persevered in their vows more faithfully than the majority of monks. To this day, it has proved nearly impossible to move them from their holy purpose by prayers, cajoling, threats, terrors, or distress.

Therefore evil interpretations of the monastic life dare not be permitted to stand. The Holy Scriptures clearly show that the monastic life, when properly observed, merits and grows in eternal life, and that such an observance is, by God's grace, possible for anyone in holy orders. Christ himself promises this: "And everyone who has left houses or brothers or sisters or father or mother or children or fields, for my name's sake, will receive a hundredfold, and will inherit eternal life," Matthew 19[:29].

As they note, the monasteries were formerly schools,[99] but it should not be overlooked that they were first schools of virtue and discipline and that the study of Scripture was added later. For "no one who puts a hand to the plow and looks back is fit for the kingdom of God," Luke 9[:62]. In other words, marriages and the breaking of vows by monks and nuns are to be condemned because they are contrary to the spirit of the Scriptures as well as church and civil law. As St. Paul says: "They incur condemnation for having violated their first pledge," 1 Timothy 5[:12]. Furthermore, that vows are not contrary to the ordinance of God has been stated above in the second article concerning alleged abuses.

Also, their reference to papal dispensations of vows is to no avail. It may be true that the Pope granted a dispensation to the king of Aragon.[100] But it should be noted that he returned to the monastery after having children. Such a dispensation would occur only to keep peace in the kingdom or province, in order to prevent war, carnage, pillage, debauchery, or murder. However, private individuals who break their vows and commit apostasy have little ground for a dispensation.

It cannot be argued, as they do, that it is impossible to keep a vow. If continence is not possible, then how did so many men and women remain faithful to their vows down through the ages? It is true that the Scripture says, "But I perceived that I would not possess wisdom unless God gave her to me," Wisdom 8[:21]. But Christ has promised that it will be given: "Search and you will find," Luke 11[:9]; Matthew 7[:7]. And St. Paul says: "God is faithful, and he will not let you be tested beyond your strength, but with the testing he will also provide the way out so that you may be able to endure it," 1 Corinthians 10[:13].

---

99. *Scholae literarum*, or schools where the Scriptures were studied.

100. For the historical context, see Immenkötter, *Der Reichstag zu Augsburg und die Confutatio*, p. 92, n. 70.

They do not present sufficient grounds for their statement that the breaking of vows may be exempt from punishment because marriage is not forbidden.[101] One should also not break a vow made in marriage. Both of these vows (monastic and marital) are upheld in civil and canon law. Moreover, their arguments from the canon *Nuptiarum* are not persuasive since this document speaks not of religious vows but of ceremonial ones, which the church observes to this day. Thus the marriages of monks, nuns, and priests have never been accepted.

Their claim that the monastic life is a human invention is an empty one. For it is grounded in the Holy Scriptures, and the Holy Spirit has inspired this teaching in the church fathers. Nor does monasticism diminish Christ. Monks observe vows for Christ's sake and seek to imitate him. Their judgment that the monastic life is godless is without merit. It is actually the most Christian form of life.

The monks have not been separated from God's grace as the Jews of whom Paul spoke in Galatians who sought justification by the law of Moses, Galatians 5[:4]. The monks seek to live—as much as possible—according to the Gospel so that they might merit eternal life. Therefore, the accusations made here against monasticism are an insult to God.

Also to be addressed is their groundless charge that those in religious orders claim to be in a state of perfection. They have never said this. Rather, they see themselves in a position to acquire perfection. The rules of their orders are aids on the way to perfection but not perfection itself. This is how Gerson must be understood in his treatises "Against the Proprietors of the Rule of St. Augustine," "Concerning Evangelical Counsels," "Concerning Perfection of the Heart," et al. He did not deny that monastic orders exist for the purpose of acquiring perfection.

Thus the princes and the civil authorities should be instructed to reform the monasteries through the offices of those who supervise these institutions rather than to close them. For the improvement of monastic life must be the goal. This has been the intention of Christian princes down through the ages. And if the arguments in favor of monasticism by the holy and pious fathers have no standing with them, then let them listen to what his Imperial Highness, the Emperor Justinian, said in *Authentica. Concerning Monasticism.*[102]

Article Twenty-Eight

Concerning Ecclesiastical Power. In this article, they discuss many things about ecclesiastical power, often with considerable acrimony. However, it must be maintained that the spiritual powers granted to the most reverend bishops and

101. The Augsburg Confession (Article XXVII) argues that, since marriage is a divine command, to break a vow in order to get married is not against God's law.

102. The reference to this document can be found in Immenkötter, *Der Reichstag zu Augsburg und die Confutatio*, p. 95, n. 78.

priest by law or custom rightfully belong to them. These privileges, preferments, and immunities were given to them by Roman emperors and kings. Thus it cannot be tolerated if anyone, whether a prince or subject of the Roman Empire, attempts to infringe upon these rights.

It has been most satisfactorily demonstrated that ecclesiastical power in spiritual matters is based on divine right as St. Paul says: "Now even if I boast a little too much of our authority, which the Lord gave for building you up and not for tearing you down, I will not be ashamed of it," 2 Corinthians 10[:8]. In the same letter, he also says: "So I write these things while I am away from you, so that when I come, I may not have to be severe in using the authority that the Lord has given me for building up and not for tearing down," 2 Corinthians 13[:10]. Paul shows his willingness to use his power to compel someone when he says: "What would you prefer? Am I to come to you with a stick, or with love in a spirit of gentleness?" 1 Corinthians 4[:21]. And regarding legal matters, he writes to Timothy: "Never accept any accusation against an elder except on the evidence of two or three witnesses," 1 Timothy 5[:19]. From these and many other passages, it is easy to see that bishops have not only the power to preach the Word and administer the sacraments but also the authority to punish as well as to direct and guide their subjects so that they might obtain eternal salvation. It necessarily follows that when someone is given the power to govern, he must also be given the authority to judge and decide what is most helpful to reach the goal mentioned above, namely, eternal life. Therefore, everything that is asserted in this article against ecclesiastical and priestly immunity is without foundation.

Subjects of the Holy Roman Empire are forbidden to bring the clergy before civil courts since this would be contrary to the imperial privileges the civil realm has yielded to the church. For example, Pope Clement the Martyr says: "If any of the presbyters have trouble with one another, let the issue be settled by the presbyters of the church."[103] In the same way, the Christian emperor Constantine the Great was unwilling at the Council of Nicea to judge secular cases [among the clergy]: "You are gods, appointed by the true God. Go and settle the case among yourselves, for it is not proper that we judge gods."

In our comments above, we have given sufficient response to the issue involving church regulations. Nor is their cause aided by their appeals to Christian liberty since this is not liberty but wanton irresponsibility by which the people are led to a dangerous and even fatal sedition. For Christian liberty does not oppose the ordinances of the church. The latter exist to promote what is good. Rather, Christian liberty is opposed to the servitude of the Mosaic law and the servitude of sin. Christ says: "Very truly I tell you, everyone who commits sin is a slave to sin," John 8[:34].

Thus the breaking of the Lenten fast and other fasts, the refusal to abstain from meats, the neglect of the canonical hours, the omission of Confession

---

103. C. 11, q. 1, c. 32 (*CIC* I:635).

(namely, at Easter), and similar things are not a proper exercise of liberty but an abuse of it. Recall the warning of St. Paul: "For you were called to freedom, brothers and sisters; only do not use your freedom as an opportunity for self-indulgence, but through love become slaves to one another," [Gal. 5:13]. Thus Christians must not hide their sins under the cloak of evangelical freedom. This was forbidden by St. Peter, who said: "As servants of God, live as free people, yet do not use your freedom as a pretext for evil," 1 Peter 2[:16].

Finally, we must give the following reply to what they have said concerning abuses in the church. The princes and the estates of the Holy Roman Empire know well that neither his Imperial Majesty, nor individual princes, nor any other Christian approve even the slightest deviation from proper Christian practice. It is the desire of all, including the princes and the estates, that together we might work to eliminate or rectify the abuses. It is also their desire that the excesses in the civil and churchly realms be abolished so that these estates can be reformed for the better. All these things are done to improve the ecclesiastical estate so that the Christian faith, which has grown cold among some, might be returned to its original lively and vigorous state. The goal of renewal is shared by his Imperial Majesty, who has devoted great care and labor to its attainment and who will continue to work assiduously in the future for its achievement.

Epilogue

On the basis of this confession and the answer that has been made to it, his Imperial Majesty perceives that the Elector, princes, and estates agree on many of the articles with the catholic and Roman church. Further, these same authorities also condemn and reject the godless teachings that have been spread by pamphlet among the German people. His Imperial Majesty also hopes and does not doubt that when the princes and estates have heard and understood this response to the articles which up to this time have been disputed, that they will now come to agreement in these things as well as the other matters mentioned above. Thus, they will prove obedient to the Christian faith and the catholic and Roman church.

For such action, his Imperial Majesty will be especially grateful, and he will bestow favor upon the princes and cities, individually and collectively, when an opportunity presents itself. However, if this generous and Christian admonition is ignored, then the Elector, princes, and cities should know that his Imperial Majesty has sufficient cause as Roman emperor and Christian king to act as a defender and advocate of the catholic and Christian faith. This office and the dictates of his conscience will determine his future course of action.[104]

---

104. In a separate edict, Charles V threatened military action against the supporters of Luther if they did not return to the Roman obedience by 15 April 1531. He made good on this threat, a renewal of the Edict of Worms of 1521, in the Smalcald War, 1546–47.

Philip Melanchthon's Disputation

We Are Justified by Faith and Not by Love

Translated by Charles P. Arand

Introduction

Since the beginning of the fourteenth century, the medieval scholastic system had used the genre "disputation" as a means of examination for promotion from one academic degree to the next. At each stage of academic progress, students proved their abilities by defending theses written by their professors or themselves before the assembled instructors and students of their faculty. By the time of Luther and Melanchthon, the "disputation" as a collection of short, thetical statements on a subject had also become a means of provoking discussion among colleagues apart from the examination. Luther's Ninety-five Theses on indulgences are an example of this use of the genre. The reformers abolished the use of the disputation for more than a decade, restoring it for academic examination in 1533. They continued throughout the intervening decade, however, to employ the genre for provoking discussion of significant issues.

In the spring of 1531, as Melanchthon was polishing the first edition of his Apology of the Augsburg Confession, he composed thirty-eight theses on the doctrine of justification and its relation to the works of the Christian life. He apparently had them printed and also distributed them to a number of friends in order to elicit reactions to the ways in which he was developing his insights into the biblical teaching on righteousness.

This English translation of his disputation on "justification by faith, not by love" is based on the text of the 1531 printing as edited by Johannes Haussleiter in 1898, "Melanchthons *loci praecipui* und Theses über die Rechtfertigung aus dem Jahre 1531," in *Abhandlungen Alexander von Oettingen zum siebenzigsten Geburtstag gewidmet von Freunden und Schülern* (Munich: Beck, 1898), 245–62.

Philip Melanchthon's Disputation, "We Are Justified by Faith and Not By Love"

We Receive Forgiveness of Sins by Faith Alone in Christ

1. Certainly our opponents must admit that the forgiveness of sins is necessary above all else in justification because we are all under sin [Rom. 3:9, 23].

2. It is impossible to obtain the forgiveness of sins without faith in Christ, that is, without grasping Christ as our mediator and setting him against the wrath of God. This faith consoles consciences and brings them to life again.

3. It is ungodly to maintain that we receive the forgiveness of sins by our love for God because that is the same as saying that we have the forgiveness of sins on account of our own work and not on account of Christ. In this way, the merit of Christ is eradicated and destroyed.

4. Indeed, it is impossible for love to exist unless mercy is grasped first; otherwise, the heart flees the wrath of God and is angry at God's judgment.

5. Therefore, it is clear that faith alone justifies, that is, out of us unrighteous human creatures it makes human creatures who are acceptable to God, and it regenerates us.

6. There are three kinds of righteousness. The first is that which is derived from reason. The second is that which conforms to the law of God. The third is that which the Gospel promises.

7. It is certain that we are justified neither by reason, nor by the law, but by the Gospel, for otherwise the Gospel has been taught in vain.

8. It is certain that Christ is the mediator. We do not have access to God by means of reason or by the law prior to having this access through Christ [Rom. 5:2].

9. Nor do we have access through Christ in any other way than by faith.

10. The righteousness of reason is the righteousness of works, and reason produces it. Human beings understand what this righteousness is.

11. It is false that we merit the forgiveness of sins through such works of reason as monastic exercises and similar practices.

12. For this would attribute the mediatorial office attained by Christ to these works of reason. We have access to God through Christ by faith, not through the works of reason.

13. The righteousness of the law consists of love toward God and neighbor. Human reason does not understand this kind of righteousness. And while the sophists speak about loving God, they cannot show what love is because human nature, under the control of concupiscence, cannot see what it means to love God.

14. The office of mediator must not be attributed to our love even if this love is present. Accordingly, we do not have access to God by virtue of our own love but by faith on account of Christ.

15. Therefore, Paul says that we are not justified by the law but by the promise [Gal. 3:18, 24].

16. It is necessary, therefore, for the righteousness of the promise to be present before the righteousness of the law or reason.

17. The promise is received by faith. For that reason we are first justified by faith, by which we receive the promise of reconciliation by faith. Thereafter we keep the law.

18. Condemned are those who approach God through the law or through reason without the mediator Christ.

On Love and the Fulfilling of the Law

19. Nevertheless, since we are born anew by faith and have received the Holy Spirit, the righteousness of the law is present in us, namely, love for God and neighbor, fear of God, obedience toward governmental authorities and parents, patience, and similar virtues.

20. This initial keeping of the law is produced in those who already have been justified and born anew.

21. Therefore, love does not regenerate.

22. Therefore, the faith which regenerates has rendered the person righteous beforehand.

23. The office of mediator dare not be subsequently shifted to human fulfillment of the law.

24. Likewise, afterwards we are not pronounced righteous in God's sight on account of that fulfillment of the law but only because we have access to him through Christ by faith.

25. And this fulfillment of the law is extremely meager and impure because the remnants of sin remain in us.

26. And yet the righteousness of the law necessarily follows faith.

27. This must be made clear lest we seek the righteousness of the law in such a way as to destroy faith and rely on the fulfillment of the law. It is certainly necessary to insist that we are pronounced righteous on account of Christ by faith.

28. The sophists only speak about the fulfillment of the law. They do not speak of faith. They imagine that we are reputed righteous on account of this fulfilling the law and not through faith.

29. And we are righteous through that righteousness [of faith], and not through a righteousness of the law, which God does not accept except on account of faith by which we take hold of Christ the mediator.

Response to the Arguments of the Opponents

30. Hence all the statements about works can easily be explained. The law can never be performed, or if it is performed, it is not acceptable unless we first

take hold of the mediator, Christ, by faith. Thus Christ says, "Without me you can do nothing" [John 15:5].

31. Therefore, whenever works are praised, it is necessary to understand that faith is present because apart from Christ no one pleases God [Rom. 14:23; Heb. 11:6].

32. It is insane to imagine that the law truly suffices without the gospel, that is, without Christ. Therefore, only on account of faith are works acceptable to God.

33. James rightly teaches, "We are justified by faith and works" [2:24], because works justify according to the righteousness of the law, which certainly ought to follow faith. Nevertheless, this righteousness of the law is not righteousness in God's sight except on account of faith.

34. And the resulting works, because they please God on account of faith, are also meritorious, not for righteousness or eternal life but for other blessings of body and soul.

35. For the law pays a wage, and those who keep the law earn certain rewards.

36. When we say that faith alone justifies, this must be understood not only to mean that in the beginning it receives the forgiveness of sins or turns to God, but also that thereafter faith alone is regarded as righteousness by God even though the fulfillment of the law necessarily follows it. Truly this fulfillment of the law is not acceptable in God's sight except on account of faith.

37. In this way, consciences have a sure consolation in Christ through faith, and they know how these works are to be performed and which works please God and that by faith through Christ they receive the Holy Spirit so that they are able to perform good works.

38. To summarize: Scripture imprisons all under sin, so that what was promised through faith in Jesus Christ may be given to those who believe [Gal. 3:22].

39. Aristotle rightly and wisely said that moderation in virtue is to be determined geometrically, not arithmetically.[1]

---

1. Melanchthon referred to Aristotle's idea of moderation or the golden mean in these terms in his *Ethicae doctrinae elementorum libri duo* of 1550 (*CR* 13:211–12). He defined the Aristotelian idea of moderation not in "arithmetic" terms, that is, as a point halfway between opposites or extremes, but rather "geometrically," that is, understood proportionately or relationally, with prudence and wisdom. See W. F. R. Hardie, *Aristotle's Ethical Theory*, 2d ed. (Oxford: Clarendon, 1980), 134–43, 189–90.

The Augsburg Interim

Translated by Oliver K. Olson

Introduction

At the Diet of Worms in 1521, Emperor Charles V outlawed Martin Luther and all who persisted in following Luther's call for the reformation of the teaching of the church. Civil war in his Spanish domains, attacks from Mediterranean pirates and the armies of the Turkish empire, continued military encounters with his French rivals, led by King Francis I, and ongoing tensions between the imperial government and the papacy distracted Charles from executing the Edict of Worms for a quarter of a century. Shortly after Luther's death in 1546, the emperor felt free to mount a military campaign against the Protestant princes and cities in his German realm. War broke out between the Lutheran league of Smalcald and the imperial government, aided by papal troops, Roman Catholic German rulers, and even a few Evangelical princes, among them Duke Moritz of Saxony. The forces of the Smalcald League were led by Moritz's father-in-law, Landgrave Philip of Hesse, and Moritz's cousin, Elector John Frederick of Saxony. Their Evangelical armies were defeated on 24 May 1547, at the battle of Mühlberg.

With these two leading Lutheran princes enchained in imperial prison, Charles felt able to redesign the religious map of Germany. He called for an imperial diet to meet in the city of Augsburg in late 1547, and he appointed a commission of theologians to devise a new religious policy for his empire. In response to pressure from Roman Catholic princes and ecclesiastical officials, Charles decided to enforce this policy only upon Evangelical lands and cities.

The original commission was led by auxiliary bishop Michael Helding of Mainz and included the head of the Carmelite province of Cologne, Eberhard Billick, the Spanish Dominican Pedro Malvenda, and Balthasar Fannemann. They were assisted by three members of Charles's Spanish circle, including two Dominican imperial confessors, Pedro de Soto and Domingo de Soto. This group prepared the first draft of the new religious policy in what scholars have called the "December Formula." Criticism from those in Charles's circle who represented the ideals of Erasmian reform managed to win the rejection of the "December Formula," and a new committee was formed, with the newly elected bishop of Naumburg-Zeitz, the reform-minded Julius Pflug; Helding; and the renegade Evangelical court preacher in Berlin, Johann Agricola, at its core. Agricola's antinomian views had separated him from Luther in the late 1530s, but now in the service of the elector of Brandenburg, he was able to support an Erasmian reform program that stood in stark contrast to his earlier position.

With help from other Roman Catholic theologians, these three produced the second draft of the new religious policy, the "March Formula," after many hours of negotiation, with the aid of reactions gathered from Electors Joachim II of Brandenburg, Frederick II of Palatinate, and Moritz of Saxony as well as representatives of the cities of Nuremberg and Strassburg. While work on the policy itself was being completed, a "Formula for Reformation" was issued separately on 14 June 1548. The text of the "Formula" appears to have been derived from earlier drafts of proposals for compromise and reform from the pen of Pflug as well as materials drafted by Helding and Johann Gropper, a theologian in Cologne, who had led efforts to bring reform within the Roman party for more than a decade. It dealt with practical issues of church life.

The Augsburg Interim was published on 15 May 1548. Imperial troops from Germany, Spain, and Italy began to enforce it in those areas that they occupied in southern Germany, above all the Duchy of Württemberg, where some three hundred pastors were driven from office into exile or hiding. Among them was the reformer Johannes Brenz. The cities of Nördlingen and Esslingen were punished for resistance to the Interim by having Spanish troops quartered in the homes of their citizens. The city of Constance lost its municipal rights and was made a provincial city of the Hapsburg realm. In a number of south German cities, the municipal governments were forced to oust leading Evangelical pastors; Andreas Osiander left Nuremberg, Nicholas Gallus left Regensburg, and Martin Bucer and Paul Fagius left Strassburg. Resistance to the Augsburg Interim was successful in northern Germany, beyond the reach of imperial troops, particularly in the cities of Lübeck, Hamburg, Bremen, and, above all, Magdeburg. The government of Brandenburg published the Interim but did not enforce it. The government of electoral Saxony attempted its own compromise with the religious policy of the Augsburg Interim, formulating it in a series of drafts that came to be known as the Leipzig Interim.

The enforcement of the Augsburg Interim declined, and the policy itself became a dead letter with the Truce of Passau of 1552, which tentatively granted adherents of the Augsburg Confession an inferior but legal status within the empire. These terms were strengthened and made permanent in the Religious Peace of Augsburg of 1555.

This translation follows Joachim Mehlhausen, ed., *Das Augsburger Interim von 1548* [Texte zur Geschichte der evangelischen Theologie 3] (Neukirchen-Vluyn: Neukirchener Verlag, 1970).

The Augsburg Interim

Preface

Although from the beginning of your reign, Your Imperial Majesty has wanted nothing more than to do and promote everything that in any way can bring together all of Christendom, especially the holy empire of the German nation, your beloved fatherland, for the sake of its honor, welfare, and happy state, and for preserving the peace, unity, and tranquillity of all estates under Your Majesty's wings and benevolent government:

Yet, on the basis of sufficient clear evidence, Your Majesty has realized for a long time and has learned from experience that without a Christian resolution or settlement of this most ruinous controversy—the religious dispute from which have already arisen all manner of discord, rancor, wars, anxiety, and trouble among the estates—within the framework of the law, there is no hope for lasting peace, justice, or public tranquillity.

Your Majesty has therefore left no stone unturned, by means of various colloquies and negotiations, to move this destructive disagreement toward Christian concord and better understanding.

When this matter was investigated, experience made it clear that this dissent has sent out such deep roots that not only Germans but many other nations as well were affected, and it was beginning to be a common problem for all. The result is that it seems impossible to settle such a grave disorder as this in any other way than by a universal catholic council. At length, responding to the entreaties of the estates, and after many discussions about the matter, Your Majesty had a general council assemble in the German nation, and it began meeting at Trent.[1] That is why also at the beginning of these meetings he negotiated with the estates and persuaded them that, in the footsteps of the holy fathers and our forefathers, who in matters of faith were always accustomed to return to the holy councils and to comply with them, they should join in consenting to adhere to and submit to this council. Beyond that, they permitted Your Majesty freedom to consider Christian and suitable means by which all estates can live and dwell together piously and peacefully for the time until the completion and determination of the council, so that no one is oppressed contrary to law and justice. And just as Your Majesty most graciously accepted the agreement of the estates to put the matter in his hands, and no less does he accept it now.

On the issue of assuming responsibility for this himself, since it is a weighty matter, Your Majesty deliberated faithfully with fatherly love, and (as they

---

1. The German-speaking episcopal city of Trent was part of the German empire. Emperor Charles V insisted that the council be held within his domains, basing his argument on the ancient tradition that councils were held in the area in which the problems they were treating had arisen.

know) examined the opinions of the estates with the greatest care, considering the matter not without sorrow in his heart, as he perceived what immense damage has been caused to this illustrious nation by the dissent mentioned above and what calamities and destruction it threatens. So until the general council has made progress and come to some resolution, to maintain peace, justice, and unity and to remove the seeds of discord, it is a matter of absolute necessity that this matter not be left in the present state of confusion, hanging in the air, but rather that greater Christian concord, moderation, and a healthier and more proper understanding be restored. This is necessary to prevent them from disturbing and impeding public peace, that the many intruding opinions to the contrary should no longer be left unnoticed.

While Your Majesty was wholly occupied with this matter, it happened that certain men of high rank and name, no doubt because of zeal for Christian concord, peace, and tranquillity, and out of genuine love for the fatherland, offered the appended document—their advice and opinion—to Your Majesty, submitted it for more precise discussion, and promised that they themselves would observe it diligently.

Your Majesty referred the document for examination to several distinguished scriptural experts and to proven teachers. From their report it is clear that, understood in the proper Christian sense, with the exception of two articles on communion under both kinds and marriage of priests, it does not vary from our true Catholic religion and ecclesiastical doctrines, statutes, and ordinances. It is conducive, rather, to promoting and achieving a fuller Christian concord in the religious controversy and conserving public peace and tranquillity in the holy empire. In the same way, in the trying nature of these times, Your Majesty wishes nothing more than that in religion all estates under your imperial rule live together and agree amicably and peacefully, just as is expected of Your Majesty in his office.

So Your Majesty graciously sets the requirements before the common estates who thus far have observed the ordinances and statutes of the universal church, graciously entreating them to observe them henceforth as well, that they continue in them resolutely, that they persevere in them, and not depart from them, or change what they have constantly promised to do in any way. In the same way, Your Majesty mercifully and earnestly demands that the remaining estates who have introduced novelties either conform to the common estates and agree with them in the observation of the statutes and ceremonies of the universal Catholic church, or immediately conform their doctrine and ecclesiastical ordinances completely to the aforementioned council, and not institute or attempt anything beyond this. In cases where they have introduced something more, they shall conform firmly in everything to the council and confession, and persevere in it. For the promotion of public peace, quiet, and unity, all estates shall support the said document for now, and not oppose it, or teach, write, or preach anything against it, and all estates shall patiently and obediently accept the declaration and decision of the universal council.

Nevertheless, Your Majesty will employ all diligence, and according to the request of the estates, leave nothing untried by which the universal council can be convoked as soon as possible, and the German nation be completely freed from the present schism. In like manner, Your Majesty is already very much engaged in publishing a specific program for catholic reformation in the present diet. It is hoped that this program will also be fruitful in abolishing abuses and scandal and for planting and preservation of Christian discipline, conduct, and virtue until the council resolves the matter.

In the recommendation mentioned, under the rubric on ceremonies, it was reported, among other things, that if anything crept in that might be a cause for superstition, it should be removed, etc. In that article, or in other articles, Your Imperial Majesty should reserve the right to restrain such superstition, so as to arrange matters properly where and to the extent that it is necessary, now and at all future times. For everything that can be undertaken, established, brought about, and improved for increasing God's honor, for settling the religious disputes, and maintaining lasting peace, justice, and unity in the holy empire of the German Nation, and finally for the welfare and benefit of the common estates, in that, according to your imperial office, with all mercy, Your Majesty shows himself most ready.

I. On the Human Condition before the Fall

In the beginning, God created the human creature in his image and likeness [Gen. 1:26-27], adorned that creature with grace, and brought about that through original righteousness he was just in all powers, of both body and soul, and driven by no shameful or perverse impulses. Rather, in him the flesh submitted to the spirit, and the inferior powers of the soul to the superior, which impelled him to the good.

Since the human soul was so well constituted, God left him free to make his own decisions [Eccles. 15:14] so that he had no less power to choose good than to choose evil.

If he had used this freedom rightly and had obeyed the commands that God gave him, the human creature would have preserved the good things and righteousness he had received for himself and his posterity, and he and his posterity would have lacked nothing for living well and blessedly. Neither hunger or thirst, heat or cold, pain or illness, or death would have afflicted him. Finally, he would have escaped all sin and guilt, and no detriment from them would have been assigned to him and his posterity as payment for sin.

II. On the Human Condition after the Fall

But after our first parent acted against God's command, he fell into punishment imposed by God and lost the most beautiful gift, original righteousness [Rom. 5:12ff.]. Hence the lack of original righteousness, together with the corrupt habitus of concupiscence, which constantly resists the Spirit and the higher powers of the soul [Eph. 2:1ff.; Gal. 5:17]. This sin (that is the deprivation of that righteousness, by which it gave up the reason which had been subject to God, together with concupiscence) spread to all his posterity, so that all people, as many as come into the world, are born with it. Nor is anyone free of it, according to the Scriptures, not even a child a day old [Job 25:4; 14:4-5].[2]

And hence the damage to our nature: natural human beings do not perceive things of the Spirit [1 Cor. 2:14; 12:3]. Prior to grace, he does not desire and choose such things since the desire and passion of the flesh that rules in him is enmity against God and abhors God's law, and hampers the good as much as it provokes and impels to evil [Rom. 5:10; 8:7].

And although such people retain free will, albeit weak and damaged, from which flow the moral virtues and actions of the heathen as from a spring, yet prior to the grace of God and restoration to the righteousness which avails before God, they are unable to attain this righteousness but are rather servants of sin, slaves of Satan, enemies of God, and guilty of the evil of this world. They are burdened with hunger, thirst, cold, heat, sorrow, death, and are finally destroyed by death itself: for "sin came into the world through one man and death came through sin" [Rom. 5:12].

But these penalties for the first lie are common to the reborn and to sinners. God applies them to the former as exercise, but inflicts them on the impious as punishment.

In addition, in such people, whom original sin has corrupted, Satan, together with evil concupiscence, reigns at the same time, so long as they live only according to nature and are not renewed by grace. Satan holds these prisoners with the chains of their slavery and works in them, so that their desires are changed, producing the will of the flesh and their own reasoning. Moreover, they crown this original sin, which they assumed from their parents, with actual sins, and according to the apostle, such people are children of wrath [Eph. 2:3]. So, if they were to die in their most wretched condition, thrown into Gehenna according to a just judgment, they would be punished in eternal torment, there where, as is written in Isaiah [66:24], their fire shall not be quenched and their worm shall not die.

III. On Redemption through Christ Our Lord

God, therefore, who is rich in mercy, not willing that those he created should perish [John 3:16], since it is impossible for human beings to save themselves [Rom. 3:9-20], sent his Son into the world, so they would have redemption in our Lord and Savior, through his blood, as it is written by the apostle [Eph. 1:7].

---

2. On the provenance of this citation, oriented to the Septuagint, see Augustine, *Confessions* 1, 7, 11 (*CSEL* 33/9:4–5; *NPNF*, ser. 1, 1:48).

For God laid our iniquities on him [Isa. 53:5-6] so that he bore sins in his body on the cross, fastening them to the wood [1 Peter 2:24]. Since he suffered as an innocent person for us sinners and made satisfaction for sins, he redeemed us and placated God the Father, so that the same Father, for the sake of his blood, would absolve us wretched people, polluted with sins, as well, and reconcile us to himself. For God, as Paul says, truly "was in Christ reconciling the world to himself, not counting their trespasses against them, and entrusting the message of reconciliation to us" [2 Cor. 5:19].

And although God is gracious to us freely and for his name's sake, and he blots out our sins for his own sake, nevertheless, to show his own righteousness [Rom. 3:26], he does not remit sin without the payment of satisfaction. Because of his incomprehensible wisdom and immense goodness, he mixed his justice with mercy and determined that the price for redeeming us would be the blood of his Son, so that that most innocent lamb bore our punishments, which we sinners ought to suffer, on the cross, and so that we could borrow the payment for our salvation we poor sinners lacked from his wounds and appropriate them for our redemption and salvation. He did this so that, although the most benign Father has mercy on us freely, yet his mercy does not take place except through the intervention of the blood of his Son. And all that happens to us here gratuitously, we have to attribute to the merit and the righteousness of Christ, so that everyone who glories may glory in him our Lord, Redeemer and Savior [1 Cor. 1:29-31].

IV. On Justification

Those who are redeemed by the precious blood of Christ and to whom the merit of Christ's passion is applied are justified immediately, that is, they find forgiveness of their sins, are absolved from the guilt of eternal damnation and renewed through the Holy Spirit. In this manner, the unrighteous are made righteous. For when God justifies, he does not act only in a human way with people, by merely ignoring their sin, forgiving them the sin, and absolving them from guilt, but he also makes them better, something that human beings are not accustomed to granting and cannot grant. For God shares with them the Holy Spirit, who purifies the heart and rouses it through the love poured out in this same heart, so that they desire what is good and just and with good works pursue what God desires.

That is the true kind of inherent righteousness that David desired when he delivered these words: "Create in me a clean heart, O God, and put a new and right spirit within me" [Ps. 51:10]. The apostle also speaks of it: "You were washed, you were sanctified, you were justified" [1 Cor. 6:11]. And when he says, "He saved us, not because of any works of righteousness that we had done, but according to his mercy, through the washing of rebirth and renewal by the Holy Spirit. This Spirit he poured out on us richly through Jesus Christ our Savior, so that having been justified by his grace, we might become heirs according to the hope of eternal life" [Titus 3:5-8].

But although this righteousness which flows from the font of the law of the Spirit is much more abundant than the righteousness of the scribes and the Pharisees [Matt. 5:20], nevertheless, in those who have such righteousness, as long as we live here on earth, lust battles against the Spirit [Gal. 5:17]. Therefore, it happens that the same people serve the law of God with their mind, but with their flesh serve the law of sin and do not live without sin [Rom. 7:22-23; 1 John 1:6-10].

Therefore, since as long as they live here on earth, people cannot attain the full perfection of inherent righteousness, Christ, whom God made our wisdom, our righteousness and sanctification and redemption [1 Cor. 1:30], most graciously hastens to help us also in this situation. Since, just as through sharing his righteousness he produces inherent righteousness in the one with whom he shares it, so also he increases it, so that it is renewed from day to day, until that person is fully perfected in the eternal fatherland. And through the merit of his precious blood and righteousness, which is perfect, he procures indulgence for people, so that what they cannot perform adequately because of their infirmity is obtained and granted through the perfection of Christ himself. Hence John's consolation: "My little children, I am writing these things to you so that you may not sin; but if anyone does sin, we have an advocate with the Father, Jesus Christ the righteous; and he is the atoning sacrifice for our sins" [1 John 2:1-2].

Thus, Christ's merits and inherent righteousness come together, and we are renewed in them by the gift of love. They are inherent, so that we may thereby live "self-controlled, upright, and godly lives in this world, while we are waiting for our blessed hope, the manifestation of the glory of our great God and Savior" [Titus 2:12-13]. But Christ's merit is involved, so that it may be a cause of our inherent righteousness, and so that in the same merit and precious blood of Christ we may recover and find that by it we are able to be strengthened in the hope of eternal life most firmly since we stumble and fall in many matters, and because of our weakness and imperfection many things happen that disturb our hearts and are able to tempt us to despair.

For in Christ Jesus the Lord, our Redeemer and Savior, whom the faithful put on, and with whom everything is given, according to the apostle [Gal. 3:27; Rom. 8:32], everything is absolutely firm, unshakable, and perfect, so that we are strengthened by him to a living hope.

V. On the Use and Fruits of Justification

Those who are justified have peace with God through our Lord Jesus Christ [Rom. 5:1], for God is appeased, merciful, and gracious to them so that they are able to hope. If God reconciled them to himself through the death of his Son, when they were enemies, much more, now that they are reconciled, they may hope that they will be saved. So we may rightly appropriate the word of the apostle, which is full of consolation [Rom. 5:10].

Likewise, those who are justified are also adopted as God's sons, heirs of the eternal Father in heaven, as St. Paul teaches [Rom. 8:14-15], coheirs of Christ, and have the right of entering into the heritage, life eternal.

VI. On the Manner by Which the Human Creature Receives Justification

Since God does not justify human beings on the basis of the works of righteousness that they do, but gratuitously, that is, without their merit, if they want to glory, let them glory in Christ alone, by whose merit alone they are redeemed from sin and justified. Yet the merciful God does not deal with such people as with a dead block of wood, but draws them through acts of will, if they are of the age of reason. For such people do not receive those benefits of Christ, unless their minds and wills are moved by the prevenient grace of God to detest sin. For since, as Isaiah says [Isa. 59:2], sins separate God from us, none can come to the throne of grace and mercy, unless through repentance they have earlier turned from the same sin. Therefore, when he prepared the way for the Lord, John said, "Repent, for the kingdom of heaven is at hand" [Matt. 3:2].

Then the same divine grace moves the mind to God through Christ, and the movement is of faith, through which people, believing without hesitation, assent to the Holy Scriptures and what they announce. For Christ himself, as soon as he urges repentance, requires such faith, saying, "The time is fulfilled, and the kingdom of God is at hand; repent, and believe in the gospel" [Mark 1:15].

People believe this and are converted out of fear of divine righteousness, by which they are disturbed in a beneficial way, moved to reflect on the mercy of God and redemption by the blood of Christ; through the moving of God's grace they are aroused and receive trust and hope, so that they believe in hope beyond hope, that is, beyond hope in their own merit and in hope for the promised mercy. Such people give God the glory and so are led to love.

And those who rest through such faith on the mercy of God and the merit of Christ and entrust themselves to his mercy and merit receive the promise of the Holy Spirit, and so they are justified through faith in God according to the Scriptures. Not only is their sin remitted, but they are also sanctified and renewed through the Holy Spirit. For this faith obtains the gift of the Holy Spirit, through which the love of God is poured out into our hearts. To the extent that love is added to faith and hope, to that extent we are truly justified by inherent righteousness. For this righteousness is made up of faith, hope, and love, so that if you would subtract any of these from righteousness, you would clearly leave it incomplete.

VII. On Love and Good Works

As soon as love, however, which is the end of the commandments and the fullness of the law, enters into justification, it is fruitful and in itself a seed of all good works [Ps. 1:3; 1 Tim. 1:5; Rom. 13:8]. As it is ready to bear good fruits of righteousness [Gal. 5:6, 22], so it bears them in the justified as soon and as often as it should, and its performance power is not taken away from it by any hindrance. Therefore, faith which does not work through love is not seen to be alive, but rather sterile and dead, as also James says [2:17]. Furthermore, no matter how much faith people have, as John testifies [1 John 3:14], if they lack love, they remain in death since especially love ought to be a part of life eternal in us. It begins in us and is finally perfected through glorification. Then, although faith and hope cease, when we travel into the eternal tabernacles, love will remain [1 Cor. 13:33], and with us it will enter into those tabernacles, so that according to it we are able to live most beatifically and to God, who will be all to us [1 Cor. 15:28], and enjoy the eternal age. Nevertheless, faith, by which Christians are distinguished from infidels, is true to the extent that they assent to the Scriptures and the revelation from God, even if the faith is separated from love.

And from this greatest gift of God (which the more it grows and increases in us, the more the old being of our flesh diminishes) flow as from a fountain all good works, which are so necessary for the salvation of everyone justified, that those who do not perform that to which they are obligated lose the grace of God and will be cut off from Christ as useless branches and thrown into fire, as Christ himself teaches in his Gospel [Matt. 7:19; John 15:6].

And indeed these works are of such a nature that God necessarily can compel them from us. Even the saints, if they do all the precepts which are commanded them, ought to know and say that they are unworthy servants [Luke 17:10]. Nevertheless, they flow from love and come about by God's grace. Because according to his will, God freely promises a reward to those who do his will, he deems them worthy of the reward of temporal goods and of eternal life, according to the testimony of the apostle, who says: be abounding in all good work "because you know that in the Lord your labor is not in vain" [1 Cor. 15:58]. "For God is not unjust; he will not overlook your work and the love that you showed for his sake in serving the saints, as you still do" [Heb. 6:10].

And those who are justified and have been made slaves of righteousness, showing their members to be slaves of righteousness toward sanctification [Rom. 6:18-19] through cooperating with grace, abound in good works, and the more they abound in them, the greater growth in righteousness is added to them, so that those who are righteous become more righteous. "Do not fear being justified until death" [Eccles. 18:22]. "Let him who is righteous still do right" [Rev. 22:11]. And whoever is fruitful in Christ will be purified by the heavenly father, so that he will bear more fruit, as Christ himself teaches [John 15:2]. And that is the righteousness that comes from the works about which James, the brother of the Lord, speaks [2:14-17].

What remains is: since works are mandated by God as necessary to salvation, they are especially to be encouraged, according to the words of Christ: If you would enter life, keep the commandments [Matt. 19:17]. So the works which are added to the commandments and honored piously and honestly should also be praised. It would be neither good nor useful to stray from the Holy Spirit, who commends many people in the Holy Scriptures to leave all and follow the Lord [Matt. 19:21], also, to preserve virginity or celibacy. Otherwise, why should not David have been ridiculed by Michol when he danced before the ark [2 Kings 6:5-7, 20-27]? And Paul would have remitted the salary of those to whom he preached the Word of God in vain [1 Cor. 9:12-15].

Briefly, the works of supererogation, which, as Chrysostom says, are works above the commandments, must be distinguished from those that are against them.[3] For Christ himself condemns the latter as the leaven of the Pharisees [Luke 11:37-41], but the Holy Spirit commends the former in the Scriptures, saying: "Accept my offerings of praise, O Lord" [Ps. 119:108].

VIII. On Confidence in the Forgiveness of Sins

Here one must take care lest people make themselves too secure, trusting themselves, or that by anxious doubt we thrust them into desperation. Thus, Paul says that he himself is conscious of no sin, but he is not thereby justified [1 Cor. 4:4]. Because of their own infirmity or indisposition people cannot believe without doubt that their sins are remitted. But just as they ought not boast in themselves, so they ought not to be afraid, so that they doubt the efficacy of God's promise and of his death and resurrection and think that they cannot arrive at the remission of sins and salvation. But all their hope and the certainty of their whole faith ought to be in the precious blood of Christ, which was shed for us and for our salvation. In this very blood, we are surely able and ought to revive and trust, confirmed by the Holy Spirit, who gives testimony to our spirit, that we are children of God [Rom. 8:16].

IX. On the Church

Now we must consider the church, the communion of believers in Christ, in which the Holy Spirit assembles and joins together the reborn and Christians to be one house, one body, from one baptism and one faith, which, according to Paul, is one in all Christians [Eph. 4:3-6]. So, although it is necessary that the life of Christians be good and pious, so that it attains to the perfect end to which the church strives, let none persuade themselves that piety of life will be of use unless it is joined and accommodated to this unity and communion of the faithful. Therefore, the church is the house of the living God and that body

---

3. John Chrysostom, Hom. in Mt. 19.16 (*MPG* 58:604; *NPNF*, ser. 1, 10:387–88).

whose head is Christ. "For we many are one body in Christ" [1 Cor. 10:16-17; Rom. 12:5; Eph. 2:22; 1 Tim. 3:15], says Paul.

For this church our same Lord Jesus Christ gave himself up, "in order to make her holy by cleansing her with the washing of water by the Word, so as to present the church to himself in splendor, without a spot or wrinkle or any thing of this kind—yes, so that she may be holy and without blemish" [Eph. 5:26-27].

And since the church is that only dove [Song of Sol. 6:8] and one body, Christ sanctifies and upholds only her with his Spirit, and outside of her he grants the gifts of his grace to no one. Therefore, whoever is not in the communion of this body will be just as little vivified by the Holy Spirit unto eternal salvation as a natural member broken or cut off from its body to natural life because it is not revived by the spirit of life that flows alone from its head. Therefore, it should be believed that no one outside the Christian church and her spiritual communion is able to come to eternal life.

But it is the nature of this community that when the Spirit of Christ flows from him as head to his body, that is, passes through the church and all its members, individual members receive from him as much as is necessary for salvation, and whatever good happens to each one comes to them all and benefits the whole community. For, as the apostle says, the members grow in love "in every way into him who is the head, into Christ, from whom the whole body, joined and knit together by every ligament with which it is equipped, as each part promotes the body's growth in building itself with love" [Eph. 4:15-16]. In this communion and community of people is the greatest communion, since one member is concerned about the other, and "if one member suffers, all suffer together; if one member is honored, all rejoice together" [1 Cor. 12:26].

And although the church, insofar as she consists of members that live according to love, is composed of saints, and therefore spiritual and invisible, yet she is also perceptible, as Christ himself indicates, saying, "tell it to the church" [Matt. 18:17]. An integral part of this church are the bishops, who rule the people whom Christ bought with his own blood [Acts 20:28], and all other ministers. For God has given that "some would be apostles, some prophets, some evangelists, some pastors and teachers" [Eph. 4:11].

Other integral parts of this church are the Word of God, which flows through the ears into the heart, the sacraments, the keys of binding and absolving, the power of coercing through excommunication, the right of ordaining ministers of the church, vocations to church offices and, finally, the power of establishing canons.

What belongs to the perceptible and external part of the church ought to serve toward the fulfilling of the saints in the work of the ministry, for edification of the body of Christ [Eph. 4:11-13].

Now in the church there are not only saints but also evil people as well as unfruitful members. Therefore, Christ compares it at one time to a net cast into the sea, which catches good and bad fish [Matt. 13:47-52]. And at another time, he compares it to a field that is sown at the same time with good and bad seed [Matt. 13:24-30]. For those who have been made members of the church by Baptism often fall again into sins and make themselves slaves of sin and guilty of everlasting damnation. And although they lose the grace of the community of the holy and the spiritual church, nevertheless they remain in the external community of Christians and of the church. They hear the Word of God, receive the sacraments, and share all perceptible aspects of the church, unless they were separated from the Christian faith through regular excommunication, schism, heresy, or defection. For those who are ill in a mortal sin and separated from the spiritual community are in a wretched condition, and they are therefore encompassed by the danger of everlasting damnation. But because they still have the possibility of hearing God's Word and using the sacraments, they can be brought again more easily to God's communion through these as instruments of God's grace, especially because the Holy Spirit works salvation through the Word of God and the sacraments also in the external church.

But the schismatics, heretics, and those fallen from the Christian faith have nothing by which to be rescued or assisted as long as they are in this dangerous state because they are separated not only from the spiritual but also from the external communion of the church. As members cut off from the whole body, they must decay into their own ruin. They are not worthy to remain in a part of the body of Christ, whose unity they so shamefully sever and divide. Here pertains the apostle's word: "After a first and second admonition, have nothing to do with anyone who causes divisions since you know that such a person is perverted and sinful, being self-condemned" [Titus 3:10-11].

X. On the Marks and Signs of the True Church

Since there are many human assemblies, it is necessary to know the marks and signs by which the church is distinguished from other human societies, especially because the schismatics and heretics who abandon the church organize assemblies, to which they do not hesitate to attribute the authority and the name "church," and some of them say that Christ is in another place [than the true church]. We should beware of them, as Christ himself warns. Therefore there are signs of the true church, that is, of the great house, "there are utensils not only of gold and silver but also of wood and clay, some for special use, some for ordinary" [2 Tim. 2:20], that is, sound doctrine and the right use of the sacraments, by which the church is distinguished from the assemblies of the heathen and the Jews, neither of which has pure doctrine and sacraments of the New Testament. The third sign is unity, which is maintained by the bond of love and peace and binds the members of the church together, so that they not only think the same about those things that the perpetual consensus of the saints from the apostles down to us has accepted and maintained, but also speak in the same way, as the apostle warns: "I appeal to you, brethren, by the name of our Lord Jesus Christ, that all of you be in agreement and that there be no divisions among you, but that you be united in the same mind and the same purpose" [1 Cor. 1:10].

The fourth sign of the true church is that it is catholic and universal, that is, propagated in all places and continued in succession through the apostles and their successors to us, spread to the ends of the earth, according to God's promises: "Ask of me, and I will make the nations your heritage, and the ends of the earth your possession" [Ps. 2:8]. Again, "many will come from east and west and will eat with Abraham and Isaac, and Jacob in the kingdom of heaven" [Matt. 8:11]. Again, "and you will be my witnesses in Jerusalem and in all Judea and Samaria, and to the end of the earth" [Acts 1:8]. And again, "I will ask the Father, and he will give you another advocate, to be with you forever; this is the Spirit of truth, whom the world cannot receive" [John 14:16-17].

These two signs distinguish the Christian church from the flocks of schismatics and heretics, who break the bond of peace and separate themselves from catholic unity to their own destruction, when they prefer their own party to the whole of the universal church.

XI. On the Authority and Power of the Church

Although, as Christ says, the Scripture cannot be broken [John 10:35] and is therefore immovable and greater than all human authority, yet it was in the power of the church to distinguish the true Scriptures from the false. From it came the canon of the Scriptures, introduced under the name of apostles and disciples of the Lord, that distinguishes the true Scriptures from the false.

And just as the church has always had authority and power of this kind, so also she has the power of interpreting and especially of drawing forth and explaining doctrines from the same Scriptures since the Holy Spirit is with her and leads her into all truth, as the Lord Christ himself promised [John 16:13]. Hence the statement of St. Peter [2 Peter 1:20-21]: "No prophecy of Scripture is a matter of one's own interpretation . . . but men moved by the Holy Spirit spoke from God." And that power of interpreting is necessary especially in those passages that are difficult to understand, as is obviously the case from the nature of the matter.

Furthermore, the church has traditions passed down to our time from Christ and the apostles by the hands of the bishops. Whoever destroys them denies that the church is the pillar and support of truth. Among such matters are the baptism of infants and others.

It is also certain that the power of coercion and excommunication belongs to the church. It derives from Christ's institution on the power of binding. It is consistent with what the apostle said: "Drive out the wicked person from among you" [1 Cor. 5:13].

It also has the power of jurisdiction. For whoever has the right of coercion cannot lack the power of jurisdiction.

And if dubious questions arise in the church, it has the power of making and coming to decisions concerning them by means of a synod. And what it decides, legitimately assembled in the Holy Spirit, is to be regarded as if the Holy Spirit himself decided, as is written about the Council of Jerusalem: "It has seemed good to the Holy Spirit and to us" [Acts 15:28]. Thus, no one ought to doubt that the authority of councils is beneficial.

And it is also clear from the same Jerusalem Council that the church has the power of making canons for the benefit of the church, for all its power is for the edification of the church and not for its destruction.

XII. On the Ministers of the Church

The church has divinely given doctrine, which must be explained to the people. It has external rites, which must be administered and taught faithfully and expediently for the benefit of Christians. Therefore, the church cannot and should not do without ministers suitable for carrying out such duties. But these offices are not common to all Christians; from the beginning, God himself ordained that "some would be apostles, some prophets, some evangelists, some pastors and teachers, to equip the saints for the work of ministry, for building up the body of Christ" [Eph. 4:11-12].

Therefore, at the time of the apostles, the power of the church's offices was not given to all, but only to certain ones, those set aside for them. For when Barnabas, Lucius, Manachem, and Saul were at Antioch, "worshipping the Lord and fasting" (as Luke writes in the Acts of the Apostles [13:2]), "the Holy Spirit said, 'set apart for me Barnabas and Saul for the work to which I have called them.'" Therefore, we should avoid confusing the spiritual priesthood which is common to all Christians whom the Holy Spirit has anointed with this external and ministerial priesthood, which does not belong to all, but only to those who are called to it and who are properly ordained. Such confusion cannot take place without grave and pernicious disorder and calamity in the churches.

XIII. On the Supreme Pontiff and the Bishops

And although the church, which is the body of the one head, Christ, has many bishops, who rule his people, whom Christ has won through his precious blood, nevertheless, in order that it can more easily be kept in unity, on the basis of divine right, to prevent schism, it has one supreme pontiff, set over all the others, with plenitude of power, through the prerogative given to Peter. How useful such a one is to guard against schisms in the church is clear since many schisms have originated from the contempt of this highest priest, as Cyprian writes[4] and the facts themselves testify. Whoever therefore occupies the chair of Peter as supreme pontiff governs and should govern the universal church by the right given to Peter by Christ when he said, "Feed my sheep"

---

4. Cyprian, Ep. 59 [54], 5 (*CSEL* 3/2: 672; *ANF* 5:340); Ep. 66 [68], 5 (*CSEL* 3/2: 730; *ANF* 5:373–74).

[John 21:17]. He should use the power not for destruction but for edification [2 Cor. 10:8; 13:10].

Christ gave to Peter and his successors plenitude of power, but in a way that did not take away from the other bishops their share of the obligation of care for the church that he entrusted to them. He willed that in their churches and dioceses they be true bishops by divine right. All Christians then should obey the supreme bishop and everyone his own bishop, as the apostle says: "Obey your leaders and submit to them; for they are keeping watch over your souls" [Heb. 13:17].

XIV. On the Sacraments in General

The sacraments were instituted by divine authority primarily for two reasons: first, to be signs and marks of the great assembly that is the church. For people cannot be brought together in one name unless they are assembled in community by some external visible signs or sacraments. For that reason, our Lord Jesus Christ gathered together the society of his new people by means of a small number of sacraments that are very easy to observe and have powerful significance, namely, Baptism, Confirmation, Eucharist, Penance, Extreme Unction, Ordination, and Marriage.

The second reason is that they not only signify but also sanctify and confer the invisible grace of God, not by virtue of external things or the merit of the minister, but by the Lord who instituted them and works in them secretly. So, although it is appropriate that ministers of the sacraments be pious, even an evil person can dispense them beneficially.

XV. On Baptism

First of all, since by nature people are children of wrath and it is necessary for salvation that they be born again as a new creature [Eph. 2:3], Christ himself instituted the sacrament of Baptism to be the washing of our regeneration [Titus 3:5]. It is no less necessary for human beings for a new and spiritual life than fleshly birth is to natural life. Nor can they be saved, as Christ himself testifies, unless they are reborn of water and the Spirit [John 3:3-8].

This sacrament washes, sanctifies, and justifies us; this sacrament brings about that we attain remission of our sins, both original and actual; and finally, this sacrament is of such a nature that whoever is washed with it, as Paul writes, puts on Christ [Gal. 3:27].

This sacrament consists of the Word of God and water. For as soon as the Word is added to the element, it becomes a sacrament;[5] through this washing, we are born again and cleansed from all sin. Therefore, as often as we see anyone's body washed outwardly, we should consider that just as often the Spirit, whom we do not see, functions inwardly even more.

---

5. Augustine, tractate 80, 3. In Johannem [15:1–3] (*CCL* 36:529; *NPNF,* ser. 1, 7:344).

Christ himself gave the apostles the form of words, without which this mystery cannot be administered, when he commanded that they should baptize in the name of the Father and the Son and the Holy Spirit [Matt. 28:19]. As often as Baptism is administered, the faith of the one receiving Baptism (if that person is an adult) rests on this command of the Lord. But for children, the faith of those who bring them and who confess for them, indeed, the faith of the whole church and the word of the minister, when he says, "I baptize you in the name of the Father and the Son and the Holy Spirit," suffices.

And it is clear to us that Baptism serves powerfully in arousing faith and consolation in adults, that they know that all those who are baptized in the name of the Father and the Son and the Holy Spirit are consecrated with the authority, might, and power of the Father and the Son and the Holy Spirit, that they are wholly reconciled to God and are made God's possession, who is Father and Son and Holy Spirit, that they come into his protection, and that when they renounce the devil and his works and promise to serve under God's command, they bind themselves in an eternal covenant with God.

And although the function of baptizing pertains primarily to priests, yet in case of emergency, a layperson can baptize legitimately and validly. And even if a heretic baptizes, if the proper material, form, and intention are employed, the sacrament should not be repeated since it consists not of the worthiness of the minister but the truth of the Word of God and the power of the Holy Spirit.

Although, according to the Scriptures, Baptism takes away all our iniquities, it does not remove all the infirmities and illness of the corrupt nature, as we have warned above. For when the guilt itself has been removed, concupiscence inclined to evil remains. This concupiscence against the good does not cease making war against the Spirit in people as long as we live on this earth [Gal. 5:17].

In that struggle, the power of Baptism does not abandon us since it not only takes away the guilt of all sin but through the Holy Spirit also strengthens our powers against all evil lusts still in our flesh. We are thereby armed against all the power of lusts, so that we are able to resist and overcome them; as the apostle says, "Walk by the Spirit, and do not gratify the desires of the flesh" [Gal. 5:16].

XVI. On Confirmation

Just as for the life of the body it is necessary that a person not only be born but also grow and be nourished, so it is not only necessary for salvation that this person be regenerated, but also be confirmed and increased in good by the power of the Holy Spirit. Therefore, the sacrament of Confirmation was instituted. It brings special benefits, and it was practiced by the apostles when they laid hands on the Samaritans, by which they obtained beneficial power, as is written in the Acts of the Apostles [8:17]. And what the apostles did here, they did in the name of Christ, and in introducing this mystery, no differently than in other aspects of their office, they are regarded as having acted in place of Christ. This mystery is based on Christ's promise of the grace of the Holy Spirit and his mission: "I am sending upon you what my Father promised" [Luke 24:49]. Again, "But the advocate, the Holy Spirit, whom the Father will send in my name, he will teach you everything" [John 14:26]. And although the sacrament of Confirmation was celebrated originally with only the laying on of hands, yet in order to point to the internal unction of the Holy Spirit, already from the time of the apostles, from the same tradition the church added chrism to the rite, with the imposition of the sign of the cross, to demonstrate the internal unction of the Holy Spirit with an external sign. This is a very ancient custom and practice that the catholic church has not ceased to approve. It believes that God regenerates those servants that are sealed in this mystery by water and the Spirit, that they receive the seven-fold Holy Spirit, the holy Paraclete, from heaven, the Spirit of wisdom and intel-lect, the Spirit of counseling and fortitude, the Spirit of knowledge and piety and fear [Isa. 11:2]. The catholic church, which is the best interpreter of God's mys-teries, believes this and gives witness to it in the administration of this mystery. And whoever believes otherwise denies that it is a pillar and a foundation of truth [1 Tim. 3:15].

The power of this sacrament is that those who are confirmed by it receive the Holy Spirit, by which they are able to make progress on the way of salvation, persevere, and resist temptations and lusts of the flesh, the world, and the devil.

And because most of those who are baptized are infants and cannot confess their faith for themselves, it would be good that children who come to their years of understanding are sufficiently instructed to understand the sacrament of Confirmation, confess the faith of Christ and obedience to the church also with their own mouth, and be initiated by fasting and confession in this sacred mystery, as was decided in the Aurelian Council.[6] But we should not think, therefore, that young children should be excluded from this sacrament since Christ himself did not hesitate to lay his hands upon them [Mark 10:13-16; Matt. 19:13-15]. Here we do not give the church a law.

The minister of this sacrament should be a bishop, as has been determined by the consensus of the whole catholic church and the practice of the apostles.

XVII. On the Sacrament of Penance

And since the reborn often fall into grave sins, Christ instituted the sacrament of Penance, which after Baptism for us is like a second plank in a shipwreck. For to this use he gave the key for loosing, saying, "Receive the Holy Spirit; if you forgive the sins of any, they are forgiven them" [John 20:22-23]. For as soon as they truly repent of their sin and with confidence approach the throne of mercy

---

6. According to Giovanni Dominico Mansi, *Sacrorum Conciliorum nova et amplissima collectio* (Florence, 1762), VIII:347–72, as well as *Monumenta Germaniae Historica Leges, Conc. I* (*Concilia aevi Merovingici*) (Hannover: Hahn, 1893), and *CCL* 148 A, the Synod of Orleans made no such conciliar decision. The reference to an Aurelian Council is taken from *Decretum*, c. 6. dist. 5, *de con-secratione* (*CIC* I:1414).

and believe that in this sacrament they receive what Christ promises, it happens to them as they believe. Nor is what is promised absent from this sacrament. For, like other sacraments, this one also has the power of sanctifying. This sacrament consists in the absolution by the priest, which rests on the institution and word of Christ, who in this matter delegates his power to the priests, saying, "As the Father has sent me, so I send you. . . . Receive the Holy Spirit. If you forgive the sins of any, they are forgiven them; if you retain the sins of any, they are retained" [John 20:21-23].

Because the priest has the power not only to loose but also to bind, since both are given by God, and because he receives the power of both keys, he receives power to judge since he cannot exercise this power unless he knows which he ought to remit or retain. This knowledge, however, cannot be gained in any other way than by oral confession and enumeration of sins. For since many sins are committed by people secretly [Ps. 18:13-14] without witness, and the secret sins also wound and even kill the soul and are sometimes graver and more dangerous than open ones, the priest cannot judge rightly unless the person who commits them recounts and confesses them and personally opens them as if opening his own wounds.

For that reason, since the remedy of repentance is appointed for healing the faults of people, confession of the penitent with enumeration of sins is commended to us. Just as the sacrament of Penance must be praised to the Christian folk as beneficial and necessary, so also should confession itself and enumeration of sins, which ought not be made too slack nor too strict. For who understands his sins [Ps. 18:13]? Sinners should enumerate those sins that they remember upon diligent reflection and examination—though they should not do so too anxiously. Those sins that are not remembered are properly included in the general confession and are remitted no less than if they had been enumerated in [private] confession. And since forgiveness is obtained from absolution, confession does not impose as much of a burden on believers as absolution offers them consolation.

Even if the satisfaction that atones for sin and eternal punishment is to be attributed to Christ alone, yet if it is carried out in faith and love, the satisfaction that consists in the fruits of penitence, especially in fasting, alms, and prayer—whether we undertake it ourselves or it is imposed by a pastor and dispenser of the sacraments—destroys the causes of sin, heals the remainders of sin, removes or mitigates the punishment of temporal sin, and serves as example.

But to return to the absolution of the priest, in which the power of the sacrament of Penance consists, its form and wording should be such that the one who confesses is able to hear and understand that in the virtue, merit, and benefit of Christ, sins are remitted to him according to his institution and Word: "If you forgive the sins of any, they are forgiven them" [John 20:23]. For this is the function of God, as St. Ambrose says, although the ministry is of the priests.[7]

---

7. Ambrose, *De poenitentia* 1, 2, 8 (*CSEL* 73:123, 45 ff.; *NPNF,* ser. 2, 10:330).

XVIII. On the Sacrament of the Eucharist

Whoever is revived in the Lord through the sacrament of Penance must also be nourished and grow in spiritual good. Therefore, Christ instituted the sacrament of the Eucharist under the visible forms of bread and wine, which gives us the true body and blood of Christ and unites us to him with this spiritual food as head and members of his body, so that in him we may be nourished and renewed to all good and with the saints, in communion with them, may increase through love. For "because there is one bread, we who are many are one body, for we all partake of the one bread" [1 Cor. 10:17], Paul says. The form of this sacrament is those solemn words given by Christ himself: "This is my body," and again, "This is my blood of the covenant" [Matt. 26:26, 28].

And if we ascribe as much to Christ and his Word as we should, there is no doubt that as soon as the Word comes to the bread and wine, they are the true body and true blood of Christ, when the substance of bread and wine are transmuted into the true body and blood of Christ. But whoever denies that calls into doubt the omnipotence of Christ and accuses him of lying.

Therefore one must carefully avoid taking the sacrament unworthily. For it is written: "For all who eat and drink without discerning the body, eat and drink judgment against themselves. For this reason many of you are weak and ill, and some have died" [1 Cor. 11:29-30]. And all those take the sacrament unworthily who think otherwise about it than they should or do not truly repent. For, as Augustine says, "Let him change his life, who wants to accept life; for if he does not change his life, he receives life unto judgment [in the sacrament], and will be more corrupted by it than healed, more killed than revived."[8] Therefore, the custom of the church should be praised according to which a person does not go to the sacrament of the Eucharist before he has been purified through the sacrament of Penance. The Eucharist has a power to strengthen in spiritual good, and that cannot take place unless cleansing from sin has preceded. In this we ought to imitate good physicians, who do not give medicines that strengthen and restore a person's energy before they can drive the bad humors out of the body. Unless they do that, the medications are not helpful to the sick but rather harmful. And so, as one ought to be careful not to take this sacrament unworthily, so those receive more consolation who take the Eucharist worthily and piously and meditate on the fact that they are eating bread come from heaven that gives life to the world, and that from it they receive true and spiritual strength against all evils.

XIX. On the Sacrament of Unction

The sacraments set forth above bring great and manifold benefit to humankind because they regenerate those who lie enfeebled by the weakness of the flesh,

---

8. (Pseudo-)Augustine (*MPL* 39:1973, cf. *MPL* 2:846).

confirm the newborn in the grace received, restore to grace those who have fallen from grace, or unite the restored more firmly to Christ. For these salutary ends, the grace of Christ is not lacking to the sacraments, but it is dispensed to the people through the sacraments as if through instruments. Although the benefit of these sacraments is widely accessible throughout life, yet should people desire special assistance when they are ill, in the most dangerous time for the body, or should they desire to fortify the soul against the fiery darts of Satan, the Holy Unction was instituted, to which is added the prayer of the church. This sacrament was first practiced by the apostles, who, sent by the command of the Lord to preach the Gospel, "cast out many demons, and anointed with oil many who were sick and cured them" [Mark 6:13]. That Unction is clearly sacramental and mystical, not a medical or bodily anointing. At the beginning of the faith, as a special sign of inward health, outward health of the body was added to it, just as in the other sacraments (to strengthen the unexercised faith) inner power is witnessed by external and perceptible signs and miracles. But now, adult and strengthened faith has no more need for the signs given to the weak.

How this salutary and mystical Unction, established by the Lord, should be administered was explained first by the apostle James: "Are any among you sick? They should call for the elders of the church, and have them pray over them, anointing him with oil in the name of the Lord, and the prayer of faith will save the sick, and the Lord will raise them up" [5:14-16].

How great should the testimony of the brother of the Lord be in the church? And without doubt Christ willed that the command James gave as legate and apostle of Christ should be obeyed as if he himself had given it. Therefore, whoever despises this sacrament despises Christ himself and spurns his grace that he offers us in a special way through this Holy Unction. The greater the danger is in which the sick person lies, the more damaging it is to despise the sacrament, not only to the body but also to the soul. The powers of darkness lead him into that danger, since in the last hours of the body, by means of incredible terrors, they all attempt to extinguish a person's salvation, to break down the soul, and to force the person into desperation.

The apostle James teaches [5:14-16] that this Holy Unction, as practiced also by other apostles, should be administered only to the sick. Not for all of them, but only for the sickest, and where the destruction of this life is feared, should this mystic Unction be administered.

XX. On the Sacrament of Ordination

As for the offices of the church, the greater they are, the more they need the gift and grace of God. Although all Christians are priests since they offer spiritual sacrifices to God and may call on his name with benefit in all places, they are not all ministers of the church. From the beginning of the church until now, some have been set aside for the service of the church, to carry out its functions. And God made distinctions among them, so that everything not be done by the same persons, and so that no disorder arise from an indiscriminate order. "For God is a God not of disorder, but of peace" [1 Cor. 14:33]. The sacrament of Order, therefore, was instituted with the sign of laying on of hands and other appropriate rites, by which those who are consecrated to the offices of the church receive the grace by which they become fit, suitable, and capable of administering the same functions. Appropriate here is what the apostle wrote to Timothy: "Do not neglect the gift that is in you, which was given you through prophecy with the laying on of hands by the council of elders" [1 Tim. 4:14].

The sacrament of Ordination is based on the words of Christ, "As the Father has sent me, even so I send you." And when he had said this, he breathed on them and said to them, "Receive the Holy Spirit. If you forgive the sins of any, they are forgiven" [John 20:21-22]. Again, "Go into all the world and proclaim the gospel to the whole creation" [Mark 16:15]. Again, "Go therefore and make disciples of all nations, baptizing them" [Matt. 28:19]. And again, "Do this in remembrance of me" [Luke 22:19; 1 Cor. 11:24-25]. Therefore, on whomever in the perpetual succession of the church the bishops place their hands, consecrating them to their orders, to them they give the power of discharging their office. That power is twofold: of order and of jurisdiction. To the former belong the office of the divine Word, the administration of the sacraments, and the ordering of the church for edification. To the latter belongs the power of excommunicating and absolving penitents. The orders recognized by the catholic church are seven: priests, evangelists [German: deacons], epistolers [German: subdeacons], acolytes, readers, exorcists, and thurifers. Separate functions ought to be assigned to each one, either those necessary or beneficial to the churches. It is clear that whoever despises or abolishes these offices brings evil on the Christian church.

XXI. On the Sacrament of Matrimony

In paradise, God instituted Matrimony, by which man and woman were joined in a perpetual and indivisible community of life, according to the Word of the Lord: "Therefore, a man leaves his father and mother and clings to his wife; and they will become one flesh" [Gen. 2:24; Matt. 19:5].

And although Matrimony was set into such a narrow human community, under patriarchal law it degenerated from its first institution in two ways. First, one could marry many wives, and second, when he had married them, he could later separate from them by a bill of divorce. The former was permitted in God's dispensation to serve the future mystery of time by showing that just as one man had many wives, so Christ would gather the church to himself both from the synagogue and from the multitude of nations and join his spouse to himself; and that they might serve Christ the Savior, who by the fecundity of many wives would be born from their seed.

Moses permitted divorce to the people because of the hardness of their hearts [Deut. 24:1-4], because he considered it less serious that a wife hated by her husband be dismissed than that she be murdered to open a way to a future marriage.

When the fullness of grace had come and Christ renewed all things in heaven and earth, he restored marriage as well when he said, "Have you not read that he who made them at the beginning made them male and female, and said, 'For this reason a man shall leave his father and mother and be joined to his wife and the two shall become one flesh? So they are no longer two but one. Therefore, what God has joined together, let no one separate'" [Matt. 19:4-5]. And a little further on, he said to them, "It was because you were so hard-hearted that Moses allowed you to divorce your wives, but from the beginning it was not so, and I say to you: whoever divorces his wife, except for unchastity, and marries another commits adultery" [Matt. 19:8-9], which the apostle interprets, saying, "To the married I give a command, not I but the Lord, that the wife should not separate from her husband (but if she does separate, let her remain unmarried or else be reconciled to her husband)" [1 Cor. 7:10-11].

And these special conditions of a Christian marriage are backed by clear testimonies of Scripture: first, that the marriage is a joining of only two, that is, a union of one man with one woman. For God says: "They become one flesh" [Gen. 2:24]. Nor is it permitted to yield power over his body to any third person to the disadvantage of his spouse. Prohibiting it, the apostle says: "For the wife does not have authority over her own body, but the husband does; likewise the husband does not have authority over his own body, but the wife does" [1 Cor. 7:4]. The second condition is that the bond of marriage, once established between the two, is not dissolved by divorce, but only by the death of the other [Rom. 7:2-3]. Christ's statement that a man may abandon a wife because of fornication does not mean that the separation of bed and table looses the bond of marriage. So, whoever puts away his wife commits adultery, just as when he touches another woman.

By his grace, Christ improved marriage and gave it narrower bonds, so that, just as Christ is the one spouse of one church, by an indivisible bond one man should be the husband of one wife, and that in perpetual union, just as Christ is eternally joined to his spouse, the church [Eph. 5:23-24]. Therefore, marriage is not only a union of a man and a woman but also a sacrament of Christ's grace, which is nevermore lacking to it. As the man is able to love his wife as Christ loved the church, so let him honor the undivided community, so that he is always content with one and does not separate against her will, with the exception of reasons explained by divine law.

And because God upholds marriage through his grace and is well pleased when people enter into it, a clear sign is thereby given for hope that their living together is both good in itself and pleasing to God. And although marriage ought to be contracted primarily for the sake of raising children, yet whoever marries also to avoid fornication does not sin. For St. Paul says: "But because of the temptation to immorality, each man should have his own wife" [1 Cor. 7:2].

The power of this sacrament is that the partners should know that they have come together not on the basis of human but rather of divine authority and have received grace, in which legitimate intercourse is not considered sin. And also a Christian man hallows a heathen woman, when she wants to remain with him, and produces saints, that is, children dedicated to God [1 Cor. 7:12]. Thereby he maintains perpetual faith with his marriage partner since the two are one flesh. And faithful women "will be saved through childbearing, provided they continue in faith and love and holiness, with modesty" [1 Tim. 2:15]. Therefore marriage can be honorable, and in it there can be an "undefiled marriage bed" [Heb. 13:4].

Because the Manichaeans, Tatianites, and Encratitians are ignorant, they do not hesitate to despise marriage. Paul the Apostle condemns that deliberate wickedness [of holding this belief] as having come from the devil's teaching [1 Tim. 4:1-3].

Since the bond of marriage is what it is and has such power to bind together, there is no human union more binding. As Adam saw that in paradise, he said about his wife, whom God had made from his rib, "This at last is bone of my bones and flesh of my flesh; this one shall be called Woman, for out of man was this one taken. Therefore a man leaves his father and his mother and clings to his wife; and they become one flesh" [Gen. 2:23-24].

Therefore, although the patriarchal power has been withdrawn from this union between marital partners for legal reasons, those who want matrimony or promised marriage be broken up or invalidated if the parents do not give their permission must not be given a hearing. Here, we do not want to diminish the obedience children owe their parents, but we also do not want parents to abuse their power by preventing or sundering the marriage. But because we recognize that it is honorable that children not marry without the counsel and consent of their parents, they should be carefully advised about their duty by the preachers.

Whether in this case the parents ought to be permitted power to punish their children for their disobedience by withholding or diminishing their inheritance, or in any other way, should be left to the proper authority.

XXII. On the Sacrifice of the Mass

Just as the law of nature instituted religion, without which no people lives, so it also instituted ceremonies, without which religion neither can nor should be practiced. And among those ceremonies, as the most important, all peoples in all ages have observed external sacrifice. And, as Cyprian testifies,[9] although the gentiles shrank from circumcision as cruel and unnatural, they did not reject the other sacrifices in the same way but followed the law of nature in many

---

9. The reference is probably to (Pseudo-)Cyprian, *De singularitate clericorum* 33 (*CSEL* 3/3: 208–9).

ways. They retained the means of expiation and persisted in the worship inborn in human beings by nature itself and divinely spread to all souls, in sacrificing animals, burning oil, and uttering vows and prayers before God with libations. All gentiles also have this in common, affixed to all hearts, that with great unanimity they value the practice of external sacrifice due to God alone.

For no one has ever considered using an external sacrifice to worship anyone other than one whom they knew, believed, or imagined to be a god. That this cult is ancient is proved by the sacrifice of the brothers Cain and Abel [Gen. 4:3-8]. For God rejected the former, together with his gifts, but was graciously pleased with the sacrifice of the younger.[10]

God (who wills that everyone be saved [1 Tim. 2:4]) planted this sacrificial rite in human hearts for this divine purpose: since because of the sin of one man, the whole human race was held guilty under the wrath of God and just condemnation, and the condemnation became graver and more threatening, the more they heaped up their sins and incited the righteous wrath against themselves. But because God did not want those he had created to perish, he appointed a mediator and reconciler for the human race, who reconciled us with our Creator and by means of a special sacrifice stilled the righteous wrath of God. Therefore, with great love God sent his Son into the world, wrapped in our flesh, who took upon himself our sins and bore them on his body on the cross [1 Peter 2:24]. He also gave himself for us as a sacrifice and, since he entered into the holy place, thereby achieved eternal redemption through his own blood [Heb. 9:11-12].

Mollified by the fragrance of this most precious victim, God the Father abated his wrath and absolved, justified, and reconciled those who were once immersed in sin, impure and unrighteous and liable to damnation, but now washed with the blood of his Son [1 Cor. 6:11].

The power and efficacy of this one sacrifice served not only the time when Christ gave himself in the flesh for one sacrifice, but embracing all times, it was enough to blot out the sins of all people from the beginning of the world and those who will be born unto the end of the world.

For "God was in Christ reconciling the world to himself" [2 Cor. 5:19]. And, "Here is the Lamb of God, who takes away the sin of the world!" [John 1:29]. And, "He is the atoning sacrifice for our sins, and not for ours only but also for the sins of the whole world" [1 John 2:2]. The term "world," however, embraces people not of one time, but of all times; hence in Revelation Christ is called the lamb slain from the beginning of the world [13:8] because his blood cleanses the sins of all times since the beginning of the world.

About this sacrifice, which by itself is enough to redeem the whole human race, St. Paul says: "For by a single offering he has perfected for all time those who are sanctified" [Heb. 10:14]. And, "For in him all the fullness of God was pleased to dwell and through him to reconcile to himself all things, whether on

---

10 Augustine, *De civitate Dei* 10.4 (*CSEL* 40/1: 451, *CCL* 47:276; *NPNF,* ser. 1, 2:182–83).

earth or in heaven, making peace through the blood of his cross" [Col. 1:19-20]. And: he was pleased that "all things were restored" in him, "things in heaven and things on earth" [Eph. 1:10]. And in Isaiah, "I have trodden the winepress" [63:3]. And, "By his bruises we are healed" [Isa. 53:5].

So that all people might participate in this most efficacious sacrifice, which has won the salvation of all fully, sufficiently, and perfectly, and in order to transfer its fruit to themselves, God aroused in human souls the rite of sacrificing, from the origin of the world, under the law of nature and by divine inspiration. When the law had been given, he demonstrated various kinds of sacrifice. Their function was not to reconcile people with God or by themselves to merit salvation, but that through this external sacrifice a continual memorial of the future sacrifice might be made in human hearts, in which God promises salvation to all. They were given so that faith might be confirmed; that its fruit might be applied to believers and, based upon the power of the coming sacrifice, to those who had hoped; and that as often as these sacrifices are celebrated, people would remember with thankful hearts the other blessings of God that they receive constantly from his kindness and their salvation, which will be obtained through the promised reconciliation.

Therefore, God was pleased with no sacrifice for himself, either under the law of nature or under the Law of Moses, since he often said that he had no need for the things that human beings offered to him. "If I were hungry, I would not tell you; for the world and all that is in it is mine. Do I eat the flesh of bulls, or drink the blood of goats?" [Ps. 50:12-13]. But as far as these visible sacrifices were sacraments of the invisible and future sacrifice, if those who sacrifice them in faith in the promised reconciler promised by God sacrifice and complete this external sacrifice to demonstrate faith in the coming Christ and in the fruit of this salutary sacrifice, they declare their gratitude to God for such blessings for the soul. Such sacrifices are surely pleasing to God, for they are not made on the basis of our own power, but of the future sacrifice, through the faith of the one who sacrifices.

So that the nature of sacrifices be clearly understood, a meritorious sacrifice is unique, having power to blot out sin, and reconciling those alienated from God and guilty of his wrath and damnation; they merit eternal salvation and redemption for all humankind. That salutary sacrifice of Christ, hanging on the cross for human sins, "perfected for all time those who are sanctified" [Heb. 10:14]. This merit does not increase because it is perfect; it is not diminished or exhausted, for it is eternal. Therefore, the other sacrifices add nothing to this unique sacrifice and by themselves merit nothing, but they bring to the faithful the fruit of this one sacrifice, and they serve to awaken and preserve the memory of this one sacrifice in human hearts, to strengthen their faith, and to show God thankfulness for all his benefits.

There are sacrifices common to all systems of laws and permitted to all people, such as the sacrifice of a contrite heart and humble spirit, accepting bodily afflictions for the sake of cultivating piety, sacrifice of the lips, of prayer, thanksgiving, praise, and the like.

Every system of law has had its own sacrifices and, for carrying them out, has appointed special persons, from whose sacrifice others were excluded by threats and punishments [1 Kings 13:9; 2 Chron. 26:16-21]. For no legal system nor any heathen religion is without sacrifices, for these three are connected and necessarily follow from each other: law, priesthood, and sacrifice [Heb. 7:11-15].

So under the law of nature, righteous people and those instructed in the promises of God, believing in him whom they knew would be the future savior, offered sacrifices. By this oblation, they declared their faith and hope in the future salvation and their gratitude for it, and they entreated that the merits of the salutary sacrifice that they expected in the future would come to their aid. Some heathen, following this custom, introduced into their minds by hidden inspiration, desired by sacrifices to placate not the true God but the one they thought was God, or the one they invented.

But the law given by Moses was added to the law of nature, not to abolish it but to improve it. It instituted external sacrifices which also prefigured Christ's future sacrifice. And as often as the Jews celebrated them, they remembered with thankful hearts both the other benefits of God, and they brought the power of the coming sacrifice upon themselves by believing, hoping, and praying.

But Christ, who did not come to abolish the law, either natural law or moral law, but rather to fulfill it [Matt. 5:17], introduced his new law into the world, as Jeremiah had promised [31:33-34]. In order not to replace the common custom of the earlier law with something defective and imperfect, he provided a special sacrifice and priesthood. For, according to the apostle's opinion, because a new law came, a new sacrifice should follow this law [Heb. 7:12], and priests must be accepted as ministers of this sacrifice [Heb. 5:1-4].

Lest anything be lacking for his church, the same Lord Jesus Christ replaced it with something that is really good, holy, and pious when in the Last Supper he gave thanks to God, instituted the sacrament of his body and blood, and immediately recommended two uses of it: "Take," he said, "and eat" [Matt. 26:26]. And so that there might be a sacrifice in memory of his passion, giving the ministry of sacrificing to the apostles as a new law, he said, "Do this in remembrance of me" [Luke 22:19].

Before the advent of Christ, God the Father gave certain sacrifices to the fathers, to kindle in their souls the memory of the great sacrifice that they expected in the future, to establish their faith, and to apply its fruit to themselves by believing and praying, and that by their sacrifice they would remember the blessings of God with grateful hearts. In like manner, Christ commended to his church the pure and salutary sacrifice of his body and blood under the forms of bread and wine, so that in our hearts we would constantly renew the memory of his body hung on the cross and his blood shed for us, and apply to ourselves the fruit of that bloody sacrifice, in which "he has perfected for all time those who are sanctified" [Heb. 10:14]. That is what is meant by "do this in memory of me," that is, with thankful hearts recall the death of the Lord, and by means of the memory and the merit of his passion implore the Father to be reconciled with us.

This is the pure and salutary memorial offering of that one sacrifice by which the salvation of all was won. It not only signifies but in itself contains the truth of those things that the offering of various sacrifices once prefigured. It is the same sacrifice of Christ's body and blood which was sacrificed on the cross, none other, the same lamb, not another, and the one Christ in both places.[11] At that time the sacrifice was offered with blood and suffering, to obtain sufficient remission of sins and redemption for all believers. But now we sacrifice the same person in a mystic and unbloody way, without suffering, not to merit remission and salvation of our souls for the first time but, remembering the passion of the Lord, to give thanks to God for the salvation won for us on the cross and to apply the remission of sins and redemption which he merited to ourselves through our faith and devotion.

Such a salutary victim was foreseen in the Spirit by Malachi: "I have no pleasure in you, says the Lord of hosts, and I will not accept an offering from your hand. For from the rising of the sun to its setting my name is great among the nations, and in every place incense is offered to my name, and a pure offering" [Mal. 1:10-11]. That prophecy cannot be understood as a spiritual sacrifice only, which belongs to no specific legal system. It was common to all times and all people, and it persisted, always mixed with the sacrifices of the ancients. The prophet's words are proof enough that he is speaking of a sacrifice that, after the old sacrifices were discontinued, would follow in their place. Therefore, these words are correctly understood as being about the most holy sacrifice of Christ. They are not about the sacrifice by which he offered himself on the cross for the sins of the human race (because that was carried out not among the heathen, nor in every place, but in Judea only), but about the sacrifice offered by the church, gathered from the heathen throughout the world, to remember the Lord's death and to pour out his power into believers.

The clear interpretation of this quotation is supported by testimonies of the fathers. Irenaeus says, "He took that which is by nature bread and gave thanks saying: This is my body. In like manner, he took the cup, which comes from the creation that pertains to us, confessed that it was his blood, and taught that it was a new sacrifice of the New Testament. Accepting that sacrifice from the apostles, the church offers it to God throughout the whole world. It was prophesied in the book of Malachi [1:11]: 'For from the rising of the sun to its setting my name is great among the nations, and in every place incense is offered to my name, and a pure offering.'"[12]

Augustine: those who read, he said, know what Melchizedek prophesied when he blessed Abraham. And if they are participants in it, they see that such a sacrifice is now being offered to God throughout the whole world; because of this, another prophet said to Israel after the flesh: "I have no pleasure in you," etc.[13]

---

11. See n. 16.

12. Irenaeus, *Adversus hereses* 4, 17, 5 (*MPG* 7/1: 1023f., SCh 100:590ff.).

13. Augustine, *Contra adversarium legis* 1.20 (*MPL* 42:627; *Works of Saint Augustine: A Translation for the Twenty-first Century* 8/18: 384).

About this sacrifice of the new law, Ambrose testifies, "Before, the lamb or a calf was sacrificed. Now Christ is sacrificed as if he takes on his suffering again and sacrifices himself as a priest."[14]

Chrysostom: "Do we not sacrifice every day? Yes, we sacrifice, but we do it to remember his death. And it is one sacrifice, not many. But how can it be one and not many? Because this sacrifice was offered once, it is sacrificed in the holy of holies, and this sacrifice is an example of the other sacrifice, which we always offer, not one lamb now and another one tomorrow, but always the same one, etc."[15]

Athanasius: "Eternal," he said, "is the priesthood of Christ because a sacrifice is made daily by the ministers of God, having Christ as both priest and sacrifice."[16]

Important witnesses testify that the sacrifice that Christ commended to the church to memorialize his death, he carried out himself in the Supper and sacrificed himself under the form of bread and wine. Among them was David, who called Christ a priest according to the order of Melchizedek [Gen. 14:18; Psalm 109:4]. He made plain that by the sacrifice of bread and wine Christ fulfilled the figure foreshadowed by the priest Melchizedek. About this, the martyr Cyprian writes, book 2, letter 3: "This order surely derives from that sacrifice and comes down from it. Melchizedek is a priest of the most high God. He sacrificed bread and wine, and Abraham blessed them. For who is a greater priest of the most high God than our Lord Jesus Christ, who offered a sacrifice to God the Father, and offered the same that Melchizedek sacrificed, that is bread and wine, namely, his body and blood. And soon thereafter: as it is written in Genesis, so that the blessing on Abraham by the priest Melchizedek could be practiced rightly, it was preceded by the image of a sacrifice made up of bread and wine. Fulfilling and perfecting this image, the Lord offered bread and a cup mixed with wine. Since he himself was the fullness, he adds truth to what is prefigured."[17]

Arnobius: Here (he says, speaking about Christ) he was made a priest forever according to the order of Melchizedek by the mystery of bread and wine. When Abraham returned as victor from battle, he was the only one among the priests who sacrificed bread and wine.[18]

John of Damascus: With bread and wine, Melchizedek, the priest of the most high God, received Abraham after the battle with the other tribes. That table prefigured this mystical table, just as that priest bore the prefigured image of Christ, the true priest. For he says, "You are a priest after the order of Melchizedek."[19]

---

14. Ambrose, *De officiis ministrorum* 1, 48, 238 (*MPL* 16:100–101; *NPNF*, ser. 2, 10:40).

15. Chrysostom, Hom. in Hebr. (9:25—10:7) 17, 3 (*MPG* 63:131; *NPNF*, ser. 1, 14:447).

16. Athanasius, *Oratio secunda contra Arianos* 9 (*MPG* 26:161–66; *NPNF*, ser. 2, 4:352–53).

17. Cyprian, Ep. 63.4 (*CSEL* 3/2: 703, 704; *ANF* 5:359).

18. Arnobius the Younger, *In Psalm 109* (*MPL* 53:496).

19. John Damascene, *De fide orthodoxa* 4, 13 (*MPG* 94:1150; *NPNF*, ser. 2, 9:81–84). Ps. 109:4; Heb. 5:6.

Many other similar testimonies are found in the letter of Jerome to Evagrius,[20] Augustine, *On Christian Doctrine*, book 4, chapter 21,[21] Ambrose, *On the Sacraments*, book 4,[22] Chrysostom,[23] and Theophylact.[24]

According to these testimonies of Holy Scripture and the holy fathers, the catholic church recognizes two sacrifices of Christ, the same according to their substance, but different according to the manner and ritual of sacrificing. The one was on the cross, a bloody sacrifice, the other is in the Supper under the form of bread and wine. In it, as the priest of the order of Melchizedek, he offered his body and blood to the Father, thereby establishing the perpetual sacrifice of the new law, which he commended to his apostles and successors, to practice in his memory to end of the age. Just as the manner of sacrificing them is different, so is the usage differentiated. By the bloody sacrifice, Christ obtained reconciliation of the whole world, propitiation for sins, and full redemption of all. The other sacrifice instituted and commended to the church for the remembrance of the bloody sacrifice, not that we merit remission of sins and redemption anew, but that with faith and devotion we apply the merit won on the cross to ourselves, following Christ's command to do this in his memory. That is, that by the memory and merit of his passion, we entreat the Father for our reconciliation, remission of sins, salvation of our souls, and the preservation of our bodies and possessions.

Up to this point, the reasons and testimonies have been presented upon which the sacrifice of the altar rests. Now a few things will be set forth about the rite.

In the celebration of the sacrifice of the altar are joined together praise of God, prayers of the faithful people, thanksgivings, and Scripture readings. It is therefore rightly called a sacrifice of praise, thanksgiving, and prayers. By this rite, the catholic church follows the example of Christ, who in the sacrifice of the Supper poured out many prayers to the Father for the preservation of the church he left behind on earth, and finally completed the mystical meal with hymns and the thanksgiving [John 17; Matt. 26:30]. Celebrating the sacrifice, the church follows fully and exactly the earnest admonition of Paul cited by Augustine "that supplications, prayers, intercessions and thanksgivings be made for everyone, for kings and all who are in high positions, so that we may lead a quiet and peaceable life, in all godliness and dignity" [1 Tim. 2:1-2].

Before beginning to consecrate what is on the Lord's table, the church makes supplications. She offers prayers when it is blessed and sanctified and makes claims or intercessions for pardon when the people are being blessed

---

20. Jerome, letter 73 to Evagrius (*CSEL* 55:13; *NPNF,* ser. 2, 6:154).

21. Augustine, *De doctrina Christiana* 4.21 (45) (*CSEL* 80:154–55, *CCL* 32:151–52; *NPNF,* ser. 1, 2:590).

22. Ambrose, *De sacramentis* 4, 3, 10–12 (*CSEL* 73:50–51; *Fathers of the Church* 44:300–301).

23. John Chrysostom, *De Melcisedeco* (*MPG* 56:257ff.).

24. Theophylact, *Expositio in ep. ad Hebr.* 5:6f. (*MPG* 125:242f.); Heb. 7:1ff. (*MPG* 125:267ff.).

and commended to the most merciful power. When that is concluded and thanks have been given for the sacrament received, the action is ended. See Augustine, letter 50 to Paulinus, where you can clearly recognize the rite of celebrating the sacrifice of the altar as the church celebrates it today.[25]

It can be seen that in all ages Catholic people have received and confirmed this rite, and with great unanimity have remembered that prayers and thanksgiving were mixed into the celebration of this sacrifice and that the host was consecrated with a solemn prayer. On this, Chrysostom, *Homily on Matthew*,[26] *On the priesthood*, book 3,[27] Basil the Great, *On the Holy Spirit*, chapter 27,[28] Theophylact on chapter 14 of Mark,[29] Gregory, letter 63 to John, bishop of Syracuse,[30] Ambrose, *On the Sacraments*, book 4, chapter 5,[31] who cites the canon the church now uses in the books he wrote now and then, almost word for word.

XXIII. On the Memorial of the Saints in the Sacrifice of the Altar and on the Intercession for Them Required in It, and Also on the Invocation of the Saints

In the sacrifice of the altar, we recall that limitless favor by which Christ made himself a victim for the preservation and salvation of his whole mystical body, that is, all believers. According to the Lord's example and the apostle's admonition, then, prayer should be made to God for the preservation of the whole church and thanks be given for all the benefits of his grace. Assembling all its members, the church remembers those who have departed from this mortality and who are living with the Lord, including especially the dear saints, with grateful veneration to God. It also gives thanks to God for those who, although weak by nature, were strong, strengthened with the gift of his grace. In courageous struggle against sin, the devil, and death, they overcame the defects of the flesh and from the righteous judge attained the crown of righteousness—not by their own but by God's strength. On the antiquity and practice of this act of thanksgiving for the saints, see Dionysius the Areopagite;[32] Cyprian, book 3, letter 6;[33] book 4, letter 6;[34] Augustine, *On the City of God*, book 8,

---

25. Augustine, Ep. 149 (*CSEL* 44:348–55; *Fathers of the Church* 20:259–66).

26. John Chrysostom, Hom in Mt. 26:26 (*MPG* 58:737ff.; *NPNF*, ser. 1, 10:491–97).

27. John Chrysostom, *De sacerdotio* 3, 4–6 (*MPG* 48:641–44; *NPNF*, ser. 1, 9:46–48).

28. Basil, *De spiritu sancto* 27 (*SCh* 17:233ff.; *NPNF*, ser. 2, 9:40–43).

29. Theophylact, *In Ev. Marci* 14, 1ff. (*MPG* 123:643ff.)

30. Gregory the Great, Ep. 9.12 (*MPL* 77:955–58; *NPNF*, ser. 2, 13:3–9).

31. Ambrose, *De sacramentis* 4, 5, 21–25 (*CSEL* 73:55f.; *SCh* 25:84ff.; *Fathers of the Church* 44:304–6).

32. Dionysius Areopagita, *De ecclesiastica hierarchia* (*MPG* 3:551ff.; J. Parker, *The Celestial Ecclesiastical Hierarchy of Dionysius the Areopagite*, 1894, 66–67).

33. Cyprian, Ep. 12 (*CSEL* 3/2: 503; *ANF* 5:285–86).

34. Cyprian, Ep. 39 (*CSEL* 3/2: 583; *ANF* 5:314).

chapter 27;[35] book 22, chapter 10;[36] *Against Faustus the Manichaean,* book 20, chapter 21.[37]

Not only do we honor the saints and thank God for them, but we also entreat that through their prayers and merit, through the help of their divine protection, we may be strengthened in all things. We rightly believe that, as citizens of the same community and members of the same body, bound together with us in the Spirit and in the bands of love, they desire our salvation, are concerned about our misfortune, and that they pray for our needs to God, our common Father, through Jesus Christ, our common mediator. They are moved by the law of community itself and by the precept of James: "Pray for one another that you may be healed" [James 5:16]. The love they have for us admonishes and drives them, and the fact that they now live secure before God and free from infirmities and defects means that there is no hindrance to their doing so. We know that they do it in the other life on the basis of the clear testimony of Scripture, where Onias is observed, hands extended and praying for the people, and another man is described, marvelous in age and glory, about whom it is said, "This is a man who loves the family of Israel and prays much for the people and the Holy City—Jeremiah, the prophet of God" [2 Macc. 15:12-14]. And in another place, an angel prays for the city of Judah: "O Lord of Hosts, how long will you withhold your mercy from Jerusalem and the cities of Judah with which you have been angry?" [Zech. 1:12].

Just as we demand prayers from those who live with us in the flesh, so we claim prayers for ourselves in this faith from the saints living with God, calling on them by name, not doubting that God who can do all things, either by the ministry of angels or by other means pleasing to him, can bring it about that the saints are aware of our prayers. For he is responsible for the angels in heaven rejoicing when they hear about the conversion of a sinner [Luke 15:10].

About the merits of the saints, we do not say that they are like those we find in Christ, who gave himself for us and poured out his blood for us to win for the world full reconciliation with God. The saints drew their own merits, by which they are saved and help us, from the same source of all salvation and of all merit, Christ's suffering. For considering the severity of righteousness, their own works, no matter how virtuous, do not suffice for the salvation of any saint, as is written: "For no one living is righteous before you" [Ps. 143:2]. And the Word of Christ: "So you also, when you have done all that you were ordered to do, say, 'We are worthless slaves'" [Luke 17:10]. And this from Paul: "I consider that the sufferings of this present time are not worth comparing with the glory about to be revealed to us" [Rom. 8:18].

But out of the mercy and generosity of God and the grace of Christ, the merits of the saints serve for salvation not only for them but also for us, for

35. Augustine, *De civitate Dei* 8.27 (*CSEL* 40/1:405–7; *CCL* 47:248–49; *NPNF*, ser. 1, 2:164–65).

36. Augustine, *De civitate Dei* 22.10 (*CSEL* 40/2: 613f.; *CCL* 48:282; *NPNF*, ser. 1, 2:491–92).

37. Augustine, *Contra faustum* 20.21 (*CSEL* 25/1:561; *NPNF*, ser. 1, 4:261–63).

protection and for obtaining divine grace. In them, God graciously fulfills what he promised when he said, "I the Lord your God am a jealous God, visiting the iniquity of the fathers upon the children to the third and the fourth generation of those who reject me, but showing steadfast love to thousands of those who love me and keep my commandments" [Exod. 20:5]. Thus, the merits of the dead Abraham came to help his son Isaac [Gen. 26:5]. And when Jacob instructed his offspring in this religion, he taught them that they should invoke his and his father's name [Gen. 46:16]. With full faith, Moses did the same when he said, "Remember Abraham, Isaac, and Israel, your servants" [Exod. 32:12]. So, for the sake of the grace by which David was counted as a man after God's heart, all his posterity, to their advantage, often experienced God's indulgence.

XXIV. On the Memorial of Those Who Have Died in Christ

Our Lord Jesus Christ, affixing himself to the cross according to the will of the Father as a salutary sacrifice for redeeming humankind, gathered to himself with faith and longing as his own members all those who from the beginning of the world had anticipated this his sacrifice, which was designed for the salvation of the world, all those who would subsequently embrace it in faith. He willed that the fruit of his passion would reach all who would become members of his body equally. Therefore, when it repeats the memorial of this common sacrifice, the church ought to call all its members equally and exclude no one who, according to the gracious will of the Lord, is able to benefit from the sacrifice. Therefore, just as once the church remembered the saints, so also afterward it brings to the sacrifice of the altar a memorial of all other Christians, whom it piously believes died in the true Christian faith, about whom, however, it is unable to be certain whether they departed hence sufficiently purified and purged. It observes one memorial for the saints and another for those who rest in the sleep of peace. For the former, not so that we pray for them, but rather that they pray for us, so that we follow in their footsteps;[38] for the latter, so that we pray to the Lord we share with them, that God would grant to all those who sleep in Christ a place of consolation, light, and peace through Christ our Lord.

And so that we do not exclude those who have departed before us in the sign of faith from the benefit of our prayer, the same kind of communion which we confess with all the saints is demanded of us. For although they have been released from their bodies, they remain joined to us by spiritual bonds and in one spirit. They are united with us as members of the same body and are connected to us with the bond of love, and the death of the body cannot divide or separate them from the structure of Christ's mystical body.

Since the Lord introduced us to such a form of prayer, that none ought to pray only for their own needs but rather as citizens for the benefit of the whole

---

38. Augustine, *In Ioannem*, tractate 84, 1 (*CCL* 36:537; *NPNF*, ser. 1, 7:350).

community, and since by the apostle he commanded us to pray for each other that we be saved [James 5:16], it would be a great atrocity against his kindred and a detestable temerity against the Lord if anyone excluded from the fellowship of our prayers those who have died in Christ. The Scripture nowhere commands us to exclude them, and on the basis of the spiritual communion with the saints, which we confess, reason clearly forbids it.

It can be shown with great and reliable witnesses that this custom was spread throughout the whole church of Christ, that the memorial of the dead during the sacrifice of the altar came out of apostolic tradition. In chapter 7 of the *Ecclesiastical Hierarchies*, Dionysius the Areopagite writes that one should pray for the dead: the tradition has come down to us from the divine leaders, that is, from the apostle. There he clearly explained the structure and rationale for these prayers. This petition appeals to the divine kindness to forgive all the sins of the dead committed in human weakness and to bring them into the light and into the place of the living, etc.[39]

In Homily 69, Chrysostom says to the people of Antioch that it is not by chance that it was ordained by the apostles that there be a commemoration of the dead in the awesome mysteries. For they knew that benefit will follow from it. When the people stand with outstretched hands and the awesome sacrifice is made, why should we not entreat God for them as we pray?[40]

John of Damascus: The apostles, he says, the disciples of the Savior, who won the circle of the whole world by preaching the word of life that they had seen with their eyes, taught that the memory of those who fell asleep in the faith should be observed in the awesome and living sacraments, something which the apostolic and catholic church of Christ and God observed heretofore firmly and without contradiction, from one end of the earth to the other, and from their time to the present and to the end of the world.[41]

Augustine: It should not be denied that the piety of the living enlightens the souls of the dead when the sacrifice of the mediator is offered for them, or alms are given for them in the church. They benefit those who, when they were living, merited such benefits.[42]

See the same in Epiphanius, book 3, *Against Heresies;*[43] Tertullian, *Ad uxorem;*[44] *de corona militia;*[45] Ambrose in the prayer for Emperor Theodosius,[46]

---

39. Dionysius Areopagita, *De ecclesiastica hierarchia* 7 (*MPG* 3:562–63; Parker, *The Celestial Ecclesiastical Hierarchy,* 89–91).

40. John Chrysostom, Hom. in 1 Cor. 15, 35–36 (*MPG* 61:361–62; *NPNF,* ser. 1, 12:249–50).

41. John Damascene, *Sermo de iis, qui in fide hinc migraverunt* (*MPG* 95:250).

42. Augustine, *In Enchiridion,* cap. 110 (*MPL* 40:283, 182); in q. 2 ad Dul. (*De octo Dulcitii quaestionibus, quaestio 2: De cura pro mortuis gerenda, CSEL* 41:619ff.; *NPNF,* ser. 1, 3:272–73).

43. Epiphanius, *Panarion (Adversus haereses)* 3, 1, 75 (*MPG* 42:513ff.; F. Williams, *The Panarion of Epiphanius of Solamis, Book II and III, Nag Hammadi and Manichaean Studies* 36:496–97).

44. Tertullian, *Ad uxorem* (*CCL* 1:373ff.); the exact reference is not clear.

45. Tertullian, *De corona militis* 3, 3 (*CCL* 2:1043; *ANF* 3:94).

de excessu fratris;[47] and book 2 of the Letter to Faustinus;[48] Cyprian, book 1, epistle 9;[49] Bernhard in the sermon on the Cantica 6, 6.[50]

After this memorial of the dead, where the church again commends the salvation which the living share with the Lord, the rest of the prayers are delivered for the worthy preparation for receiving the Most Holy Eucharist. This part of the Mass serves primarily those who are present and receive the sacrament either sacramentally or at least spiritually, without actually partaking of the elements. For just as no one can be baptized for another, so no one can profitably receive the sacrament for another. When the sacrament has been administered and all other things have been properly performed, the thanksgiving concludes the service (as Augustine says).[51]

XXV. On the Communion, to Be Joined with Sacrifice

And when that most true and unique sacrifice is offered, it is useful to recall the ancient custom of the church by which not only the celebrant himself but also the deacons and the other ministers of the church, who on high feast days are used as witnesses of the sacrifice and as assistants to the holy ministers who must be present, offer themselves as participants in the reception of the body and blood of our Lord Jesus Christ, as the canon earnestly requires. But also all the faithful who come together for this sacrifice of our redeemer to recall the death of the Lord and the memory of our redemption should also be admonished and roused by diligent exhortation, after examination, confession, and absolution, to receive the grace of the Most Holy Communion, and together with the priest, with zeal and devotion, come often to participate in the most divine Eucharist.

XXVI. On the Ceremonies and the Use of the Sacraments

All the ancient ceremonies practiced at Baptism shall be retained: exorcism, renunciation of Satan, confession of faith, chrism, and others, for they demonstrate the efficacy and significance of this sacrament.

Also, in the ancient ceremonies practiced by the catholic church that apply to the Mass shall nothing be changed since they all are particularly appropriate to what occurs in the Mass.

And what pertains to the use of this holy office, in each city and place that has its own priests and where large numbers of people attend, at least two masses

---

46. Ambrose, *De obitu Theodosii* 17ff. (*CSEL* 73:380ff.; *Fathers of the Church* 22:323).

47. Ambrose, *De excessu fratris* (*CSEL* 73:209ff.; *NPNF*, ser. 2, 10:165–66).

48. Ambrose, ep. 39 (58) (*MPL* 16:1145ff.; *Fathers of the Church* 26:417).

49. Cyprian, ep. 65 [63] (*CSEL* 3/2: 721ff.; *ANF* 5:364–65).

50. Bernhard, in cant. 3, 3 (6, 6), sermo (*MPL* 184:42; *Cistercian Fathers Series* 4, *Bernard of Clairvaux*, 2:35–36).

51. Augustine, *De spiritu et littera* 11, 18 (*CSEL* 60, 170, 12 ff.; *NPNF*, ser. 1, 5:90).

ought to be celebrated every day (even if there are many churches in a city or a place). One of them should be celebrated early, to which manual laborers may come and receive the Eucharist or piously commend themselves to God. The other should be sung more solemnly, about the eighth hour of the morning. Similarly, those who either want to commune or to commend themselves to God should attend this mass. But in the villages, at least one mass should be celebrated every Sunday and feast day.

And so that the people be recalled to the use of masses in an appropriate way, preachers ought to urge the people according to the rationale about this sacred office set forth above, so that they attend voluntarily. Certain meditations should be prescribed for them, appropriate to each part of the Mass. And the priest or deacon, if there is one, should explain the true use of the Mass before the preface, and do it from a specific instruction sheet, to be agreed upon [by the priest and deacon], according to the way the sacred office is explained above.

The canon, in which nothing is to be changed, should also be explained clearly and succinctly, first, so that the priests understand the function of their office better, and so that they are able to explain what they understand to the people.

The ceremonies of the other sacraments should be conducted according to the directions of the ancient agendas. But if anything has slipped in that can give cause to superstition, it should be eliminated. Altars, priestly vestments, church vessels, banners, crosses, candles, and pictures are to be retained in the church, but in such a way that they are only reminders, and that no divine honor is rendered to these things, nor shall any superstition be attached to pictures and statues.

The canonical hours and the pious recitation of the psalmody, which the apostle himself commanded to us [1 Cor. 14:26], should by no means be excluded from the church, but restored, especially for appointed times, on Sundays, and on other ancient and more solemn feasts.

But details that have been added concerning the saints to the *Commune sanctorum*[52] should be removed, and matters that seem to have gone beyond what is proper [in the prayers to the saints] should be corrected.

Vigils, too, and funeral rites for the dead should be celebrated according to the custom of the ancient church. For it would be monstrous not to retain any memory of them in the church, as if their souls had perished with their bodies.

Feast days, received from the church, should be retained; and if not all, at least the principal ones:

Sundays
The Birth of the Lord
The Circumcision of the Lord

---

52. The *Commune sanctorum* consists of those parts of the liturgy of the Mass that bring prayer and veneration before the saints. The authors of the Augsburg Interim were opposed to the use of such superstitious passages in these liturgical elements.

Epiphany
Palm Sunday
Easter and the two days following
The Ascension of the Lord
Pentecost and the two days following
Corpus Christi
and the feast days of the Blessed Virgin Mary and the Holy Apostles:
St. John the Baptist
Mary Magdalene
Stephen
Lawrence
Martin
Michael
All Saints

And in each church, [the day of its] own patron saints, so that we honor God in his saints on the same saints' days, are stimulated to imitate them and desire to be helped by their prayers and associated with their merits.

Rogation days before the Ascension of the Lord and the litany on St. Mark's Day and all customary processions should be held throughout the year in the ancient manner, and similarly in Holy Week and on the other feasts of the church the usual solemnities should be observed. And on the vigils of Easter and Pentecost, baptismal water should be prepared in all churches with the solemn benediction.

And abstinence from meat is accepted, not because meat is impure but for the sake of temperance since it is good in itself and suitable for chastising the flesh. Even public welfare demands that we abstain from meat at certain times since otherwise there are hardly enough cattle for constant consumption. Therefore, the custom and institution of the ancient church of abstention from meat on fast days, on Fridays and Sundays, should be retained. For the church did not take over this abstention from food at certain times from any superstition, nor because any food was unclean (knowing that "to the pure all things are pure" [Titus 1:15] and "not what goes into the mouth defiles a person" [Matt. 15:11]), but in order to subdue the flesh, so that the soul would be better humbled, drawn away from perverse desires and evil affections.

The church instituted this abstention especially for Fridays and Saturdays, so that, prepared by the two-day abstinence, people would go more prepared and worthy to the worship of God required of them, to hear the Word of God, and to receive the Most Holy Eucharist (which was once celebrated on Sundays more frequently). And so they crucified their own flesh by this voluntary chastising, as if joined to Christ (the memory of whose passion is remembered by the faithful especially on these days). The practice of fasting should be observed as well, with the exception of those excused by necessity: those engaged in hard work, pilgrims, pregnant women, nursing mothers, children, the elderly, and the sick.

Nor should the blessing of those things prepared for human use by exorcism and prayers be despised, but [care must be taken] that the results are attributed not to the things themselves but to divine power, and that no kind of magic and superstition is practiced.

And although one should hold with the apostles that the unmarried man be anxious about the affairs of the Lord, etc. [1 Cor. 7:32], and that it is to be hoped that many of the clergy, since they are celibate, will be found to be truly continent; yet, since many who have functions as ministers of the church, in many places, now have wives, whom they do not want to dismiss, a statement of a general council is expected on this matter. No change in this matter, therefore, can be made at this time without grave disruption. Still, it cannot be denied, although according to the Scripture, marriage is good in itself, that he who is not married and is truly continent does better, according to the same Scripture [Matt. 19:20-22; 1 Cor. 7:1, 8, 26].

The same reasoning applies to the reception of the Eucharist under both kinds, to which many are now accustomed, and from which they cannot be turned away at this time without great distress. And because the ecumenical council, to which all estates of the empire have submitted themselves, will without doubt give this matter pious and careful diligence, so that in this concern the consciences of many and the public peace will be given proper attention, therefore those who have up to now received the two kinds and do not want to give it up, and who are waiting for the deliberation and judgment on these things by the ecumenical council, may receive both kinds.

But those who practice the use of both kinds should not condemn that ancient practice of communing under one kind, and no one should disturb anyone else, until the ecumenical council decides on the matter.

And, although the sacrament of the Eucharist was instituted under two kinds, it should not be held that the true body of Christ is divided in the flesh, an idea to which the inspired Scripture testifies [1 Cor. 1:13], but rather that the whole Christ is contained in each kind.

And because the true body of Christ and the true blood of Christ are in the sacrament of the Eucharist, Christ properly ought to be adored in this sacrament.

Again, since the sacrament of the Eucharist was once consecrated by the word of Christ, the sacrament remains the body and blood of Christ, even if it is kept for a long time, until it is consumed.

The matter of the discipline of clergy and people seems to be particularly necessary for removing scandal from the church, for that is something that furnishes great cause for disturbance, as is clear from the situation itself. So, if the Imperial Majesty creates a useful reform for the church, no one zealous for the holy religion and public peace wants to repudiate it, but all ought to beg humbly and with all their strength that it might be promoted and procured.

And we, Charles, emperor of the Romans, etc., recognize that the consultation given above is the one which was reported in our and the imperial recess of this diet, celebrated here in Augsburg. In testimony of which, we have ordered our imperial seal attached here. Dated in our and the empire's city, Augsburg, the last day of July, 1548, and of our life the forty-eighth and of our rule the thirty-third year.[53]

Charles Sebastian, Archbishop of Mainz, signed by the German
  Archchancellor.
By the order of the Imperial and Catholic Majesty, [Johann] Oldenburger.

---

53. Emperor Charles was born in 1500 and began assuming the regal duties of his deceased father Philip in 1515, after the death of his maternal grandfather, Ferdinand of Aragon.

The Leipzig Interim

Translated by Robert Kolb

Introduction

Because the religious policy dubbed by its opponents the "Leipzig Interim" was never officially enacted by the Diet of Electoral Saxony and because its provisions were only selectively enforced, some modern scholars reject the term.[1] However, the concept of a "Leipzig Interim" did play an important role in the polemic among Lutheran theologians in the period between 1548 and 1577, and it is therefore worthwhile to assess the concept and the text that lies behind it.

Emperor Charles V and his brother King Ferdinand had given an oral promise to Duke Moritz of Saxony that he would not have to abandon his religious faith if he supported them in the Smalcald War. Nonetheless, after their military success and the enactment of the Augsburg Interim, the Hapsburg brothers insisted that Moritz bring his domains in line with this new religious policy for the empire. Moritz was under pressure, however, from the populace and the estates of electoral Saxony to remain faithful to the Lutheran confession of the faith. In a series of negotiations between his secular counselors and his theological staff during the summer of 1548, the electoral Saxon government drafted a compromise intended to stave off imperial invasion and retain the pulpits of the churches of Saxony for Lutheran preachers.

The goal was to formulate a statement of faith and practice that would seem to comply with the policies of the Augsburg Interim while still preserving a doctrine of justification that faithfully conveyed Luther's teaching. However, the statement of the final draft regarding justification, which had been prepared at a conference in the Saxon town of Pegau in August 1548, contained ambiguous language regarding the doctrine. In fact, parts of it had been borrowed directly from the Augsburg Interim. Most of the Leipzig Interim was prepared at similar conferences at Meissen in July, Torgau in October, and Altencelle in November 1548; there Moritz's advisors developed treatments of the doctrines of the sacraments and of church and ministry as well as of ceremonies and usages that Melanchthon and his colleagues at Wittenburg regarded as adiaphora—things that are neither commanded nor prohibited by Scripture. Throughout these negotiations, Melanchthon and the other Wittenberg theologians fought hard to minimize the amount of compromise with the Roman Catholic position, with some success.

---

1. On the document itself, see *Melanchthons Briefwechsel, Kritische und kommentierte Gesamtausgabe, Band 5*, ed. Heinz Scheible, with assistance from Walter Thüringer (Stuttgart-Bad Cannstatt: frommann-holzboog, 1987), 400–401, #5387.

The text of Moritz's new religious policy was laid before the diet of his lands in December 1548. The diet did not officially adopt the policy. In July 1549, Elector Moritz issued an *Excerpt* of the provisions of the Leipzig Interim for use in guiding church practice, but even its prescriptions were enforced only selectively.

After the Truce of Passau, the Leipzig Interim became a dead letter, but the compromise intended with its formulation and the principle of "making no concession at a time when the faith is being persecuted" remained issues of sharp dispute for a quarter of a century within German Lutheranism.

This text is taken from *CR* 7:258–64 with portions printed in the preceding documents, *CR* 7:51–64 (Pegau on justification) and *CR* 7:217, 219–20 (Altencelle on Confirmation, the Mass, and the festivals).

"The Leipzig Interim"

Our concern is based upon our desire to be obedient to the Roman Imperial Majesty and to conduct ourselves in such a way that his Majesty realize that our interest revolves only around tranquillity, peace, and unity. This is our counsel, made in good faith; it is what we ourselves want to serve and promote wherever possible. For in contrast to what some say and write about us—without any basis—our concern and our intention are always directed not toward causing schism and complications, but rather toward peace and unity. We testify to that in the very presence of God, to whom all human hearts are known. Our actions will demonstrate that.

Accordingly, our first consideration is that everything that the ancient teachers regarded as adiaphora, that is, things that are neither commanded nor forbidden by God, may still be regarded as adiaphora without compromising Scripture. Even when they are still in use by the other party, they may continue to be observed. No one should try to make them a burden or regard them as such or as something to be avoided since they may be observed without harming good consciences.

Secondly, in reference to public teaching regarding the state and nature of the human creature before and after the fall, there is no dispute.

The Article on Justification

was agreed upon at Pegau.[2]

---

2. The counselors of Elector Moritz had met at Pegau in August 1548.

How the Human Creature Becomes Righteous before God

After it has been said that God's Son has been appointed as mediator and Savior by the wondrous, unfathomable counsel of God and that for his sake forgiveness of sins, the Holy Spirit, righteousness, and eternal life are given in all certainty, the people should further know how this great grace and these great benefits are received:

Although God does not make human creatures righteous through the merit of their own work, which they perform, but through his mercy, freely, without our merit—so that we boast not of ourselves but of Christ, through whose merit alone we are redeemed from sin and made righteous—nonetheless, the merciful God does not deal with human creatures as with a block of wood but draws them in such a manner that their will cooperates, if they are of the age of reason. They do not receive Christ's benefits if the will and heart are not moved by prevenient[3] grace, so that they stand in fear of God's wrath and detest sin. For because sin creates enmity between God and human creatures, as Isaiah says [55:2], no one can come before the throne of grace and mercy without turning from sins through genuine remorse. Therefore, John, as he was preparing the way for the Lord, preached with utmost seriousness: "Repent, for the kingdom of heaven has come near" [Matt. 3:2]. And there is absolutely no doubt, there must be regret and terror in the face of God's wrath in conversion. As long as a person remains secure and persists in sinning against conscience, there is no conversion and no forgiveness. Why does Isaiah say, "In whom does God want to dwell? In the one who has a stricken heart, which trembles before God's Word" [66:2]? And Moses says, "The Lord your God is a devouring fire" [Deut. 4:24], that is, he is truly wrathful and angry over all sin, and he announced his judgment soon after the fall with his Word and with punishments, and thereafter gave the law for that reason with indisputable testimonies. In this law, it is taught that death, destruction, and other plagues are reminders thereof, so that we can recognize his wrath. God wants sin condemned in human hearts in his church through the Word and the Holy Spirit until the final redemption, as it is written: "The Holy Spirit will convict the world of sin" [John 16:8].

God has not only revealed his wrath, however, but alongside it has given his gracious promise, the gospel of the Son of God. It is his eternal, unchangeable will, confirmed by his own oath and by the blood of his Son and his resurrection and many miracles, that he in all certainty wants to forgive sins, wants to give his Holy Spirit, and to accept us, renew us, and make us heirs of eternal salvation, for the sake of his Son, not because of our merit or worthiness. Thus, in this fear and remorse we truly believe and trust that he will forgive our sins for the sake of this mediator.

---

3. The medieval term "gratia praeveniens" is rendered here through the German "vorgehende Gnade." The term was used in medieval theological systems to indicate that grace precedes all human actions in the relationship between God and the human creature.

This true faith believes all the articles of faith. For it must recognize God correctly and believe along with the other articles of faith the following: "I believe in the forgiveness of sin, that it is conveyed to me and not only to others." For although many who live with a bad conscience also confess Christian teaching and boast of their faith, it is nevertheless not a living and justifying faith. For such a heart does not believe that forgiveness of sins is given to it, and it does not accept the promise but flees from God's presence and has no comfort and cannot call upon God. And there is no doubt that this devil's faith, which is terrified in the face of God's judgment, is a far different thing than the true faith. True faith accepts the promise and its gracious comfort, as Paul clearly testifies, Romans 4[:13]; there he speaks of this faith which accepts the promise, which is not only the knowledge that the devils or human beings who live with a bad conscience have, but this faith believes, together with the other articles of faith, in the forgiveness of sins. It accepts the promise and has in the heart a true trust in God's Son, who bestows trust and the ability to call on God and other virtues. Of this faith the words of Isaiah speak [28:16], which Paul cites in Romans 10[:11]: "Whoever trusts in him shall not be put to shame." And it is certainly true that there is no other way to God and to the forgiveness of sins, no other way to receive grace, than the way through God's Son, as it is written: "No one comes to the Father apart from coming through the Son" [John 14:6]. And the Holy Spirit is given into our hearts at the same time, so that we may grasp the divine promise with faith and be comforted and set upright, as is clearly expressed in Galatians 3[:2, 14], that we receive the promise of the Holy Spirit through faith. In the heart, the Holy Spirit produces a steadfast faith, comfort, and life, and arouses all necessary virtues, firm faith, the invocation of God, fear of God, love, good intentions, hope, and other virtues. And these are they who have received the forgiveness of sins, and in whom the Holy Spirit has begun faith and trust in God's Son, love, and hope, as heirs of eternal salvation for the sake of the Savior, as Paul says in Romans 6[:23]: "Eternal life is God's gift through Jesus Christ our Lord."

And because throughout time, after he accepted Adam and Eve again and had given them the promise of a future Savior [Gen. 3:15], God has graciously built a church for himself and preserved it, he has continually preserved this understanding of forgiveness and faith. Although it has often been obscured in many who have sought forgiveness through their own works or have remained stuck in doubt, as is the case with the heathen, among whom no memory of the promise has remained, so God has indeed expressed this understanding clearly in his Scripture, and again and again had it explained in his church, so that the knowledge and the honor of his Son has not been destroyed, and so that he continued to gather a church for himself and saved many people.[4]

---

4. The following paragraph from the Pegau document is omitted from the manuscripts of the Leipzig Interim: "It is not correct to say that one should doubt the forgiveness of sins and remain in doubt, for it is God's unchangeable command that we accept God's Son and believe the promise,

Thus, in the Christian church, all people should know these two aspects of the matter and truly believe them: those who live in sin against conscience should certainly recognize that they are in God's wrath and if they do not convert, they will fall into eternal punishment. On the other hand, it is God's serious intention and command in true conversion that we accept his promise and believe that not because of our worthiness but because of the reconciler and mediator God is gracious, wants to forgive us our sin, and to accept us and come to our aid, etc.

That some speak against that and say that this is a peculiar way of speaking, and that every person finds there to be much doubt of God stuck and remaining in the heart, is unfortunately true. All human beings continue to doubt, tremble, and flee from God. This weakness is the damage done by original sin. Against that, God has given his promise to comfort us and to strengthen us that we may overcome doubt and find refuge in him. Paul says, "I am conscious of nothing, but I am not thereby righteous" [1 Cor. 4:4]. With these words he teaches not that we should doubt but rather that we may conclude both points: the conscience should stand upright, but there is still much weakness in us, and therefore we should know that we are at the same time righteous, that is, God-pleasing, for the sake of the Son, and it is correct, as Augustine says, "The certainty of faith ought to rest in the precious blood of Christ." And it is the divine unchangeable truth that in the heart which receives the forgiveness of sins through faith, the Holy Spirit initiates invocation of God, love, hope, and other virtues, and these must be accompanied by good intention and a good conscience, as Paul says, faith and a good conscience must go together [1 Tim. 1:19]. John says, "Who does not love remains in death" [1 John 3:14].

This is most certainly true. And even if we would like to live without vice and mortal sin by means of divine grace, we must know that in this infirm life there are many inclinations against God's commandments, much lack of knowledge, doubt, and various disorders, as St. Paul says in Romans 7[:23]: "I see another law in my members which strives against the law of my reason." And the Psalm [143:2] says, "No one living is righteous in your sight." And Daniel [9:18] says,

---

and as St. Paul says, 'the promise must be accepted through faith' [Gal. 3:22] and John says, 'those who do not believe God regard him as a liar' [1 John 5:10]. This is a very harsh statement against the false teaching which states that we should remain in doubt. But it is very comforting for all believers in Christ to know that it is God's will and command that everyone should believe in the forgiveness of his or her own sins. Some object and say that that the promise is conditional: God alone knows who is worthy or unworthy. This counterargument stems from blindness, from the fact that many do not know the difference between law and Gospel. For the wondrous counsel regarding God's Son was concluded, and the promise is given, because we are unworthy, and therefore God has revealed his will in the promise that we may know his gracious will and not live in doubt, as the heathen, who even have the law, doctrine, and some wonderful virtues but doubt that God wants to pay attention to them, to accept them, and to hear them."

"Not because of our righteousness, but through your mercy, for the sake of the Lord, hear us."[5] People hardly understand this.

Therefore, although new obedience has been begun, we should not think that the person who has forgiveness of sins, and is therefore pure, has no need for forgiveness of sins and a mediator. The Son of God is and remains at every moment our mediator and stands in the divine secret council and prays for us, that the severe wrath of God against our sin may not be poured out upon us. It is not enough to say that God does not want to credit to our account the remaining weakness, that he acts as if the person is without sin; this creates a false trust in our own righteousness. Instead, both must be in us, a good conscience and initial obedience, and with them this humility and faith, that we confess that we still have sin and that in us there is serious regret and displeasure over our sin. We confess as well that we have merited punishment, and that in it we submit to God, as Daniel says, "You, O Lord, are righteous; we are ashamed" [9:7]. Along with that there must exist the necessary comfort, that God most certainly wants to accept this person and be gracious for the sake of his Son. This trust, that looks to the mediator in the face of the divine judgment, must at all times overshadow the other virtues in this life of weakness. Therefore Paul says, "Through faith we are righteous" [Rom. 5:1]; this phrase is not to be understood as if faith is only a preparation, or a confession, or as if it attains other virtues on the basis of which the person thereafter becomes truly righteous. Rather, we should give God's Son the honor of being and remaining our mediator. We should remain so humble that we confess that we still have sin and need grace, and that God most certainly wants to be gracious to us, so that we believe in this humility that he is gracious to us for the sake of the Son.

All find in their hearts that this comfort is necessary for all God-fearing people. In all anxiety and in earnest invocation of God, we all cry out, "Oh, I am a miserable sinner. I am not worthy that God listens to me." In this need, we should not direct people to fashioning a prayer such as, "I have many wonderful new virtues, and therefore I am pure," but we should find refuge in God's Son and know that we should trust in him according to his promise, as Daniel [9:18] says, "not because of our righteousness but through mercy for the Lord's sake," that is, for the sake of the promised Savior.[6]

---

5. The following sentence from the Pegau document is omitted from the manuscripts of the Leipzig Interim: "And from our weakness even in God-fearing, reasonable people there arises in this life much lack of knowledge, security, doubt of God, false trust in one's own wisdom, power, and many sinful works."

6. The following paragraph from the Pegau document is omitted from the manuscripts of the Leipzig Interim: "This understanding is clearly expressed in God's Word and in many authors and is without doubt known to all reasonable Christians. St. Paul presents to the whole world the holy Abraham, who was adorned with great virtues, and the apostle teaches of him that his faith was reckoned as righteousness [Rom. 4:3]. That cannot be understood as if faith were only a preparation, and that thereafter true righteousness proceeds from other virtues. Paul also calls attention to David, who had great virtues. At the same time he says, in Psalm 32, that he needs forgiveness of sins and that he is righteous because his sins are forgiven and covered and this forgiveness is accepted

From all of this it is clear that it is true that in us new obedience must be initiated, and that nonetheless faith and trust in God's Son must continually remain and must hang on to this comfort, that God is gracious to us for the sake of his Son. Where this faith disappears, there can be no love, no taking refuge in God, no proper invocation of him. For this faith creates comfort, love, and the ability to call on God, as is said, and it is not to be found without love.

The virtues and good works in those who have been reconciled are called righteousness, but not in this sense, that a person has forgiveness of sins because of them, or that a person stands therefore before God's judgment without sin, but rather that God wants to take pleasure in this weak, initial obedience in this miserable, vulnerable, impure nature in believers for the sake of his Son. John calls such works righteousness when he says, "Whoever performs righteousness, is righteous" [1 John 3:7]. And it is true that where these works are done in hostility toward God, God despises them, and no conversion to God takes place in the heart. As the tree is, so are the fruits, as we will comment later.

On Good Works

We do not doubt that our teaching and understanding of good works is in agreement with Holy Scripture and the understanding of the catholic church in all times, and because our writings on this subject are public, it is not necessary to give an extensive report here. But to offer a reliable rule, we declare that those works are good and necessary which God has commanded, according to the Ten Commandments and the explanation of these commandments, which is sufficiently expressed in the writings of the apostles. A good conscience and a bad conscience are to be distinguished according to this rule. And, as said above, it is God's solemn command that we live with a good conscience; as St. Paul says, "Retain faith and a good conscience" [1 Tim. 1:19]. Whoever remains in sins against that conscience is not converted to God and is still God's enemy, and the wrath of God remains upon such a person as long as conversion does not take place. That is certain according to the saying in Galatians 5[:21]: "From these things I have spoken and say it still, whoever does such will not inherit the kingdom of God." And God has comprehended both of these elements in his oath, that this conversion is necessary and that we should believe in forgiveness: "So truly as I live, I do not want the sinner to die but to be converted and receive life" [Ezek. 33:11]. Therefore, where there is no conversion, there is no grace. This all reasonable people know without a long explanation.

---

through faith. There is no doubt that thinking Christians at all times have continued to hold this understanding. Although authors often use different ways of expressing it, many explain their positions and understanding in a way that agrees with ours. Augustine [Ps. 89:5; *MPL* 37:1123; *NPNF*, ser. 1, 8:430] said regarding Psalm 88, 'the Savior Christ will rule eternally in his saints.' God has said this, promised it, confirmed it with an oath. Because this promise is firm and certain, not on account of our merit, but rather on account of his mercy: that is the reason we should believe and call on God in all confidence."

Further, if anyone who has been in God's grace acts against God's command against conscience, he troubles the Holy Spirit and loses grace and righteousness and falls under God's wrath. If he is not converted, he falls into eternal punishment, like Saul and many others. This is clearly expressed in Romans 8[:12-13]: "You are obligated to live not according to the flesh, for those who live according to the flesh will die," that is, if you follow your evil inclinations against conscience, you will fall into eternal punishment. Such sins merit not only eternal punishment after this life but also terrible punishments in this life, which fall upon the one who commits the sin and many other people at the same time, as David's adultery and murder were punished.

For this reason, to say it briefly, it is easy to understand that good works are necessary, for God has commanded them. Those who act against them are discarding God's grace and the Holy Spirit. Such sins merit eternal damnation. God takes pleasure, however, in the virtues and good works of the reconciled because they believe that God accepts a person for Christ's sake and wants to take pleasure in this imperfect obedience. It is true that eternal life is given for the sake of the Lord Christ by grace, and that at the same time all are heirs of eternal salvation who are converted to God and receive forgiveness of sins and faith through the Holy Spirit. At the same time, these new virtues and good works are also most necessary so that, if they are not awakened in the heart, there is no reception of divine grace. The reception of divine grace must take place in us in this way, and the comfort is not an idle thought, but it is life and rescue from great anxiety, as King Hezekiah said, Isaiah 38[:13, 17]: "God has smashed my bones like a lion, but he has saved my soul and thrown away my sins." St. Paul says [2 Cor. 5:3]: "We will be clothed once again so that we are not found naked." Revelation 2[:10]: "Be faithful and believing until death, and I will give you a crown of life." In these verses the two parts are comprehended: first, that in this life the beginning of eternal salvation must take place, and second, that we must not fall away before our end.

Therefore, rebirth and eternal life are in themselves a new light, fear of God, love, joy in God, and other virtues, as the verse says, "This is eternal life, that they recognize you, the true God, and me, Jesus Christ" [John 17:3]. Just as this true knowledge must enlighten us, so it is certainly true that these virtues, faith, love, hope, and others, must be in us and are necessary for salvation. For all this is easily understood by the God-fearing who seek and experience comfort in God. Because the virtues and good works please God, as has been said, so they merit reward in this life, both spiritual and temporal, according to God's plan, and more reward in eternal life on the basis of the divine promise.

In no way does this confirm the error of the monks that eternal salvation is merited through the worthiness of our works, nor does it confirm that we can convey our merit to others. Instead, faith recognizes our own weakness and takes refuge in God's Son and receives this eternal comfort and his merit and treasure according to his gracious and immeasurably rich promise. It knows that we are bound to believe God at all times in conversion, for God has promised grace and has confirmed his promise with an oath, and he regards despair as blasphemy and the greatest sin.

Further, good works are adorned with many temporal promises and great praise in Holy Scripture, and we have offered Christian instruction on this in great detail in our writings and want to continue to do that always by God's grace. For God wants to be recognized in his temporal gifts and wants us to call on him and wants this invocation of him to take place in faith and in a good conscience.

To speak further of those works which God has not commanded, out of which bishops and monks have made a special service of God, we can simply mention the verse "In vain do they worship me with human commandments" [Matt. 15:9]. Therefore it is necessary to retain the truth that proper understanding remains regarding which works are necessary and provide God-pleasing service and which are to be rejected. We shall give a reminder of this later.[7]

On the Power and Authority of the Church

Whatever the true Christian church, assembled in the Holy Spirit, recognizes, determines, and teaches in matters of faith shall continue to be taught and proclaimed. For the church neither can nor shall determine anything against Holy Scripture.

On the Ministers of the Church

As in the past, learned people who have a good deal of understanding in Holy Scripture are to be presented and appointed to the office of prebend in foundations.[8] They are to administer episcopal offices, and they are to take leadership in the care and administration of the office of archdeacon[9] and in the jurisdiction of the church. God-fearing people who would be useful to the episcopal office shall not be prevented from being appointed as canons[10] on the basis of their qualifications by the use of statutes and customs which exist in certain foundations. That is said above all because such people have been discharged and dismissed on the basis of papal ordinances and decrees. Thus it was found that such foundations became filled with idle, unlearned people. Likewise, learned pastors and ministers shall be placed into service who are equipped and able to teach the Word of God and to lead the people in a Christian manner.

---

7. This concludes the text taken over from the Pegau document.

8. The office of prebend in a foundation, or special group of clergy appointed to say Mass and exercise other duties at a church, had become a political plum for prominent families.

9. The office of archdeacon had been created in the fourth century; archdeacons aided bishops in the administration of the diocese and had special responsibilities, e.g., the care of the poor.

10. Canons were members of a council of clergy appointed to office at an episcopal seat in a cathedral. They advised the bishop and exercised other duties, e.g., holding Mass at the cathedral.

All other ministers shall be subjected and obedient to the highest bishop and other bishops who carry out their episcopal office according to divine command and who use that office for the edification of the church, not for its destruction. These ministers of the church shall be ordained by these bishops after presentation by the patron of the congregation.[11] These ministers of the church when they transgress (and we speak here particularly of priests who live in a dishonorable way or teach false doctrine) shall be punished with proper means, such as with deprivation of office and finally with excommunication.

On Baptism

The baptism of infants, along with exorcism, the support and confession of sponsors, and other ancient Christian ceremonies, is taught and held.

[On] Confirmation

Confirmation shall be taught and practiced, and particularly the youth who are of age shall be examined by their bishop or someone to whom he entrusts the examination so that they may confess their faith to this person and reaffirm the promise and the renunciation of the devil which their sponsors made for them in Baptism. Thus, they may be confirmed and strengthened in their faith by means of God's grace through the laying on of hands and with Christian prayer and ceremonies.

[On] Repentance

Repentance, Confession and absolution, and everything associated with them are diligently taught and proclaimed. The people are admonished and held responsible for going to Confession, to the priest, and receiving absolution from him in God's stead. They are admonished to do that with diligence. They are also to pray, fast, and give alms. None are permitted to come to the most precious sacrament of the body and blood of Christ without confessing their sins to the priest and receiving absolution from him. The people are diligently taught and instructed that in this sacrament we are united with Christ our Savior as members of his body with him, the head, and that we are raised and nourished in him to all good deeds. Likewise, the people are taught and instructed that we grow in community with the saints. For we are one bread and one body, as St. Paul says [1 Cor. 10:17].

The people are also reminded and taught that whoever receives this sacrament unworthily eats and drinks it as judgment [1 Cor. 11:27]. Therefore, they are fervently urged to abandon their sinful way of life and to practice true

---

11. Placement in a parish pastorate in the Late Middle Ages regularly took place upon nomination by a patron—usually a nobleman or municipal council—and confirmation by a bishop.

repentance, prayer, almsgiving, moderation, and all other parts of the Christian way of life. For all those who want to receive and cling to life must avoid the causes of death and must obediently follow the physician who has preceded us in the practice of virtues and the good and who impels us to practice them.

On Unction

Although in these lands, the Unction has not been used for many years, nonetheless, it may be observed in the manner in which the apostles made use of it, as it is treated in Mark and James; as James [5:14] says, "If there are people sick among you, call the priests of the church to them and have them pray over them, anointing them with oil in the name of the Lord. The prayer of faith will save the sick, and the Lord will raise them up." Christian prayers and words of comfort from Holy Scripture may be spoken over the sick. The people may be advised of this so that they may grasp the proper understanding of this custom and be shielded and protected from all superstition and misunderstanding.

[On] [t]he Ordination of Ministers of the Church

As stated above, henceforth ministers appointed by those bishops who conduct their episcopal office as described above shall be ordained upon presentation by the patron with Christian ceremonies, and no one shall be permitted to hold any ecclesiastical office unless he has, as stated previously, been presented by the patron and admitted to office by the bishop so that no one barge into an ecclesiastical office in an unfitting fashion or be placed in that office in an unorderly fashion. Spurious examinations,[12] through which many unlearned and unsuitable people have been admitted to pastoral care and ecclesiastical offices with resulting burden and damage to consciences, shall be abolished. Bishops shall personally examine candidates for ordination carefully and extensively, with the counsel, assistance, and support of God-fearing, learned people. Particularly those who have been presented for an ecclesiastical office by the patron shall be so examined that they may be found apt and capable in their teaching, understanding, life, and conduct, so that they may feed the flock of the Lord with God's Word, oversee it with good teaching and good example, and conduct their office properly.

---

12. Examinations for favorite candidates of patrons or bishops had become farces. Melanchthon himself prepared a text for the examination of pastoral candidates. It was published in the Mecklenburg ecclesiastical constitution of 1552, "Der Ordinanden Examen, wie es in der Kirchen zu Wittemberg gebraucht wird," both in German (*CR* 23:21–110) and Latin (*CR* 23:111–128, 1–102).

On Marriage

Marriage shall be observed in these lands according to God's institution at every level of society.[13]

On the Mass

The Mass shall be observed in these lands with bells, lights, vessels, chanting, vestments, and ceremonies. In places where there are enough people, the priests and ministers shall go before the altar in their customary ecclesiastical vestments and robes in a reverent manner. They shall begin by speaking the *Confiteor* and the *Introit,* the *Kyrie Eleison,* the *Gloria in Excelsis Deo et In Terra* etc., the *Dominus vobiscum,* the Collects, and the Epistle shall be said along with the associated parts, and all this in Latin. When the Epistle is sung in Latin, the people shall have it read to them in German as well. The Gradual, the Hallelujah, the Sequence or a *Tractus* according to the time and the festival [shall be sung]. The Gospel shall be sung in Latin and read aloud to the people in German. The *Credo in unum Deum* shall be sung as the entire creed, as is customary in the foundations. In parishes where there are no canons, the Gradual may be sung in the form of an old German song: at Christmas, "A child so praiseworthy," at Easter, "Christ is risen," at Pentecost, "We now pray the Holy Spirit." And for the Creed, "We all believe in one true God," etc. The sermon is to be on the Gospel. The *Dominus vobiscum,* the *Oremus,* the *Offertorium,* the *Praefatio,* the *Sanctus,* the *Consecratio,* the Lord's Prayer in German, the *Agnus Dei,* the *Communio* and administration of the sacrament, the *Communicatio* or partaking, the Collects, the Benediction [shall be sung].

[On] Images

Images and pictures of the suffering of Christ and of the saints may be kept in the church. The people should be taught that they are only reminders, and so they are to give them no divine honor. No superstitious recourse to them shall take place in the use of images and the pictures of the saints.

[On] Singing in the Church

The canonical hours, the singing of pious psalms in foundations and in the churches in towns, shall be observed as they have been observed, at appropriate times and on high feasts and also on Sundays. The ancient customary hymns for specific times and the chief festivals shall be maintained. The hymns for and after burial may be sung at the request of those who desire it for remembering the dead and for the sake of the promise to us and the certainty of the resurrection.

---

13. German: *Stand,* the "estate" or social situation.

[On] Festivals

Sundays
The Birthday of the Lord
The Day of St. Stephen
The Day of St. John the Evangelist
The Circumcision of the Lord
Epiphany
Easter and the two following days
Ascension
Pentecost with the two following days
Corpus Christi
The Festival days of the Blessed Virgin Mary
The Days of the Holy Apostles
The Day of St. John the Baptist
The Day of St. Mary Magdalene
The Day of St. Michael,

and such others that may be observed with preaching and a mass with communicants: the conversion of Paul, the beheading of John the Baptist, Thursday, Friday, and Saturday in Holy Week.

[On] [t]he Eating of Meat

Likewise, on Fridays and Saturdays and also in Lent, the eating of meat should be omitted, observed as an external ordinance commanded by his Imperial Majesty. In special cases, this regulation shall not be binding where special needs excuse people, such as those who do heavy labor, pilgrims, pregnant women, those with young children, old, weak people, and children.

[On] [t]he Conduct of Ministers of the Church

We regard it as honorable and good that pastors and ministers conduct themselves in an honorable way, appropriate for the priesthood, as exhibited in their clothing and in their discipline and conduct, and that among themselves, with the suggestions and advice of their bishops or consistories, they make ordinances regarding clothing which marks the difference between ministers of the church and persons in secular ways of life and hold to them, so that proper reverence may be given to the priestly walk of life, as is fitting. Each and every person is to hold pastors, preachers, and ministers of the church in respect and also their teaching and conduct, and when they find something lacking, they should report this to the bishop or the consistory, who should abolish what is wrong.

Conclusion

In the other articles, we are open to discussion and prepared to look diligently at Scripture and the ancient teachers and to explain to our friends and
gracious lords, the bishops, our thinking, and to conduct discussions with their
dear princely Graces in a friendly manner befitting subjects and to come to
Christian agreement.

Judgment on Certain Controversies concerning Certain Articles of the Augsburg Confession Which Have Recently Arisen and Caused Controversy

Martin Chemnitz

Translated by J. A. O. Preus and Robert Kolb

Introduction

Martin Chemnitz (1522–86) was already claiming a place among the leading participants in contemporary theological discussion in 1561 when, at age thirty-nine, he set down his thoughts on the controversies besetting the Lutheran churches of Germany. For more than six years, he had provided theological leadership to the ministerium of the city of Braunschweig, as the confidant of its superintendent, his friend Joachim Mörlin (1514–71). The two had begun to work together a decade earlier in Königsberg, in the dukedom of Prussia, where Mörlin had been serving as pastor and Chemnitz as ducal librarian. Mörlin was ousted from his pastorate there in early 1553 by Duke Albrecht of Prussia because of his opposition to the teaching of the duke's favorite, Andreas Osiander (1498–1552), on the doctrine of justification. Chemnitz, who had been among the first and harshest critics of Osiander's teaching, had resigned his position in late 1552 and returned to Wittenberg, where he had studied before his mentor, Philip Melanchthon, had recommended him to Duke Albrecht. There, with Melanchthon's full support, he pursued his theological studies and, at Melanchthon's request, assumed the lecture course on his preceptor's *Loci communes theologici*, providing students with basic instruction in dogmatics. At the end of 1553, he departed to join his friend Mörlin in Braunschweig against the wishes of Melanchthon and his colleagues in Wittenberg.

Chemnitz was immediately drawn into the activities of the church in Braunschweig. In 1557, he served as a member of a team constituted under Mörlin's leadership that sought to reconcile Melanchthon and the Wittenbergers with Matthias Flacius and other critics of Wittenberg ecclesiastical policy and teaching. This attempt at mediation angered Melanchthon and brought the close relationship between his preceptor and Chemnitz to an end. The same year,

Chemnitz served the Evangelical dialog partners at the Colloquy of Worms as a recorder. There he forged important relationships with leading theologians from other parts of Germany, including his later partner in composing the Formula of Concord, Jakob Andreae.

Under Mörlin's leadership, the church of Braunschweig generally defended positions held by the Gnesio-Lutherans. When the churches of the cities of Lower Saxony had to deal with the doctrine of the Lord's Supper taught by the pastor of Bremen, Albert Hardenberg (ca. 1510–74), Melanchthon's close friend, Braunschweig stood against his spiritualizing views of the real presence of Christ's body and blood. Chemnitz prepared written defenses of his ministerium's teaching on the Lord's Supper, his *Repetition of the Sound Teaching on the True Presence of the Body and Blood in the Supper*[1] (Leipzig, 1561) and *Surgery Performed on the Propositions of Albert Hardenberg concerning the Lord's Supper*.[2]

About this time, Chemnitz also recorded his reactions to other controversies that Lutheran theologians were confronting at that time. His manuscript contained analyses of the disputes over the proper understanding of the term "Word of God," directed largely against the Antitrinitarian Michael Servetus; the freedom of the will; the definition of the terms "gospel" and "repentance"; justification through faith; good works; and adiaphora. He prefaced the nine chapters on aspects of these topics with a treatment of standards for judging the public teaching of the church and concluded the manuscript with reference to his *Repetition* for his solution to the disputes regarding the Lord's Supper and the person of Christ.

In this volume are included the chapters from this manuscript entitled "On Free Choice" and "On the Article of Justification," as well as the initial chapter, "Concerning a Certain Body of Teaching." The term "body of teaching" (or "body of doctrine" [Latin: *corpus doctrinae*]) would become the title used for collections of writings that were to determine the public or official teaching of Lutheran churches. In 1560, shortly before his death, colleagues had published a collection of Melanchthon's own most important doctrinal writings under the title *Corpus doctrinae*. Chemnitz himself helped prepare such a collection of doctrinal standards for the church in Braunschweig in 1563, a volume that bore the title *Corpus doctrinae*. Furthermore, he aided Mörlin in composing the *Prussian Body of Doctrine* in 1567 and in 1576 prepared a *Corpus Doctrinae* of confessional documents for two dukedoms, Braunschweig-Wolfenbüttel and Braunschweig-Lüneburg.[3]

---

1. *Repetitio sanae doctrinae de vera praesentia corporis et sanguinis in Coena. . . . Additus est Tractatus complectens doctrinam de Communicatione idiomatum* (Leipzig, 1561), translated as *The Lord's Supper*, trans. J. A. O. Preus (St. Louis: Concordia, 1979).

2. *Anatome propositionum Alberti Hardenbergii de Coena Domini . . .* (Eisleben, 1561).

3. *Corpus doctrinae Christianum* (Braunschweig, 1563); *Repetitio Corporis Doctrinae Ecclesiasticae* (Königsberg, 1567); *Corpus doctrinae, das ist, die Summa, Form und Vorbilde der reinen Christlichen Lere* (Ülzen, 1576), the "Corpus Wilhelmanum" and the similarly entitled "Corpus Julianum" (Heinrichstadt, 1576).

In 1561, the term "body of doctrine" was in use among the students of Melanchthon and Luther—however, in another sense. In the previous decade, it had been used to refer to a list of documents like the one actually compiled in Melanchthon's volume, a list that always included the Augsburg Confession and its Apology, along with a variety of other titles. That usage developed out of another definition of the term, at least three decades old. The term in its root sense had been employed by Melanchthon and Luther to designate the analogy of faith, the fundamental core teaching of the Bible, as it was understood as a standard for public teaching.[4] To make clear how this "body of doctrine" was to be defined and used among the Lutheran churches was a critical question in 1561—and the decade and a half following—particularly since a key expression of this "body of doctrine" was found in the Augsburg Confession.

With Luther's approval, Melanchthon had felt compelled to improve the text of the Confession in order to guide and shape Lutheran teaching more effectively in response to Roman Catholic attacks during the 1530s and early 1540s. However, Calvinists had used his alterations to Article X, on the Lord's Supper, to justify their inclusion under the protection of the Religious Peace of Augsburg (1555), and therefore many of Chemnitz's colleagues had attacked the use of the "Altered Augsburg Confession." Chemnitz's comments in this manuscript represent his own view in 1561, a view that he changed somewhat in subsequent years. These observations on the fundamental standard for judging controversy shed light as well on the developing discussion of the use of secondary authority for governing church life and adjudicating doctrinal disputes. This discussion led to the introductory comments on doctrinal standards in the Formula of Concord. This initial chapter of Chemnitz's analysis of the situation of the church in his day, along with his treatments of two significant controversies of the time, those over the freedom of the will and justification by faith, are offered here as examples of how this principal author of the Formula of Concord assessed the controversies that the Formula addressed fifteen years earlier and how his theological method functioned.

This translation is based upon the first printing of Chemnitz's manuscript, issued in 1594 by his successor in Braunschweig, Polycarp Leyser.[5]

---

4. On the development of this concept among the Wittenberg theologians, see Irene Dingel, "Melanchthon und die Normierung des Bekenntnisses," in Heinz Scheible, ed., *Der Theologe Melanchthon* (Stuttgart: Thorbecke, 2000), 195–211.

5. *De Controversiis quibusdam, quae superiori tempore circa quosdam Augustanae Confessionis articulos motae et agitatae sunt, Iudicium d. Martini Chemnitii*, ed. Polycarp Leyser (Wittenberg, 1594).

Judgment on Certain Controversies concerning Certain Articles of the Augsburg Confession Which Have Recently Arisen and Caused Controversy . . .

I. Concerning a Certain Body of Teaching

Some engage in dispute over controversies of the time in such a way that they think they have done well when they are able to reconcile conflicting opinions with [no more than] rhetorical flourish and skill. Others, on the contrary, seem to act in such a way that they are always provoking new, and often unnecessary, quarrels, and in this way they gradually distort the body of teaching set forth as a sufficient and appropriate form for teaching. Both of these approaches must be condemned. For the sake of those who teach and for the sake of those who learn—indeed, even for the sake of our opponents—it is necessary to have a proper form and systematic summary of godly teaching. By God's grace, our churches have confessed the correct interpretation of this teaching as it was purged from error through Luther's ministry with divine help on the basis of the prophetic and apostolic writings. This teaching is expressed in the Confessions, which we have approved. If any opinions diverge from this norm, clever interpretations and fancy compromises should not be sought. Instead, they should be decisively condemned and rejected. Otherwise, the purity of teaching cannot be retained. Thus, at the Diet in Regensburg, in 1541, where clever compromises of conflicting dogmas were proposed, accompanied by convincing demonstrations of moderation, our side wisely and faithful responded: "In religious controversies certain ideas are proposed in a milder form in the search for harmony, but in the church it is of utmost importance to establish what limits are to constitute the defining elements of this harmony. Often in the church not only princes and political advisors, but even theologians have sought harmony on the basis of human judgment which led people away from the purity of the Gospel. Therefore, it is necessary in the church that the rule for such harmony be the Word of God, so that we may bring controversies to an end, but according to the norm of God's Word and the proper, approved testimonies of the apostolic church."[6]

---

6. In 1541, representatives of the Roman Catholic party and the Evangelical churches in Germany met at the imperial diet held in Regensburg, after preparatory meetings over the previous year in Hagenau and Worms. At Regensburg, a common statement on justification was worked out that supporters of both sides found unsatisfactory. This citation is taken from a document addressed to Emperor Charles V by the Evangelical representatives at Regensburg on 12 July 1541, "Responsio principum et Statuum coniunctorum Augustanae Confessionis de libro exhibito Imperatori Carolo" (*CR* 4:481–82). Chemnitz here brought together two passages from the document into a single citation.

For this reason, we must reject the impertinence of those who for no good or necessary reason make light of or nibble away at that which has been handed down in orderly fashion and can be explained clearly. They pick away at one position in the body of teaching here and at another way of expressing an idea there. In this way, they gradually distort and undermine the entire system. Philo's elegant observation was correct: "The same principle obtains in the teaching of religion as in building, where if one small stone is removed, the rest of the building may not collapse immediately and may seem to be in good shape. Nonetheless, it begins to crack; little by little the building begins to fall apart, and the cracks become gaping fissures."[7] When our people have wanted to show what kind of teaching is being passed on everywhere in our churches, they have always testified that they embraced the Augsburg Confession as presented to the emperor and the Apology which was associated with it. Then they have listed the Smalcald Articles prepared in 1537 by Luther officially in the name of our churches;[8] in the preface of that work, Luther explained why these articles were written and accepted by us alongside the Augsburg Confession. He explained that the several attempts at conciliation both in Augsburg and afterwards had led many to think that certain things in the articles of the Augsburg Confession could be discarded and conceded to the papal party. In addition, fanatics and sectarians were foisting off their crazy ideas as Luther's own ideas upon the common people, as if Luther understood the teaching in a different way than he actually did. Therefore, he wrote the Smalcald Articles as a confirmation and a true, certain, enduring explanation of the Augsburg Confession and how its content was understood and taught in all our churches while Luther was living. Earlier, only a few had subscribed to the Augsburg Confession. From the subscription to the Smalcald Articles it may be seen that all our churches approved and received the Augsburg Confession, its Apology, and the explanation joined to them in the Smalcald Articles as a public confession and true form of teaching. In this way, opposition to both the papal council and all fanatics was clearly expressed.

The ancients had their creeds, which set down the form and norm for sound expressions against the corruptions of the heretics for the sake of both teachers and learners. In the same way, the body of teaching of our churches, which we judge to be the true and lasting doctrinal content of the prophetic and apostolic writings, is expressed in the content of the confessions which we accept, that is, the Augsburg Confession, its Apology, and the Smalcald Articles. There are good and serious reasons for our wanting the Smalcald Articles to be joined to the other two, for they offer fuller explanations regarding the Pope, the power of the

---

7. Philo of Alexandria, a first-century Jewish philosopher and theologian, was often cited by Chemnitz.

8. In fact, the Smalcald Articles were not officially adopted by the Evangelical estates or churches in 1537. From the 1540s on, the Articles were added to the "body of doctrine" that was accepted in various Lutheran principalities and cities as the standard of public teaching.

bishops, Zwinglianism, transubstantiation, and sins which drive out the Holy Spirit.[9]

Ever more often in controversy and dispute, our papalist opponents mention that copies of the Augsburg Confession, in the editions of 1530, 1531, 1537, and 1542, do not agree with each other but differ considerably.[10] The same issue has aroused a great deal of contention among our own people. This is a matter of highest importance, for it is necessary to determine what is correct in this case, both because of the controversies of the present and especially for the sake of posterity. For by using a different edition as a pretext, it is always possible to create new controversies.

Calvin and his adherents have grabbed onto the tenth article in the edition of 1542 with glee (because it a is boot which fits either foot and can even be put on Zwingli's foot).[11] He, however, condemned and rejected the article in the form in which it was presented to the emperor and as it stood in the 1531 edition, because it affirmed that the body of Christ is truly present in the Supper, and it condemned those who teach otherwise.

On the other hand, some approve the first edition of 1531 in order to undermine, repudiate, and reject what was added in the 1542 edition for the sake of clarification concerning the definition of the gospel, although this definition is also found in the first edition of the Apology.

Therefore, it is necessary to take care so that the churches not be unnecessarily troubled and threatened. The edition of 1531 cannot and ought not be rejected, for it is the true Augsburg Confession, as it was presented to Emperor Charles in 1530. It is the version that should always be cited. All our churches subscribed to this edition in 1537.[12] On the other hand, I do not see how it can be useful or proper to reject and condemn the edition of 1542. For when it was prepared for the colloquy at Hagenau in 1542,[13] it was found to be most useful and was presented as a body of doctrine, a standard for the teaching of our churches, as well as the basis of discussion at the colloquy. It was printed in the same year at Wittenberg, with some additions inserted as a fuller explanation. This edition of 1542 was presented at Worms under the title "Augsburg Con-

---

9. See Smalcald Articles II:iv (papacy), III:vi (Lord's Supper), and III:iii (repentance).

10. Melanchthon published revised versions of the German text of the Augsburg Confession in 1533 and of the Latin in 1540 and 1542, but some alterations were found in printings of the intervening years. Chemnitz may have referred to 1537, however, not because of significant changes but because of the formal subscription of the Evangelical estates at the diet in Smalcald in that year.

11. Chemnitz here uses a common sixteenth-century designation for something that was ambiguous or capable of various interpretations, the boot that fit both right and left feet, a "cothurnus."

12. At the diet of the Smalcald League of Evangelical governments in Smalcald, February 1537.

13. The colloquy, actually held in 1540, which began preparations for negotiations between Roman Catholic and Evangelical theologians in Regensburg the following year. The Latin Variata of 1540 contained the new version of Article X, which had aroused controversy, and it was in use at Hagenau in 1540. The 1542 edition contained expansions of sections on justification and good works that Chemnitz wanted to preserve.

fession."[14] At the colloquy in Regensburg, the same edition was placed before our opponents as the standard of teaching in our churches. This was done at Luther's advice and with his approval and agreement. In 1546 and subsequently, our people used this edition at meetings and in various activities concerning the faith, and they called it the Augsburg Confession. It cannot be demonstrated that there are any errors or distortions in the explanations which were added in the edition of 1542, except for the truncation of Article X. Indeed, in 1540, Cochlaeus at Worms,[15] and in 1542, Pighius at Regensburg,[16] argued vigorously that a little more light should be shed on several articles of the Confession through more extensive explanations. Because of this, our people saw that statements that were true in themselves could be made even clearer, and the shameful outrage of the Babylonian whore[17] could be clearly exposed. They would have preferred simply to stick to the edition of 1531, as their writings testify. Indeed, the edition of 1540 was circulating in the hands of everyone, and many were oblivious to and had never seen the edition of 1531. In the 1540 edition, certain parts were expanded as necessary explanations, and it contained nothing false. I do not know how it could be rejected or condemned totally and simply without disturbing the churches. Therefore, it seems to be the wisest possible course for the churches to return to the edition of 1531 and to recommend it to them as having full and primary authority. The edition of 1540 and its explanations should be retained, for they ought not be seen as contradicting but rather agreeing with the first edition in every article. Article X should be restored [to its form in the 1531 edition] so that reference is made to the fundamentals, and the other elements of the first edition are present. Even the passage of Paul in the tenth article of the Apology should be restored.[18] The words that have been added to it from the Greek canon and from the Vulgate concerning transformation in the sacrament should be moderated, for the Vulgate clearly and crassly asserts transubstantiation. It would be better to omit these passages or to explain them correctly so that transubstantiation is clearly rejected. In this way, the body of teaching can remain correct and be commended to posterity, and the churches will not be disturbed.

14. This may be a reference to the colloquy between Roman Catholic and Evangelical theologians held at Worms in 1557, but it probably refers to the preparatory colloquy at Worms in 1540, where the revised Augsburg Confession published in that year was used.

15. Johannes Cochlaeus (1479–1552) was one of the leading representatives of the Roman Catholic party in Germany and as a representative of the Roman Catholic Duke George of Saxony engaged in fierce polemic against Luther. He was among the negotiators at the colloquies of Hagenau, Worms, and Regensburg, 1540–41.

16. Albert Pighius (ca. 1480–1542), a Roman Catholic official from Utrecht, took part in the colloquies of 1540–41.

17. "Thaidis Babylonicae," a reference to the papacy.

18. The citation of 1 Cor. 10:16 in Apology X:5 was omitted from the second (octavo) edition of the Apology of the Augsburg Confession of 1531.

III. On Free Choice

The controversies on this article of faith are not idle hair splitting or disputes about nothing. As Luther rightly recognized, the church cannot retain the purity of the doctrine of the law concerning the corruption and perversion of human powers by the fall, and the doctrine of the Gospel concerning the benefits of God's Son, if the treatment of free choice is not held free from all distortions according to God's Word. It is not difficult to show from Justin, Irenaeus, Tertullian, Clement, Origen, [and] Chrysostom that the chief topics of Christian teaching—sin and justification—are either perverted or certainly terribly obscured when they deviated from the standard of God's Word in the teaching on free choice and strayed off to natural ways of thinking about it. By God's grace, some light concerning grace was restored at Augustine's time. During that period the beginning, the initiation, of the purification of the treatment of free choice took place.

In the same way, God began the restoration of pure teaching on the basis of God's Word through Luther's ministry by purifying the teaching on this topic. There is no doubt that if the fog had rolled in over this subject again, darkness would have engulfed the purity of teaching which was once again made most clear through Luther's ministry by God's limitless grace. I must say this so that this controversy will not be tossed onto the pile of idle and unnecessary disputes. Instead, a proper, clear, and prudent decision may be reached on the basis of Scripture, a decision that pleases God and works for the good of the church, so that such a decision may be handed down to posterity.

Many questions are connected with this topic, and they must be distinguished from one another to avoid confusion. The ancients made a learned distinction, posing four questions concerning human freedom of choice: (1) before the fall, (2) after the fall before renewal, (3) after new birth before glorification, (4) in glorification. But since there are now no disputes over the first and fourth stages, we treat here only those questions which require an explanation and a decision because of the controversies of our time.

[1.] The question concerning the cause of sin. Luther predicted that there would be battles over this question. He wrote on Genesis 26, "I have wanted to teach and transmit this in such a painstaking and accurate way because after my death many will publish my books and will prove from them errors of every kind and their own delusions. Among other things, however, I have written that everything is absolute and unavoidable; but at the same time I have added that one must look at the revealed God. . . . But they will pass over all these passages and take only those that deal with the hidden God. Accordingly, you who are listening to me now should remember that I have taught that one should not inquire into the predestination of the hidden God but should be satisfied with what is revealed through the calling and through the ministry of the Word."[19]

---

19. WA 43:463; *LW* 5:50.

Here we hear allusions to absolute necessity and to the idea that God effects all things, evil as well as good works, in human creatures. Although such disputes may be suppressed at this time, there can be no doubt that they will break into public view sometime. Especially disputes regarding the compulsion of the will that has not been reborn will arise.

Therefore, in order to counter the arguments of malicious spirits and to hand the truth down to posterity, it is necessary to formulate a single, true, proper, and specific doctrinal position, which is faithful to the analogy of faith, pleasing to God, and useful and beneficial for the church. Otherwise, new and absurd disputes will arise on the basis of certain opinions which are to be found in Luther's and Philip's earliest writings. At Augsburg and Regensburg, Eck[20] provoked arguments which lasted whole days with citations from the earliest writings of Luther and Philip. It is therefore useful to retain the standard to teaching and expression which is found in the nineteenth article of the Augsburg Confession. So that it may be understood how best to counter specific words of this type in disputes, I will sort out the matter in this way.

When we turn to ideas about God's providence, which sustains nature, and about the foreknowledge of God, which cannot err, or when we consider that nothing happens if God does not will it, or that God determines things, things do not determine God, then we assemble a multitude of inexplicable ideas. It then seems logical that there is an absolute necessity that governs all things, whether in good actions or in evil actions. Luther refers to such speculations with the term "Deus absconditus" ["the hidden God"]. On Genesis 17, he made the following comments: ". . . about the God who has not been revealed and disclosed through the Word. What he is, what he does, and what his will is does not concern me. But this does concern me, that I know what he has commanded, what he has promised, and what he has threatened."[21] In regard to this question, we must not believe and speak speculatively, according to the logical consequences drawn from the hidden and unknown God, but according to the revealed word.

2. The negative side of the proposition must be clearly set forth. God is not the author or the cause of sin. This proposition must be explained. God did not create sin in the beginning, and he does not now will sin. He does not approve it. He does not support it. He does not effect it. He does not drive anyone into sinning.

3. Nevertheless, sinners cannot for this reason be regarded as exempt from God's rule, providence, and governance. For God's act of determining sets the limits of what may be permitted. His decision determines when and where he

---

20. John Eck (1486–1543), professor at Ingoldstadt, one of the foremost Roman Catholic opponents of Luther, played a leading role at the negotiations between Roman Catholic and Evangelical theologians at Augsburg in 1530 and in the negotiations of 1540–41, which climaxed in the colloquy at Regensburg.

21. WA 42:647; *LW* 3:139.

stops the ungodly. He frustrates and overturns many of their plans, and he puts a halt to many of the things they attempt to do. In other cases, he directs things either for the sake of the church or so that the ungodly call destruction upon themselves. For he often turns the very worst plans and endeavors of the ungodly to the good of the church, for example, in the case of Joseph (Gen. 45:8). At other times, God used evils which the devil had caused or which arose out of the will of the ungodly to impose punishments which they had earned upon them whom he wished to visit with his judgment, for example, in the case of Shimei (2 Sam. 16:5ff.). Finally, sins are often punishments for sinners according to the just judgment of God. In this sense, Scripture often uses active verbs when it speaks of this subject. Although we cannot peer into the hidden governance of God, we ought to reverently abide by this axiom: God is not the author of sin.

4. The affirmative side of this proposition must be set forth also: the cause of sin is the will of the devil and the ungodly. The devil is the cause of sin, not only because he sinned from the beginning, John 8:44, or because due to the devil's envy sin came into the world through one human creature, Wisd. 2:24, Rom. 5:12, but also because he is at work in the children of unbelief, Eph. 2:2. He who commits sin is of the devil, 1 John 3:8. He has blinded their minds, 2 Cor. 4:4. He has filled their hearts, Acts 5:3. They are held captive by the devil to do his will, 2 Tim. 2:26. The ungodly may not try to use this tyranny as a pretext or excuse, as if they were forced against their will to wantonness and therefore did not deserve punishment but rather deserved favor. James identifies the immediate cause of sin: "One is tempted by one's own desire, being lured and enticed by it; then, when that desire has conceived, it gives birth to sin," James 1:14. Two things are joined together in this article of confession: the will of the devil and the will of ungodly people.

Therefore, the argument that the will which has not been reborn is compelled to sin must be rejected, for it diminishes original sin, as if it were not a perversion in the mind and defiance in the will but rather a punishment, by compulsion. Thus, the ungodly would be absolved, if not totally, at least to a certain extent, as the scholastic theologians argued, as they transferred the cause of sin from the human mind and will to the devil's will. Original sin and the devil's tyranny consist, however, in this: Not that in those who have not been reborn the mind is ignorant and the will is coerced, not willing, and resisting, as if its neck were being twisted to force it to wantonness. Instead, human nature is corrupted by the original malady. The result is that blinded and bewitched by the devil's tricks, they compliantly yield to all sorts of leadings in mind, will, and affections, as James 1:14 and Prov. 2:13 say. They rejoice in doing evil. Indeed, Scripture says in Rom. 1:24 of those that have been given up to their evil lust, "He gave them over to the desires of their hearts." Psalms 81:12: "I gave them over to the desires of their hearts." Ephesians 2:3 describes the devil's tyranny and clearly refers to the passions and desires of flesh and senses. Only to the reborn can the words of Rom. 7:15 be attributed: "I do not do what I want, but

I do the very thing I hate." Similarly, Gal. 5:17 speaks of "preventing you from doing what you want."

Augustine wrote in book 1, chapter 10, of *Against the Two Letters of Pelagius*, "Free choice has not at all disappeared in the sinner but rather all those who delight in sin and who love to sin use it to commit sin. They find it pleasing that they may use it so. . . . This will, which is free in the practice of evil deeds, is not free to practice good deeds because it has not been liberated. . . . They have free choice in evil, and when [the deceiver][22] grafts a delight in evil, either more secretly or more openly, into them, they persuade themselves."[23] In this sense, the ancients said that the human creature has free choice in evil, but when it is not reborn, this free choice is able only to sin, as Augustine shows in book [chapter] 2 of *On Grace and Free Choice:* "No one blames God in his heart, but ascribes it to himself when he sins."[24]

The distinction made by John of Damascus and Bernhard of Clairvaux is applicable here.[25] One kind of necessity is the necessity of compulsion. Its origin and cause lie outside the human creature. Human beings do not motivate themselves and do not cooperate but offer strong resistance throughout the compulsion. Bernhard correctly said that this kind of compulsion does overwhelm the will. Augustine thought it absurd that the will be said to be compelled by necessity, as if something could become warm apart from heat. Luther said, "If the will is forced, it is not a will, but a nill."[26] The second kind of necessity is the necessity of immutability. Human beings are willing as they choose and do something, but they do not have the ability to choose between two opposites; instead, they are immutably bound to act in one direction. Augustine rightly attributes this kind of necessity to the will that has not been reborn. For, as Bernhard says, they do not have the ability or the faculty to turn to either good or evil. They are instead perverted by sin so that they can do nothing else of themselves but think sin, choose sin, and delight in sin. Bernhard explained this with a most appropriate expression in *Song of Solomon,* sermon 81: "I do not know in what a perverted and extraordinary way the will experiences necessity, altered as it is by sin for the worse, but it is not a necessity because it is a matter of the will. It does not give the will an excuse. Nor does the will reject this necessity when it is seduced. For this necessity is in some way a matter of the

22. The word "deceptor" is not found in Chemnitz's citation but is present in the *MPL* text.

23. *MPL* 44:552–53 (with a different chapter numbering than that of Chemnitz).

24. *MPL* 44:884.

25. The terms "necessity of compulsion" and "necessity of immutability" had been appropriated by Luther, e.g., in his *On the Bondage of the Will* (WA 18:634–35; *LW* 33:64–65); and by Melanchthon in the Apology of the Augsburg Confession, IV:11. The concepts, although not the terms, appear in the *Tractatus de gratia et libero arbitrio,* chs. 3 and 4, of Bernhard of Clairvaux (*MPL* 182:1004–8), and in the *De fide orthodoxa,* bk. II, ch. 25, of John of Damascus (*MPG* 94:955–58).

26. Luther here invented the word "noluntas," contrasted with "voluntas," will. Chemnitz paraphrases Luther's words from *On the Bondage of the Will* (WA 18:635, 12–14; *LW* 33:64–65).

will. It is in a certain way a pleasant force, which charms as it forces and forces as it charms. Thus, its voice is carping, as if groaning under the burden of this necessity. It says, 'Lord, I am suffering violence. Respond in my behalf. But I know that I cannot justly lay blame on the Lord since the will itself is rather to blame. Look upon the burden that I, in my carefree way, am carrying. What shall I say? or what kind of answer will I receive since I myself am doing it? I was being pressed, and therefore I bind myself, but to nothing other than this voluntary servitude, a miserable servitude but one inexcusable for the will.' For the will is free in itself but acts as bound to sin, assenting to sin. For the will is nothing when it is held under sin for a slavery to which it submits."[27] Augustine expresses a similar opinion in *Confessions*, book 8, chapter 5.[28]

Therefore, in summary: we must conclude that there is free choice in evil things or our teaching regarding original sin and the tyranny of the devil will be either weakened or obscured. The tyranny of the devil in those who are not reborn must be emphasized in such a way, in accord with Scripture, so that the will of the impious is not freed from guilt and the cause of sin is not made into a punishment for something that has been compelled. Thus, discussion of necessity must be so formulated that we do not make God the author and cause of sin. If this standard is observed, it is not difficult to reach a proper understanding of these questions.

VIII. On the Article of Justification

The chief controversy regarding this article of faith concerns Osiandrism. The crass corruption of this article on justification by Andreas Osiander (who was in other regards an outstanding man) has gained notoriety and destroyed our teaching.[29] Even the common people who have at least learned the basic catechetical material regarding proper teaching are able to see that, and his errors were considered and condemned by the judgment of nearly all the churches. The author of these errors clearly admitted that he disagreed with the Augsburg Confession on the doctrine of justification. We who called attention to his errors that were properly condemned did not do so because we sought to be involved in never-ending battles but because various publications in both Latin and German were being distributed, appearing not just occasionally over the course of several years but almost every month. In them, the pernicious Osiandrian corruption of the doctrine of justification was being painted in attractive colors and set forth in new ways. These publications were written sometimes by

27. *MPL* 183:1174.

28. *MPL* 32:753–54.

29. Osiander (1498–1552), reformer in Nuremberg, had fled as a result of the enforcement of the Augsburg Interim to Königsberg, in Prussia, where Chemnitz was ducal librarian, in 1549. He quickly fell into controversy with colleagues and with theologians throughout Germany over his definition of the righteousness of faith. He defined this justifying righteousness as the indwelling, essential righteousness of the divine nature of Christ.

his supporters, sometimes by his opponents, and even for the common people in German tracts. Therefore it is necessary, in order to give the church edifying counsel, that a true and certain doctrinal position be maintained and that it be useful for retaining and proclaiming the truth in the proper doctrine of justification against the virus of all corruptions of this teaching—what ought to be believed on the basis of the standard of God's Word concerning this controversy. For what, I ask, are we building if, when we cannot defend our positions, we paint over them with defective paint, as Ezekiel said, "smearing whitewash on flimsy walls" [Ezek. 13:10], so that the flaws are not apparent to the buyer, just as paid orators sought to demonstrate their genius with disreputable material?

If Osiander's position on justification by faith, which is opposed to that of the Augsburg Confession, is true, then it clearly would have to be approved. If indeed it does not agree with the teaching of the prophets and apostles, why are we trying to use fallacious drugs for a sick person to the great harm of the church by employing the same word [even though the concepts behind them are different]? For such a tricky way of proceeding, which the prophet called whitewash, is not useful or beneficial for the church. In this way, many who previously had fallen captive to false opinions find confirmation of them. This only arouses and nourishes careless thinking which undermines the truth and contrives absurd ideas. Some even began to doubt our whole approach to teaching when they saw that in the chief article of our faith some affirmed what others denied. Our papist foes reproached us for this inconstancy, and they were not altogether wrong in doing so. If any think that the purity of teaching can be retained in this way and handed on to posterity, they are in dangerous error. For Christ requires both that we listen to his true voice and that we flee other voices. Paul requires that a teacher of the church be able both to hold fast to proper teaching and also to refute those who contradict it [Titus 1:9]. In 1 Tim. 6:3, he forbids "teaching otherwise." He means by that not only holding false positions; he is also referring to the form of teaching which the apostles handed down. It should not be changed arbitrarily nor carelessly undermined.

It is worth the trouble, however, to consider the arguments by which they tried to defend Osiander's case to prove that his position concerning the righteousness of faith had been unjustly condemned by so many of the churches. Such a refutation is necessary as a warning for the sake of posterity, lest it be thought that this battle was not important and only a harmless game of some intellectuals who wanted to "teach otherwise" concerning the article of justification. As the church grows old, it is its fate to be threatened in such ways, but they are most certainly not to be confirmed through public acceptance.

To pull things together: it is certain that the summary of the teaching of the Gospel is that there are two kinds of benefits which Christ bestows, grace and truth, John 1:17, grace and the gift given through grace, Rom. 5:17, or the benefit of reconciliation and the benefit of renewal or sanctification. They say Osiander never denied these benefits of Christ, which are the substance and essence of the Gospel (as I like to say). They say that he confessed that in the

Gospel we receive by faith remission of sins and the Spirit of renewal because of Christ. They say that this is the only difference: what the Augsburg Confession calls renewal—in line with the standard of speaking set by the apostles—Osiander calls justification and the righteousness of faith. Osiander shifts the testimonies of Scripture, which the Augsburg Confession correctly refers to the benefits Christ bestows, to the concept of renewal—in what he offers as an excuse for his point of view. The argument runs: as has been the case with all authors, ancient and recent, many expressions which are unusual have to be condoned because their positions are essentially correct. So it is with Osiander. His position could not be justly condemned just because he used some improper phrases and inappropriate arguments, when there was agreement in the substance of the teaching, since in the writings of all the fathers there are many things awkwardly or improperly formulated that have to be tolerated. That is a summary of their defense of Osiander.

This is fawning of the first order, for human nature delights more in defending itself than confessing its error. If this argument is considered more carefully, they will see that it is nothing other than a cloak made of fig leaves invented for just such cleverly constructed corruptions of the article concerning the righteousness of faith. I find the same ideas clearly expressed in Gropper's writings.[30] He confirms that he believes and confesses that we receive both reconciliation and renewal by faith because of Christ alone. These benefits come from Christ alone. But then he says that he contends that the testimonies concerning justification or the righteousness of faith consist equally of the remission of sins and renewal since the Gospel proclaims a single integral benefit of Christ consisting of grace and what is given through grace. Here it is clear that if we permit Osiander to use that defense of which we have spoken, we have no right to disagree with Gropper. This is clearly a corruption of the teaching concerning the righteousness of faith. I mention this example simply to point out how dangerous and inappropriate it is to construct artificial agreement.

It dare not be thought that this is some vain battle over words since in the article on justification the language is being twisted from its true, proper, and apostolic sense into another meaning, just as the *Historia Tripartita* contains this farcical harmonization of "cot" and "bunk."[31] In every age, the church must be reminded again and again [of the course of history]. Augustine had actually shed some light on the subject in comparison to others of that age, but even he bent the meaning of the words "justification" and "righteousness" just a little out of their native, apostolic sense. After him, under the rule of the papacy, a tragic and

---

30. Johann Gropper (1503–59) served and then opposed Hermann von Wied, the archbishop of Cologne who tried to turn his archdiocese to the Evangelical faith in the early 1540s. He strove to mediate between more conservative Roman Catholic theologians and the Evangelicals and was active in the negotiations between the two parties in the 1530s and early 1540s.

31. Chemnitz cites the comparison in the *Historia Tripartita* of the Greek words σκίμποδος and κράββατος *MPL* 69:896, from Sozomon's history, bk. 1, ch. 11.

horrible darkness fell upon the concept of the righteousness of faith. Luther confessed that he sweat much in the most oppressive agonies of soul until he could establish from Scripture that the righteousness of faith did not refer to some substance or quality in us but the relationship [with God]. To summarize: in his limitless mercy, God once again lit the light of the Gospel so that the words "justification," "righteousness," "grace," and "faith" might be restored to their true, apostolic meaning. How easily we might lose this light again if through public statements we approve the idea that there is no danger to the faith in using and interpreting these words in this way or that, however we please. For the elements that necessarily stand at the heart of the article on justification cannot be retained in their true purity without observing the rules of grammar.

There are abnormal ways of expressing the doctrine which may be granted as true expressions without doing any harm. These are very much different from those which alter and shift the very words which Scripture uses to express the heart of this topic to mean something else—especially in those passages in which the most important grounding and foundation of an article of faith lie, for instance, in the passages on the righteousness of faith. Thus Pelagius departed from the meaning of the words of Romans 5 although he did not per se extract from this an ungodly position regarding the transmission of vices. Nevertheless, he was justly condemned since the basis of the teaching on original sin lies in this passage. Thus the fundamental elements of the matter are set forth through the words, and without the true, apostolic meaning of the words, these elements cannot be understood or retained. This is especially true in those passages in which the articles of faith are grounded, as if in their own seedbed. Such passages include (apart from every controversy) Gen. 15:6; Rom. 3:22, 24, and 25; 4:3; Rom. 5:1; John 16:8; [and] Phil. 3:9. Osiander corrupted all of these with his interpretation. This is certainly clear, and no sophistical argument can avoid this conclusion.

If this is indeed the case, then Osiander's work, along with all that he did, dare not be defended in print. Osiander himself did not want his defenders to make any sort of concession. Thus it is useful to take note of the issues in the battle with Osiander on the basis of his own writings for the sake of posterity. In his own *Confession* and his *Confutation against Philip,* Osiander himself clearly stated that the points of controversy or the issues of the battle did not lie in our acceptance of the remission of sins by faith and God's accepting us into eternal life because of the obedience of Christ. Nor was the issue of the controversy the renewal which takes place through divine indwelling in us. He correctly confessed this teaching as it has been handed down by our people. Nor was the question that of righteousness in the life to come. This is found in Osiander's *Confutation against Philip,* leaves E2, L2, M2 and 3, N2, P2 and 3, and S3.[32] He stated that the issue in this battle was the definition of the righteousness of

---

32. *Widerlegung: der vngegrundten vndienstlichen Antwort Philipi Melanthonis* . . . (Königsberg: Hans Weinrich, 1552), edited in *Andreas Osiander d. Ä. Gesamtausgabe, Band 10: Schriften und*

God or the righteousness of faith which is revealed in the Gospel, which is grounded in the passages in Genesis 15; Romans 3, 4, and 5; Philippians 3, and John 16. He was not contending so much regarding the vocabulary. Rather, he attributed to this righteousness concerning which he was disputing the characteristics which Paul attributed to the righteousness which results from the righteousness that justifies us in God's sight for eternal life and frees us from death. But this is a righteousness that results from—and must necessarily result from—life and eternal salvation. Osiander states this in his *Confession,* leaves G1, H3, O3, S4, T2–4, V1, 4, and in his *Confutation,* D4, G3, H1, M2.[33]

That means that the controversy was not about the question of whether the remission of sins and renewal come through Christ's benefit. The question was about what is—what the heart is of—the righteousness for the sake of which we are justified in God's sight to eternal life and are liberated from death. Is it the imputation of Christ's obedience, or is it the renewal effected by the Holy Spirit? This most important issue is what the battle was all about. There is no greater treasure, neither in heaven nor on earth, than the teaching which reveals to us most miserable sinners how we are justified freely in God's sight by faith to eternal life.

In this regard, Osiander shamefully lashed out against the teaching of the Augsburg Confession, contradicting it, rejecting it, condemning it. He did so because it affirmed that the righteousness of faith in God's sight is the imputation of Christ's obedience. He called this teaching of the Augsburg Confession carnal, natural, deceptive, idolatrous. He said it is a teaching which falsely depicts Christ in the devil's realm, and he added to this many wild ideas. These are to be found in a great many passages in Osiander's writings, in the *Confession,* leaves G1 and 2, I4; in the *Confutation,* K1, O4; in the *Taste of Beer,* H2.[34] On the contrary, he affirmed that the righteousness of faith which frees from death, which Paul calls the righteousness by which the ungodly are justified in God's sight to eternal life (for Osiander attributes this liberation to the righteousness concerning which he is disputing), is an infused righteousness, in which all virtues are included. This righteousness causes us to be made righteous and does away with sin. This righteousness is the divine essence which dwells in believers, and it causes us to act righteously. That is Osiander's position, and his defenders dare not deny that.

Briefe September 1551 bis Oktober 1552, ed. Gerhard Müller and Gottfried Seebass (Gütersloh: Gütersloher Verlagshaus, 1997), 597–98, 631–32, 636–39, 642–43, 654–56.

33. *Von dem Einigen Mitler Jhesu Christo vnd Rechtfertigung des Glaubens. Bekantnus Andreas Osiander* (Königsberg, 1551), in *Gesamtausgabe,* 146/148, 162/164, 210/212, 244/246, 248/250/252, 252/254, 258/260; *Widerlegung,* in *Gesamtausgabe,* 611–12, 614–15, 636–37.

34. *Bekantnus,* in *Gesamtausgabe,* 146/148/150, 172/174; *Widerlegung,* in *Gesamtausgabe,* 624–25, 651–52; *Schmeckbier. Aus D. Joachim Mo[e]rlins Buch . . . Das sein kurtze Anzaigung/ etlicher furnemblicher Stuck/ vnd Artickeln/ Die in Iren Buchern wider mich begriffen sein . . .* (Königsberg: Hans Weinrich, 1552), in *Gesamtausgabe,* 790–92.

It is certainly regrettable, indeed it is the deplorable lot of our age, that there is doubt and dispute about whether such perversions must be reviewed and condemned even though they outrageously and blatantly contaminate, cripple, and conflict with the chief article of our teaching. To say it as gently as possible, it is sophistical to whitewash these very notorious, very horrible perversions as simply an unusual usage of inappropriate passages—as if those who hold the correct position let those expressions which are inappropriate disappear either out of neglect or because they were doing something else.

If such an approach to reaching agreement were accepted and put to use in ecclesiastical controversies, the best creator of agreement would be Postel. He has written his *Pantenōsia,* in which all religions of all people are regarded as equally true and are brought into agreement, and in this manner he promises harmony on earth, as he entitles his book.[35] What will posterity learn from these examples if it is so in the future? I do not wish to burden my conscience by either approving or excusing such perversions. They certainly clash with true teaching and provide a seedbed for many errors in this article, which is the very basis and foundation of our entire religion. So much concerning Osiandrism.

To continue: in the same way, we must clearly reject the most significant formulations which obscure or pervert the purity of the article on justification that have been introduced out of the depths of the papacy through the zealots of this ungodly mediating religion into the crystal-clear fountains of the Augsburg Confession. We must reject them both because of the battles in which we are now engaged and as a reminder for posterity. For instance, there is the comment of Gropper that is found in certain of our own writings: "The righteousness of faith, by which we are reconciled to God and by which we are accepted into eternal life, consists in and is completed by these two parts, reconciliation and renewal, from which good works, that is, the fruit of the Spirit, result." This is a clear perversion of the righteousness of faith.

For although renewal ought to be the result—and it undoubtedly is the result—of the righteousness of faith, it is nevertheless certain on the basis of God's Word that they are not reconciled in God's sight or accepted to eternal life because of the new life which results from that righteousness. Instead, they receive the free promise of the remission of sins in, through, and because of Christ by faith alone. Therefore, that dogma must be rejected which teaches that the reception of the freely given promise takes place at the same time through faith in the heart and the confession of the mouth. For this is nothing other than to say that the promise of grace is not grasped and applied by faith alone.

These two ideas are mutually exclusive (therefore the papalists must be rebutted because they teach as if human creatures are not completely righteous

---

35. Guillaume Postel (1510–81), French humanist scholar, briefly a member of the Society of Jesus but also imprisoned by the Inquisition in Rome for his universalist ideas. Among his works are those mentioned here by Chemnitz, *De orbis terrae concordia libri quatuor* (Basel, 1544); and *Panthenosia seu compositio omnium dissidiorum circa aeternam veritatem* (Basel, n.d.).

and acceptable in God's sight by faith but because of their own virtues). For by whatever means they excuse it, it is ambiguous and inappropriate to say that the form of sound words is not to be defended. The position which is found in one of Philip's disputations concerning the antitheses of human opinions and the true expression of the doctrine of justification must be repeated and retained, and the opinion that teaches that human creatures are righteous principally by faith, that is through trust in God's mercy, but also because of the worth of human works, must be rejected and condemned.[36] No one can satisfy the law; indeed, trust in God's mercy makes up for this satisfaction because it is lacking.

It is sometimes asked whether it is correct to say that we ought not fight for the exclusive term "sola" ["alone"]. It is true that in one disputation on faith conquering doubt, held years ago, at Luther's time, it was said of the exclusive term "sola": "We are not going to fight about words. We want to retain the heart of the matter so that people of good will recognize they are not condemned but are pleasing to God because of God's Son, by faith in him, not because of the law or because of the merit of virtues."[37] This is a correct statement, for the battle over the proposition that we are justified by faith alone is not a war of words but is especially necessary because of the seriousness of the subject and for the sake of consciences. This said, at the time of the Interim when the teaching concerning justification was combated with various tricks, the exclusive term "sola" was either obscured or omitted, and other forms of expression were used in its place.[38] It was not denied, but there was a profound silence regarding this proposition, and rarely was the exclusive term "sola" heard with even a whisper. In this way, the issue was not properly defended.

There are genuine and necessary reasons why this exclusive term "sola fide" ["by faith alone"] must be retained. 1. It attributes the appropriate honor to God's Son, for he is the only sacrifice and ransom for us. 2. Consciences have firm consolation through it. 3. It focuses clearly on the distinction of law and Gospel. 4. It makes it possible for us to pray even when our weakness impedes us. Especially and above all in the battle against the papalists concerning these matters, the exclusive term "sola" should not be obscured or rejected in any way.

Furthermore, there is argument over this proposition: faith justifies when joined with love, hope, and other virtues. It is clear that this proposition is very dangerously ambiguous. For with this formula the papalists present their formed faith,[39] and they say, if asked, that it is not faith alone but faith with the

---

36. *CR* XII:449–452.

37. *CR* XII:465, thesis 18 in Melanchthon's disputation "de Fide vincente dubitationem."

38. See the treatment of justification in the Augsburg Interim and the Leipzig Interim in this volume.

39. In the scholastic analysis of the biblical concept of faith, "formed faith," *fides formata*, designated "faith given form by love," that is, the combination of trust in God and the resulting acts of obedience and love that it produces. The reformers found this concept a confusion of what God does in creating the relationship of trust and love between himself and human creatures and what they do as a result of living out the Christian life.

other virtues which justifies. A godly and religious caution should be urged upon posterity. At the colloquy in Regensburg, the book prepared there stated, "Through a living and effective faith the sinner receives justification."[40] On Luther's advice and warning, our people did not want to accept this proposition because of its ambiguous and equivocal language. For it is easy to pervert this proposition by equating an effective faith with faith at work, and thereby saying that faith together with works justify.

Against this position must be considered whether such antitheses for the proposition should be formulated and tested. Faith, which is without works, or which does not produce good works, or which is not effective through love, justifies. Here it could be said that a dead or hypocritical faith justifies. The Apology of the Augsburg Confession rightly says [IV:250], "Faith without works does not justify." Luther commented on the third chapter of Galatians that it is necessary to distinguish between true and theological faith and a false or counterfeit faith: "If they were to distinguish between a 'formed faith' and a false or counterfeit faith, their distinction would not offend me at all. But they speak of faith formed by love, and they posit a double faith, namely, formed and unformed. This noxious and satanic gloss I cannot help detesting violently."[41] Therefore the ambiguity of this proposition must be made clear so that we do not stumble either into a concept of formed faith or into that of a dead faith.

It is also necessary to add that love is not that which constitutes the life of faith, but rather faith grasping Christ. It is in itself not a condition in which we are snoring but a condition which is on the move, glowing, consoling, making alive, for it has a hold on Christ, who is life eternal. Indeed, the life of faith does demonstrate itself and is at work through love and other virtues.

We must also repudiate the proposition that it is necessary for the other virtues, such as hope, patience, and the like, to be joined to this virtue, although trust ought not find its footing on them but on God's Son. But it is not proper to reject this proposition in this way, as if faith alone excludes the other virtues. Indeed, they have no merit, cause, or part in justification, but it is not as if faith simply excludes the presence of the other virtues so that they are not at all present. There is a very clear difference between the time when Abraham was first called out of the idolatry of Chaldea and when he was reborn a few years later, Gen. 15:6. In the first situation, he had not a trace of good works. Then he was pronounced righteous, and his faith certainly had in itself a collection of the finest virtues, even though he was justified by faith alone. Paul carefully chose the example of Abraham, not as he was first called from Ur of the Chaldeans but as, some years later, he obeyed God through faith, Heb. 11:8ff. Although Abraham had many very outstanding and very fine good works, in the article—the matter, the question, the act—of his justification Paul says of him, "not by

---

40. The text is found in the modern edition of the Regensburg Book's treatment of justification, in *Martin Bucers Deutsche Schriften, Bd. 9,1. Religionsgespräche (1539–1541)* (Gütersloh: Gütersloher Verlagshaus, 1995), 399, 8 = CR 4:99.

41. WA 40/1:421–22; *LW* 26:269.

works." Abraham believed in God, who justifies the ungodly [Romans 4]. Without works! For there is no attention paid to works in the article of justification, not to works performed before justification or works performed at the time of justification or the works that result from justification. This proposition is simply false: faith necessarily requires the presence of good works to justify or while it is justifying. For this constructs a formed faith which does not justify apart from works, while Paul clearly affirms the opposite. This rule is true: good works do not precede justification but follow from it or are its product. Faith is the mother of good works; as Christ says: "Make a good tree and then good fruits" [Matt. 7:17]. Paul is justified, however, by faith alone. That was true not only in his first conversion, when he was overtaken in the midst of his actions as a persecutor and clearly had no truly good works at all, but also when the Spirit of God was at work in him and he was walking in good works, as it is stated in Acts about Thabita [9:36]: "She was devoted to good works," so that he could truly say, "I am not conscious of them at all" [1 Cor. 4:4]. There, in the article and the matter of justification, faith turns completely from looking at Paul's works and grasps the works and merits of the mediator Christ alone. In them, it finds righteousness and salvation. Truly this is what Paul speaks of in Rom. 4:5: "But to one who without works trusts him who justifies the ungodly, such faith is reckoned as righteousness apart from works." Thus faith is joined with many other virtues, but faith alone justifies apart from works. It is absolutely necessary to maintain this distinction. When faith acts in God's sight in the article or matter of justification, it does not bring its works along with it to elicit the act of justification, but it justifies apart from works. Faith is not performing works, but it is believing in him who justifies the ungodly, Rom. 4:5.

It is indeed another question how we determine—whether by argument or testimony—that it is a true faith, not a false faith which we have invented and by which we seduce ourselves. Here it is correctly said, faith has the power to work through love, Gal. 5:6. Without works, faith is dead. But faith does not justify because our works play a part in it or are regarded in connection with it. Faith alone justifies in that it grasps the merit of Christ alone in the promise. Thus these points should be declared clearly, without ambiguity or sophistry, lest brevity either produce battles or provide a seedbed for perversions of the doctrine. Luther said the following regarding Genesis 15: "I know that these virtues are outstanding gifts of God; . . . I know that faith does not exist without these gifts, but the question now before us is: What is characteristic of each? In your hand you are holding a variety of seeds, yet I do not ask which are related to which; I ask what virtue is characteristic of each? State clearly here what faith alone does, not with what virtues it is closely connected. Faith alone lays hold of the promise. . . . This is the characteristic function of faith alone. The other virtues are concerned with other matters, and they stay within these bounds."[42] A bit later he stated: "We know indeed that faith is never alone but

---

42. WA 42:565; *LW* 3:24.

brings with it love and other manifold gifts. . . . Thus, faith brings with it a multitude of the most beautiful virtues and is never alone. But matters must not be confused on this account, and what is characteristic of faith alone should not be attributed to other virtues. Faith is the mother, so to speak, from whom that crop of virtues springs. If faith is not there first, you would look in vain for these other virtues."[43] Such statements must be repeated and handed on because they edify and are necessary.

It is more dangerous than useful to argue about the initial movements in conversion: contrition, hatred of sin, sorrow over sin, recognition of God's wrath and judgment against sin, spiritual struggles, and exertions are not good works just because they are present as we grasp the freely given promise. Good works do not precede being justified but are a result of having been justified. So it is certain that all these are gifts bestowed through the activity of the Holy Spirit.

Above all, some contend that the concept of being made alive again is to be removed altogether from the article of justification, and under this pretext they criticize Philip for including the process of making alive again in his definition of justification in his commentary on Romans 3, leaf 8, with these words: "At the same time as we are accepted, the Son of God is at work, consoling us with the word of the gospel in our minds and making us alive as believers, and he pours the Holy Spirit into our hearts."[44] This is quite plainly the same way of speaking as is found in the Apology where justification and being made alive again are joined together, among other places folios 16, 31, 22, 30. The *Confession and Apology* of Magdeburg of 1556 states, "By trust alone the heart is also made alive for life eternal more fully, receives new and true consolation."[45] It continues, "Properly speaking, faith is the justification of the person who believes in its righteousness, the consolation of the terrified, the making alive of one whose conscience has been killed by the law." The Apology of the Augsburg Confession clearly declares that it understands the concept of making alive as part of the article of justification. It states [Ap IV:100]: "When Habakkuk says, 'The righteous live by their faith' it means that faith justifies, and as it justifies, it makes alive at the same time, that is, it lifts up, it consoles consciences, and it produces eternal life and joy in the soul." It also states [Ap IV:115]: "Properly speaking, faith lifts up and makes terrified spirits alive," and [Ap IV:62] "It conquers the terrors of sin and eternal death, frees from death, and produces a new life in the heart. For the consolation of faith is spiritual and new life."

This way of speaking is not without scriptural warrant.[46] For Habakkuk [2:4] says, "The righteous live by their faith." Ephesians 2:5, "Even when we

43. WA 42:567; *LW* 3:25–26.

44. In his commentary of 1543 (*CR* 15:884).

45. *Confessio et apologia pastorum & reliquorum ministrorum Ecclesiae Magdeburgensis. Anno 1550. Idibus Aprilis* (Magdeburg: Lotther, 1550), B4b, C1a.

46. Chemnitz here uses the Greek term ἀγραφή.

were dead through our trespasses, God made us alive together with Christ—by grace you have been saved." 1 Samuel 2:6, "The Lord kills and brings to life." Isaiah 57:15, "He makes the spirit of the humble and the heart of the contrite alive." Psalm 70:20, "When you have turned me around, you will give me life again." Shortly thereafter he adds this explanation: "When you have turned me around, you will console me." There are similar passages throughout the Psalms. It is clear that this is a proper definition.

They argue that it is possible to understand the term "making alive" as new obedience. I answer, the proper meaning has to be sought. Therefore we demonstrate on the basis of Scripture that it does not actually mean new obedience. It is, of course, true that new life produces new actions, as Paul says, Rom. 6:5 and 7:4. But the new way of life which follows justification is not a part of the definition of justification. An explanation must therefore be added: what the "making alive" that is joined to justification is, and that the new way of life which follows justification is not a part of justification. Then there will be nothing dangerous or inappropriate.

In the same way concerning regeneration, some argue that it is to be completely separated from justification; they understand it as referring to the renewal that results from justification. But Luther clearly said in the first disputation concerning faith, "Justification is indeed regeneration."[47] The Apology [IV:72] states, "To justify means to regenerate." Paul indicates, when he calls Baptism a washing of rebirth and renewal, that rebirth and renewal are simply not the same thing. He adds soon thereafter, "So that having been justified by his grace, we might become heirs of eternal life." Certainly we do not attain this because of the renewal which follows justification. Therefore, Paul's way of speaking makes justification and new birth synonyms. The same usage is found in 1 Peter 1:3. Often it must be understood in this way to retain the proper meaning of the word "regeneration." For when Scripture says, John 1:12, "He gave power to become children of God," it refers to those who are born of God. John 3:5, "No one can enter the kingdom of God without being born of water and the Spirit." If this being born again in this passage is understood as the renewal which follows justification, the article of justification will be undermined. Indeed, it cannot be so understood on the basis of the usage of Scripture.

It must be added that regeneration, as Luther said, embraces first of all adoption or acceptance. Then the new creature or renewal results from this. Regeneration makes a new human being, or a new creature; it bestows a new heart. From this, new actions or new motivations result. It is clear, however, that the new creature in us is not the thing because of which we are justified, that is, accepted to eternal life. Thus, lest that give the occasion for error, clarifying statements, in agreement with Scripture, should always be added so that the

---

47. In the theses for the doctoral promotion of Hieronymus Weller and Nicholaus Medler (WA 39/1:48, thesis 65).

word "regeneration" is correctly understood. For in the church we ought never speak with craftiness and deceitful scheming, but rather all things should serve to edify, Ephesians 4[:14].

Still others have no use for the not inappropriate formula in this article that faith is called our justification. Luther spoke in this manner in the Galatians commentary, and so does the Apology, fol. 19 and 41.[48]

They also reject the expression "Righteousness is believing that Christ died and rose for you." But Paul said precisely that.

There are others who contend that we must disapprove, reject, and refuse to say, "Christ, or Christ's death, or Christ's blood is our righteousness," but Scripture itself describes the righteousness of faith with various words, which nevertheless all refer to the clear and fuller explanation of what the righteousness of faith is.

---

48. The page numbers in the edition Chemnitz used are unclear but may refer, e.g., to Ap IV: 61, 69.

Catalog of Testimonies

Translated by Thomas Manteufel

Introduction

Following the example of Luther and Melanchthon, the Lutheran theologians of the later sixteenth century frequently employed citations from the ancient fathers of the church to reinforce their own arguments and to demonstrate the continuity of their teaching with that of the early church. One of the authors of the Formula of Concord, Andreas Musculus, had written both a dogmatics textbook and a popular catechism, as well as a popular prayer book, composed of citations of the fathers. Martin Chemnitz had used extensive patristic argumentation in his works on the Lord's Supper and Christology. Their contemporaries also knew the ancient fathers well and quoted them frequently. Therefore, it was natural that the authors of the Formula of Concord would respond to criticism that their understanding of the Lord's Supper, particularly their christological doctrine, was not in line with that of the ancient church. Such criticisms came from Calvinist quarters and also from Philippist theologians in various lands.

After Jakob Andreae had frequently encountered such objections in his negotiations aimed at winning acceptance of the Formula Concord in 1577–79, he and Martin Chemnitz took on the assignment to prepare a "catalog of testimonies" from Holy Scripture and the ancient teachers of the church to lend support to the christological teaching of Article VIII of the Formula of Concord, particularly its use of the *genus maiestaticum.*

Chemnitz and Andreae worked together on the assembling of these citations, based on a similar list that Andreae had compiled for his own use and on Chemnitz's wide-ranging study of the ancient patristic texts, particularly his *On the Two Natures of Christ* (2nd ed., 1578). Chemnitz himself expressed the hope that this catalog might be included as an appendix in the Book of Concord. In some early editions, it appeared under the title "Appendix," with the expectation that it would be part of the authoritative text of the Book of Concord. However, it did not remain so and became simply a supplement that could be used to support and explain the basis of Article VIII of the Formula. Nonetheless, it traditionally appeared as part of some editions of the Book of Concord.

This English translation is based upon the text in *Die Bekenntnisschriften der Evangelisch-Lutherischen Kirche*, 11th ed. (Göttingen: Vandenhoeck & Ruprecht, 1992), 1001–1135.

Catalog of Testimonies
of Holy Scripture and the Ancient Pure Church Fathers,
As They Have Taught and Spoken of the Person and
Divine Majesty of the Human Nature of Our Lord
Jesus Christ, Exalted to the Right Hand
of the Almighty Power of God.

To the Christian Reader

Some have asserted—without any basis—that the language in the Book of Concord, especially in the article on the Person of Christ, deviates from the manners and modes of speaking in the ancient pure church and fathers; on the contrary, that new, strange, arbitrarily devised, unusual, and unheard-of expressions are introduced in it. However, the testimonies of the ancient church and fathers to which this book appeals (which were later presented to several electors and princes, with careful notations) would have been somewhat too long to be incorporated into the Book of Concord. These are appended in abundant number at the end of this book, under several headings, as a correct and thorough account for Christian readers, in which they may see for themselves and readily discover that in the book mentioned above nothing new has been introduced either in content or formulation, either in the doctrine or the mode and manner of speaking, but that we have taught and spoken of this mystery just as, first of all, Holy Scripture, and, later, the ancient pure church have done.

The affirmations of the Book of Concord about the unity of the person of Christ and the distinction of the two natures in Christ and their essential attributes are written just as the ancient pure church, its fathers and councils, have spoken, namely, that there are not two persons, but one Christ, and in this person two distinct natures, the divine and the human nature. These two natures are not separated or intermingled or transformed the one into the other, but each nature has and retains its essential attributes and never lays them aside; the essential attributes of either nature, which are truly and rightly attributed to the entire person, never become attributes of the other nature. All of this is proved, in the first place, by the following testimonies of the ancient pure councils.

In the Council of Ephesus, canon 4: "If any one interprets the words of Scripture in such a way as to divide Christ into two persons or beings, and applies some of them to him as a human being, who should be understood by himself as apart from the Word of God, but assigns others to the Word of God the Father, because they are appropriate only for God, let him be accursed."

Canon 5: "If any one dares to say that the human being Christ is the Bearer of God, and not rather that he is God, so as to say that he is truly the Son by nature, because the Word became flesh and shares flesh and blood, like us, let him be accursed."

Canon 6: "If any one does not confess that the one Christ is at the same time God and human being, since, according to the Scriptures, the Word became flesh, let him be accursed."

Canon 12: "If any one does not confess that the Word of God suffered in the flesh and was crucified in the flesh and tasted death in the flesh and became the First-born from the Dead because as God he is the Life and the Life-Giver, let him be accursed."[1]

And the decree of the Council of Chalcedon says, as quoted in the *Ecclesiastical History* of Evagrius, book 2, chapter 4:[2] "Following, therefore, the holy fathers, we confess one and the same Son, our Lord Jesus Christ, and in total agreement we teach that he is perfect in divinity and he is perfect in humanity; that he is truly God and truly a human being, composed of rational soul and body, the same in substance as the Father as far as the divinity is concerned, and the same in substance as we are as far as the humanity is concerned, like us in all things except sin, begotten from the Father before the ages as far as the divinity is concerned, but born in the last days, for us and for our salvation, from Mary, the virgin and the one who bore God, as far as the humanity is concerned; that one and the same Jesus Christ, the Son, the Lord, the Only-begotten One, is recognized in two natures. These two natures are not intermingled; they are not transformed one into the other; they are not divided; they are not separated; nor is the distinctiveness of each nature abolished in any way because of the union. Instead, the distinctiveness of each of the two natures was preserved as they came together in one person and one being, not in such a way as to be split or divided into two persons, but one and the same Only-begotten Son, God, the Word, and the Lord Jesus Christ. Thus we confess as the prophets from the beginning and Christ himself taught us about himself, and as the Creed of the fathers has handed down to us."

Thus, too, the Tenth Synodical Epistle of Leo (to Flavianus) [German: which amounted to a formal instruction for the Council of Chalcedon] says (chapter 3):[3] "Since the distinctiveness of each nature is intact and the two come together with each other in one person, lowliness has been assumed by Majesty, infirmity by Power, mortality by Eternity, and for the purpose of paying the debt of our [sinful] condition the nature which cannot suffer has been united to the nature which can suffer, so that our one and the same Mediator could be both able to die by virtue of the one and unable to die by virtue of the other."

Likewise (chapter 4):[4] "The same One who is true God is a true human being since the lowliness of the human being and the nobility of deity are shared in common. For just as God is not changed by compassion, so the human being is not consumed by Dignity, for each nature does what is characteristic of it, in

1. Denzinger, 255–57, 263.
2. *MPG* 86:2507/8C–2509/10A.
3. Denzinger, 293–95.
4. Marginal note: "Here a concrete term is used in place of an abstract term."

communion with the other, namely, the Word performs what is appropriate for the Word, and flesh accomplishes what is appropriate for the flesh. The one blazes forth in miracles, the other collapses under assault. He is God because in the beginning was the Word, and the Word was God, through whom all things were made. He is human because the Word became flesh and because he was born of a woman. Also, because of this unity of the person, which must be understood as embracing each nature, we read that the Son of Man came down from heaven, when the Son of God took flesh from the Virgin Mary."

And again (chapter 5): "The Son of God was crucified and buried, although he suffered these things not in his divinity itself, by which he is the same in substance as the Father, but in the infirmity of his human nature, etc."

These are the words of the two councils of Ephesus and of Chalcedon, with which also all the other holy fathers agree.

This is precisely what the scholars in our schools have up to now desired to indicate and express with the words "abstract" and "concrete." The Book of Concord refers briefly to this when the statement is made: "All of which scholars know right well." These words, rightly understood, must necessarily be retained in the schools.

For concrete terms are words which designate the entire person in Christ, such as "God," "human being." But abstract terms are words by which the natures in the person of Christ are understood and expressed, such as "deity," "humanity."

According to this distinction, it is correctly said in concrete terms that "God is a human being," "a human being is God." On the other hand, it is incorrect to say in abstract terms: "deity is humanity," "humanity is deity."[5]

The same rule applies also to the essential attributes, with the result that the attributes of the one nature cannot be attributed to the other nature in abstract terms, as though they were attributes also of the other nature. Therefore the expression "the human nature is omnipotence" or "is from eternity" would be false and incorrect. So also the attributes themselves cannot be identified with each other, as if one were to say: "Mortality is immortality, and immortality is mortality." For by such expressions, the distinction of the natures and their attributes is abolished, and they are confused with one another, changed one into the other, and thus made equal and alike.

But one must not only know and firmly believe that the human nature assumed in the person of Christ has and retains to all eternity its essence and natural essential attributes; it is especially important and constitutes the highest comfort for Christians that we also know from the revelation of Holy Scripture, and in faith embrace, without doubt, the majesty to which this, his human nature, has been elevated in fact and in truth and in which it thus personally participates, as extensively explained in the Book of Concord.

---

5. A marginal note refers the reader to FC SD VIII:43.

Therefore, in order that everyone may likewise see that also on this subject this book [the Book of Concord] has introduced no new, foreign, arbitrarily devised, unheard-of paradoxes [German: "dogmas"] and expressions into the church of God, the following Catalog of Testimonies—drawn first of all from Holy Scripture, and then also from the ancient pure teachers of the church (but especially those fathers who were the most distinguished and the leaders in the four major councils)—will clearly show how they have spoken of this matter.

And in order that Christian readers may the more easily find their way through these testimonies and orient themselves, they have been arranged under several distinct headings, as follows.

I

First, that the Holy Scriptures, as also the fathers, when they speak of the majesty which the human nature of Christ has received through the personal union, use the words *communicatio, communio, participatio, donatio, traditio, subiectio, exaltatio, dari,* etc., that is, the words "communication," "communion," "sharing," "bestowed and given," etc.

Daniel 7:13: "I saw one like a Son of Man coming with the clouds of heaven. And he came to the Ancient One and was presented before him. To him was *given* dominion and glory and kingship, that all peoples, nations and languages should serve him. His dominion is an everlasting dominion that shall not pass away, and his kingship is one that shall never be destroyed."[6]

John 13:3: "Jesus, knowing that the Father had *given* all things into his hands . . ."

Matthew 11:27: "All things have been *handed over* to me by my Father."

Matthew 28:18: "All *authority* in heaven and earth has been *given* to me."

Philippians 2:9: "Therefore God also highly *exalted* him and *gave* him the name that is above every name, so that at the name of Jesus every knee should bend, in heaven and on earth and under the earth," etc.

Ephesians 1:22: "He has *put all things under* his feet. Psalm 8:6; 1 Cor. 15:27; Heb. 2:8."

Eusebius, *Evangelical Demonstration,* book 4, chapter 13:[7] "The Word *communicated,* however, what belongs to him out of his very self to the human being he had assumed. For he *imparted* divine power to the mortal, but did not receive in turn from the mortal anything of that which belongs to it."

The same source, chapter 14:[8] "The Word . . . there making this very one"—human being—"worthy of eternal life as he always had been, and of communion in deity and blessedness."

---

6. Marginal note: "Here a concrete term is used in place of an abstract term."

7. *MPG* 22:288A/B; W. J. Ferrar, *The Proof of the Gospel: Being the Demonstratio Evangelica of Eusebius of Caesarea* (New York: Macmillan, 1920), 1:188.

8. *MPG* 22:289A; Ferrar, *The Proof of the Gospel,* 1:190–91. Marginal note: "Here a concrete term is used in place of an abstract term."

ATHANASIUS, in his letter to Epictetus, quoted also by Epiphanius against the Dimoeritae (*Heresies,* 77):[9] "The Word did not become flesh in order to add anything to the deity, but that the flesh might rise. Nor did the Word proceed from Mary that he might be improved. . . . But a great addition has rather been made to the human nature itself due to the communion and union of the Word with it."

EPIPHANIUS, *Heresies,* 69, against the Ariomanites:[10] "It is manifest that the flesh which was from Mary and from our race was also transfigured into glory"—in the transfiguration—"so that it acquired the addition of the glory of the Godhead, heavenly honor, perfection, and majesty, which the flesh did not originally have but received here in the union with God the Word."

CYRIL, *Dialogue,* book 5:[11] "How, then, does the flesh of Christ bestow life?" And he replies: "On account of the union with the living Word, who is accustomed to make what belongs to his nature *common property* shared with his own body."

THEODORET, *Interpretation of the Epistle to the Ephesians,* on Ephesians 1:[12] "However, the fact that the nature which is assumed from us *shares* in the same honor with him who assumed it, so that there is no difference in the way they are worshiped, but the divinity which is not seen is worshiped through the nature which is seen—this indeed surpasses every miracle."

JOHN OF DAMASCUS, *On the Orthodox Faith,* book 3, chapters 7 and 15:[13] "It"—the divine nature—"*communicates* or imparts all that glorifies it to the flesh, but in itself it remains free from suffering and does not share in the sufferings of the flesh."

The same source, chapter 19:[14] "The flesh *has communion* with the deity of the Word which is at work, because the divine activities are carried out in the same way as [activities are carried out] through an organ of the body, and because it is the same One who works in both a divine and a human way. For it ought to be recognized that, just as his holy mind also carries out its natural activities . . . it has communion with the deity of the Word, which works and arranges and governs, perceiving and knowing and arranging all things, not as a mere human mind, but as one personally united with God and called the mind of God."

9. *MPG* 42:656C, 26:1065A/B; *NPNF,* ser. 2, 4:573.

10. *MPG* 42:332D; J. M. Robinson and H. J. Klimkeit, eds. *Nag Hammadi and Manichaean Studies 26 (The Panarion of Epiphanius of Salamis, Books II and III)* (Leiden: Brill, 1994), 398–99.

11. *MPG* 75:962B–963C.

12. *MPG* 82:517A.

13. *MPG* 94:1012C, 1058C; *NPNF,* ser. 2, 9 (pt. II):52.

14. *MPG* 94:1080B/C; *NPNF,* ser. 2, 9 (pt. II):68.

II

That Christ, moreover, has received this majesty in time, not according to the divinity, or the divine nature, but according to the human nature he assumed, or according to the flesh as a human being or as the Son of Man, humanly, with respect to the body or humanity, on account of the flesh, because he is human or the Son of Man.

Hebrews 1:3: "When he had made purification for sins *by himself,* he sat down at the right hand of the Majesty on high."

Hebrews 2:8-9: "We do not yet see everything in subjection to him, but we do see *Jesus,* who for a little while was made lower than the angels, now crowned with glory and honor because of the *suffering* of death."

Luke 22:69: "From now on *the Son of Man* will be seated at the right hand of the power of God."

Luke 1:32-33: "And the Lord God will give *to him* the throne of his ancestor David. He will reign over the house of Jacob forever, and of his kingdom there will be no end."

ATHANASIUS, quoted by Theodoret, in *Dialogue* 2:[15] "Now, whatever Scripture says that the Son received or was glorified with, it says it *in regard to his humanity,* not in regard to his divinity."

John 5:26-27: "He has granted the Son also to have life in himself, and he has given him authority to execute judgment because he is *the Son of Man.*"

ATHANASIUS, *Discourse against the Arians* 1 and 3:[16] "Scripture does not mean that the substance of the Word has been exalted, but this is said in view of his humanity, and he is said to be exalted in regard to the *flesh.* For since it is his own body, he himself is properly said to be exalted and to receive things *as a human being, with respect to his body, humanly,* because the body receives those things which the Word always possessed according to his own deity and perfection, which he has from the Father. He says, therefore, that *as a human being* he received the power, which as God he always has. And he who glorifies others says, '*Glorify* Me,' in order to show that he had a flesh that lacked such things. And, therefore, when *the flesh of his humanity receives* this glorification, he so speaks as if he himself had received it. For we must bear in mind everywhere that none of those things which he says that he 'received,' namely, in time, he received in such a way as if he had not had them; for he always had them *inasmuch as he is God and the Word.* But now he says that he '*received*' them *humanly,* in order that, *since his flesh has in itself received them,* he might in time to come hand them over from his flesh to us so that we may possess them."

The same author, on the humanity which Christ took on himself, against Apollinaris:[17] "When Peter says that Jesus was made Lord and Christ by God, he

---

15. *MPG* 83:181A.
16. *MPG* 26:95C, 98–99, 406B/C, 410A/B; *NPNF,* ser. 2, 4:330, 415.
17. *MPG* 26:1022A/B.

does not speak of his divinity but of his *humanity*. His Word always was Lord, and he did not first become Lord after the cross, but his divinity *made the humanity Lord and Christ.*"

Also:[18] "Whatever Scripture says that the Son has '*received,*' it understands as 'received' *with respect to his body,* and that body is the first fruits of the church. The Lord, then, first raised up and *exalted his own body,* but later the members of his body." By these words, Athanasius explained what a little later he applied also to the entire church.

BASIL THE GREAT, *Against Eunomius,* book 4:[19] "That the Lord is honored and receives a name above every name [Phil. 2:9]; also: 'All authority is given to me in heaven and on earth' [Matt. 28:18]; 'I live because of the Father' [John 6:57]; 'Glorify me with the glory that I had in your presence before the world existed' [John 17:5]; etc.—these sayings must be understood as related to the *incarnation,* and not to the deity."

AMBROSE, *On the Faith,* book 5, chapter 6:[20] "You have learned that he certainly can subject all things to himself according to the way the deity works. Learn now that *according to his flesh he receives all things in subjection,* as it is written, Ephesians 1[:2]. According to the flesh, therefore, all things are delivered in subjection to him."

The same source, book 5, chapter 2:[21] "For God does not grant possession of his throne to the apostles, but he grants *Christ, according to his humanity,* possession of the divine throne."

And chapter 6:[22] "In Christ the nature which we have in common with him, *according to the flesh,* has obtained the prerogative of the heavenly throne."

CHRYSOSTOM, *On the Epistle to the Hebrews,* homily 3:[23] "[German: The Father] saying, with respect to the flesh: 'Let all God's angels worship him [German: Christ].'"

THEOPHYLACT, *Explanation of the Gospel of John,* on John 3:[24] "And he has given all things into the hand of the Son, *according to his humanity.*"

OECUMENIUS, *Commentary on the Epistle to the Hebrews,* on Hebrews 1, from Chrysostom:[25] "For as God, he has the eternal throne. 'Your throne,' God says, 'is forever and ever.' For after the cross and suffering it was not as God that he was regarded as worthy of this honor. But he received *as a human being* what he has as God." And a little farther on: "Therefore as a human being he hears: 'Sit at My right hand.' For as God he has eternal power."

---

18. *MPG* 26:1003B.
19. *MPG* 29:694C, 597C, 701A/B.
20. *MPL* 16:714B; *NPNF,* ser. 2, 10:307. *MPL* numbers this chapter "15."
21. *MPL* 16:691B; *NPNF,* ser. 2, 10:294.
22. *MPL* 16:713B; *NPNF,* ser. 1, 14:307. *MPL* numbers this chapter "4."
23. *MPG* 63:28; *NPNF,* ser. 1, 14:375.
24. *MPG* 123:1225A.
25. *MPG* 119:289A/B.

CYRIL, *Thesaurus,* book 9, chapter 3:[26] "*As human being* he ascended to the power of governance."

The same source, book 11, chapter 17:[27] "*As human being* he sought his glory which he always had as God. Nor are these things said by him because he had ever been without his own glory, but because he *wished to bring his own temple into the glory* which is always his as God."

The same author, *To the Queens,* book 2:[28] "The fact that he received glory, power, and sovereignty over all things must be understood as referring to the conditions of humanity."

THEODORET, *Interpretation of the Psalms,* on Psalm 2:[29] "Though Christ is Lord by nature as God, he receives power over all things also *as a human being.*"

On Psalm 110[:1]:[30] "'Sit at my right hand': this was said *with respect to his humanity.* For as God he has eternal power; so it is *as a human being* that he has received what he had as God. As a *human being,* therefore, he hears: 'Sit at my right hand.' For as God he has eternal power."

The same author, *Interpretation of the Epistle to the Hebrews,* on Hebrews 1:[31] "Christ always received worship and adoration from the angels, for he always was God. Now, however, they adore him also *as a human being.*"

LEO says in letter 23, discussing Ephesians 1:[32] "Let the adversaries of the truth say when, or according to what *nature,* the almighty Father raised his *Son* above all things; or to which he subjected all things. For all things have always been subject to Deity, as to the Creator. If power was added to Deity, if Highness was exalted, it was inferior to the One who exalted and did not have the riches of that nature whose generosity it needed. But anyone who thinks such things, Arius receives into his fellowship."

The same author, letter 83:[33] "Although in Christ there is absolutely one and the same person [constituted] of the divinity and the humanity, nevertheless we understand that the exaltation and the "name above every name" [Phil. 2:9] *belong to the form which was to be enriched by the addition of so great a glorification.* For nothing had been withdrawn from the Word through incarnation which would be returned to it by the gift of the Father. But *the form of a servant* is human lowliness, which has been *exalted* to the glory of divine power, so that divine things would not be done without the human being, nor human things without God."

---

26. *MPG* 75:363C.

27. *MPG* 75:439/40A, a passage that expresses the idea of this citation, though not in its precise words.

28. *MPG* 76:1359C, a passage that expresses the idea of this citation, though not in its precise words.

29. *MPG* 80:880A.

30. *MPG* 80:1768B.

31. *MPG* 82:686C.

32. *MPL* 54:869; *NPNF,* ser. 2, 12:59.

33. *MPL* 54:1066; *NPNF,* ser. 2, 12:94.

In the same place:[34] "Whatever Christ has received in time he has *received as a human being,* upon whom are conferred those things which he did not have. For, according to the power of the Word, the Son also has all things that the Father has, without distinction."

Vigilius, *Against Eutyches,* book 5:[35] "The divine nature does not need to be elevated to honors, to be augmented by advancements in dignity, to receive the power of heaven and earth by the merit of obedience. Therefore, it was *according to the nature of the flesh that he acquired* these things; according to the nature of the Word, he lacked none of them at any time. Did the Creator have no power and dominion over his creatures, so that in the last times he should obtain them as a gift?"

Nicephorus, *Ecclesiastical History,* book 1, chapter 36:[36] "Christ is seen by the disciples on the mountain in Galilee and there affirms that the highest power of heaven and earth has been committed to him by the Father, obviously, *according to his humanity.*"

III

That Holy Scripture, first of all, and then also the holy fathers of the ancient pure church, speak of this mystery in abstract terms, that is, in words which expressly point to the human nature in Christ and refer to it within the personal union, where clearly the human nature actually and truly has received and uses such majesty.

John 6[:55, 54]: "*My flesh* is true food and *my blood* is true drink. Those who eat my flesh and drink my blood have eternal life."

1 John 1[:7]: "*The blood of Jesus* his Son cleanses us from all sin."

Hebrews 9[:14]: "How much more will *the blood of Christ,* who through the eternal Spirit offered himself without blemish to God, purify our conscience from dead works, to worship the living God!"

Matthew 26[:26-28]: "Take, eat; this is *my body.* . . . Drink from it, all of you; for this is *my blood* of the covenant."

Eustathius, quoted by Theodoret, in *Dialogue* 2:[37] "Therefore he prophesied that 'he'—Christ the human being—would sit upon a holy throne, indicating that he has revealed himself as the one who shares the throne with the most divine Spirit because God continually dwells in him."

The same author, quoted by Gelasius (*On the Two Natures in Christ*):[38] "The *human being* Christ, who increased in wisdom, age, and favor [Luke 2:52], received dominion over all things."

---

34. *MPL* 54:1066–67; *NPNF,* ser. 2, 12:94.
35. *MPL* 62:141A/D, 142B.
36. *MPG* 145:742B.
37. *MPG* 83:176B.
38. *Epistolae Romanorum Pontificum Genuinae et quae ad eos Scriptae Sunt* I (Braunsberg: Peter, 1868), 544.

The same author, in the same place:[39] "Christ, in his very body, came to his own apostles, saying: 'All power is given to me in heaven and on earth.' The *external temple received* this power, not God, who built that temple of extraordinary beauty."

ATHANASIUS, *On the Arian and the Catholic Confession:*[40] "God was not changed into human flesh or substance, but in himself he glorified the nature which he assumed, *so that the human, weak, and mortal flesh and nature advanced to divine glory,* so as to have all power in heaven and on earth, which it did not have before it was assumed by the Word."

The same author, on the humanity which Christ took upon himself, against Apollinaris:[41] "Paul, in Philippians 2[:9-11], is speaking about the *temple* which is *his body.* For not he who is the Most Exalted One, but the *flesh,* is raised on high. And to his flesh he gave a name which above every name, that at the name of Jesus every knee should bow, and every tongue confess, *that Jesus Christ is Lord, to the glory of God the Father.*" And he adds a general rule: "When Scripture speaks of the glorification of Christ, it speaks of the *flesh,* which has received glory. And whatever Scripture says that the Son has received, it says *with respect to his humanity,* not his divinity. So, for instance, when the Apostle says that in Christ dwells all the fullness of the Godhead bodily [Col. 1:19; 2:9], it is to be understood that this fullness dwells *in the flesh* of Christ."

The same author, quoted by Theodoret, in *Dialogue* 2:[42] "'Sit at my right hand' has been said to the Lord's body" [Ps. 110:1]. Also: "It is, therefore, the body to which he says: 'Sit at My right hand.'"

ATHANASIUS, *On the Incarnation,* as quoted by Cyril in his defense of Anathema 8 and in his book *On the True Faith, to the Queens:*[43] "If any one says that the flesh of our Lord, as the flesh of a human being, is not to be adored, so that it should not be adored *as the flesh of the Lord and God,* the holy and catholic church pronounces that person accursed."

The same author:[44] "Whatever Scripture says that the Son has *received,* it understands as received *with respect to his body,* and that body is the first fruits of the church. The Lord, then, first raised up and *exalted his own body,* but afterwards the members of his body."

HILARY, *On the Trinity,* book 9:[45] "That thus the human being Jesus would remain in the glory of God the Father, if *the flesh were united* to the glory of the Word, and *the flesh he assumed possessed the glory of the Word.*"

39. *Epistolae Romanorum Pontificum Genuinae* I, 554.

40. This work was traditionally assigned to Athanasius in the Middle Ages but was in fact composed by Vigilius of Thapsus, *MPL* 62:305B.

41. *MPG* 26:987–90.

42. *MPG* 83:180B.

43. *MPG* 76:350C, 1211.

44. *MPG* 26:1003B.

45. *MPL* 10:326–27; *NPNF,* ser. 2, 9:167. Marginal note: "Here a concrete term is used in place of an abstract term."

Eusebius of Emissa, in his *Homily on the Sixth Festival Day after Easter:*[46] "He who, according to his divinity, had always, with the Father and the Holy Spirit, power over all things, now, also *according to his humanity,* has received *power* over all things, so that this *human being,* who suffered not long ago, rules over heaven and earth, and indeed does here and there whatever he pleases."

Gregory of Nyssa, quoted by Gelasius, *On the Two Natures in Christ,* and Theodoret, *Dialogue* 2:[47] "'Exalted, therefore, by the right hand of God' [Acts 2:33]. Who, then, was exalted? The Lowly One or the Highest? But what is lowly if not the human? And what else than the divine is the Highest? But God, who is the Highest, does not need to be exalted. Therefore the apostle is saying that the *human nature* was *exalted*—exalted, moreover, by becoming Lord and Christ. Therefore by the word 'made' [Acts 2:36], the apostle does not designate the eternal essence of the Lord, but the remaking of the *lowly* into the Highest, at the right hand of God." And a little farther on: "For the right hand of God, which is the Maker of all things, the Lord himself, through whom all things were made, and without whom nothing exists which was made, has itself, through the union, raised up *the human being united with it* to its own high status."[48]

Basil the Great, *Against Eunomius,* book 2:[49] "When Peter says, in Acts 2:36, 'God has made this Jesus, whom you crucified, Lord,' by the demonstrative word 'this' he designates the *humanity* of Christ and says that *to it* power and dominion were entrusted by the Father."

Epiphanius, against the Ariomanites (*Heresies,* 69):[50] "[Peter adds:] 'This Jesus, whom you crucified,' in order that the holy plan for the incarnation might not be set aside by the Word, which is uncreated and free from suffering, but that this plan might be brought into conjunction from above with the uncreated Word. For this reason God made that [human] nature God and Lord, which was conceived of Mary and united to deity."

Ambrose, *On the Holy Spirit,,* book 3, chapter 11:[51] "The angels adore not only the divinity of Christ, but also the *footstool of his feet.*" And afterwards: "The prophet says that the earth which the Lord Jesus took upon himself, when he took on flesh, should be adored. Therefore by 'footstool' we understand the earth, and by this *earth* we understand the *flesh,* which we today also adore in the celebration of the Lord's Supper[52] and which the apostles adored in the Lord Jesus, as we have said above."

Augustine, *On the Words of the Lord,* discourse 58:[53] "If Christ is not God by nature, but a creature, he is not to be worshiped or adored as God. But they will

---

46. *MPG* 86:486–88.

47. *MPG* 83:193, 195. See also *Epistolae Romanorum Pontificum Genuinae,* I:549.

48. Marginal note: "Here a concrete term is used in place of an abstract term."

49. *MPG* 29:577A/B.

50. *MPG* 42:268B/C; Robinson and Klimkeit, *The Panarion of Epiphanius,* 360.

51. *MPL* 16:827A, 828B–829A; *NPNF,* ser. 2, 10:145–46. *MPL* numbers this chapter "11."

52. Literally, "in the mysteries."

53. *MPL* 39:2200.

reply and say to this: Why, then, is it that you adore his *flesh*, along with his *deity*, when you do not deny it to be a creature, and why are you no less devoted to it than to the deity?"

The same author, *Explanation of the Psalms*, on Psalm 98:[54] "'Worship the footstool of his feet' [Ps. 99:5]. His footstool is the earth, and Christ took upon himself earth from the earth, because flesh is of the earth, and he received flesh from the flesh of Mary. And because he walked here in this very flesh, he also gave this very flesh to be eaten by us for salvation. But no one eats *that flesh* unless he has first *worshiped* it. Therefore we have discovered how such a footstool of the Lord may be worshiped, so that not only do we not sin by worshiping it, but we sin by not worshiping it."

CHRYSOSTOM, *On the Epistle to the Hebrews*, on Hebrews 2:[55] "For it is really great and astonishing and full of wonder that *our flesh* should be seated above and be worshiped by angels and archangels and the seraphim and the cherubim. Often, when I reflect on this, I am awestruck."

The same author, *On the First Epistle to the Corinthians*, on 1 Corinthians 10:[56] "The Magi venerated *this body*, even when it was lying in the manger. . . . And they made a long journey, and when they had come, they worshiped with much fear and trembling."

The same author, quoted by Leo, in letter 95: "Let us recognize *which nature it is* to which the Father said: 'Share my seat.' *It is that nature* to which it has been said, 'Dust you are, and to dust you shall return.'"

THEOPHYLACT, *Explanation of the Gospel of Matthew*, on Matthew 28:[57] "Since the *human nature*, which was previously condemned, sits in heaven, united in person with God the Word, worshiped by angels, he properly says: 'All power is given to me in heaven.' For precisely the *human* nature, which previously was subservient, in Christ now rules over all things."

The same author, *Explanation of the Gospel of John*, on John 3:[58] "He has also given all things into the hand of the Son, *according to his humanity*."

CYRIL, *On the Incarnation*, chapter 11:[59] "The Word inserted himself into that which he was not, in order that *the nature of the human being* might also become that which it was not, resplendent, with the honors of divine majesty, through this union. It has not cast the unchangeable God beneath its own nature, but rather has itself been raised above its nature."

The Council of Ephesus, canon 11:[60] "If anyone does not confess that *the flesh of the Lord* is life-giving, because it has become the flesh of the Word him-

---

54. *MPL* 37:1264; *NPNF*, ser. 1, 8:485.

55. *MPG* 63:47; *NPNF*, ser. 1, 14:388.

56. *MPG* 61:202; *NPNF*, ser. 1, 12:143.

57. *MPG* 123:484D; *The Explanation by Blessed Theophylact of the Holy Gospel according to St. Matthew* (House Springs, Mo.: Chrysostom Press, 1992), 257–58.

58. *MPG* 123:1225A.

59. *MPG* 75:1383A; *Library of the Fathers*, 44:198.

60. *MPG* 76:311.

self, who gives life to all things, let him be accursed." Cyril says in his explanation of this anathema[61] that Nestorius was unwilling to attribute the power to make alive to *the flesh of Christ*, but explained the sentences in John 6 as referring only to his divinity.

THEODORET, *Dialogue* 2:[62] "And it"—the *body* of the Lord—"was considered worthy of the seat on the right hand of God and is worshiped by every creature because it is called the body of the Lord by nature."

The same author, *Interpretation of the Psalms*, on Psalm 8:[63] "Such an honor, namely, dominion over the universe, the *human* nature in Christ has received from God."

LEO, letter 11:[64] "[When it is written] that God has highly exalted him, and given him a name which is above every name, that at the name of Jesus every knee should bow, and every tongue confess that Jesus Christ is Lord, to the glory of God the Father [Phil. 2:9-11], it refers to the elevation of that which is assumed [Christ's human nature], and not of the One who assumes it."

JOHN OF DAMASCUS, *On the Orthodox Faith*, book 3, chapter 18:[65] "Therefore his"—Christ's—"divine will was both eternal and omnipotent. . . . But his *human* will began in time and sustained its own natural disposition, unaltered, and indeed was not omnipotent by nature. But *truly and according to its nature as God the will of the Word has been made omnipotent*." This means, as a commentator explains: "The divine will has, by its own nature, the power to do all things which it wishes. *But Christ's human will has power to do all things, not by its own nature, but as a will united with God the Word*."

The same source, chapter 19:[66] "*The flesh has communion with the deity of the Word which is at work*, because the divine activities are carried out in the same way as [activities are carried out] through an organ of the body, and because it is the same One who works in both a divine and a human way. For it ought to be recognized that, just as *his holy mind* also carries out its natural activities . . . it has communion with the deity of the Word, which works and arranges and governs, *perceiving and knowing and arranging all things, not as a mere human mind*, but as one personally united with God and called the mind of God."

The same source, in the same book, chapter 21:[67] "*The human nature* does not essentially possess or have knowledge of things to come; but *the soul of the Lord*, because of the union with the Word, was endowed, along with the other divine powers, also with the knowledge of things to come." And at the end of the chapter: "We say that he, as Master and Lord of all creation, *the one Christ, who*

61. *MPG* 76:311; *NPNF*, ser. 2, 14:217.

62. *MPG* 83:168C.

63. *MPG* 80:920B.

64. *MPL* 54:807; *NPNF*, ser. 2, 12:49.

65. *MPG* 94:1076–77; *NPNF*, ser. 2, 9 (pt. II):66.

66. *MPG* 94:1080B/C; *NPNF*, ser. 2, 9 (pt. II):68.

67. *MPG* 94:1085A/C; *NPNF*, ser. 2, 9 (pt. II):69.

is at the same time God and human, also knows all things. For in him are hidden all the treasures of knowledge and wisdom."

NICEPHORUS, *Ecclesiastical History,* book 18, chapter 36:[68] "Christ is seen by the disciples on the mountain in Galilee and there affirms that the highest power of heaven and earth has been committed to him by the Father, namely, *according to his human nature.*"

IV

That Holy Scripture and the fathers have understood this majesty, which Christ has received in time, as not only consisting of created gifts, of finite qualities, but as the glory and majesty of the divinity, which is God's own, to which his human nature, in the person of the Son of God, has been exalted and thus has received the power and efficacy of the divine nature, which belongs to divinity.

John 17:5: "So now, Father, glorify me in your own presence with the glory that I had in your presence before the world existed."

Colossians 2:9: "In him the whole fullness of deity dwells bodily."

HILARY, *On the Trinity,* book 3:[69] "The Word that became flesh prayed that *that which began in time* might receive the glory of that splendor which is timeless."

GREGORY OF NYSSA, quoted by Gelasius, *On the Two Natures in Christ,* and Theodoret, *Dialogue* 2, concerning the saying of Peter in Acts 2[:33]:[70] "Exalted by the right hand of God," etc.: "It"—the right hand of God—"has itself, through the [personal] union, raised up *the human being, united* with it to its own high status."

The same author, *On the Soul:* "God the Word is never changed by the communion which he has with *body and soul,* nor does he partake of their limitation, but, *transmitting to them the power of his divinity,* he remains the same that he was before the union."

BASIL THE GREAT, *On the Holy Nativity of Christ:*[71] "In what manner is the deity in the flesh? As fire is in glowing iron, not by transformation, but by impartation. For the fire does not flow into the iron, but, remaining in its place, imparts to or bestows on the iron its own natural power, which is not diminished by the impartation and which fills the whole mass of iron which partakes of it."

EPIPHANIUS, in *Ancoratus:*[72] "Empowering an *earthly body* with divinity, he *united it into one power,* brought it into one divinity, being one Lord, one Christ—not two Christs, nor two Gods," etc.

---

68. *MPG* 145:742B.

69. *MPL* 10:85B; *NPNF,* ser. 2, 9 (pt. I):66.

70. *MPG* 83:196; *Epistolae Romanorum Pontificorum Genuinae,* I:549.

71. Pseudo-Basil, *MPG* 31:1460C.

72. *MPG* 43:168C/D.

CYRIL, *On the Gospel of John*, book 4, chapter 23:[73] "You are not completely off the mark in denying that the flesh makes alive. For if considered by itself, it can make nothing whatever alive, in fact needs someone to give it life itself. But when you have examined the mystery of the incarnation in an honorable way, and have learned to know the Life dwelling in the flesh, *you will believe that, although the flesh is able to do absolutely nothing by itself, it has nevertheless become life-giving.* For since it has been united with the life-giving Word, it has been made fully life-giving. For it has not dragged down to its corruptible nature the Word of God which has been joined to it, but it has itself been elevated to the power of the better nature. Although, therefore, the nature of the flesh, inasmuch as it is flesh, cannot give life, nevertheless it does this because *it has received the entire mode of performance which belongs to the Word.* For the body of Peter or Paul or others cannot do this, but the body of Life itself, in which the fullness of the godhead dwells bodily, can do this. Therefore the flesh of all the others produces nothing, but only *the flesh* of Christ can give life, because in it dwells the only-begotten Son of God."

AUGUSTINE, *Against Felicianus the Arian*, chapter 11:[74] "I do not hold that the deity is affected by the violence to his body in the same way that we know his flesh was glorified by the *majesty of deity.*"

THEODORET, *Compendium of the Fables of the Heretics,* chapter on Antichrist:[75] "The Word that became human did not confer grace piecemeal upon the *nature* it assumed, but it pleased [God] that the whole fullness of deity dwell in it."

The same author, *Interpretation of the Psalms,* on Psalm 21:[76] "If the nature which was assumed has been joined with the divinity which assumed it, it has also come to participate and share in the same glory and honor."

The same author, *Interpretation of the Epistle to the Hebrews,* on Hebrews 1:[77] "The *human nature* itself, after the resurrection, attained divine glory."

JOHN OF DAMASCUS, *On the Orthodox Faith,* book 3, chapters 7 and 15:[78] "It"—the divine nature—"communicates its own glories to the flesh, but in itself remains free from suffering and does not share in those of the flesh."

V

That Christ has the same divine majesty in one way as God, namely, essentially and as an essential characteristic, in and of himself, but as a human being he has it in another way, namely, not essentially in and of himself, but on account of and according to the nature of the personal union.

---

73. *MPG* 73:602C; *Library of the Fathers* 43:435.
74. *MPL* 42:1165.
75. *MPG* 83:530–31.
76. *MPG* 80:1023C.
77. *MPG* 82:683B.
78 *MPG* 94:1012C, 1058C; *NPNF,* ser. 2, 9 (pt. II):52.

John 14:6: "I am the Life."

John 5:26-27: "He has granted the Son also to have life in himself . . . *because he is the Son of Man.*"

CYRIL, *Thesaurus*, book 12, chapter 15:[79] "The creature has one condition and set of characteristics as the creature, and the Creator has another, but *our nature,* assumed by the Son of God, has transcended its limit and by grace has been transferred into the condition of the One who assumed it."

The same author, *On the Gospel of John*, book 2, chapter 144:[80] "Christ added the reason why he said that life and the power of judgment were given him by the Father, saying: '*Because he is the Son of Man,*' that we may understand that all things were given him as *human being.* But in fact the only-begotten Son does not partake of life, but is Life by nature."

The same source, book 3, chapter 37:[81] "*The body of Christ* gives life because it is the body of Life itself, which retains the power of the incarnate Word and is full of the power of him by whom all things exist and live."

The same source, book 4, chapter 14:[82] "Since the *flesh* of the Savior was joined to the Word of God, who is Life by nature, it has been made life-giving."

And chapter 18:[83] "I have filled *my body* with life. I have assumed mortal flesh. But because I, who exist by nature as Life, dwell in this flesh, *I have formed it all anew in keeping with my own life.*"

Chapter 24:[84] "*The flesh's nature* itself cannot of itself give life, nor is it understood to be by itself in Christ, but it has joined with itself the Son of God, who is Life in himself. Therefore when Christ calls his flesh life-giving, he does not ascribe the power of giving life to it in the same sense as he does to himself or his own Spirit. For the Spirit gives life of himself. The flesh rises to his power by being united [with the Son of God]. *But how this takes place we can neither understand with the mind nor express with the tongue, but we receive it in silence and firm faith.*"

The same source, book 10, chapter 13:[85] "The flesh of Life, since it has been made the flesh of the Only-begotten, *has been brought to the power of Life.*"

The same source, book 11, chapter 21:[86] "*The flesh of Christ* itself was not holy of itself, but having been transformed in a certain way by being united with the Word to the power of the Word, it is the cause for salvation and sanctification to those who partake of it. Therefore we ascribe the power of the divine activity not to the flesh as flesh, but to the nature of the Word."

---

79. *MPG* 75:535, 538.
80. *MPG* 73:383A/B; *Library of the Fathers* 43:272.
81. *MPG* 73:519D-522A; *Library of the Fathers* 43:376.
82. *MPG* 73:566D; *Library of the Fathers* 43:410.
83. *MPG* 73:586C; *Library of the Fathers* 43:424.
84. *MPG* 73:603C/D; *Library of the Fathers* 43:437.
85. *MPG* 74:343A/B.
86. *MPG* 74:519A.

Dialogue, book 6:[87] "He was glorified by the Father, not because he was God, *but because he was human.* Not having the power to act with divine efficacy as the fruit of his own nature, he received it in a certain way by the union and the inexpressible joining which God the Word is understood to have with the humanity."

The same author, *On the True Faith, to Theodosius:*[88] "He has transfused his life into the assumed body by the very plan for the union [of the two natures]."

In the same place:[89] "The Word gives life on account of the ineffable birth from the living Father. Yet we should see where *the efficacy of divine glory is ascribed also to his own flesh."* Also: "We will confess that the earthly flesh is unable to give life, as far as its own nature is concerned."

EPIPHANIUS, against the Ariomanites (*Heresies,* 69):[90] "For his humanity was not something existing apart by itself, and he did not speak of the deity separated [from the humanity] and the humanity existing apart [from the deity], as if they were two different persons, but he spoke of the humanity united with the deity, one holy being, which knows in itself those things which are absolutely perfect, inasmuch as it is now united in God and joined to the one deity."

AUGUSTINE, *On the Words of the Lord,* discourse 58:[91] "I indeed adore *the Lord's flesh,* yes, the perfect humanity in Christ, because it has been assumed by the divinity and united to deity, and I do not confess that there are two different persons, but that the one and same Son of God is God and human being. In short, if you separate the human being from God, I will never believe in him or serve him."

Also:[92] "If any one disdains worshiping humanity, *not alone or by itself,* but united to divinity, namely, the one Son of God, true God and true human being, he will die eternally."

Augustine, *On the City of God,* book 10, chapter 24:[93] "The flesh of Christ, therefore, does not *of itself* cleanse believers, but [it cleanses them] through the Word, by which it has been assumed."

THE COUNCIL OF EPHESUS, canon 11:[94] "If anyone does not confess that the flesh of the Lord is life-giving *because it has become the flesh of the Word himself,* who gives life to all things, let him be accursed."

THEOPHYLACT, *Explanation of the Gospel of John,* on John 3:[95] "The Father has given all things into the hand of the Son *according to his humanity.* For if

---

87. *MPG* 75:1026A.
88. *MPG* 76:1190A/B.
89. *MPG* 76:1190A/B.
90. *MPG* 42:305C/D; Robinson and Klimkeit, *The Panarion of Epiphanius,* 383.
91. *MPL* 39:220.
92. *MPL* 39:220.
93. *MPL* 41:301; *CSEL* 40:486, 11; *NPNF,* ser. 1, 2:195.
94. Denzinger, 262.
95. *MPG* 123:1225A.

this is stated according to his divinity, what is meant? That the Father has given all things to the Son *by reason of his nature, not by reason of grace.*"

The same author, *Explanation of the Gospel of Matthew,* on Matthew 28:[96] "If you understand the saying, 'All power is given to me,' as spoken about God the Word, the meaning will be: Both the unwilling and the willing who previously served me with involuntary obedience now acknowledge me as God. But if you take it as spoken of the human nature, understand it thus: *I, previously the condemned nature,* but being God *according to the union with the Son* of God, *without confusion of natures,* have received all power."

JOHN OF DAMASCUS, *On the Orthodox Faith,* book 3, chapter 17:[97] "For *not according to its own mode of operation,* but on account of the Word united to it, it"—*the flesh of the Lord*—"effects divine things, the Word displaying his own mode of operation through it. For the glowing iron burns, not by possessing the power to burn by reason of its own nature, but by acquiring it from its union with the fire. Therefore it"—*the flesh of the Lord*—"was *by itself* mortal and *life-giving* on account of personal union to the Word."

The same source, chapter 18:[98] "Therefore his"—Christ's—"divine will was both eternal and omnipotent. . . . But his *human* will began in time and sustained its own natural disposition, unaltered, and indeed was not omnipotent by nature. But *truly and according to its nature as God the will of the Word has been made omnipotent.*" This means, as a commentator explains: "The divine will has, by its own nature, the power to do all things which it wishes. *But Christ's human will has power to do all things, not by its own nature, but as a will united with God the Word.*"

In the same book, chapter 21:[99] "*The human nature* does not essentially possess or have knowledge of things to come; but *the soul of the Lord,* because of the union with the Word, was endowed, along with the other divine powers, also with the knowledge of things to come." And at the end of the chapter: "We say that the one Christ, Master and Lord of all creation, *who is at the same time God and human, also knows all things.* For in him are hidden all the treasures of knowledge and wisdom."

The same source, book 2, chapter 22:[100] "For although it"—*the soul of the Lord*—"was of a nature that was ignorant of things to come, nevertheless, being personally united to God the Word, *it had the knowledge of all things,* not by grace, but on account of the personal union." And a little farther on: "And since in our Lord Jesus Christ the natures are distinct, likewise the natural knowledge and will of the divinity and humanity [are also distinct]."

96. *MPG* 123:484–85; *Explanation of St. Matthew,* 258.
97. *MPG* 94:1069B/C; *NPNF,* ser. 2, 9 (pt. II):66.
98. *MPG* 94:1076–77; *NPNF,* ser. 2, 9 (pt. II):66.
99. *MPG* 94:1085A/C; *NPNF,* ser. 2, 9 (pt. II):69.
100. *MPG* 94:948A/B; *NPNF,* ser. 2, 9 (pt. II):69.

VI

That now the divine nature powerfully manifests, actually exerts, its majesty, power, and efficacy (which are and remain the property of the divine nature) in, with, and through the humanity which is personally united to it and thus has such majesty because of the fact that all the fullness of the Godhead dwells personally in the flesh and blood of Christ which he has assumed.

Romans 3:25: "Christ Jesus, whom God put forward as a sacrifice of atonement by his *blood*."

Romans 5:9: "We have been justified by his *blood*."

Colossians 1:20: "Through him God was pleased to reconcile to himself all things, whether on earth or in heaven, by making peace through the blood of his cross."

ATHANASIUS, *Discourse 5 against the Arians:*[101] "Why should *the body of the Lord* not be adored since the Word healed the person with a fever by stretching out his bodily hand; by speaking *with a human voice* he raised Lazarus; *by extending his hands on the cross* he overthrew the Prince of the Air?"

The same author, *Dialogue 5, On the Trinity:*[102] "God the Word, united with the human being, performs miracles, and he performs them not separated from that human nature, but *exercising his own divine power through it and in it and with it.*" And a little farther on: "And by his own good pleasure he perfects the creature beyond its own nature and yet did not prevent it from being a rational creature."

CYRIL, *On the True Faith, to Theodosius:*[103] "His soul, which had been united with the Word, descended into hell; but, *using the power and ability* he has as God, *it said* to the fettered ones, 'Go out.'"

The same author, *To the Queens*, book 1:[104] "Christ as God makes alive *through his own flesh*."

VII

And that this communication of the divine majesty takes place without mingling, destruction, or denial of the human nature, even in glory.

Matthew 16:27: "The Son of Man is to come with his angels in the glory of his Father."

Acts 1:11: "This Jesus, who has been taken up from you into heaven, will come in the same way as you saw him go into heaven."

---

101. *MPG* 26:1082B; *NPNF,* ser. 2, 4:577.

102. *MPG* 28:1280–81. Marginal note: "Here a concrete term is used in place of an abstract term."

103. *MPG* 76:1166A.

104. *MPG* 76:1282B.

Athanasius, *Dialogue 5, On the Trinity:*[105] "And by his own good pleasure he perfects the creature *beyond its own nature* and yet did not prevent it from being a rational creature."

Theophylact, *Explanation of the Gospel of Matthew*, on Matthew 28, from Chrysostom:[106] "I, previously the condemned nature, but being God according to the union with the Son of God, *without confusion of natures*, have received all power."

Cyril, *On the Gospel of John*, book 4, chapter 24:[107] "He has shown that his whole body is filled with the life-giving power of the Spirit, *not because it has lost the nature of flesh and been changed into Spirit*, but because, united with the Spirit, it has received the whole power to give life."

The same author, *On the Incarnation*, chapter 8:[108] "In burning wood, taking that as an illustration, we can see how God the Word, united, in fact, to humanity, has *transformed the nature it assumed into his own glory and power*. As the fire penetrates the wood, so has God been united to humanity in an inconceivable manner, *conferring on it even the mode of operation of his own nature*."

Theodoret, *Dialogue 2:*[109] "The body of the Lord, therefore, rose incorruptible, incapable of suffering, immortal, and *glorified with divine glory*, and it is adored by the heavenly powers. *Nevertheless, it is a body* and is circumscribed as it was before."

The same author, in *Dialogue 3*,[110] quotes this sentence of Apollinaris with approval: "If the combination of fire with iron, which makes it appear that the iron is fire, so that it also does those things which are characteristics of fire, *does not change the nature of the iron*, so the union of God with the body is not a change of the body, although it imparts divine powers to the body."

John of Damascus, *On the Orthodox Faith*, book 3, chapter 17:[111] "*The flesh of the Lord* was provided with divine powers on account of its complete personal union with the Lord, *without having suffered any loss of those things that are its own by nature*."

The same source, book 2, chapter 22:[112] "For although it"— *the soul of the Lord*—"was of a nature that was ignorant of things to come, nevertheless, being personally united to God the Word, *it had the knowledge of all things*, not by grace, but on account of the personal union." And a little farther on: "And since in our Lord Jesus Christ the natures are distinct, and likewise the natural knowledge and will of the divinity and humanity [are also distinct]."

105. *MPG* 28:1280–81.
106. *MPG* 123:485A; *Explanation of St. Matthew*, 258.
107. *MPG* 73:603B; *Library of the Fathers* 43:437.
108. *MPG* 75:1379; *Library of the Fathers* 44:194.
109. *MPG* 83:163A.
110. *MPG* 83:215B.
111. *MPG* 94:1069B; *NPNF*, ser. 2, 9 (pt. II):66.
112. *MPG* 94:948A/B; *NPNF*, ser. 2, 9 (pt. II):37.

VIII

Also, that the human nature shares in and is capable of [assuming] the divine majesty which belongs to God, according to the nature of and because of the personal union.

Colossians 2:9, 3: "In him the whole fullness of deity dwells bodily. In him are hidden all the treasures of wisdom and knowledge."

JUSTIN, in *Exposition of the Faith:*[113] "Nor do we say that he is in the Father in the same way as he is in other beings, not because his essence, which is in the others, is brought together with them in fact, but because these other creatures are incapable of receiving the divine." Again: "For a defiled body does not receive rays of divinity." And a little farther on:[114] "Thus consider with me that the Sun of Righteousness is in substance equally present to all things because he is God, but that we all, being weak and made bleary-eyed by the filth of sins, cannot receive the light, but *his own temple* is the purest eye and *has the capacity for the splendor of all the light,* because it has been fashioned by the Holy Spirit and is separated from sin in every part."

ORIGEN, *On the Principal Doctrines,* book 2, chapter 6:[115] "The whole soul of Christ receives the whole Word and yields to his light and splendor."

And in book 4:[116] "*The soul of Christ,* which is united with the Word of God, has full *capacity to receive the Son of God.*"

AUGUSTINE, letter 57:[117] "Although God is entirely present in all creatures, and dwells especially in believers, nevertheless they do not entirely receive him. But in relation to the difference of their capacity, some possess and receive him more, and others less. But concerning our head, Christ, the apostle says: *In him the whole fullness of deity* dwells bodily" [Col. 2:9].

IX

It is well known and undeniable that the Godhead, together with its divine majesty, is not locally enclosed by a circumscription of the flesh, as though it were enclosed and circumscribed in a vessel, as Athanasius, Origen, Gregory of Nyssa, and others correctly wrote.[118] Likewise, also in the Book of Concord it is expressly rejected as an error to teach that the humanity of Christ has been locally spread out into all places, or that the human nature in Christ has been transformed by the personal union into an infinite essence.[119]

113. *MPG* 6:1237–39.
114. *MPG* 6:1240.
115. *MPG* 11:211C; *ANF* 4:282.
116. *MPG* 11:405D; *ANF* 4:378.
117. *MPL* 33:837, 383, 847; *CSEL* 52:113, 115–16; *Fathers of the Church* 30:252.
118. A marginal note refers the reader to FC SD VII, 9–10; see also FC Ep VIII, 27–29, and SD VIII, 90–92.
119. This position was frequently ascribed to Andreae and his associates in the church of Württemberg, above all, Johannes Brenz, under the label "ubiquitarianism."

Nevertheless, since the divine and human natures are personally and inseparably united in Christ, Holy Scripture and the holy fathers testify that Christ, wherever he is, is not present there as half a person, or only a half or only a part of his person is present, such as the divinity alone, separate and bare, apart from and outside the humanity he assumed and with which he is personally united, separated from that humanity and outside the personal union with the humanity; rather, his entire person, namely, as God and human being, according to the nature of the personal union with the humanity, which is an unsearchable mystery, is present everywhere, in a way and measure which is known to God.

Ephesians 4:10: "Ascended far above all the heavens, so that he might fill all things." This passage Oecumenius explains thus:[120] "For he, in fact, also filled all things long ago merely with his divinity. And after becoming incarnate, he descended and ascended *in order that he might fill all things with his flesh.*"

THEOPHYLACT on the same passage (in his *Exposition of the Epistle to the Ephesians*):[121] "So that he might fill all things by ruling and performing his tasks, and so that he might *do this in the flesh* since already before this [the incarnation] he filled all things with his divinity. These things, however, are contrary to Paul of Samosata and Nestorius."

LEO, letter 10:[122] "In this faith the catholic church lives and thrives, that in Christ Jesus *neither* the humanity is believed *without the true divinity*, nor the divinity *without the true humanity.*"

The same author, *Sermon 3, on the Passion:*[123] "This the catholic faith teaches, this it requires: that we recognize that in our Redeemer two natures have come together, and because their characteristics remain, a union of both natures has been produced in such a way that, from the time when the Word became flesh in the womb of the blessed virgin, *we are not to think of this God apart from this fact, that he is human, nor of this human apart from the fact that he is God.*"

In the same place:[124] "Each nature, indeed, expresses its true character by distinct modes of operation, but neither separates itself from its connection with the other; here *neither is without the other* in anything. But God has assumed the whole human being and thus united himself to the latter and the latter to himself, *so that each nature is in the other and neither enters into the other without its own set of characteristics.*"

120. *MPG* 118:1217/1220.
121. *MPG* 124:1083D.
122. *MPL* 54:777; *NPNF,* ser. 2, 12 (pt. I):42–43.
123. *MPL* 54:319B; *NPNF,* ser. 2, 12 (pt. I):165.
124. *MPL* 54:319B/C; *NPNF,* ser. 2, 12 (pt. I):165.

X

But since in this article such teaching is purposely directed toward this point: where we should seek and may grasp the whole person of the Mediator, God and human being, the Book of Concord, as also all other holy fathers, directs us, not to wood or stone or any such thing, but to that to which Christ has pointed and directed us in and with his Word.[125]

CYRIL, *On the Gospel of John*, book 12, chapter 32:[126] "The clothes of Christ were divided into four parts, and his tunic alone remained undivided. This, I may say, was a sign of a mysterious reality. For the four quarters of the world, which have been brought to salvation, *have shared the garment of the Word, that is, his flesh, among themselves* in an indivisible way. For the Only-begotten One, who passes into each person in such a way that each partakes of him, and he sanctifies each person's soul and body by his flesh, *he exists indivisibly and entirely in all since he is in no way divided, because everywhere he is one.*"

THEOPHYLACT, *Explanation of the Gospel of John*, on John 19:[127] "Therefore the holy body of Christ is *indivisible*, though 'divided' and distributed to the four quarters of the world. For the Only-begotten One, who is distributed among them to each person and sanctifies the soul of each person together *with the body, by his own flesh*, is entirely and indivisibly in all, *existing everywhere*. For he is by no means divided, as Paul also proclaims [1 Cor. 1:13]."

CHRYSOSTOM, *On the Epistle to the Hebrews*, homily 17 (and Ambrose, *On the Epistle to the Hebrews*, chapter 10):[128] "Are there many Christs, just because he is offered in many places? By no means. Rather, *there is one Christ everywhere*, who is both completely here and completely there, as *one body*. Just as the One offered[129] in many places is one body, and not many bodies, so also there is but one sacrifice. He is our high priest, who has offered the sacrifice that cleanses us. We also now offer that sacrifice which is offered and yet is incapable of being consumed. This is done in remembrance of what was then done. For he says, 'Do this in remembrance of me.' We do not perform another sacrifice, like the high priest, but always repeat the same sacrifice. Rather, we are engaged in the remembrance of the sacrifice." [German: Do you think that because this sacrifice is performed at many places, there should be many Christs? That does not follow. For there is one Christ, and he is omnipresent, completely here and completely there, and has but one body. For as the body is one, which is sacrificed in every place, and there are not many bodies, so is there only one sacrifice, which is a model and reminder of the sacrifice which was performed on the cross.]

---

125. A marginal note refers the reader to FC SD VIII, 76–79, 87.
126. *MPG* 74:659B/C.
127. *MPG* 124:278A/B.
128. *MPG* 63:131; *NPNF*, ser. 1, 14:449. Marginal note: "Against the papistic propitiatory sacrifice of the Mass."
129. In the Lord's Supper.

Conclusion

Christian reader, these testimonies of the ancient teachers of the church have not been set forth here with the idea that our Christian faith is founded upon human authority. For the true saving faith should not be founded upon any teachers of the church, old or new, but only and alone upon God's Word, comprised in the Scriptures of the holy prophets and apostles as unquestionable witnesses of divine truth. But the erring spirits, by the characteristic, tricky craft of Satan, want to lead the people from Holy Scripture (which, thank God! even a common layman can now profitably read) to the writings of the holy fathers and teachers of the ancient church, as if into a broad sea, so that one who has not read them cannot know for sure whether they and their writings teach in the way that these new teachers construe their words, and so is left in grave doubt. Because of this, we have been compelled to indicate with this catalog, and show for everyone to see, that this new false doctrine has as little foundation in the writings of the ancient pure church teachers as in Holy Scripture. Instead, it is directly opposed to them. They quote the testimonies of the fathers with a false understanding, contrary to the fathers' purpose, just as they purposely and willfully pervert the plain, evident, and clear words of Christ's testament and the pure testimonies of Holy Scripture. On account of this, the Book of Concord directs everyone to Holy Scripture and the simple Catechism. For the person who clings to this simple form with true, simple faith provides best for the soul and conscience, since it is built on a firm and immovable rock, Matthew 7 and 17; Galatians 1; Psalm 119.

Martin Luther's Torgau Sermon on Christ's Descent into Hell and the Resurrection

Translated by Robert Kolb

Introduction

In the final stages of composing the Formula of Concord, at their meeting in Torgau in May 1576, the committee charged with its drafting decided to add as an appendix to its long article on Christology a brief treatment of the descent into hell. In the 1530s, the Wittenberg theologians Martin Luther, Philip Melanchthon, and their colleague Johannes Bugenhagen did not agree on the explanation of the Creed's confession, "he descended into hell,"[1] and in the following years disagreement and debate over the proper way to understand this doctrine plagued Lutheran ministeria, for example, in Hamburg (1544–53), Pomerania (1554), and Augsburg (1565).[2] In 1564, the ministerium of Mansfeld had dedicated part of one chapter of its confutation of false teaching to a critique of the position of the new Heidelberg Catechism on the issue.[3]

In order to provide guidance for teaching on Christ's descent into hell, the Formula of Concord directed readers to a sermon by Martin Luther, preached in Wittenberg on Easter day, 31 March 1532, and published with an undated sermon given at the electoral Saxon court in Torgau the following year. (Because the title of the printed version states that it contains "a sermon on Jesus Christ, preached at the court in Torgau," the third sermon in the little volume, that on the descent into hell and the resurrection, has been called the "Torgau sermon.") The three sermons were printed together as an exposition of the second article of the Creed.[4] Jakob Andreae copied a long section of the

---

1. See Melanchthon's and Luther's comments on Bugenhagen's explanation of 1 Peter 3:18 in a letter from Melanchthon, with marginal notes from Luther, to Georg Spalatin, 20 March 1531 (*CR* 2:490).

2. On these controversies, see David G. Truemper, "The *Descensus ad Inferos* from Luther to the Formula of Concord," S.T.D. thesis, Lutheran School of Theology at Chicago, 1974, 218–91.

3. *Confessio de sententia ministrorum verbi in comitatu Mansfeldensi, de dogmatis quorundam proximo triennio publice editos* (Eisleben: Urban Gaubisch, 1565), 47a–58b.

4. All three have been falsely attributed to 16 and 17 April 1533; see WA 37:XXI. The sermon printed in 1533 as the third section of *Von Jhesu Christo eine Predigt/ D. Mart. Luthers/ zu Hofe zu Torgaw gepredigt* (Wittenberg: Nikolaus Schirlentz, 1533) is a polished version of the sermon found in the notes of Georg Rörer from 31 March 1532 (WA 36:159–64). It is likely that the first and perhaps the second of these sermons was preached in Torgau during one of Luther's several stays there in 1532 and 1533, and that the three were brought together to present a complete treatment of the

sermon into the margin of his own manuscript copy of the Solid Declaration, but this text was not included in the final version of the Formula.[5] Its ninth article simply referred readers to this sermon.

This English translation is based upon the printed text of 1533 that was partially cited by Andreae in the marginal notes of his manuscript copy of Solid Declaration IX, as that 1533 printing is reproduced in WA 37:62–72.

Martin Luther's Torgau Sermon on Christ's Descent into Hell and the Resurrection

The Third Sermon on Easter Day

Because we have buried the Lord Christ and have heard how he departed this life, we must also get him out of the grave again and celebrate the day of Easter. On that day, he entered into a new life, from which he cannot die anymore. For this is the day on which he became Lord over death and over all things in heaven and earth. This is disclosed to us by the article of faith in which we say, "descended into hell, on the third day risen from the dead."

For[6] before he rose from the dead and ascended into heaven—while he was still in the grave—he descended into hell so that he might redeem us who lay imprisoned there, just as he came into death and was laid in the grave that he might bring us out of it. I do not want to preach this article with sublime or precise language, describing exactly how it happened or what it means to descend into hell. Instead, I want to stick to the simple meaning of the words as they must be presented to children and simple people. Many have wanted to grasp these words with their reason and five senses, but without success. They only wandered further from the faith. Therefore it is certainly the case that if we want to proceed correctly and not become confused, we must remain with these words and present them in the most simple way, as best we can.

The customary way of depicting how Christ descended into hell on church walls represents him with a cape and with banners in his hand as he makes his descent and stalks and assaults the devil, as he storms hell and rescues his own people from it. The children's play presented at Easter depicts it in a similar way. It seems better to me that you depict, act out, sing, and recite the story in a very simple way and let it remain at that and not concern yourself with sublime and precise ideas about how it actually took place. For it did not happen in a physical manner, since he indeed remained three days in the grave.

---

second article. See Truemper, "The *Descensus ad Inferos*," 95–111; and Erich Vogelsang, "Luthers Torgauer Predigt von Jesu Christo vom Jahre 1532," *Lutherjahrbuch* 13 (1931): 114–30.

    5. *BSLK*, 1049–52.

    6. The section of the sermon that Jakob Andreae copied in the margin of his manuscript of the Formula of Concord began here.

Therefore, even though we might formulate precise and subtle descriptions and definitions of the descent into hell and pose the questions certain teachers of the faith have disputed—whether he was personally present in his soul or only effectively present—our thinking will not attain such knowledge or fathom it. These teachers did not understand it themselves. That I should be able to grasp how it actually happened in such a way that I can speak about it or perceive with my senses is far and above what is possible in this life. So I would simply set this subject aside since I cannot even grasp everything that takes place within this sphere of life—for instance, what Christ was thinking and feeling in the Garden [of Gethsemane] when he sweat great drops of blood. This sort of thing must remain a matter of faith. How he descended into hell is much less a matter to be comprehended with words or thoughts. But because we must comprehend this with our own thinking and picture it to ourselves so that it can be presented to us in words, and because nothing can be understood or thought of without images, it is appropriate that we view these things in words that depict how he descended into hell, broke the gates of hell, and destroyed them. We should be hesitant about formulating sublime and inexplicable ideas.

For such paintings show well how powerful and useful this article is, why it took place, why it is to be preached and believed that Christ destroyed hell's power and took all his power away from the devil. When I have that, then I have the true core and meaning of this article of faith, and I should not ask further nor rack my brain about just how it happened or how it was possible—just as I should not rack my brain in regard to other articles of faith. Mastering such things with reason is forbidden and cannot attain anything. If I wanted to be as smart as some who like to soar to the heights and who mock our simplicity, I could make jokes and ask what kind of a banner he had and whether it was from cloth or paper and how it happened that the banner did not burn in hell. I could ask what kind of gates and locks hell had, and I could mock Christians in a pagan fashion as the greatest fools because they believe such things. That is a simple skill which everyone could practice without having to learn it; even a sow or cow could do such things. And I could also fashion superb allegories in explaining what the banner and the staff and the cloth and the doors of Hell really mean.

We, praise God, are indeed not so crude that we believe or say that it happened physically, with a great display of splendor or with wooden placards and cloth banners, or that hell is a building made of wood or iron. We leave such questioning and fussing and interpreting aside and speak simply with that which can be comprehended through the crude pictures that this article offers. This is similar to the way we present teaching on other divine matters—through crude, outward images as Christ himself presented the secret of the kingdom of heaven through such images and parables to the people throughout the Gospels. Similarly, the child Jesus is painted treading on the head of the serpent, .

and Moses is depicted in the wilderness with a bronze serpent.[7] Another example is John the Baptist being depicted as a lamb since he called Jesus the Lamb of God.[8] For such images are quite clear, and it is easy to comprehend and remember something through their use, and to do so in a way that is winsome and comforting. Even though they would have no other use, they serve to defend against the devil with his fiery arrows and temptations, for he wants to lead us with sublime thoughts away from God's Word and enchain us with reason and have us fuss about the sublime articles until he finally brings us down.

Without doubt, such a description has come to us from the ancient fathers who spoke and sang in the language of the old hymns as we still read and sing on Easter Day, "He broke hell and bound the accursed devil" and so forth.[9] When children or simple people hear something like this, they think of nothing else than that Christ has conquered the devil and taken all his power from him. That is the proper, Christian way to think and expresses the correct truth and meaning of this article, although it is not precisely what is being said and expressed in these words. But what difference does that make if my faith is not damaged and if the correct understanding is clearly presented and I can comprehend it? Should I spend a long time conducting an intense search for an explanation that I cannot grasp and instead lose the right understanding of the true meaning? These things must be presented to the general public in a simple childlike way; otherwise, one of two things will happen: either they will not learn or understand anything, or they will want to be smart and use their reason to move on to sublime thoughts that do not arise out of faith.

I am talking about these things because I see that the world still wants to be smart in the devil's name and to establish and master everything in the articles of faith according to its own head. Therefore, when it hears that Christ descended into hell, it sallies forth and immediately wants to speculate how that might have happened and poses many complicated, useless questions: Did the soul descend alone, or was the divine nature with it? What did he do in hell, and how did he interact with the devil, and many similar questions, regarding which nothing can be known. We want to ignore such unnecessary questions and bind and fix our hearts and thoughts simply on the word of faith, which says "I believe in the Lord Christ, God's Son, dead, buried, he descended into hell." That means I believe in the entire person, God and human creature with body and soul inseparable, born of the virgin, suffered, dead and buried. Therefore I am not supposed to divide up his person but instead simply to believe and to say that this very Christ, God and human creature in one person, descended to hell. But he did not remain there as the sixteenth psalm [:10] says of him, "You do not give my soul up to Sheol, or let your holy one see the pit." In the language

---

7. See Num. 21:8-9.

8. See John 1:29.

9. *Analecta Hymnica Medii Aevi: I: Cantiones Bohemicae*, ed. Guido Maria Dreves (Leipzig: Fues, 1886), 99, #65.

of Scripture, "soul" here means not that we have an essence divided from the body; it refers to the whole person, as he calls himself the "Holy One of God."

However it may have actually happened that this human creature was lying in the grave and then descended into hell, we should and must let stand. We cannot fathom or understand it. For it is indeed not to be comprehended in a physical way. We have to depict it in a crude and physical manner and speak of it in parables. For instance, it is as if a strong hero or giant comes to a well-protected castle with his army and banners and weaponry and wants to destroy that castle, taking his enemy captive and binding him, and so forth. Therefore, just simply say when someone asks about this article: I really don't know how it happened, and I will not and cannot think that through and formulate a good explanation. But I can depict it in a crude way and fashion an image which can speak clearly of this mysterious matter, that he went to hell with his banner in hand as a victorious hero, and he tore down its gates and charged into the midst of the devils, throwing one through the window and another out the door.

So you come, you inopportune smart aleck, with your rotting wisdom, and you mock, "If it is true, as I hear, that hell has wooden doors, made by a carpenter, how have they stood so long without being burned up, and so forth?" Answer: that I knew long before you got your wisdom, and you dare not teach me that hell is not built of wood and stone and does not have doors and windows, locks and deadbolts, like a house or a castle on earth, and that he did not destroy it with a banner of cloth. Praise God, I can speak in as much detail as any such smart aleck and interpret and explain everything with such images and representations and interpret exactly what they mean. But I want to stick by the childlike understanding and simple clear words which depict this article to me very well rather than to soar with them to such sublime ideas—which they don't understand themselves and which the devil uses to lead them from the straight and narrow. For such images cannot harm nor deceive me, but they serve and help me to comprehend and to hold on to this article ever more strongly, and then the meaning remains pure and unperverted—whether the portal's doors and the banners were wood or iron or weren't even there. We, of course, have to grasp all things that we cannot really know through images, whether they fit exactly or not, whether they precisely convey the truth as they depict it or not. Therefore, I believe also in this case that Christ personally destroyed hell and bound the devil whether banners, portals, doors, and chains were made of wood or iron or did not exist at all. It doesn't depend on whether I hang on to what is depicted with the image but rather that I believe these things of Christ. Believing in him is the chief thing. It is useful and gives the power that we have from this: that neither hell nor the devil can take us and all others who believe on him captive nor can they do us harm.

That is speaking of this article of faith as simply as possible, sticking to the words and remaining with this chief point: that through Christ hell has been torn apart as far as we are concerned, and that the devil's reign and power has been destroyed. That is why he died, was buried, and descended into hell, so that they might not harm us or overpower us anymore, as he said in Matthew 16[:18]. To be sure, hell in and of itself remains hell and holds the unbelievers imprisoned there, as well as death, sin, and all evil. They remain there and rot, and they may terrify and harass us in the flesh, in our outward persons, beating us and biting us. Nonetheless, in faith and in the spirit, they are completely destroyed and torn apart, so that they cannot harm us anymore.

That was all accomplished by this one man in our Lord Christ's descent into hell. Otherwise, the world with all its powers would never have been able to redeem anyone or liberate anyone from the devil's bonds nor take away the power and suffering of hell for our sins—even if all the saints had proceeded into hell for one person's sin. Instead, all who had ever come to this earth would have had to remain in hell eternally if the holy, almighty Son of God had not descended there in his own person and with his might and through divine power conquered it and destroyed it. No Carthusian cowl, no Franciscan cincture, nor the holiness of all of the monks, nor the power and might of all the world could have quenched one little spark of the hellish fire. But that was accomplished when this man descended with his banner. All the devils had to run away. They had to flee as if they'd met their own death and poison. His presence quenched all the fires of hell. The result is that no Christian need fear these things, and because he went there, they shall not suffer hell's pain just as they do not taste of death because of Christ. Instead, they press on through death and hell to everlasting life.

But our Lord Christ did not simply leave it at that, that he died and descended into hell (for in the end that would not have done us any good). He also came back from death and hell. He was brought again to life, and he opened heaven. Thus, he publicly demonstrated his victory and triumph over death, the devil, and hell in that, according to this article, "on the third day he rose again from the dead." That is the culmination and the very best of what he has done, and in it we have everything. For therein lies all power, strength, and might and everything that is in heaven and earth.[10] Through the fact that he is risen from the dead, he has become a mighty Lord over death and everything that lay in death's power or that served death. Thus, death can no longer gobble him up nor hold him in its grip. Sin cannot fall upon him anymore and drive him to death. The devil cannot bring an accusation against him anymore; nor can the world or any other creature harass or harm him. And none of them can do anything against us anymore, for they serve death and hell as the judge's flunky and the hangman's toady; they usher us to the judge and hangman and hand us over to them. All those who have escaped death are outside its control, and therefore they cannot trap us or hang on to us. We have also escaped all these other enemies and are lord over world, devil, every trap, sword, fire, gallows, and all afflictions, and we can defy and deride them.

---

10. The section of the sermon that Jakob Andreae copied in the margin of his manuscript of the Formula of Concord ended here.

The praise for this belongs alone to the Lord Christ. For through his almighty divine power, he has brought this to pass. But he did not do so for himself; rather, he did it for his poor miserable people who would have had to remain eternally captive to death and the devil. Beforehand, in and of himself, he had had nothing to fear from death and all other misfortune. He did not have to die and to descend into hell. But because he stuck himself into our flesh and blood and took all our sins, punishment, and misfortune upon himself, he had to help us escape. And then he grabbed hold of life again. In his own body, according to his human nature, he became the lord of death so that we might escape in him and through him from death and every misfortune. Therefore Scripture speaks of him as "the firstborn of the dead"[11] as he broke the trail for us and went ahead of us into eternal life so that through his resurrection we might come through and experience a glorious victory over death and hell. For we whom death and hell had held captive are not only redeemed; we also have become victors and lords through faith. Through this faith we are clothed in his resurrection, and we shall all someday rise physically and visibly and shall soar above; all things shall lie eternally under our feet.

It is characteristic of a strong faith to make this article of faith strong and sure and to write these words, "Christ is risen," with large letters onto the heart and make them as large as heaven and earth. As a result, our hearts will be able to see, hear, think, and know nothing else than this article, as though there were nothing else written in all of creation. Faith should submerge itself totally in this article and live from it alone, as St. Paul was accustomed to say; he was a true master at setting forth this article. His heart and mouth were always filled with descriptions of how Christ is risen. He slipped so easily into words like these: "He has made us alive together with Christ and raised us up with him and seated us with him in the heavenly places," Ephesians 2[:5, 6]. In Galatians 2[:20], he wrote, "It is no longer I who live, but Christ lives in me." In Romans 8[:33, 34], he wrote, "Who will bring any charge against God's elect? It is God who justifies. Who is to condemn? It is Christ who died, yes, who was raised," and so forth.

If we would believe this, then we would live well and die well. For such a faith would teach us properly that he not only is risen for himself but that his resurrection is inseparably connected with ours. It is also valid for us, and we also stand in the "He is risen"[12] and are enwrapped in it. Through it and because of it we must also rise and live with him eternally. Our rising and living (as St. Paul also says) has begun in Christ. Even though it is still hidden and not revealed, it is as certain as if it had already happened. Henceforth, we should fix our gaze on this article so firmly that everything else in our view is nothing by comparison, so firmly that you see nothing else in earth or heaven. So when you see a Christian dying and being buried, lying there like nothing else than a dead piece of

---

11. This phrase occurs in both Latin and German. See 1 Cor. 15:20.
12. The Latin word *Resurrexit* is used here.

wood, dead to both your eyes and your ears, nonetheless, through faith you see another image instead of that image of death. You see not a grave, not a dead piece of wood. You see nothing but life and a beautiful, lovely garden or a green meadow, and in it nothing but new, living, happy human creatures.

For it is so that Christ is risen from the dead, and because of this we have the best part, the foremost piece of the resurrection already. Our own physical resurrection from the grave in the flesh (which is still future) is not very important by comparison. For what are we and all the world alongside Christ our head? Hardly a droplet alongside the sea, or a little fleck of dust alongside a large mountain. For Christ, the head of the Christian church, through whom it lives and has everything and has grown so great, fills heaven and earth. He is risen from the grave and through his resurrection has become a mighty lord of all things, including death and hell, as we have heard. So because we are his members, his resurrection also makes its impact in our lives and engages us, for we share it with him. He has arranged that. His resurrection happened for our sakes. He has taken everything along with himself. Through his resurrection, both heaven and earth, sun and moon, must become new. Likewise, he will also take us along with himself, as St. Paul said in 1 Thessalonians 4[:14] and then in Romans 8[:11, 20]. The same God who raised Christ from the dead will make our mortal bodies alive. Along with us, all creatures who now are subjected to futility, and who long for the glory that is ours, will be freed from this decaying existence and be glorified. Therefore, we already have more than the half of our resurrection because the head and heart are already above. What is yet to take place is the smallest part: the body must be buried in the earth so that it may be made new. For where the head is, there the body must also follow, as we see in the birth of all animals.

And there is the other half, yes, far more than a half: that we have already risen spiritually in faith through Baptism. The best part for us is not only that physically the very best has taken place—our head has ascended out of his grave into heaven—but also that in its spiritual essence, our soul already has its part and is with Christ in heaven (as St. Paul was accustomed to say). Now only the husks and the peelings or the shards are here below, but because of the chief part they must also follow into heaven as well. For this body is, as St. Paul says, only a hovel for the soul, made of earth or clay, a worn-out piece of clothing, an old, mangy fur. However, because the soul is already in the new heavenly life through faith and cannot die and be buried, we expect nothing more than that this poor hovel and this old fur will become new and never pass away. For the best part is above and cannot leave us behind. He who is called "Resurrexit" has taken off, has left death and the grave behind. Those who say the Creed and cling to it shall follow after, for Christ has gone before us that we should follow after him. He has initiated this so that we might daily rise in him through the Word and Baptism.

Look! we should get used to thinking such thoughts of faith against outward, physical perspectives of the flesh, which simply place death before our eyes.

They want to terrify us with its image and cause us to doubt the article of the resurrection and destroy this article of faith. We can really set ourselves up for a fall when we let our reason with its ideas hang before our eyes, and when we do not clutch the word in our hearts against reason. For we cannot have thoughts of anything else but death when we see a corpse lying there. It is more heartrending and ghastly than a dead piece of wood, sordid, rotting, and stinking so badly that no person on earth can stand it. There is no medical treatment that can help, nothing to be done apart from burning the body or burying it as deep under the earth as possible.

But when you grasp the word in faith, you get another point of view. It can see through this death into the resurrection and form nothing but thoughts and images of life. This is indeed a part of the resurrection and the beginning of new life. It creates a new way of thinking and conceiving of things. No one could think this way who had not already made this transition through faith and come to understand the resurrection and brought the outward self along, so that it has to think and live in this way, too. Therefore, against everything in human nature and human thinking, we can conclude, "If I want to orient myself according to reason as I see and understand things, then I am lost. But I have a higher level of understanding, for my eyes see and my senses feel what faith teaches me. There stands the text, "He is called Resurrexit," "He is risen," and not for himself but for our sakes. His resurrection is our resurrection, and we have been raised in him. We shall not remain in the grave and in death, but we shall observe the eternal Easter day with him in our bodies.

For look at what the farmer does. He sows in his field and throws the grain onto the earth, where it has to spoil and rot. It looks as though it has been lost. But he is not worried, as if all had been in vain. He actually forgets where the grain is. He does not ask about it, or whether the worms are eating it or it is being spoiled in some other way. He proceeds simply with the idea that by Easter or Pentecost there will be beautiful stalks coming up, and even more that they will be bearing grain, for he has thrown the seed into the field. If others, who had never seen grain growing before, would see that, they would certainly say to the farmer, "What are you doing, you fool? Are you crazy and stupid that you throw away your seed onto the earth in such a wasteful fashion, for it is certainly going to rot and decay and will be of use to no one?" If you did ask him, he would give a very different answer. He would say, "Friend, I knew beforehand, before you asked, that I was not supposed to throw away the grain for no good purpose. But I did not do it so that it would rot, but rather so that by decaying in the earth, it would take on another form and produce much fruit." That is the way all think who see or do such things. We do not take our orientation from what we see with our eyes but rather what we have seen and experience as the work of God year after year, even if we may not know or understand how it takes place, and much less have the ability with our own power to bring one little stalk out of the earth.

Because we have to conduct ourselves according to this kind of earthly procedure, how much more should we learn this article (which we can grasp and understand much less) because we have the Word of God and with it the experience that Christ has risen from the dead. We do not take our orientation from that which we see before our eyes as our body is buried, burned, or in some other way returns to the earth. Instead, we should let God do and take care of what is supposed to come of it. For if we immediately comprehend what is before our eyes, we would not need to believe, and God would not have the opportunity to demonstrate his wisdom and power over our wisdom and understanding. Therefore, it is called the skill, the art, and the wisdom of the Christian that in the midst of mourning and lamentation, we can draw comforting and joyful thoughts regarding life: God lets us be buried in the earth and rot for the winter, so that in the summer we shall once again emerge much more beautiful than this sun. It is as if the grave were not a grave but rather a garden planted with wonderful carnations and roses that remain green and blossom the whole lovely summer through. Similarly, the grave of the Lord Christ had to be emptied, stop stinking, and become lovely, glorious, and beautiful.

In this manner, the dear, holy martyrs and virgins have spoken and thought as they were led into jail and to death, as can be read about St. Agatha, who convinced herself that she was going to a dance and that all torture and suffering with which she was threatened should not be regarded in any other way as that they were whistling a dance tune for her so that she could dance.[13] It is also written of St. Vincent and others that with joy and laughter they went to their death and mocked their judges and hangmen.[14] For they had a far firmer image of the resurrection than any farmer has of his harvest in the field. They grasped it so firmly that they could only mock the hangmen, death, and the devil.

Let us learn this in such a way that we drive this article into our hearts. We can take comfort in it and use it to spite the devil when he sharpens his spear against us and threatens us with death and hell. For, as we said, since our head, upon whom everything rests, has risen and lives, and since we are baptized in him, we already have more than half the matter behind us. Only a tiny little part remains that has to be fulfilled as we lay aside the old skin that it might become new. For because we already have taken complete possession of the inheritance, the husks and peelings will follow most certainly.

For this time, that is enough on this article of our Lord Jesus Christ. Here can be seen how to summarize and recapitulate all the wisdom and knowledge which a Christian should know. This is indeed a sublime wisdom, above all wisdom and knowledge, but it is not created on earth, nor does it develop in our own heads. It is revealed from heaven and is a divine spiritual wisdom. It lies hidden in mystery (as St. Paul says [Rom. 11:33]). For reason and this world cannot attain the tiniest piece of this wisdom, cannot grasp it, cannot under-

---

13. This story is related of Agatha, a Sicilian martyr of uncertain date, in the *Golden Legend,* a collection of stories of the saints assembled by Jacob of Voragine. Her cult was being practiced by the end of the fifth century in Sicily.

14. A Spanish priest and martyr, died 304.

stand it even if it is placed directly before it. Instead, reason and the world do the very opposite. They get angry with such teaching and regard it as no more than a great foolishness. God with his Word must simply be their fool and be a liar in their eyes. They have to condemn what he says and teaches in every point. They have to label it the worst of heresies and the seduction of the devil, as we are now experiencing from our own people. But we teach nothing other than this text, which they also recite and say with us each day. There is no other reason for them to slander us as heretics, for we have proclaimed the article on the Lord Jesus Christ so clear and so powerfully, and we have extolled it as the only thing and everything that matters that we have him and have his name as Christians and want to know no other righteousness or holiness. That is our great comfort because we are certain that we are being afflicted for no other reason on earth than because of the Lord Christ and the faith which we have received from the apostles and which has gone into all the world and stands fast to this day. That is our sin. That is what makes us heretics in the world's sight. In God's sight, it is what makes us—and all other saints from the beginning of the Christian church—defiant, boastful, and joyful. We stand upon this and learn day in and day out no other skill than this, for in it rests our wisdom, our salvation, and our blessedness. Where this article remains, everything remains. It grants us assurance, and in it we have the correct foundation for speaking about all other matters and living. On the other hand, where this part of Christian teaching is lost, our entire salvation, comfort, and wisdom are lost. No one can come to a right judgment or assessment in either teaching or living. May God help us through his dear son Jesus Christ, our Lord. May he be praised eternally.

The Saxon Visitation
Articles of 1592

Translated by Charles P. Arand

Introduction

In 1574, Elector August of Saxony dismissed theologians in his employ who were striving to introduce a spiritualizing understanding of the Lord's Supper and a Christology that supported that view into his lands. Though labeled "Crypto-Calvinist" by their opponents, because of similarities between their teaching and that of John Calvin, this group, led by Christoph Pezel and Caspar Peucer, actually were only working out the implications of positions expressed by their preceptor Philip Melanchthon. These positions were extended and elaborated in directions closer to Luther's view by other students of Melanchthon, such as Martin Chemnitz and David Chytraeus, to be sure, but the Wittenberg theological faculty of the late 1560s and early 1570s, along with its supporters in the electoral Saxon ministerium, were also formulating their theology in the shadow of their Wittenberg professors. They owed relatively little apart from friendship and support to the theologians of Geneva or Heidelberg, the centers of Calvinist theology in their day.

However, when August died in 1586, the circle around his young son, Christian I, did include lay counselors and theologians who stood under the influence of Calvin and other like-minded theologians. These Crypto-Calvinists were led by Christian's chancellor, Nikolaus Krell (ca. 1550–1601), a bureaucrat in the Saxon government since 1580, who assumed the chancellorship in 1589.[1] He and his supporters abolished the legal authority of the Book of Concord and removed its leading adherents (including Nikolaus Selnecker and Polycarp Leyser) from office, replacing them with Calvinist teachers and pastors. The Krell party banned books supporting Lutheran theology and introduced a new catechism that advanced Calvinist theology. The new Saxon government introduced changes in baptismal practice, including the abolition of the baptismal exorcism. Popular opposition to this program was widespread.

At Christian's death in 1591, his cousin Duke Friedrich Wilhelm, the regent for his son Christian II, restored Lutheran theologians to key positions in the electoral Saxon court. To return parishes to the Lutheran confession of the faith, he commissioned a new professor at Wittenberg, Aegidius Hunnius (1550–1603), and others to compose the Visitation Articles in 1592. They were

---

1. See Thomas Klein, *Der Kampf um die zweite Reformation in Kursachsen, 1586–1592* (Cologne: Böhlau, 1962).

used to reaffirm the theology of the Formula of Concord through a visitation of parishes. Its four articles treated the controverted issues involved in the attempt to "Calvinize" the Saxon church: the Lord's Supper, the person of Christ, Baptism, and election. Positive expressions of the doctrines are presented first, followed by four sets of rejections of false teaching. Within electoral Saxony, these Visitation Articles were appended to the Book of Concord and were a part of the tradition that Saxon church leaders, including those of the Evangelical Lutheran Synod of Missouri, Ohio, and Other States, brought to the United States.

The text of the Visitation Articles may be found in *Die symbolischen Bücher der evangelisch-lutherischen Kirche,* ed. J. T. Müller (12th ed., Gütersloh: "der Rufer," 1928), 779–84, and in *Concordia Triglotta,* ed. F. Bente (St. Louis: Concordia, 1921), 1150–57. Bible passages in brackets were not in the original text, but they do reflect common usage of the time for making the points of this document.

Christian Visitation Articles

Article I: The Holy Supper

The pure and true doctrine of our church concerning the Holy Supper

1. The words of Christ, "take and eat, this is my body" and "drink, this is my blood" [Matt. 26:26-28] are to be understood simply and literally, just as they read.

2. In the sacrament, two things are given and received with each other: one earthly, that is, the bread and wine; and one heavenly, that is, the body and blood of Christ.

3. This [union of the bread and the body, the wine and the blood] takes place on earth and not above in heaven.

4. This is the true, natural body of Christ, which hung on the cross, and the true natural blood, which flowed from the side of Christ.

5. The body and blood of Christ are not only received spiritually by faith, which can also take place outside the Supper, but they are received here orally with the bread and wine, yet in an inscrutable and supernatural manner, as a pledge and assurance of the resurrection of our bodies from the dead.

6. Not only the worthy partake orally of the body and blood of Christ, but also the unworthy, who approach without repentance and true faith. Nevertheless, they receive it with different results: the worthy for salvation, the unworthy for judgment.

Article II: The Person of Christ

The pure and true doctrine of our churches on this article concerning the person of Christ

1. In Christ there are two distinct natures, the divine and the human. These cannot be mixed together or separated and never will be into eternity.

2. These two natures are personally united with each other in such a way that there is only one Christ, one person.

3. On account of this personal union, it is correctly said—and it is so in fact and in truth—that God is a human being and a human being is God, that Mary gave birth to the Son of God [Gal. 4:4], and that God redeemed us through his own blood [Acts 20:28].

4. Through this personal union and after that exaltation that followed upon it, Christ has been placed at God's right hand according to his flesh and has received all power in heaven and on earth [Matt. 28:19], and shares in all divine majesty, honor, power, and glory [Matt. 25:31].

Article III: Holy Baptism

The pure and true doctrine of our churches concerning Holy Baptism

1. There is but one Baptism and one washing, not of the kind that removes dirt from the body [1 Peter 3:21] but rather that washes away our sins.

2. Through Baptism as a washing of regeneration and renewal in the Holy Spirit, God saves us and effects in us righteousness and cleansing from sins [Titus 3:5-7], so that whoever perseveres in this covenant and confidence unto the end is not lost but has eternal life.

3. All who are baptized into Christ Jesus are baptized into his death and through Baptism are buried with him into his death [Rom. 6:3-4] and have put on Christ [Gal. 3:27].

4. Baptism is the washing of regeneration because in it we are born anew and sealed with and graciously given the Spirit of adoption [Rom. 8:23].

5. Unless born of water and the Spirit [John 3:5], a person cannot enter the kingdom of God. However, this does not refer to emergency situations [in which a person dies before Baptism is possible].

6. That which is born of flesh is flesh. By nature, we are all children of God's wrath, for we are begotten of sinful seed and are all conceived in sins.

Article IV: Election and the Eternal Providence of God

The pure and true doctrine of our churches on this article

1. Christ has died for every human being, and as the lamb of God, he has borne the sins of the entire world [John 1:29].

2. God created no one for condemnation but wants every human being to be saved and to come to the knowledge of the truth [1 Tim. 2:4]. Therefore, he

commands everyone to hear his Son Christ in the Gospel [Matt. 3:17] and promises the power and efficacy of the Holy Spirit for conversion and salvation through such hearing.

3. Many are condemned by their own guilt who are either unwilling to hear the gospel of Christ or who fall from grace again, whether by error against the foundation of the faith or by sin against conscience.

4. All sinners who repent are received into grace, and none are excluded even though their sins were as scarlet, for God's mercy is much greater than the sins of the entire world, and God has compassion on all he has made.

False and Erroneous Doctrine of the Calvinists

Concerning the Holy Supper

1. The words of Christ cited above are to be understood in a figurative way and not as they sound.

2. In the Supper, there are only bare signs. The body of Christ is as far from the bread as the highest heaven is from the earth.

3. Christ is present there with his power and efficacy, and not with his body, just as the sun is present and powerful here below on earth with its shining and effect, while the sun itself is above in heaven.

4. [This body] is only a type of the body, a figurative body, which is only signified and symbolized [in the Supper].

5. [The body] is received only by faith, which soars into heaven, and is not received orally.

6. Only the worthy receive the body. The unworthy who do not have the faith to ascend into heaven receive nothing but bread and wine.

False and Erroneous Doctrine of the Calvinists

Concerning the Person of Christ

which conflicts especially with the third and fourth articles of pure doctrine[2]

1. In the first place, the expressions "God is a human being" and "a human being is God" are figurative.

2. The human nature has communion with the divine not in fact and in truth, but only rhetorically.

3. It is impossible for God, with all his omnipotence, to cause the natural body of Christ to be simultaneously present in more than one place.

4. Through his exaltation, Christ has received according to his human nature only created gifts and finite power; according to his human nature, he neither knows nor can do all things.

---

2. That is, of the third and fourth items in Article II of the positive confession of the faith above.

5. Christ rules in absentia according to his human nature in the same manner as the king of Spain rules the new islands.

6. It is damnable idolatry to place confidence and faith of the heart in Christ not only according to his divine nature but also according to his human nature, and to direct the honor of adoration toward the human nature.

False and Erroneous Doctrine of the Calvinists

Concerning Holy Baptism

1. Baptism is an external washing of water by which an inner washing away of sins is only signified.

2. Baptism neither effects nor confers regeneration, faith, the grace of God, and salvation but only signifies and seals these things.

3. Not all who are baptized with water receive in it the grace of Christ or the gift of faith. Only the elect do.

4. Regeneration does not occur in and with Baptism, but it first occurs later, when a person is grown up, and in the case of some not until old age.

5. Salvation does not depend on Baptism. Accordingly, emergency Baptism should not be permitted in the church. If a minister of the church cannot be found, the child should be allowed to die without Baptism.

6. Children of Christians are holy before Baptism, from their mothers' wombs. Indeed, while still in their mothers' wombs, they are brought into the covenant of eternal life. Otherwise, Holy Baptism could not be administered to them.

False and Erroneous Doctrine of the Calvinists

Concerning Election and the Providence of God

1. Christ did not die for all humankind but only for the elect.

2. God created the greater part of humankind for eternal condemnation, and he is unwilling to have them converted and saved.

3. The elect and regenerate cannot lose faith and the Holy Spirit or be condemned even though they commit great sins and crimes of every kind.

4. Those who are not elect must be condemned and cannot attain salvation even if they are baptized a thousand times, go daily to the Lord's Supper, and in addition live as holy and irreproachable lives as possible.

Index of Biblical Passages

Biographical Index

Subject Index